Blockchain Development with Hyperledger

Build decentralized applications with Hyperledger Fabric and Composer

Salman A. Baset
Luc Desrosiers
Nitin Gaur
Petr Novotny
Anthony O'Dowd
Venkatraman Ramakrishna
Weimin Sun
Xun (Brian) Wu

BIRMINGHAM - MUMBAI

Blockchain Development with Hyperledger

First Published: March 2019

Production Reference: 1250319

Published by Packt Publishing Ltd.
Livery Place, 35 Livery Street
Birmingham, B3 2PB, U.K.
ISBN 978-1-83864-998-2

www.packtpub.com

mapt.io

Mapt is an online digital library that gives you full access to over 5,000 books and videos, as well as industry-leading tools to help you plan your personal development and advance your career. For more information, please visit our website.

Why Subscribe?

- Spend less time learning and more time coding with practical eBooks and Videos from over 4,000 industry professionals

- Improve your learning with Skill Plans built especially for you

- Get a free eBook or video every month

- Mapt is fully searchable

- Copy and paste, print, and bookmark content

Packt.com

Did you know that Packt offers eBook versions of every book published, with PDF and ePub files available? You can upgrade to the eBook version at www.packt.com and as a print book customer, you are entitled to a discount on the eBook copy. Get in touch with us at customercare@packtpub.com for more details.

At www.packt.com, you can also read a collection of free technical articles, sign up for a range of free newsletters, and receive exclusive discounts and offers on Packt books and eBooks.

Contributors

About the Authors

Salman A. Baset is the CTO of security in IBM Blockchain Solutions.

Luc Desrosiers is an IBM-certified IT architect with 20+ years of experience.

Nitin Gaur is the director of IBM's Blockchain Labs, and an IBM Distinguished Engineer.

Petr Novotny is a research scientist at IBM Research, with an MSc from University College London and PhD from Imperial College London, where he was also a post-doctoral research associate.

Anthony O'Dowd works in IBM's Blockchain team and is based in Europe.

Venkatraman Ramakrishna is an IBM researcher with a BTech from IIT Kharagpur and PhD from UCLA.

Weimin Sun is an expert in designing data-driven solutions.

Xun (Brian) Wu is an author, founder, and board advisor for several blockchain start-ups.

Packt Is Searching for Authors Like You

If you're interested in becoming an author for Packt, please visit authors.packtpub.com and apply today. We have worked with thousands of developers and tech professionals, just like you, to help them share their insight with the global tech community. You can make a general application, apply for a specific hot topic that we are recruiting an author for, or submit your own idea.

Table of Contents

Preface

This Learning Path is your easy reference for exploring and building blockchain networks using Ethereum, Hyperledger Fabric, and Hyperledger Composer. It begins with an overview of blockchain and shows you how to set up an Ethereum development environment for developing, packaging, building, and testing campaign-decentralized applications. You'll learn Solidity – the de facto language for developing decentralized applications in Ethereum. You'll configure the Hyperledger Fabric and use these components to build private blockchain networks and applications that connect to them. Starting with the principles first, you'll learn to design and launch a network, implement smart contracts in chaincode, and much more.

By the end of this Learning Path, you'll be able to build and deploy your own decentralized applications by handling the key pain points encountered in the blockchain life cycle.

Who This Book Is For

This Learning Path is designed for blockchain developers who want to build decentralized applications and smart contracts from scratch using Hyperledger. A basic familiarity or exposure to any programming language will be useful to get started with this course.

What This Book Covers

Chapter 1, *Blockchain - Enterprise and Industry Perspective*, you've heard about blockchain and you are wondering, what is all the fuss about? In this chapter, we explore why blockchain is a game changer, what innovation it brings, and what the technology landscape is.

Chapter 2, *Exploring Hyperledger Fabric*, starts with an understanding of the blockchain landscape, then we turn our attention to Hyperledger Fabric. The aim of this chapter is to walk you through the deployment of each component of Hyperledger Fabric while unveiling/building the architecture.

Chapter 3, *Setting the Stage with a Business Scenario*, describes a business use case and then focuses on understanding the process of creating a good business network, using blockchain from requirements to design.

Chapter 4, *Designing a Data and Transaction Model with Golang*, aims to define what makes up a smart contract in Hyperledger Fabric. It will also introduce you to some terms regarding smart contracts and get you to experience the development of a chaincode using the Go language.

Chapter 5, *Exposing Network Assets and Transactions*, leveraging the smart contract written in the previous chapter, this chapter looks at the required integration of application to the network. It takes the readers through the process of configuring a channel, and installing and invoking chaincode, from a client application and considers the various integration patterns that might be used.

Chapter 6, *Business Networks*, has an objective to introduce and uncover the skills and tools needed to model a business network. Working at a higher level of abstraction, the foundation, tools, and framework will provide the reader with a way to quickly model, design, and deploy a complete end-to-end business network.

Chapter 7, *A Business Network Example*, putting the concepts of the previous chapter into practice, this chapter walks through the steps to deploy a full business network from end-user application to smart contracts.

Chapter 8, *Agility in a Blockchain Network*, focuses on the aspects required to maintain agility in a blockchain network. Applying DevOps concepts, the reader is presented with a continuous integration / continuous delivery pipeline.

Chapter 9, *Life in a Blockchain Network*, aims to raise the reader's awareness on the key activities and challenges that organizations and consortium may face when adopting a distributed ledger solution, ranging from management of application changes to maintenance of adequate performance levels. A successful network deployment will hopefully see that many organizations join it and that the number of transactions increase.

Chapter 10, *Governance –The Necessary Evil of Regulated Industries*, governance is a necessary evil for regulated industries, but governance is not required only for business network that deal with use cases for regulated industries. It is also a good practice to ensure longevity and scalability of a business network. This chapter explores vital considerations for production readiness for any founder-led blockchain network.

Chapter 11, *Hyperledger Fabric Security*, lays the foundation for security design of blockchain networks. Various security constructs are discussed and Hyperledger Fabric security is explained in detail. An essential chapter to understand security design considerations.

Chapter 12, *Introduction to Blockchain Technology*, gives an overview of the key concepts, such as cryptography and hash algorithms, the distributed ledger, transactions, blocks, proof of work, mining, and consensus. We cover Bitcoin, the mother of blockchain technology, in detail. We briefly introduce Ethereum by pointing out some limitations of Bitcoin and how they are addressed by Ethereum. While Bitcoin and Ethereum are examples of public blockchains, IBM's Hyperledger is used as an example of enterprise blockchains. Toward the end of this chapter, we look at the evolution of blockchain, through 1.0, 2.0, 3.0, and beyond, and we examine their use cases.

Chapter 13, *Ethereum Fundamentals*, covers the basic concepts of Ethereum, such as smart contracts, ether, consensus algorithms, EVM, gas, and accounts. We will discuss Ethereum performance and review ideas on how to improve the overall performance via proof of work, casper, plasma, and sharding.

Chapter 14, *Overview of Solidity Programming*, discusses what solidity is, as well as the tools for the solidity development environment. We then discuss smart contracts and their common patterns. We cover the important topic of smart contract security. Finally, we show how to write a smart contract with a use case of crowdfunding.

Chapter 15, *Building an Ethereum Blockchain Application*, looks at what a DApp is. We give a quick overview of web3.js. We explain how to set up an Ethereum development environment, as well as how to develop and test a DApp.

Chapter 16, *Exploring an Enterprise Blockchain Application Using Hyperledger Fabric*, gets into the key concepts of Hyperledger Fabric, along with the core components. We explain how to create a Hyperledger Fabric environment, how to write a chaincode, and how to set up Hyperledger Fabric configuration.

Chapter 17, *Implementing a Business Network Using Hyperledger Composer*, provides an overview of Hyperledger Composer and talks about how to set up a Hyperledger Composer environment. We discuss business scenarios, the business network archive, and how to implement a business transaction function.

Chapter 18, *Blockchain Use Cases*, first talks about popular blockchain use cases across industries, including the financial sector, civil services, supply chains, the **Internet of Things (IoT)**, and healthcare, at a high level. We will then proceed to a discussion of the proper use cases for DApps, before then developing a successful DApp. Finally, we take the health data-sharing use case and comment at a high level on building a DApp for it.

To Get the Most out of This Book

We've focused on organization and flow. The content is made to ensure not only an easy-to-follow and natural flow but also topical modularity. Each chapter explores a facet of blockchain. While Hyperledger projects are specifically discussed, the core areas of focus are universal to blockchain technology discipline.

This learning path aims to be a development path into the world of blockchain technology. The chapters are arranged to ensure that they can be followed easily and flow naturally.

Business users can skip the chapters with detailed descriptions on how to develop blockchain applications and, instead, focus on the chapters with general descriptions of the technology and use cases.

It is recommended that IT users download the code and make modifications for adopting to their own use cases or exercises.

Download the Example Code Files

You can download the example code files for this book from your account at `www.packt.com`. If you purchased this book elsewhere, you can visit `www.packt.com/support` and register to have the files emailed directly to you.

You can download the code files by following these steps:

1. Log in or register at `www.packt.com`.
2. Select the **SUPPORT** tab.
3. Click on **Code Downloads & Errata**.
4. Enter the name of the book in the **Search** box and follow the onscreen instructions.

Once the file is downloaded, please make sure that you unzip or extract the folder using the latest version of:

- WinRAR/7-Zip for Windows
- Zipeg/iZip/UnRarX for Mac
- 7-Zip/PeaZip for Linux

The code bundle for the book is also hosted on GitHub at `https://github.com/PacktPublishing/Blockchain-Development-with-Hyperledger`. In case there's an update to the code, it will be updated on the existing GitHub repository.

We also have other code bundles from our rich catalog of books and videos available at `https://github.com/PacktPublishing/`. Check them out!

Conventions Used

Code words in text, database table names, folder names, filenames, file extensions, pathnames, dummy URLs, user input, and Twitter handles are shown as follows: "The orderer belongs to its own organization called `TradeOrdererOrg`."

A block of code is set as follows:

```
- &ExporterOrg
  Name: ExporterOrgMSP
  ID: ExporterOrgMSP
  MSPDir: crypto-config/peerOrganizations/exporterorg.trade.com/msp
  AnchorPeers:
    - Host: peer0.exporterorg.trade.com
      Port: 7051
```

When we wish to draw your attention to a particular part of a code block, the relevant lines or items are set in bold:

```
pragma solidity ^0.4.15;
import 'zeppelin/contracts/math/SafeMath.sol';
....
contract ExampleCoin is ERC20 {
  //SafeMath symbol is from imported file SafeMath.sol'
  using SafeMath for uint256;
    ...
}
```

Any command-line input or output is written as follows:

```
mkdir ~/insurance-claim && cd ~/insurance-claim
```

Bold: Indicates a new term, an important word, or words that you see onscreen. For example, words in menus or dialog boxes appear in the text like this. Here is an example: "When the preceding request is validated by mining nodes, the **HelloWorld** smart contract is invoked."

Warnings or important notes appear like this.

Tips and tricks appear like this.

Get in Touch

Feedback from our readers is always welcome.

General feedback: If you have questions about any aspect of this book, mention the book title in the subject of your message and email us at customercare@packtpub.com.

Errata: Although we have taken every care to ensure the accuracy of our content, mistakes do happen. If you have found a mistake in this book, we would be grateful if you would report this to us. Please visit www.packt.com/submit-errata, selecting your book, clicking on the Errata Submission Form link, and entering the details.

Piracy: If you come across any illegal copies of our works in any form on the Internet, we would be grateful if you would provide us with the location address or website name. Please contact us at copyright@packt.com with a link to the material.

If you are interested in becoming an author: If there is a topic that you have expertise in and you are interested in either writing or contributing to a book, please visit authors.packtpub.com.

Reviews

Please leave a review. Once you have read and used this book, why not leave a review on the site that you purchased it from? Potential readers can then see and use your unbiased opinion to make purchase decisions, we at Packt can understand what you think about our products, and our authors can see your feedback on their book. Thank you!

For more information about Packt, please visit packt.com.

Blockchain - Enterprise and Industry Perspective

1

Blockchain promises to fundamentally solve the issues of time and trust to address inefficiencies and costs in industries such as financial services, supply chains, logistics, and healthcare. Blockchain's key features include immutability and a shared ledger where transactional updates are performed by a consensus-driven trust system, which can facilitate a truly digital interaction between multiple parties.

This digital interaction is not only bound by systemic trust, but ensures that the provenance of the transactional record maintains an immutable track record of interaction between parties. This very characteristic lends itself to culpability and non-repudiation, and incentivizes fair play. With the blockchain system design, we are attempting to build a system that has implied trust. This trust system leads to reduced risks, and various applied technology constructs such as a cryptography, encryption, smart contracts, and consensus essentially create gates to not only reduce risk but to also infuse added security into the transaction system.

We will be covering the following aspects of blockchain in our discussion for this chapter:

- Defining a blockchain
- Building blocks of blockchain solutions
- Fundamentals of the secure transaction processing protocol
- Applications of blockchain
- Blockchain in an enterprise
- Enterprise design principles
- Business considerations for choosing a blockchain framework
- Considerations for choosing a blockchain framework

Defining the terms – what is a blockchain?

At a technical level, a blockchain can be defined as an immutable ledger for recording transactions, maintained within a distributed network of mutually untrusting peers. Every peer maintains a copy of the ledger. The peers execute a consensus protocol to validate transactions, group them into blocks, and build a hash chain over the blocks. This process forms the ledger by ordering the transactions as is necessary for consistency. Blockchain has emerged with bitcoin (`http:// bitcoin.org/`) and is widely regarded as a promising technology to run trusted exchanges in the digital world.

A blockchain supporting a cryptocurrency is public, or permissionless, in the sense that anyone can participate without a specific identity. Such blockchains typically use a consensus protocol based on **proof of work** (**PoW**) and economic incentives. In contrast, permissioned blockchains have evolved as an alternative way to run a blockchain between a group of known, identified participants. A permissioned blockchain provides a way to secure interactions between a group of entities who share a mutual goal but don't fully trust each other, such as businesses that exchange funds, goods, or information. A permissioned blockchain relies on the identities of its peers, and in so doing can use the traditional **Byzantine-fault tolerant** (**BFT**) consensus. BFT is a protocol that has been widely used in IT solutions to reach a consensus on the state of faulty nodes of a network. This protocol is based on the Byzantine General's Problem, whereby a group of general need to reach a consensus on their strategy but one of them maybe treacherous.

Blockchains may execute arbitrary, programmable transaction logic in the form of smart contracts, as exemplified by Ethereum (`http://ethereum.org/`). The scripts in bitcoin were predecessors of this concept. A smart contract functions as a trusted, distributed application and gains its security from the blockchain and underlying consensus among its peers.

Discerning permissions from a permissionless blockchain is vital for enterprises looking to utilize the blockchain platform. The use case dictates the choice of technology, which depends on consensus systems, governance models, data structure, and so on. With permissioned blockchains, we can do some of the things we already do but in an incrementally better way, which can be significant. In the chart that follows, you can see how a consortium of banks could use Hyperledger, a type of permissioned blockchain, for clearing and settlement without relying on a central clearing house:

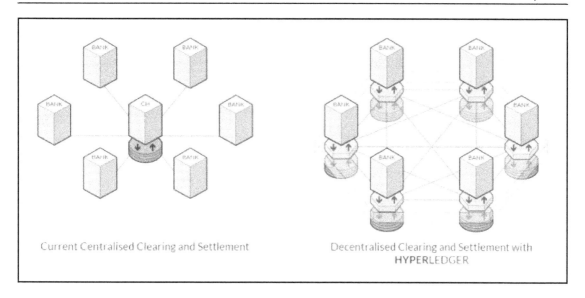

Current Centralised Clearing and Settlement

Decentralised Clearing and Settlement with
HYPERLEDGER

Clearing house have been created because banks do not fully trust each other and thus as the intermediary between trades, reduces the risk the one party does not honor his terms leads to a never-ending debate around permissioned versus permissionless blockchains, and while this chapter will not address the debate, blockchain can present a way to either transform or disrupt the current business and business models. Most use cases in regulated industries embark on permissioned blockchain models.

This is due to regulatory requirements and the economic viability of transaction processing, and while permissionless blockchains provide a platform for new business models such as **Peer-to-Peer (P2P)** transactions and disintermediation-led models, by definition permissionless blockchain architecture relies on a very compute-intensive compute model to ensure transactional integrity. Regardless of the choice in blockchain models, blockchain provides a lot of possibilities for transformation and disruption.

Blockchain has extraordinary potential as a technology platform. In the enterprise, blockchain can provide:

- A design approach that keeps transaction data, value, and state inherently close to the business logic
- Secure execution of business transactions, validated through a community, in a secure process that facilities the trust and robust transaction processing that are foundational to blockchain
- An alternative, permissioned technology that conforms to existing regulations

Blockchain promises to solve longstanding industry concerns—and this is where its potential can really be seen, with issues such as modernizing financial and trade systems, and speeding up securities and trade settlements.

Four core building blocks of blockchain framworks

Blockchain frameworks typically include the following four building blocks:

- **A shared ledger**: The shared ledger appends only the distributed transaction record. Bitcoin blockchain was designed with the intent to democratize visibility; however, with blockchain, consumer data regulations also need to be considered. Using a properly configured SQL or noSQL distributed database can achieve immutability, or append-only semantics.

- **Cryptography**: Cryptography in a blockchain ensures authentication and verifiable transactions. Blockchain design includes this imperative because of the focus on assuming computational hardness and making encryption harder for an adversary to break. This is an interesting challenge with bitcoin blockchain because of the economic incentive and its system design. When you're working in a less democratic or permissioned business ledger network, considerations around cryptography change.

- **Trust systems or consensus**: Trust systems refer to using the power of the network to verify transactions.
  Trust systems are central to blockchain systems in my view; they are at the heart of blockchain applications, and we believe trust system is the preferred term over **consensus system** since not all validation is done through consensus. This foundational element of trust dictates the overall design and investment in a blockchain infrastructure. With every new entrant in the blockchain space, the trust system is modified, forming variations that are specialized for specific blockchain use cases. Trust, trade, and ownership are staples of blockchain technology. For inter-company transactions, the trust system governs transactions for trade between participating companies.
  Much work still needs to be done to define the best trust system for specific use cases, such as P2P and sharing economy models with B2B models.

- **Business rules or smart contracts**: Smart contracts are the business terms that are embedded in a blockchain transaction database and executed with transactions. This is also the rules component of a blockchain solution. It is needed to define the flow of value and state of each transaction.

The following use diagram gives a good idea of these concepts:

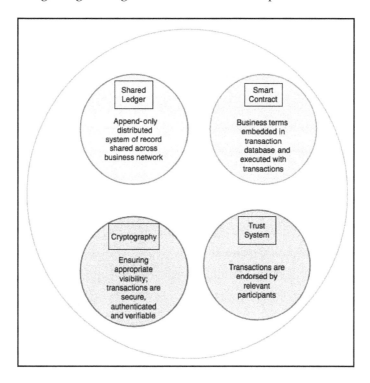

The four building blocks are generally accepted and well understood. They have existed for decades prior to blockchain. Shared ledgers are an evolutionary change, similar to the move to computer-based spreadsheets, but the underlying business rules have stayed the same.

Additional capabilities to consider

What else should be included in enterprise blockchain proposals? Here is a non-exhaustive list of other capabilities to consider:

- **Auditing and logging**: Including auditing and logging in a blockchain solution can help with addressing regulations for the purposes of non-repudiation, technology root cause analysis, fraud analysis, and other enterprise needs.
- **Enterprise integration**: It's also worth considering how the solution will be integrated into the enterprise:
  - **Integration with the incumbent Systems of Record** (**SoR**): The goal here is to ensure that the blockchain solution supports your existing systems such as CRM, business intelligence, reporting and analytics, and so forth
  - **Integration as a transaction processing system**: If you want to preserve the system of record as an interim approach to adopting blockchain, integrating it as a transaction processing system makes sense
  - **Design with the intent to include blockchain**: The path of least disruption to your existing systems will accelerate enterprise adoption of blockchain
- **Monitoring**: Monitoring is an important capability for addressing regulations and ensuring high availability, capacity planning, pattern recognition, and fault identification.
- **Reporting and regulatory requirements**: Being prepared to address regulatory issues is also very important, even for interim adoption of a blockchain as a transaction processing system. It's recommended that you make connectors to your existing SoR to offload reporting and regulatory requirements until blockchain is enterprise-aware, or the enterprise software is blockchain-aware.
- **Enterprise authentication, authorization, and accounting requirements**: In a permissioned enterprise world (unlike permissionless bitcoin blockchains), all blockchain network participants should be identified and tracked. Their roles need to be defined if they are to play a part in the ecosystem.

Fundamentals of the secure transaction processing protocol

We mentioned previously that cryptography is one of the core building blocks of a blockchain solution. The fundamental security of the bitcoin blockchain is the elegant cryptographical linkage of all major components of the ledger. Specifically, transactions are linked to each other, mainly through the Merkle tree. A Merkle tree is based on the concept of a tree data structure where every leaf node has a hash calculated of its data and where the non-leaf node have a hash of all of their underlying child. This method provides a way to ensure the integrity of the data, but also provides privacy characteristics by allowing one to remove a leaf that is deemed private but leave the hash, thereby preserving the integrity of the tree. The Merkle tree has its roots incorporated into the block header. The block header includes a reference to the block headers that precede it.

That cryptographically enforced interconnectivity fosters the stability and security of distributed ledgers. At any point, if a link between any of the components is broken, it leaves them exposed to malicious attacks:

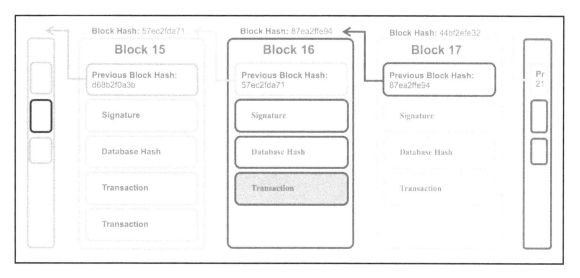

Transactions are also cryptographically connected to the rest of the blockchain structure, mainly through the Merkle tree. Once a transaction is modified within a block, with all other parts remaining stable, the link between all transactions of the block and its header are broken:

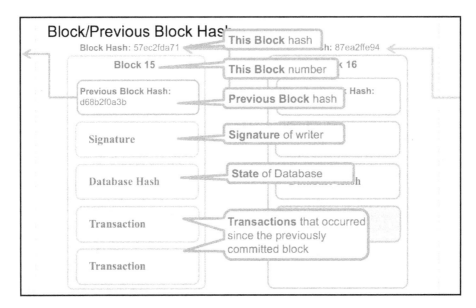

The new resulting Merkle tree root does not match the one already in the block header, hence providing no connectivity to the rest of the blockchain. If we proceed to change the Merkle tree root in the block's header, we will in turn break the chain of headers and thus the security model of the blockchain itself. Therefore, if we only change the contents of a block, the rest of the blockchain components remain stable and secure, especially as the block headers provide the connecting links by including a hash of the previous block header in the header of the next block.

Where blockchain technology has been and where it's going

Blockchain has already been a business disruptor, and I expect it to significantly transform industries, the government, and our lives in the near future.

The great divide

A significant divided exists between the cryptocurrency and **Initial Coin Offering** (**ICO**) world, and the world of regulated business. The latter consists of banks and financial institutions working collectively to assess market potential and operational efficiencies.

Both sides of this division have taken advantage of the momentum around blockchain to further their interests. The blockchain ecosystem has challenged the status quo and defied all odds to make a point—often behaving like an adolescent. It is driven by new business models, promises of disintermediation, and interesting technological innovations. As blockchain gains momentum, the value of bitcoin and other cryptoassets is seeing a meteoric rise, and now that ICO has emerged, it has defied the traditional regulatory framework around fundraising.

On the enterprise side, there are a growing number of industry initiatives around clearing and settlement to enable faster settlement and interbank transfers, transparency through digitization, symmetric dissemination of information in supply chains, and creating adhoc trust between **Internet of Things** (**IoT**) devices.

There's a common theme here—that blockchain is here to stay. As it continues to evolve and generate innovative solutions for industry use cases, it will keep inching towards maturity and deliver on its promises of efficiency and significant cost savings built on the foundation of trust.

An economic model for blockchain delivery

Business networks, underpinned by blockchain technology, may bring transformation or disruption to industries, but in any case, in order to thrive, blockchain needs an economic model. If disruption is the aim, investments in technology, talent, and market synergy can be combined with the lure of economic incentives. ICOs, for example, typically rely on tokenomics, a term that describes the economic system of value generation in those networks. The token is the unit of value created by the system or network, either through making a platform for providers or consumers, or through co-creating a self-governing value network in its business model that various entities can use to their advantage for creating, distributing, and sharing rewards that benefit all stakeholders.

The ICO front, largely funded by cryptocurrencies, has defied current fundraising mechanisms in venture capitalism (led by crowdfunding projects), and, importantly, the struggle to discern the difference between a security and utility coin is disruptive in principle.

ICOs are looking to create an economic system built on the principles of **decentralization**, **open governance** (or self-governance), and transparency, a system that rewards innovation and eradicates disintermediation. ICOs saw some initial failures and some successes, but they nevertheless provided a preview of the future, where cryptoassets will become a basic unit of value—with valuation and fungibility defined by the network they originate from—fueling an economy built for and around innovation.

On the enterprise front, there's been more focus on understanding the technology and reimagining ecosystems, business networks, regulations, confidentiality and privacy, and the business models that impact blockchain networks in various industries. Enterprises looking to explore blockchain want to see quick proof points, use cases that can demonstrate results quickly and help them innovate with blockchain.

Blockchain is helping industries move to a more symmetric dissemination of information by providing built-in control of transactional data, provenance, and historical context. This can lead to more efficient workflows and transformed business processes. Many early projects, however, didn't focus on the core tenets of blockchain, leading to disintermediation, decentralization, and robust self-governance models. There's a good reason for it, though: industries and conventional businesses tend to be focused on their current business agenda, models, growth, and preceding all, regulatory compliance and adherence. This emphasis on current business operations means they're not naturally inclined towards disruptive models.

Learning as we go

With any new technology, there is always a learning curve. As blockchain evolved and we began to work with regulated industries, we quickly recognized that in such industries, there are important design considerations to address, things such as confidentiality, privacy, scalability, and performance. These elements can have significant cost implications when it comes to designing blockchain networks, as well as the business models that govern these networks. These challenges have not only been interesting to solve; they've had a positive effect on conventional, regulated industries and businesses by re-energizing innovation in these organizations and inviting the best talent to join in tackling these challenges. Businesses are seeing that ecosystems and networks driven by blockchain technology will contribute to progress and success.

Permissioned networks (regulated, conventional, and enterprise business networks) may also need to begin uncovering an incentive model to motivate organizations to join a platform that promotes the idea of creation, distribution, and sharing of rewards, benefiting all stakeholders. The economic incentives behind tokenomics can't be blindly adopted by a lot of conventional businesses and industries, but that doesn't mean those industries shouldn't start the journey of exploring possible business models that will enable value creation and elevate some desperately needed modernization efforts.

The promise of trust and accountability

Blockchain technology promises to be the foundation for a secure transaction network that can induce trust and security in many industries that are plagued with systemic issues around trust and accountability. From a technology point of view, blockchain facilitates a system of processing and recording transactions that is secure, transparent, auditable, efficient, and immutable. These technology characteristics lend themselves to addressing the time and trust issues that current-day distributed transaction systems are plagued with.

Blockchain fundamentally shifts the multi-tier model to a flat-tier transaction processing model. This carries the promise to fundamentally disrupt industries by disintermediation, by inducing efficacy in new system design or simply by creating new business models.

Disintermediation indicates reducing the use of intermediaries between producers and consumers, such as by investing directly in the securities market rather than going through a bank. In the financial industry, every transaction has historically required a counter party to process the transaction. Disintermediation involves removing the middleman, which by definition disrupts the business models and incentive economies that are based on mediation. There's been a wave of disruption in recent years as a result of digital technologies, which have, in turn, been driven by marketing insights and the desire for organizations to provide a richer user experience.

Blockchain is a technology that aims to catapult this disruption by introducing trade, trust, and ownership into the equation. The technology pattern represented by blockchain databases and records has the potential to radically improve banking, supply chains, and other transaction networks, providing new opportunities for innovation and growth while reducing cost and risk.

Industries putting blockchain technology to work

Let's briefly look into blockchain use cases:

Blockchain use cases are emerging in every industry

Banking
- Supply chain and trade finance
- Know your customer
- Transaction banking, payments and digital currencies

Supply Chain
- Workflow digitization
- Supply chain visibility
- Provenance and traceability

Governance
- Asset Registry
- Citizen Identity
- Fraud and compliance

Financial Markets
- Post trade
- Unlisted security and private equity funds
- Reference data
- Cross currency payments
- Mortgages

Healthcare
- Mediated health data exchange
- Clinical trial management
- Outcome based contracts
- Medicine supply chain

Insurance
- Complex Risk coverage
- Group Benefits
- Parametric insurance
- Asset usage history
- Claims filing

Retail
- Supply chain
- Loyalty programs
- Information sharing (supplier – retailer)

Manufacturing
- Supply chain
- Product parts
- Maintenance tracking

Blockchain in the enterprise

Now that we've looked at where blockchain is emerging in various industries, let's talk about what principles should guide the use of blockchains in an enterprise. Why would an enterprise want to apply blockchain technology to one of its systems or applications?

What applications are a good fit?

Organizations will need to establish criteria for use during the application design process to help them assess where they can best apply blockchain technology. The following are some examples of criteria that could help an enterprise determine which applications or systems would benefit from it:

- **Applications that adhere to trade, trust, and ownership**: As described previously, these three tenets—trade, trust and ownership—are fundamental to any blockchain system. Trade and ownership imply the churn and the transfer of ledger entries, while trust points to the trustless nature of a transaction system.

- **Applications that are fundamentally transactional in nature**: There is often a debate about why we can't achieve the benefits of blockchain from a distributed database, that is, a no-SQL or a relational database. But a multi-party transaction is what makes an application suitable for blockchain. There needs to be long-running processes with numerous micro-transactions that will be verified and validated by the blockchain-powered transaction system. However, databases can still be used for persistence or replication to fit enterprise systems. Other considerations include small data set sizes that could increase over time, logging overhead, and so on.

- **Business networks that are comprised of non-monopolistic participants**: This third criteria addresses distributed versus decentralized computation models. Blockchain trust systems can work within any model; however, the trust aspect of a blockchain business network comes from multi-party participants with non-monopolistic participation (the consortium permissioned network model). Oligopolistic participation might be acceptable (the private permissioned network model), but it's essential to devise a trust model that assures the prevention of centralized control, even with rational behavior of the participants. Many internal use cases do not adhere to this principle and are more for distributed application models.

For enterprises trying to either understand or determine where to employ blockchain meaningfully, there's a simple approach to thinking through use case selection. An appropriate use case for a sustainable blockchain solution will achieve long-term business objectives and provide a strong return on technology investment.

This starts with an **enterprise problem**—an issue big enough for the enterprise to expend resources/time—and the recognition of cohorts that have the same problem. When companies realize that an enterprise problem is also an **industry problem** (such as security lending, collateral lending, and so on), they've found a use case where the promise of blockchain has the most potential.

While organizations are determining the benefits of various aspects of blockchain for their enterprise applications, they also need to recognize the fragmentation of the whole blockchain landscape. There are numerous innovative approaches available for solving a specific challenge with blockchain. A lot of vendors offer variants of the trust system that are specialized to address particular use cases, and they've defined the use cases that will benefit most from blockchain in a given industry, for example. Such specialized vendors often promise a fast solution to meet consumer demands for quick digital interactions.

The tenets of blockchain can be instrumental in delivering rapid consumer-driven outcomes such as decentralized, distributed, global, permanent, code-based, programmable assets, and records of transactions. We should exercise caution with regards to thinking of blockchain as a hammer to solve every enterprise application challenge, but it can be of use in many transactional applications.

Now, let's discuss how blockchain is perceived in the enterprise and some of the challenges that arise with enterprise adoption of the technology. In the following section, I'll focus on three areas that help set the tone for blockchain in an enterprise context.

How does the enterprise view blockchain?

Radical openness is an aspect of blockchain as a digital trust web, but in an enterprise, it's vital to consider the impact and implications of radical openness.

A public blockchain can operate with extreme simplicity, supporting a highly distributed master list of all transactions, which is validated through a trust system supported by anonymous consensus. But can enterprises directly apply the model of the trustless system without modifying the fundamental tenets of blockchain?

Do organizations view this disruptive technology as a path to their transformation or merely a vehicle to help them improve their existing processes to take advantage of the efficiencies that the trust system promises? No matter what, enterprises will want the adoption of blockchain to be as minimally disruptive to the incumbent system as it can be, and that won't be easy to achieve! After all, the design inefficiencies of the incumbent system are what have compelled the enterprise to consider this paradigm shift. A lot of the concepts and use cases for blockchain are still distant from enterprise consumption.

The first industry to experiment with and adopt blockchain was the financial services sector, as it has been facing down the fear of being disrupted by another wave of start-ups. Like many industries, it is also driven by consumer demands for faster, lower-cost transactions. Financial services has a well-defined set of use cases including trade financing, trade platform, payment and remittance, smart contracts, crowd funding, data management and analytics, marketplace lending, and blockchain technology infrastructure. The uses for blockchain we've seen in this industry will likely permeate to other industries such as healthcare, retail, and the government in the future.

The blockchain is a nascent technology that brings together a lot of good ideas, but it still has some maturing to do for enterprise use. The lack of defined standards to promote interoperability between multi-domain chains could be a challenge. Enterprises that adopt it will therefore need to build competency so that they can contribute to further innovation and help with necessary blockchain standards development. This, in turn, could help bring unique opportunities to both improve existing business practices and develop new business models built in a blockchain-powered trust web:

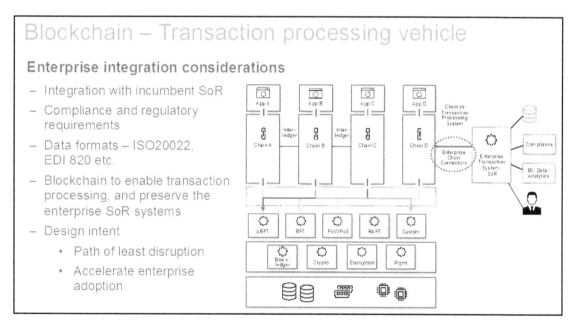

Litmus testing to justify the application of blockchain technology

Fundamentally, blockchain addresses three aspects of the transaction economy:

- Trade
- Ownership
- Trust

The notable technology elements of blockchain are:

- **Technology behind the trust system**: Consensus, mining, and the public ledger
- **Secret communication on open networks**: Cryptography and encryption
- **Non-repudiation systems**: Visibility to stacks of processes

While the implications of blockchain technology may be profound, organizations should devise a set of enterprise-specific criteria that can be applied to existing or new projects that may gravitate towards enterprise blockchains.

Given the versatility of blockchain technology and the current hype curve, enterprises should use a chain decision matrix as a tool to ensure that they have a structured approach to apply a foundational technology to a business domain. This approach will also lend itself to a consistent blockchain infrastructure and trust system management, which will prove vital as many application-driven chains evolve and the demand for enterprise visibility, management, and control grow.

Integrating a blockchain infrastructure for the whole enterprise

Any enterprise adoption of blockchain should have the goal of disrupting incumbent systems. Thinking about integration with enterprise systems of record is one way to work towards this. In this manner, an enterprise can implement blockchain-driven transaction processing and use its existing systems of record as an interface to its other applications, such as business intelligence, data analytics, regulatory interactions, and reporting.

It's vital to separate the infrastructure for enterprise blockchain technology from the business domain that uses chain technology to gain competitive advantage. Blockchain can be seen as an enterprise chain infrastructure that's invisible to businesses and operating behind the scenes, while promoting the **interprise synergy** between various business-driven chains. The idea is to separate the business domain from the technology that supports it. A chain application ought to be provisioned by a business domain that has a suitable trust system. The trust system, as I've stated repeatedly, is central to any blockchain endeavor, and therefore it should be appropriate to the needs of a given business application. The cost of the infrastructure and compute requirements will be dictated by the choice of trust system available to an enterprise.

By separating out the blockchain technology infrastructure, designing an architecture around a pluggable trust system by using trust intermediaries and a design that promotes flexibility, and a modular trust system, the business can focus on the business and regulatory requirements, such as AML, KYC, nonrepudiation, and so on. The technology infrastructure for blockchain applications should be open, modular, and adaptable for any blockchain variant, thereby making the blockchain endeavor easy to manage.

Interprise synergy suggests driving synergies between numerous enterprise blockchains to enable inter and intra enterprise chain (interledger) connections. In this model, the transactions would cross the various trust systems, giving visibility into the interactions to enterprise governance and control systems. Fractal visibility and the associated protection of enterprise data are important to consider when looking at these interactions between business units and external enterprises. An invisible enterprise chain infrastructure can provide a solid foundation to evolve enterprise connectors and expose APIs to make incumbent systems more chain-aware.

Interprise synergy will flourish due to conditional programmable contracts (smart contracts) between the business chains:

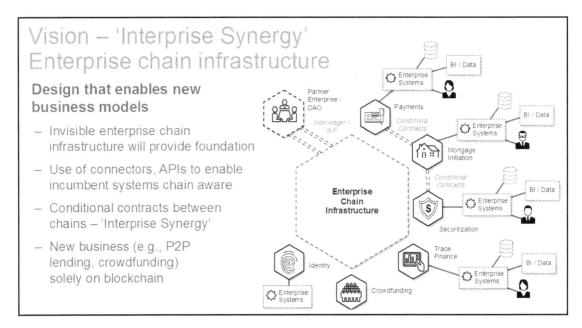

How can an enterprise know if it is ready for blockchain? More importantly, when considering blockchain consumption, should its focus be on integration with incumbent transaction systems, or an enterprise-aware blockchain infrastructure?

To take full advantage of the promise of enterprise blockchain, an integrated enterprise will need more than one use case and will need to drive **interprise synergy**. The most successful blockchain consumption strategy should focus on technology initially and then consider integration with existing enterprise business systems. This will facilitate collective understanding and accelerate enterprise adoption of the blockchain, hopefully on the path of least disruption.

Enterprise design principles

As stated previously, blockchain technology promises to be the foundation for a secure transaction network that induces trust and security in industries that are plagued with systemic issues around trust and accountability. It aims to generate market and cost efficiencies.

In the past few years, as blockchain technology has come to maturity, we've focused on how enterprises and businesses can use the technology to relieve pain points and herald new business models. Organizations that have begun to see blockchain's potential are now beginning to reshape business networks that are burdened by the systemic costs of archaic processes, paperwork, and technology.

Business drivers and evolution

In the recent past, organizations would run internal business systems and IT infrastructure out to the internet to harness the collaborative potential of interconnected and accessible systems. Blockchain technology is taking this to the next level, offering true digital interaction facilitated by trusted business networks. In the internet era, successful enterprises adopted and adapted to technological challenges, whereas in the blockchain era, business, rather than technology, is the driver for proliferation.

While blockchain technology is interesting on its own, there are a lot of other mechanics of a business network that ought to be evaluated as well, including:

- **Consensus models**: Which trust system is most fitting for your business network?
- **Control and governance**: What entities are permitted to do what? Who will own the investigative process if there's a system anomaly?
- **Digital asset generation**: Who creates an asset in the system? Who governs it?
- **Authority for issuance**: In a system that's truly decentralized, the notion of authority does not hold together. So in a blockchain network, who would be responsible for governance, culpability, and eventually regulations?
- **Security considerations:** How will the network address enterprise security, including new security challenges imposed by a shared business network?

We imagine a purpose-built blockchain network that's focused on a plurality of business domains, for example, mortgages, payments, exchanges, clearing, and settlement of specific asset types. In an enterprise context, we visualize a centralized network in which like-minded business entities share a consensus consortium. There are several practical reasons to back this idea of a centralized network, including the following:

- The use of domain-specific business language, which leads to the construction, management, and governance of smart contracts as proxy business representations
- A defined asset type, which leads to governance, management, and valuation (for exchange, fungibility, and so on) of the digital representation of assets

- Appropriate regulation, given that every industry and business network is regulated separately, and therefore the burden of adhering to regulations and other related costs can be shared in the business network
- Other related business functions such as analysis, analytics, market data, and so on

We've now covered the business drivers for enterprise blockchain, so next let's consider what can ensure the sustainability and longevity of a blockchain network.

Ensuring sustainability

Blockchain-based business networks are continuing to evolve and grow, and as they do, there will be no turning back on core issues such as trust models, data visibility, and exploiting a network for competitive advantage.

Focusing on sustainability can seem paradoxical because it promotes open collaborative innovation while at the same time locking down constructs such as consensus or trust systems and the governance systems for managing assets, smart contracts, and overall interaction in a multiparty transaction network. Blockchain system design needs to take all of this under consideration.

A business network with a successful system design needs to align well with the blockchain tenets of trade, trust, ownership, and transactionality in a multi-party scenario. Without building on these core tenets, business networks may not realize the promise of blockchain technology in a sustainable way.

Here are seven design principles to support and sustain growth in a blockchain business network:

- The network participants need to have control of their business
- The network has to be extensible, so that participants have flexibility to join or leave the network
- The network must be permissioned but also protected, to safeguard competitive data while facilitating peer-to-peer transactions
- The network should allow open access and global collaboration for shared innovation
- The network must be scalable for both transaction processing and encrypted data processing

- The network has to be able to accommodate enterprise security and address new security challenges
- The network needs to coexist with established systems of record and transaction systems in the enterprise

We will list the design principles graphically as follows:

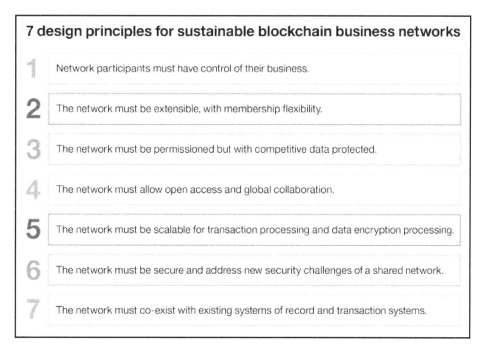

The principles that drive blockchain adoption

In any enterprise, blockchain adoption is driven by three principles: the business blueprint, the technology blueprint, and enterprise integration.

The following are some indispensable things to consider when choosing a blockchain framework according to these three principles:

- **Business blueprint**: Blockchain promises to create a business network of value based on trust. To do this, it's vital to understand how various blockchain frameworks handle network interaction patterns, inefficiencies, and vulnerabilities.
- **Technology blueprint**: If technology is to align with business imperatives, organizations need to make appropriate technology and architecture choices for their needs. **Transactions per second** (**TPS**), enterprise integration, external system integration, and regulatory and compliance requirements may be taken under advisement here. These decisions are all part of the technical due diligence necessary to properly budget for blockchain adoption.
- **Enterprise integration**: Integrating blockchain into enterprise systems, especially an adjacent system, is an important business and technology consideration (because downstream transaction systems affect critical business systems) as well as a cost point. Based on my experience, if organizations don't focus on adjacent system integration early in the planning, it can impede adoption, because it has a significant cost impact on blockchain projects.

In the following sections, I cover each of these design considerations in a bit more detail.

Business considerations for choosing a blockchain framework

Numerous criteria come into play when organizations are evaluating whether to adopt blockchain to address their pain points. Here are some considerations from a business perspective:

- **Open platform and open governance**: The technology standards a business chooses will set the stage for enterprise blockchain adoption, compliance, governance, and the overall cost of the solution.
- **Economic viability of the solution**: Whatever blockchain framework an organization chooses should provide cost alignment to its existing business models, chargebacks, compute equity, and account management. This flows into ROI.

- **Longevity of the solution**: As organizations aspire to build a trusted network, they'll want to ensure that they can sustain the cost and operation of the network so that it can grow and scale to accommodate additional participants and transactions.
- **Regulatory compliance**: Compliance issues are closely tied to transaction processing and can include events such as industry-specific reporting and analysis for business workflows and tasks, both automated and human-centric.
- **Coexistence with adjacent systems**: A blockchain network needs to be able to coexist with the rest of the enterprise, network participants, and adjacent systems, which may have overlapping and complementary functions.
- **Predictable costs of business growth**: Business growth depends upon predictable metrics. Historically, a lot of industries have focused on transactions per second, but that measurement differs from system to system based on system design, compute costs, and business processes.
- **Access to skills and talent**: The availability of talent affects costs as well as maintenance and the longevity of a blockchain solution as the industry and technology evolve with continued innovation.
- **Financial viability of technology vendors**: When choosing vendors, it's vital to think about their viability when it comes to long-term support and the longevity of your blockchain solution. You should examine the long-term vision and the sustainability of the vendor or the business partner's business model.
- **Global footprint and support**: Blockchain solutions tend to involve business networks with a global reach and the related skills to support the network's expansion with minimal disruption.
- **Reliance on technology and industry-specific standards**: Standards are critical, not only in helping to standardize a shared technology stack and deployment, but also in establishing an effective communication platform for industry experts to use for problem solving. Standards make low-cost, easy-to-consume technology possible.

Blockchain vendors offer various specializations, including:

- **Variant trust systems**: Consensus, mining, proof of work, and so on.
- Lock-in to a single trust system
- Infrastructure components that are purpose-built for particular use cases
- Field-tested design through proof of concept

The technological risk of a vendor not adhering to reference architecture based on standardized technology set is a fragmented blockchain model for the enterprise.

From a business point of view, an open standards-based approach to blockchain offers flexibility, along with a pluggable and modular trust system, and therefore is the most ideal option. This approach keeps an enterprise open to specialized blockchains such as Ripple, provides a provisioning layer for the trust system, and offers a separate business domain with the technology to support it.

Technology considerations for choosing a blockchain framework

When organizations consider the technology implications of blockchain, they should start with the premise that it is not just another application. It's a production network that involves risks and costs to ensure correct upkeep and maintenance.

Here are some important things to ponder when evaluating blockchain's technological impact.

Identity management

Identity management is a complicated, involved topic, especially in regulated industries where identities must be managed and have significant business consequences, such as around activities including **Know Your Customer** (**KYC**), **Anti-Money Laundering** (**AML**), and other reporting and analytics functions:

- **Permissioning** is the concept of **member enrollment certificates** (**eCerts**) and **transaction certificates for each member** (**tCerts**); these enable an entity to be permissioned and identified while transactions are completed
- **End user identity**, which is maintained by a participating entity in the blockchain network, is the mapping of the LDAP/User registry to the tCerts or transaction ID for the sake of tracing (Know Your Customer, as well as Know Your Customer's Customer)

Other identity management considerations include:

- An LDAP or existing user registry won't go away and has to be considered as a design point, since there's typically been significant investment and security policies in place for mature authentication and authorization systems
- Trust systems are at the heart of blockchain technology and must pave the way for trust with identity insertion (for use cases that require transactional traceability)
- The identity on blockchain and for blockchain
- Identity acquisition, vetting, and life cycle
- Alignment with trust systems based on use cases

Scalability

Scalability is both a business and a technology consideration, given the way downstream transaction systems can affect critical business systems. Technology choices for scalability, for example database choices for the shared ledger, adjacent system integration, encryption, and consensus, bring about a system design that can accommodate the predictable costs of growth in network membership or transactions.

Enterprise security

There are three layers of enterprise security to think about:

- The **physical IT infrastructure layer**, which includes use case-specific issues such as EAL5, network, and infrastructure isolation requirements.
- The **blockchain middleware layer**, which includes requirements for crypto modules, encryption levels, encryption on data storage, transfer and data at rest, and visibility of data between participants in the network.
- The **blockchain consensus** (trust system layer), which is central to blockchain and necessary to guarantee basic **data store** properties. If there are more players in the network, they have to bring capital equity to scale. This is about building a **shared data store** with enterprise data qualities at a lower barrier to entry. Consensus, even minimal consensus, is necessary to ensure this on the architecture in place. There's now a divide between cryptocurrency-based trust systems and non-cryptocurrency-based trust systems. The former models, such as POW/PoS, aren't sustainable for enterprise use cases aspiring to create permissioned blockchains.

Development tooling

Considerations for development tooling include an integrated development environment, business modeling, and model-driven development.

Crypto-economic models

The crypto-economic model refers to a decentralized system that uses public key cryptography for authentication and economic incentives to guarantee that it continues without going back in time or incurring other alterations. To fully grasp the idea of blockchain and the benefits of cryptography in computer science, we must first understand the idea of **decentralized consensus**, since it is a key tenet of the crypto-based computing revolution.

Decentralization with systemic governance

The old paradigm was centralized consensus, where one central database would rule transaction validity. A decentralized scheme breaks with this, transferring authority and trust to a decentralized network and enabling its nodes to continuously and sequentially record transactions on a public block, creating a unique chain—thus the term blockchain. Cryptography (by way of hash codes) secures the authentication of the transaction source, removing the need for a central intermediary. By combining cryptography and blockchain, the system ensures no duplicate recording of the same transaction.

Blockchain system design should preserve the idea of decentralized digital transaction processing, adapting it into a permissioned network, while centralizing some aspects of regulatory compliance and maintenance activity as needed for an enterprise context.

Enterprise support

Having enterprise support for blockchain is important for the same reasons as the reconsideration of estimation effort. Remember that blockchain should not be thought of as just another application. It's a production network that involves risks and costs for upkeep and maintenance, and it won't be able to simply use existing applications for development, infrastructure, and services.

Use case-driven pluggability choices

To make sure your blockchain solution can allow for use case-driven pluggability choices, consider the following issues.

Shared ledger technology

The use cases, design imperatives, and problems you're trying to address through blockchain will all help determine the choice of shared ledger and database technologies.

Consensus

Consensus guides the trust system and drives technology investment in blockchain application infrastructure, and therefore is at the heart of blockchain. Also, there isn't one consensus type that fits all use cases. Use cases define the interaction between participants and suggest a most appropriate trust system through consensus models.

Consensus is a way to validate the order of network requests or transactions (deploy and invoke) on a blockchain network. Ordering network transactions correctly is critical because many have a dependency on one or more prior transactions (account debits often have a dependency on prior credits, for example).

In a blockchain network, no single authority determines the transaction order; instead, each blockchain node (or peer) has an equal say in establishing the order, by implementing the network consensus protocol. Consensus consequently ensures that a quorum of nodes agree on the order in which transactions are appended to the shared ledger. Consensus, by resolving discrepancies in the proposed transaction order, helps guarantee that all network nodes are operating on an identical blockchain. In other words, it guarantees both the integrity and consistency of transactions in a blockchain network.

Crypto algorithms and encryption technology

Choosing a blockchain system design may be guided by crypto library and encryption technology as well. An organization's use case requirements will dictate this choice and drive technology investments in blockchain application infrastructure:

- **Asymmetric**: RSA (1024-8192), DSA (1024-3072), Diffie-Hellman, KCDSA, Elliptic Curve Cryptography (ECDSA, ECDH, ECIES) with named, user-defined, and brainpool curves
- **Symmetric**: AES, RC2, RC4, RC5, CAST, DES, Triple DES, ARIA, SEED
- **Hash/message digest/HMAC**: SHA-1, SHA-2 (224-512), SSL3-MD5-MAC, SSL3-SHA-1-MAC, SM3
- **Random number generation**: FIPS 140-2 approved DRBG (SP 800-90 CTR mode)

Use case-driven pluggable choices

As previously stated, use cases will define the interaction between participants and will suggest the most appropriate trust system using consensus models.

Enterprise integration and designing for extensibility

Designing a blockchain network to coexist with existing systems of record in an organization is important as a cost consideration. Integration should be through both business and technology issues, since downstream transaction systems impact essential business systems. By working with many enterprises, I've found that integrating blockchain with the adjacent systems has a significant cost impact on their blockchain projects. It really needs to be addressed early in the planning stages, so not to adversely affect enterprise adoption.

It's also important to think about operational issues. By safeguarding the elements of trade, trust, and ownership—and the inherent properties of blockchain such as immutability, provenance, and consensus—a trust system promises to help eliminate redundant and duplicate systems and processes. These duplications cost an organization significant resources, leading to slower transaction processing and associated opportunity costs. One goal with blockchain adoption should be to address the central pain point of the existing process. The aspiration is for a transparent ledger that increases trust, saves time and significant costs, and provides better customer service.

As for network extensibility, designing for extensibility means taking future growth into consideration as you plan the implementation. Extensibility measures a system's ability to extend and the level of effort that will be required to implement extensions. Extensibility is important with blockchain business network design, not only to accommodate for the dynamic nature of business (with all its regulations, competitive pressures, and market dynamics), but also to accommodate for network growth (the addition of regulators, market makers, disruptions, service providers, and so on).

The following are some design considerations to help ensure network extensibility:

- **Flexibility with membership**:A blockchain network may start with a finite group of participants and roles, but new participants could later want to join the network, and others may want to leave. Therefore, you have to consider the mechanics of membership changes, including access to (shared) data. The member type is also an important thought when designing for extensibility, as the roles and type of members may change over time.
- **Compute equity**: There's a split between trust systems based on cryptocurrency and trust systems based on compute equity, so this is a fairly new concept. The types of participants and their business interests in the network are determinants of long-term sustainable infrastructure costs and maintenance. For instance, cost models of regulators may differ greatly from cost models of the primary beneficiary of a blockchain-powered business network.
- **Shared business interests**: Blockchain networks promise specific advantages for businesses, such as reduced risk, a reliable and predictable transaction network, lower compliance costs, and so on. But these shared interests can lead to other operational issues, such as data sharing and ownership as entities join and leave the network. Since regulations around data ownership evolve, as well as industry requirements for the durability of data, these should be evaluated carefully when you design a blockchain system.
- **Governance**: Governance includes managing technical artifacts such as technology infrastructure and governing data and smart contracts in a blockchain network. Layering governance in the following categories is recommended:
  - Blockchain network/technology governance
  - Blockchain data governance
  - Blockchain smart contract governance
  - Blockchain transaction management governance

When designing for extensibility, the goal should be to ensure that the blockchain network has sustainable operational elements and business growth elements. For example, in a sustainable model, every participant could deploy the chaincode that governs its own business process as it accepts and deals with digital assets, while also putting business participants in control of changing business processes, policies, and regulatory requirements.

Other considerations

There are a few other considerations to keep in mind apart from the previously mentioned aspects. They are briefly explained in the following sections.

Consensus, ACID property, and CAP

A consensus model will never go to 0 because when NoSQL became the standard, various NoSQL systems solved their problems by understanding this CAP theorem, and the RDBMS enterprise community held steadfast to their ACID properties. Blockchain might well provide the primitives to break CAP and maintain ACID. Here are some thoughts.

CAP

Cap stands for:

- **C—Consistency**: Consensus guarantees only one truth of what happened and in what order
- **A—Availability**: The fact that all calls to the blockchain are asynchronous allows the *invoking* application to make progress while ensuring consensus and durability (chaining also guarantees this)
- **P—Network partition**: Consensus, again, prevents split-brain with conflicts when things get back together after a network partition

ACID

ACID stands for:

- **A—Atomicity**: The chaincode programming model is an all-or-nothing behavior, which allows you to group activities together. Either everything happens, or it doesn't.
- **C—Consistency**: We believe the new world of NoSQL fudges this one. I believe this means the same as the C in CAP.
- **I—Isolation**: Isolation indicates that two transactions are serialized, which is exactly what block construction and chaining does.
- **D—Durability**: The chaining and replication all over the network ensures that if one or more nodes go down, data won't be lost. This is why everyone wants to bring a node and why those nodes should not be not co-located.

Attestation – SSCs are signed and encrypted

In **secure service containers** (**SSC**s), the software, operating system, hypervisors, and Docker container images cannot be modified. Certificates may be included in the SSC so that they can probe themselves into being genuine to a remote a party. For example, including an SSL certificate when building SSCs helps ensure that you're speaking with a genuine instance, since the SSL certificate always stays protected (encrypted) within the SSC.

Use of HSMs

According to `Wikipedia`, a **hardware security module** (**HSM**) is a physical computing device that safeguards and manages digital keys for strong authentication and provides cryptoprocessing. These modules traditionally come in the form of a plugin card or an external device that attaches directly to a computer or network server.

Administering a high-security device such as an HSM can be a real challenge in relation to sufficient security and controls. In fact, today's standards mandate certain methods and levels of security for HSM administrative (and key management) systems.

Summary

Adopting blockchain in an enterprise will require a balancing act. Organizations will not only have to run, manage, and maintain their existing infrastructure; they'll also need to help pave the way for this new computational model that promises to bring transformation.

In regulated industries, organizations could face a dual impact on the cost of compliance, since even a new technology platform still needs to adhere to established regulatory frameworks and proven technology architecture standards and design. Enterprises considering blockchain can look towards a pragmatic approach by adopting a doctrine of layered defense, combining multiple mitigating security controls to help protect their resources and data. With the layered defense approach, digital assets/smart contracts as well as ledger data will be guarded.

2
Exploring Hyperledger Fabric

The focus of this chapter is the Hyperledger Fabric project—its components, design, reference architecture, and overall enterprise readiness. We will also discuss the broader aim of **Linux Foundation** (**LF**) hosted Hyperledger projects and the importance of open source and open standards. The goal is to build an understanding of the diversity of various Hyperledger projects, and what frameworks and tools may be suitable for particular enterprise use cases and software consumption models. While the blockchain technology landscape is constantly in flux, Hyperledger projects represent a structure that supports a mature and peer-reviewed technology geared toward enterprise consumption and fueled by a diverse set of talent and community interests.

This chapter will cover the following topics:

- Hyperledger frameworks, tools, and building blocks
- Hyperledger Fabric component design
- Hyperledger Fabric – the journey of a sample transaction
- Exploring Hyperledger Fabric
- Understanding governance in business networks powered by blockchain

Hyperledger frameworks, tools, and building blocks

Now that we've looked at Hyperledger's foundations in the open computing movement, as well as its benefits for industry, let's talk about the frameworks, tools, and building blocks of Hyperledger.

Hyperledger frameworks

There are five blockchain frameworks, as follows:

- **Hyperledger Iroha**: Iroha, designed for mobile development projects, is based on Hyperledger Fabric and was contributed by Soramitsu, Hitachi, NTT Data, and Colu. It features modern, domain-driven C++ design as well as a new chain-based Byzantine fault tolerant consensus algorithm called **Sumeragi**.

- **Hyperledger Sawtooth**: Sawtooth was contributed by Intel and includes a novel consensus algorithm that Intel came up with that's called **Proof of Elapsed Time (PoET)**. PoET aims to achieve distributed consensus as efficiently as possible. Hyperledger Sawtooth has potential in many areas, with support for both permissioned and permissionless deployments and recognition of diverse requirements. Sawtooth is designed for versatility.

- **Hyperledger Burrow**: Hyperledger Burrow, which was contributed by Monax and Intel initially, is a modular blockchain that was client-built to the specification of the **Ethereum Virtual Machine (EVM)**.

- **Hyperledger Fabric (HLF)**: Hyperledger Fabric, contributed by IBM, is designed to be a foundation for developing applications or solutions with a modular architecture. It allows for plug-and-play components, such as consensus and membership services, and leverages containers to host smart contracts called **chaincode** that comprise the application logic of the system. The remainder of this chapter will focus on Hyperledger Fabric and its design, components, architecture, and overall enterprise design.

- **Hyperledger Indy**: Contributed initially by the Sovrin Foundation, Indy is a Hyperledger project made to support independent identity on distributed ledgers. Hyperledger Indy provides tools, libraries, and reusable components for providing digital identities rooted on blockchains or other distributed ledgers:

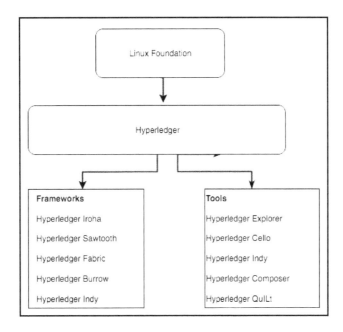

Hyperledger tools

There are also five tools currently in the Hyperledger project—all of which are hosted by the LF. These tools are as follows:

- **Hyperledger explorer**: Hyperledger explorer, which was originally contributed by IBM, Intel, and DTCC, can view, invoke, deploy or query blocks, transactions and associated data, network information (name, status, list of nodes), chain codes and transaction families, as well as other relevant information stored in the ledger.

- **Hyperledger cello**: Cello was also contributed by IBM. It seeks to bring the on demand as-a-service deployment model into the blockchain ecosystem in order to reduce the effort required to create, manage, and terminate blockchains. Cello efficiently and automatically provides a multi-tenant chain service on top of various infrastructures, such as bare metal, virtual machine, and other container platforms.
- **Hyperledger composer**: Hyperledger composer (contributed by IBM and Oxchains) is a set of collaboration tools for building blockchain business networks that accelerate the development of smart contracts and blockchain applications, as well as their deployment across a distributed ledger.
- **Hyperledger quilt**: Hyperledger quilt, from NTT data and Ripple, is a Java implementation of the interledger protocol by ripple, which is designed to transfer values across distributed and non-distributed ledgers.
- **Hyperledger caliper**: Caliper, a blockchain benchmark tool that allows users to measure performance of a specific implementation with predefined use cases, is in incubation status and was contributed by developers from numerous organizations.

The building blocks of blockchain solutions

As noted in `Chapter 1`, *Blockchain – Enterprise and Industry Perspective*, blockchain promises to fundamentally solve the issues of *time* and *trust* in industries such as financial services, supply chain, logistics, and healthcare. It seeks to streamline business processes and thereby address inefficiencies. It's a technology for a new generation of transactional applications built on trust, accountability, and transparency. There are several characteristics shared by every industrial blockchains, including the following:

- A shared single source of truth
- Secure and tamper-proof
- Private unlinkable identity
- Scalable architecture
- Confidential
- Auditable

The diagram that follows summarizes these characteristics into four tenets:

Append-only distributed system of record shared across business network
- Shared between participants
- Participants have own copy through replication
- Permissioned, so participants see only appropriate transactions

Business terms embedded in transaction database & executed with transactions
- Verifiable, signed
- Encoded in programming language
- Analogous to a stored procedure call on a database

Ensuring appropriate visibility; transactions are secure, authenticated & verifiable
- Cryptography central to these processes
- Access permission controlled via certification management

Transactions are endorsed by relevant participants
- Endorsed transactions are added to the ledger with appropriate confidentiality
- Assets have a verifiable audit trail
- Transactions cannot be modified, inserted or deleted

Blockchain solutions are comprised of four building blocks—a shared ledger, privacy, trust, and smart contracts. Allow me to elaborate a bit on each of these building blocks:

- **Shared ledger**: With bitcoin blockchain, the intent was to democratize visibility; however, enterprise blockchain requires a different approach due to the regulation of consumer data. Append-only distributed transaction records can be achieved by SQL or no-SQL distributed databases.
- **Privacy through cryptography**: Privacy through cryptography is essential for ensuring that transactions are authenticated and verified. It is imperative to include cryptography in blockchain design for the sake of hardening security and making it more difficult to breach the distributed system. Considerations about cryptography change when you're working with a less democratic or permissioned ledger network.

- **Trust systems or consensus**: Trust means using the power of the network to verify a transaction. Trust is essential in any blockchain system or application, and I prefer the term *trust* system over *consensus* system since trust is the foundational element that dictates a stakeholder's investment in any blockchain infrastructure. The trust system is modified whenever new entrants come into the blockchain space and apply blockchain technology to a new use case or specialization. The trust model is truly the heart of blockchain—it's what delivers the tenets of *trust*, *trade*, and *ownership*. Trust is what enables blockchain to displace the transaction system, but this can only happen when trade and ownership are addressed by distributed/shared ledgers. There's still much work needed to define an optimized trust system for various use cases. Database solutions are in the works to address scale and mobile use cases, but more work is require around P2P and sharing economy models, as well as B2B models.

- **Smart contracts**: In the context of blockchain, a smart contract is a business agreement embedded into the transaction database and executed with transactions. Rules are needed in business to define the flow of value and state of a transaction, so that's the function of the contract here. The contract is smart because it's a computerized protocol to execute the terms of the contract. Various contractual clauses (such as collateral, bonding, delineation of property rights, and so forth) can be codified so as to enforce compliance with the terms of the contract and ensure a successful transaction—this is the basic idea behind smart contracts. Smart contracts are designed to reassure one party that the other will fulfill their promise. Part of the objective of such contracts is to reduce the costs of verification and enforcement. Smart contracts must be observable (meaning that participants can see or prove each other's actions pertaining to the contract), verifiable (meaning that participants can prove to other nodes that a contract has been performed or breached), and private (meaning that knowledge of the contents/performance of the contract should involve only the necessary participants required to execute it). Bitcoin made provisions for smart contracts; however, it lacked some capabilities such as Turing-completeness, lack of state, and so on. Ethereum improved upon bitcoin's limitations by building a blockchain with a built-in Turing-complete programming language, so that anyone can write smart contracts and decentralized applications by creating their own arbitrary rules for ownership, transaction formats, and state transition functions. These advances made it possible for complex contracts to be codified in a blockchain, such as instant transfer of credit to a traveler's bank account when a flight is delayed beyond a certain duration or payment of employee compensation if performance goals are achieved.

- How does this work practically? Well, smart contracts are deployed as code on the blockchain nodes, which we might more appropriately call smart contract code. This code is a way of using blockchain technology to complement, or replace, existing legal contracts. This smart contract code is deployed on the blockchain node in a programming language such as Solidity or Golang. Deploying the code on the blockchain provides three important properties:
  - Permanence and censorship resistance inherited from the blockchain,
  - The ability of the program itself to control blockchain assets, such as by transferring ownership or quantities of an asset among participants
  - Execution of the program by the blockchain, ensuring that it will always execute as written and no-one can interfere

In the enterprise world, smart contracts would probably involve blockchain's smart contract code, accompanied by a more traditional legal contract. For example, a smart contract code may execute on a land registry blockchain network to transfer ownership of a house from one party to another, so that land registry records are updated in real time and all participants such as the city, realtors, lawyers, and banks can all update their own records upon completion of the sale. However, the home buyer will insist on a legal contract with indemnity clauses to cover any undiscovered liens.

Hyperledger Fabric component design

Let's discuss various components that facilitate the blockchain technology tenets of shared ledger, encryption, the trusts system, and smart contracts. The components represent the Hyperledger Fabric infrastructure components and provide isolation from chain code or smart contract development constructs. Chain code or smart contract development details will be discussed in detail in a separate chapter.

The following diagram depicts the Hyperledger Fabric infrastructure components:

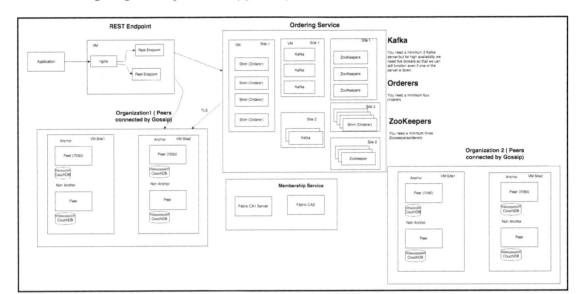

Hyperledger Fabric infrastructure components

Following are the infrastructure components:

- **Hyperledger Fabric CA** is an implementation of membership services but is not required to be used (that is, any X509-based PKI infrastructure that can issue EC certificates can be used)
- **Dedicated orderer nodes**
    - Implements atomic broadcast API
    - Orders and batches transactions and signs each batch (block) to create a hash chain
    - Hyperledger Fabric provides two implementations—Solo (for dev/test) and a Kafka-based implementation for production/fault tolerance
    - The ordering service is pluggable—the implementer needs to only provide an atomic broadcast API based on the gRPC interface definition

- **Peers** are now responsible for existing smart logic (chaincode) and maintaining the ledger
    - Endorsement simulates transactions (that is, it executes them, but does not commit them)
    - Peers receive batches of endorsed transactions from the orderer nodes and then validate and commit transactions (this eliminates non-determinism)

Principles of Hyperledger design

Hyperledger Fabric, again, is a blockchain implementation that is designed for deploying a modular and extensible architecture. It has a modular subsystem design so that different implementations can be plugged in and implemented over time. This section covers the Hyperledger Fabric reference architecture and describes the details on the various components/modules and their interactions and functions. Understanding the reference architecture facilitates better solution and technology design decisions, especially around scalability, security, and performance.

While in this book we will discuss the reference architecture of Hyperledger Fabric, please note that all the Hyperledger projects (the frameworks referred to previously) follow a design philosophy that includes the following principles:

- **Modular and extensible approach**: This implies modularity in all components of all frameworks. Components defined by Hyperledger for all projects include (but are not limited to) the following:
    - Consensus layer
    - Smart contract (chain code) layer
    - Communication (gossip) layer
    - Data store (persistent, log, and ledger data)
    - Identity services (root of trust—to identify the participants)
    - APIs
    - Pluggable cryptography
- **Interoperability**: This principle is around backward interoperability and NOT the interoperability between the various Hyperledger project-powered blockchain systems or business networks.

- **Focus on secure solutions**: Enterprise and therefore business network security is paramount, hence the focus on security-and not just of the crypto abstraction-but the interaction between components and the structure that governs the permissioning nature of permissioned blockchains. Most industries embarking on the permissioned blockchain are established and regulated industries.
- **Token (or coin or crypto-asset) agnostic approach**: This is discussed in great length in the governance section, but Hyperledger projects do not use crypto-assets, cryptocurrency, tokens, or coin-like constructs as incentive mechanics to establish trust systems. While there is a notion of asset tokenization that represents a physical, virtual, or dematerialized asset, tokenization of assets is a vastly different concept than a systemic token that is generated in the system as a virtualization of incentive economics.
- **Focus on rich and easy-to-use APIs**: The focus here is to ensure that blockchain systems have not only enterprise middleware access, but access to business networks, existing participants, and new systems without exposing the details of blockchain powered business networks.

CAP Theorem

The CAP Theorem as postulated by Eric Brewer in 2000 at ACM Symposium on Principles of distributed computing (PODC) (`https://dl.acm.org/citation.cfm?id=343502`) states that in a distributed data store it is impossible to guarantee more than any two of the following three properties: Consistency (C), Availability (A), and Partition Tolerance (P). A distributed data store thus can be characterized on the two properties it guarantees namely CA, CP or AP.

More specifically, the theorem is aimed at distributed systems deployed across unreliable networks (networks with faults and delays such as the Internet) leading to a partitioning of the system components. According to CAP, in these environments, the system design must focus on the balance between availability and consistency. For example, the ACID (Atomicity, Consistency, Isolation, Durability) approach typically provided by RDBMS (Relational Database Management Systems) guarantees consistency on a single node on the expense of availability across multiple nodes (CP type of systems). However, note that, different configurations may yield different combinations namely CA or AP as well.

In contrast, Fabric is designed similarly as many other Blockchain platforms as AP type of system with Eventual Consistency also referred to as BASE (Basically Available, Soft state, Eventual consistency).

In context of blockchain CAP properties can be defined as following:

- **Consistency:** The blockchain network avoids any forks of the ledger
- **Availability:** Transactions submitted by clients are permanently committed into the ledger and available on all the network peers
- **Partition tolerance:** The blockchain network continues to operate despite an arbitrary number of transaction proposals or blocks are being dropped (or delayed) by the physical network medium between the peers

Fabric achieves the CAP properties as follows:

- **Consistency:** By a total order of transactions and version control using MVCC
- **Availability:** By hosting a copy of the ledger on each of the peers
- **Partition tolerance:** By maintaining operation despite failed nodes (up to a threshold)

As you can see, availability and partition tolerance (AP properties of the CAP theorem) are guaranteed by default in most blockchain systems. However, consistency is harder to provide.

Fabric achieves consistency by combining the following elements:

- The transaction processing is split into a sequence of steps across multiple components of the network.
- Clients connect to a communication channel and submit transaction proposals to endorsing peers and then to the ordering service.
- The ordering service orders transactions into blocks with a total order i.e. the order of the transactions is guaranteed to be consistent across the whole network. The blocks once created are broadcasted to each member peer of the channel. The broadcasting protocol guarantees reliable delivery of the blocks to the peers in a correct order namely total-order broadcast.
- As we will explain in Multiversion concurrency control, upon reception of the block on the peer, the peer uses MVCC to validate each transaction based on the key versions stored in the transaction ReadSet. The MVCC validation guarantees consistency of the resulting ledger and of the Worldstate and prevents attacks such as double spending. However, it can also lead to elimination of otherwise valid transactions, which have been submitted in an order violating the `ReadSet` version validation check. The transactions are then marked either valid or invalid in the ledger.

- The ledger then contains a sequence of totally ordered blocks, where each block contains a sequence of totally ordered transactions (either valid or invalid), yielding a ledger imposing a total order across all transactions.

Hyperledger Fabric reference architecture

Hyperledger Fabric follows a modular design, and the following are some of the possible components or modules that can be plugged in and implemented. Note that this list is not exhaustive:

- **Membership services**: This module is essentially a permissioning module and acts as a vehicle to establish a root of trust during network creation, but this is also instrumental in ensuring and managing the identity of members. Membership services are essentially a certificate authority as well as utilized elements of the **public key infrastructure** (**PKI**) for things such as key distribution, management, and establishing federated trust as the network grows. The membership services module provides a specialized digital certificate authority for issuing certificates to members of the blockchain network, and it leverages cryptographic functions provided by Hyperledger Fabric.

- **Transactions**: A transaction is a request to the blockchain to execute a function on the ledger. The function is implemented by a chaincode. Cryptography ensures integrity of transactions by linking the transaction to previous blocks and ensuring the transactional integrity, if protected, by linking the cryptogram or hash from previously linked blocks. Each channel in Hyperledger Fabric is its own blockchain.

- **Smart contract or chaincode services**: Chaincode is an application-level code stored on the ledger as a part of a transaction. Chaincode runs transactions that may modify the world state. Transaction logic is written as chaincode (in the Go or JavaScript languages), and executes in secure Docker containers. The transaction transforms data, scoped by chaincode on the channel from which it operates.

Here are the smart contract or chaincode elements enabled by chaincode services. Chaincode is installed on peers, which require access to the asset states to perform reads and writes. The chaincode is then instantiated on specific channels for specific peers. Ledgers within a channel can be shared across entire networks of peers or include only a specific set of participants. Peers are able to participate in multiple channels:

- **Events**: The process of validating peers and chaincodes can produce events (pre-defined events and custom events generated by chaincode) on the network that applications may listen for and take actions on. These events are consumed by event adapters, which may further deliver events using vehicles such as WebHooks or Kafka. Fabric-committing peers provide an event stream to publish events to registered listeners. As of v1.0, the only events that get published are Block events. A Block event gets published whenever the committing peer adds a validated block to the ledger:

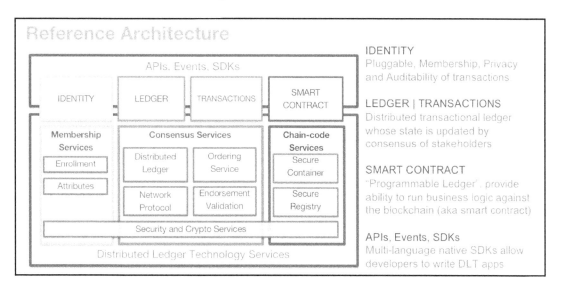

- **Consensus**: Consensus is at the heart of any blockchain system. It also enables a trust system. In general, the consensus service enables digitally signed transactions to be proposed and validated by network members. In Hyperledger Fabric, the consensus is pluggable and tightly linked to the endorse-order-validation model that Hyperledger proposes. The ordering services in Hyperledger Fabric represent the consensus system. The ordering service batches multiple transactions into blocks and outputs a hash-chained sequence of blocks containing transactions.
- **Ledger**: Another component is a distributed encrypted ledger, including an append-only data store. This provides the ability to query and write data across distributed ledgers. There are two options:
    - Level DB (default embedded KV DB) supports keyed queries, composite key queries, and key range queries
    - Couch DB (external option) supports keyed queries, composite key queries, key range queries, plus full data rich queries
- **Client SDK**: A client SDK enables the creation of applications that deploy and invoke transactions atop a shared ledger. The Hyperledger Fabric Reference Architecture supports both Node.js and Java SDK. A software developer kit is like a programming kit or set of tools that provide developers with the environment of libraries to write and test chaincode applications. SDKs are critical in blockchain application development and will be discussed in detail in further chapters. Specific capabilities included in the SDK are the application client, chaincode, users, events, and crypto suite.

Hyperledger Fabric runtime architecture

Now that we've looked at the reference architecture, let's consider the runtime architecture for Hyperledger Fabric:

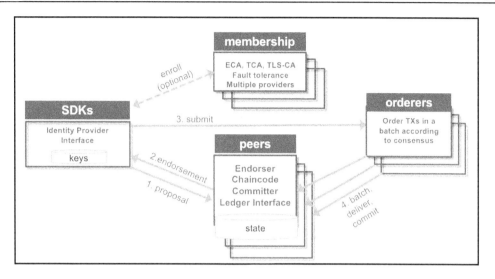

The following outline demonstrates a Hyperledger Fabric runtime transaction processing flow:

- **Transaction proposal (application SDK)**:
    1. Transaction proposal is submitted by application SDK
    2. It receives a transaction proposal response back (includes ReadWrite set) post endorsement
    3. It submits the transaction (includes ReadWrite set) to the ordering service

- **Transaction endorsement**:
    1. The transaction is sent to the counter-parties represented by endorsing peers on their channel
    2. Each peer executes the transaction by calling the specified chaincode function and signs the result, which becomes the read-write-set of the transaction
    3. Each peer may participate in multiple channels, allowing concurrent execution

- **Transaction submitted to the ordering service**:
    1. The ordering service accepts endorsed transactions and orders them according to the plug-in consensus algorithm, and then delivers them on the channel
    2. Peers on the channel receive transactions and validate before committing to the ledger

- **Transaction validation**:
    1. Validates each transaction and commit block
    2. Validates the endorsement policy
    3. Validates ReadSet versions in state DB
    4. Commits the block to blockchain
    5. Commits the valid transaction to state DB

Strengths and advantages of a componentized design

Hyperledger Fabric's component design offers several advantages. Many of these strengths relate to business network governance, which is an important compliance and costs consideration for Hyperledger Fabric in the enterprise.

These benefits include the following:

- **Delineates development design from runtime design**: Separating development and runtime design is important because the delineation is important from development best practices and infrastructure/hybrid cloud variations, and ensuring adherence to the current enterprise and their connectivity to the business network's application development, as well as DevOps practices.
- **Discerning between design imperatives and infrastructure/deployment capabilities**: Componentized design allows us to separate infrastructure design, which includes things such as network connections, security, permissioning, and contractual vehicles, from the overall application design of the business network blueprint that dictates the technology blueprint.

- **Incorporates network design principles**: The modularity of Hyperledger Fabric can address infrastructure scaling issues, such as the number of connections, co-location, security, container deployment practices, and so on. There are various considerations when it comes to network design, such as cloud deployment, hybrid and/or on premises, and a combination of any of the available options, which are dependent on the requirements of individual members in a business network. Network design also addresses the business challenges of network growth and the resulting performance and security driven **Service Level Agreements** (**SLA**) to its members.

- **Addresses channel design principles**: Modularity, or componentized design, can also address isolation, data privacy, and confidentiality between participants and controlled/permissioned access with robust audit capability. Channel constructs in Hyperledger Fabric enable us to address the business blueprint requirements around implementing business-defined transactions that may be bilateral, trilateral, or event multilateral. Channels also provide an avenue to limit the visibility of transaction data to a few participants or provide full access when required, such as to a regulator. Channel design also addresses critical business requirements around transaction processing, data visibility, business rules enforcement, and so on. It also has technology implications, such as a scalability, security, and the costs of the infrastructure that supports the business network. Finally, channel design addresses the business challenges of network growth and the resulting performance and security-driven SLAs to members.

- **Adopts Hyperledger Fabric composer model-driven development**: Hyperledger Composer, one of the tools discussed previously under Hyperledger tools, provides an avenue to modular development with a portable, standardized vehicle to add governance and control, similar to JEE constructs such as JAR/WAR/RAR, and so on. **Business network archive** (**BNA**) is an archive that can be integrated into DevOps practices for cross-enterprise team development and collaborative life cycle management capabilities. The idea is to separate chaincode development from infrastructure design and separate the competencies needed to maintain the two facets of enterprise or business network application technology practices. More details around Hyperledger Fabric composer will be discussed in a separate chapter dedicated to the composer and tooling.

Each of the advantages of componentized design described previously have cost implications in terms of runtime/infrastructure design (that is, use of resources and resulting costs), flexible design (such as products and relationships morphs), and the longevity of the solution (the global footprint of the enterprise cloud infrastructure, including robust access to technical and business SMEs in the form of maintenance and support)—all of which are essential for compliance, governance, and longevity of the solution, and resulting business networks powered by blockchain.

Hyperledger Fabric – the journey of a sample transaction

Now, let's look at the journey of a sample transaction with Hyperledger Fabric. This section will help lay the foundation of Hyperledger Fabric concepts and components in order to facilitate a better understanding of the layers involved in transaction processing:

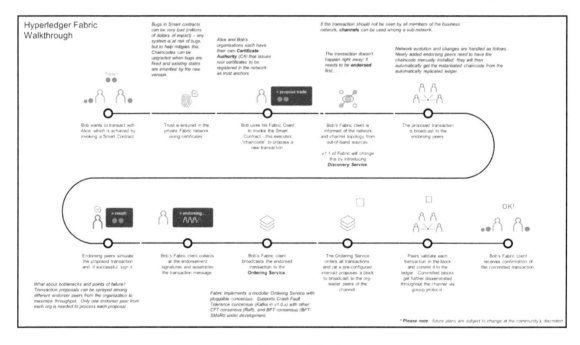

Hyperledger Fabric walkthrough

Fabric introduces a newly designed blockchain, preserving the transaction processing architecture and aiming at a secure, scalable, resilient, modular, and confidential design. Hyperledger Fabric (at the time of writing this book, the current version is 1.1) supports the execution of distributed applications supporting enterprise-friendly programming models. The components in Hyperledger Fabric provide a modular design, optimally suited for a business network made of various enterprises. Hyperledger Fabric introduces a model based on three steps, an *endorse-order-validate* architecture, designed for the distributed execution of untrusted code in an untrusted environment. This separation not only allows for provisioning at scale, but also ensures security by separation at every layer.

The transaction flow is separated into three steps, which may be run on different entities in the system:

1. **Endorsement of a transaction and checking its validity** (**validation step**): This step includes members of a channel to inspect and adhere to endorsement policies which define the acceptable agreed upon approach to validate a transaction proposal. Since peers need to update the ledger (upon transaction finality) the peers (that are subscribed to a channel) review the proposal and provide their ledgers version of (R)ead and (W)rite set. This validation step is vital as it provides the first step on transaction validation. This check also acts as a gate and prevents form erroneous downstream processing of transaction, which can be computationally expensive.
2. **Ordering through an ordering service**: This is a consensus protocol which is meant to be pluggable, irrespective of transaction semantics. The pluggability of the consensus provides enterprise and business networks with tremendous flexibility, as there are consensus mechanism considerations for various types of industries, use cases, and interactions between network participants.
3. **Validation or transaction commitment**: This implies committing a transaction and therefore going through a final set of validations per application-specific trust assumptions.

A Hyperledger Fabric transaction involves three types of nodes:

- **The committing peer** is the node that maintains the ledger and state. The committing peer is the party that *commits* transactions and may hold the smart contract or chaincode.
- **The endorsing peer** is a specialized committing peer that can grant or deny endorsement of a transaction proposal. The endorsing peer has to hold the smart contract.

- **The ordering nodes** (service) communicate with the committing and peer nodes; their main function is to approve the inclusion of transaction blocks into the ledger. Unlike the committing peer and endorsing peer, the ordering nodes do not hold the smart contract or the ledger.

Validation can be divided into two roles, endorsement and ordering:

- Endorsing a transaction means verifying that it obeys a smart contract; endorsers sign the contract to complete this aspect of validation
- Ordering verifies transactions for inclusion in the ledger; this form of validation helps to control what goes in the ledger and ensure its consistency

What about chain code invocation? In a Hyperledger Fabric transaction, simulation (chaincode execution) and block validation/commit are separate.

There are three phases involved in carrying out a chaincode operation (in other words, a business transaction) with Hyperledger Fabric:

1. The first phase is chaincode operation execution through simulation on endorsing peers. It's possible to enable parallel simulation on endorsers to help improve concurrency and scalability since simulation won't update the blockchain state.
2. Next, simulation determines the business transaction proposal, that is, the read set/write set, and broadcasts this to the ordering service.
3. A transaction proposal is then ordered in regard to others and broadcasts to committing peers (includes endorsing peers) who validate that its read set has not been modified since simulation and applies its write set automatically.

Channels are also an important aspect of the transaction journey, since peers exchange messages using consensus by way of channels, and they ensure privacy between different ledgers. The following are a few notes regarding channels:

- They don't have to be connected to by all nodes
- Peers connect to channels through an access control policy
- The ordering services orders a transaction broadcast to a channel
- Peers receive transactions in exactly the same order for a channel

- Transactions are delivered in cryptographically linked blocks
- Every peer validates the delivered blocks and commits them to the ledger

Hyperledger Fabric explored

Actors in the blockchain network: A blockchain is a network-based infrastructure where network-centric design, development, deployment, management, and support constructs apply. It is therefore vital to understand various actors and their roles that interact with the blockchain network for various purposes such as management, support, business users, regulator, and so on:

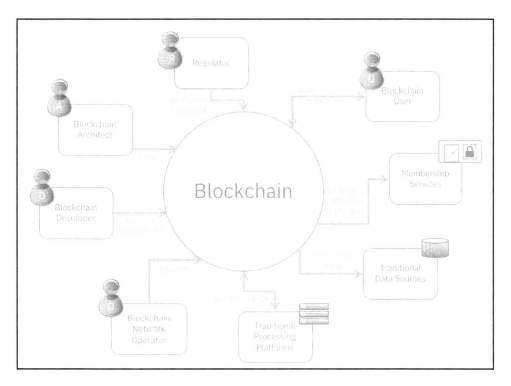

Each actor has a role and entry point and defines a governance structure that aids in network governance, audit, and compliance requirements. Business network governance (covered in detail in the following points) is an important compliance and costs consideration. Users are the parties who are users of the blockchain. They create and distribute blockchain applications and perform operations using the blockchain. These actors are consistent, and are based on cloud computing actors and roles from ISO/IEC 17788:

- **Developers**: Blockchain developers are the actors who create applications for users (client-side) and develop the smart contracts (server-side) that interact with the blockchain, which are then used by blockchain users to initiate transactions. They also write code to enable the blockchain to interact with legacy applications.
- **Administrators**: Blockchain administrators perform administrative activities, such as deployment and configuration of the blockchain network or application.
- **Operators**: Blockchain operators are responsible for defining, creating, managing, and monitoring the blockchain network and application.
- **Auditors**: Blockchain auditors have the responsibility of reviewing blockchain transactions and validating their integrity from a business, legal, audit, and compliance perspective.
- **Business users**: This term refers to users operating in a business network. They interact with the blockchain using an application, but may not be aware of the blockchain since it will be an invisible transactional system.

Components in a blockchain network

In general, a blockchain system consists of a number of nodes, each of which has a local copy of a ledger. In most systems, the nodes belong to different organizations. The nodes communicate with each other in order to gain agreement on what should be in the ledger.

The process of gaining this agreement is called **consensus**, and there are a number of different algorithms that have been developed for this purpose. Users send transaction requests to the blockchain in order to perform the operations the chain is designed to provide. Once a transaction is completed, a record of the transaction is added to one or more of the ledgers and can never be altered or removed. This property of the blockchain is called **immutability**. Cryptography is used to secure the blockchain itself and the communications between the elements of the blockchain system. It ensures that the ledger cannot be altered, except by the addition of new transactions. Cryptography provides integrity on messages from users or between nodes and ensures operations are only performed by authorized entities:

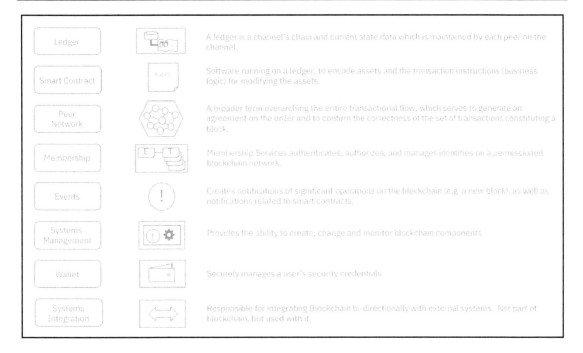

Ledger		A ledger is a channel's chain and current state data which is maintained by each peer on the channel.
Smart Contract		Software running on a ledger, to encode assets and the transaction instructions (business logic) for modifying the assets.
Peer Network		A broader term overarching the entire transactional flow, which serves to generate an agreement on the order and to confirm the correctness of the set of transactions constituting a block.
Membership		Membership Services authenticates, authorizes, and manages identities on a permissioned blockchain network.
Events		Creates notifications of significant operations on the blockchain (e.g. a new block), as well as notifications related to smart contracts.
Systems Management		Provides the ability to create, change and monitor blockchain components
Wallet		Securely manages a user's security credentials
Systems Integration		Responsible for integrating Blockchain bi-directionally with external systems. Not part of blockchain, but used with it.

The authority to perform transactions on a blockchain can use one of two models: permissioned or permissionless. In a permissioned blockchain, users must be enrolled in the blockchain before they are allowed to perform transactions. The enrollment process gives the user credentials that are used to identify the user when they perform transactions. In a permissionless blockchain, any person can perform transactions, but they are usually restricted from performing operations on any data but their own. Blockchain owners developed an executable software module called a **smart contract**, which is installed into the blockchain itself. When a user sends a transaction to the blockchain, it can invoke a smart contract module, which performs functions defined by the creator of the smart contract module.

Developer interaction

As discussed in the introduction of *Hyperledger Fabric Explored* section, blockchain developers can have many roles including creating applications for users (client-side) and developing smart contracts. Developers also write code to enable the blockchain to interact with legacy applications:

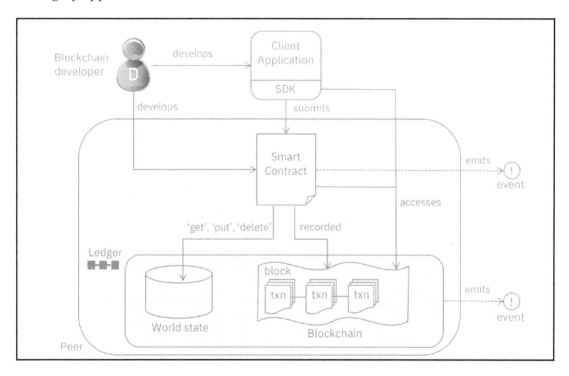

A blockchain developer's primary role is to create an application (and integration) and **Smart Contracts** and their respective interaction with ledgers and other enterprise systems of the business network and their participants. Due to the separation of the Hyperledger Fabric infrastructure, there is a clear separation between infrastructure constructs, such as peers, consensus, security, channels, policies, and developer-led activities, such as smart contract development, deployment, enterprise integration, API management, and front end application development.

From a developer's point of view, the following outline represents an example of developer interaction with Hyperledger Fabric constructs:

- The developer creates an application and a smart contract
- The application can invoke calls within the smart contract through an SDK
- The calls are processed by the business logic built into the smart contract through various commands and protocols:
    - A `put` or `delete` command will go through the selected consensus protocol and will be added to the blockchain
    - A `get` command can only read from the world state but is not recorded on the blockchain
- An application can access block information using rest APIs such as `get block height`

Note the use of **delete** here—**delete** can delete keys from the world state database, but not transactions from the blockchain, which we've already established are immutable.

The following diagram summarizes all key roles:

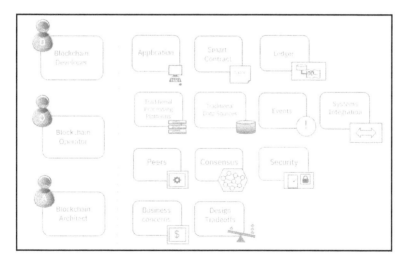

Understanding governance in business networks powered by blockchain

Governance can be defined as the centralized or decentralized body whose sole responsibility is establishing a set of rules or laws in a given system to make binding decisions. Governance in blockchain networks comes with a set of challenges and, in this section, we want to discuss those challenges along with governance structures in blockchain networks. Within the context of blockchain, the topic of governance presents an interesting paradox.

When a blockchain network is created, the governance structure is generally distributed, with input from the various stakeholders. Blockchain networks are characterized by decentralization and self-governance, with built-in control points and incentives to help maintain the right balance. Transactions go through a series of decentralized processing steps, with a decision that offers transaction finality as the output. This governance structure is based on incentive economics and consensus.

Blockchain began with largely permissionless networks (for example, crypo-asset-based networks such as bitcoin, litecoin, and so on) that relied on technology-based systemic governance through incentives and coordination. This kind of systemic governance poses several challenges in the business world when it attempts to apply the tenets of blockchain. The enterprise world is highly regulated and therefore relies on permissioned blockchain models with checks and balances; this can become rather complicated given the various data regulations, fiduciary responsibilities, and the potential conflicts of interest among competing entities that are transacting together. There can't necessarily be the same kinds of incentives or coordination, due to confidentiality and privacy concerns.

The enterprise focus has often been on understanding blockchain technology and its potential impacts on business. Governance has now become an interesting emerging discipline in the enterprise blockchain world—and an important one. As you can see from the discussion of blockchain business models, there's a range of possible governance structures, from full decentralization and quasi-decentralization to fully centralized blockchain networks. The governance structure actually determines many other aspects of the blockchain adoption, from design to operations to the growth model. Business models and governance structures are close-knit and mutually dependent; both direct various facets of how a blockchain network operates.

Governance structure and landscape

The kind of systemic governance that relies on incentives and coordination among network participants is inadequate for addressing more regulated industries and their use cases. So, I'm attempting to define a governance structure and landscape for the more traditional enterprise, which is a modular approach that leverages existing best practices.

This model aims to facilitate progress and growth, but provide the necessary separation of participants in a network. The simplified governance structure I'll outline is built upon the core tenets of blockchain as well as principles of incentive, penalties, flexibility, delegation, and coordination. Keep in mind that the goal of leveraging blockchain is to develop networks of trust while enforcing certain rules of engagement. Generally, blockchain projects aim to motivate upgrades to technology and security and to penalize non-compliance, with the hope of ensuring continued participation and shared business benefits for the network powered by blockchain. The business governance model I again describe aids not only fair participation in such networks but also an equitable cost structure. This section provides a high level context. We have discussed additional details in a chapter dedicated to Governance.

Information technology governance

The discipline of IT governance focuses on IT infrastructure, performance, cost structure, and risk. This creates some challenges in a decentralized blockchain network, since the governance framework should establish accountability to encourage desirable behavior and optimal functioning of the network's IT infrastructure. The technical design and infrastructure choices of the blockchain network ought to be able to adapt to the needs of its participants. Because blockchain networks thrive on at least some level of decentralization, IT governance should include distributed flexibility and distributed control.

IT governance should provide at least the following:

- A distributed IT management structure
- A model for distributed maintenance, upgrades, and so on
- Utilization of industry standards — COBIT, ITIL, ISO, CMMI, FAIR, and so on
- Resource optimization—this includes technology procurement, supplier-vendor relations, SLA management, skills, and talent management

- Technology adoption and evaluation to keep up with technology evolution
- A network deployment strategy to encourage and enforce regular updates and upgrades
- Network support services — IT SLA enforcement and membership services
- Risk optimization — **operational support services** (**OSSs**) and **business support services** (**BSSs**), IT infrastructure continuity services/planning, technology alignment to legal and regulatory requirements, and so on

Blockchain network governance

Governance can involve the following:

- Managing participation in the network
- Forming an equitable cost structure that's distributed fairly based on the activity of the participants
- Allowing for like-minded participating entities to engage in transactions and value creation
- Managing rules of engagement and social contracts with the aim of promoting fairness

Governance of the blockchain network's governance includes the following:

- Onboarding and offboarding members
- Establishing a fair cost structure
- Detailing how data ownership works
- Regulatory oversight and compliance reporting
- Managing a permissioning structure with central management and a voting process, a federated structure, and a delegated structure
- Managing business operations and SLAs
- Network support services (the same as for IT governance)
- Risk optimization (the same as for IT governance)

Business network governance

Governing blockchain powered business networks will require a model that is, again, specific to the use case and industry, factoring in the evolution and particularities of that industry. This governance structure will be multi-organizational, and participating organizations need to have a wide understanding of how the network functions through their collective contributions in order to achieve the best outcomes. As new participants are added or removed, and the blockchain network evolves, its dynamics change, too.

The concept of co-creation implies bringing parties together to produce a mutually advantageous and valuable outcome. One example could be uniting a company with a group of customers to generate new ideas and hear fresh perspectives.

What follows is a non-exhaustive list of what business network governance might include:

- Formulating business models, rules for how the network will operate, and legal charters
- Service management that is common/shared in the network, such as knowing your customer processes, audits, reporting, and so on
- Communication related to the network
- Quality assurance and performance measurement
- Monitoring and managing network security
- Plans for product and business network evolution
- Legal and regulatory framework enforcement
- Strategies for ensuring compliance with industry-specific requirements
- Establishing stewards of the technology and network

The governance structure in a blockchain network can be an interesting challenge. As I've shown, there remains considerable debate about full decentralization, quasi-decentralization, and full centralization of blockchain networks, and this really hinges on the governance structure. By this, I mean that the governance structure of a blockchain network helps decide what kind of interaction, growth, technology choices, and operations are the best fit for that network. Blockchain, as I've stated before, is a platform that enables co-creation, and the new synergies that are generated from it will require some management through SLAs and a robust governance structure. Governance will be covered in detail in `Chapter 10`, *Governance, Necessary Evil of Regulated Industries*.

Summary

All of this helps you attract new participants to the network, as well as sustain the confidence of founding and existing participants, all while maintaining business benefits and value.

The business models and governance structures depend on each other to properly govern the operation of blockchain networks. A carefully planned governance model will ensure harmony between the involved entities, who may function as competitors, co-creators, or collaborators at different times.

3
Setting the Stage with a Business Scenario

The first two chapters were focused on setting the stage and defining the landscape of a blockchain project. We now understand how the technology works within a business framework and how the various Hyperledger projects aim to solve the problem of time and trust.

With an understanding of the components that make up Hyperledger Fabric, we will now delve into application design and implementation considerations. The next few chapters will take you through the steps of creating your very own smart contract and then integrating it to an application.

In order to make these exercises relevant, we will leverage a business use case with its roots in some older civilizations: trading and letters of credit.

The chapter's objective will be to introduce the business concept of letter of credit, walk you through the sample scenario we selected, and conclude by setting up our development environment.

In this chapter, we will:

- Explore letters of credit
- Review our simplified business scenario
- Set up our development environment

Trading and letter of credit

Step back in history to a time when merchants traveled across continents to buy cloth in one country to sell in another country. As a Florentine wool merchant, you might make a journey to Amsterdam to buy fine wool in that newly formed city-state, whose port collected resources from the whole of Northern Europe and beyond. You could then transport the wool to Florence, where it could be sold to tailors making fine garments for their wealthy clients. We're talking about 1300 AD—a time when it was not safe to carry gold or other precious metals as a form of currency to buy and sell goods. What was necessary was a form of currency that worked across country boundaries, one that could be used in Amsterdam and Florence, or anywhere!

Marco Polo had been to China and had seen how commerce was conducted in that thriving economy. At the heart of the successful Khan empire were advanced financial techniques that we would recognize today. Fiat currencies, paper money, promissory notes, and letters of credit all arrived in Europe by way of China. Marco Polo brought these ideas back to Europe—they helped form and grow a merchant banking industry for a Europe emerging after the fall of the Roman Empire.

The importance of trust in facilitating trade

Our Florentine merchant could now contact his banker to say that he wanted to buy wool in Amsterdam, and the bank would in return give him a letter of credit, in exchange for payment on account. This letter could have various stipulations, such as the maximum amount for the trade, how it would be paid (at once or in parts), what goods it could be used for, and so forth. The merchant would now travel to Amsterdam, and after selecting wool from a wool merchant, he would offer the letter or credit as payment. The Amsterdam merchant would happily exchange the wool for the letter because Florentine bankers were famed throughout Europe as being trustworthy when it came to money. The Amsterdam merchant could bring the letter of credit to his banker, who in turn would credit their account. Of course, the Florentine and Amsterdam bankers charged their respective clients—the merchants—for this service! It was good for everyone.

Periodically, Amsterdam bankers and the Florentine bankers would meet up to settle their accounts, but this was of no importance to the wool trader and wool merchant. Effectively, what was happening was that the Florentine and Amstel merchants were using the trust between their respective bankers to establish a trust relationship with each other—a very sophisticated idea when you think about it. This is why the letter of credit process remains a fundamental way of conducting business worldwide to this day.

The letter of credit process today

However, over time, due to massive globalization of trade and the explosion of the financial industry, the number of financial institutions involved in the letter of credit process has exploded! Nowadays, there could be over 20 intermediary financial institutions involved in the process. This requires coordination of many people and systems, resulting in excessive time, cost, and risk throughout the process for both merchants and banks alike.

 The promise of blockchain is to provide a logically singular but physically distributed system that provides a platform for a low-friction letter of credit process. The characteristics of such a system would include greater transparency, timeliness, and automation (resulting in lower cost), and new features such as incremental payment.

Business scenario and use case

International trade includes the kinds of situations that illustrate the inefficiencies and distrust in real-world processes that blockchains were designed to mitigate. So, we have selected an element of an import-export scenario with simplified versions of transactions carried out in the real world as our canonical use case for practical exercises in the next few chapters.

Overview

The scenario we will describe involves a simple transaction: the sale of goods from one party to another. This transaction is complicated by the fact that the buyer and the seller live in different countries, so there is no common trusted intermediary to ensure that the exporter gets the money he was promised and the importer gets the goods. Such trade arrangements in today's world rely on:

- Intermediaries that facilitate payments and physical transfer of goods
- Processes that have evolved over time to enable exporters and importers to hedge their bets and reduce the risks involved

Real-world processes

The intermediaries that facilitate payment are the respective banks of the exporter and the importer. In this case, the trade arrangement is fulfilled by the trusted relationships between a bank and its client, and between the two banks. Such banks typically have international connections and reputations to maintain. Therefore, a commitment (or promise) by the importer's bank to make a payment to the exporter's bank is sufficient to trigger the process. The goods are dispatched by the exporter through a reputed international carrier after obtaining regulatory clearances from the exporting country's government.

Proof of delivery to the carrier is sufficient to clear payment from the importer's bank to the exporter's bank, and such clearance is not contingent on the goods reaching their intended destination (it is assumed that the goods are insured against loss or damage in transit.) The promise made by the importer's bank to pay the exporter's bank specifies a list of documents that are required as proof of dispatch, and the precise method of payment to be made immediately or over a period. Various regulatory requirements must be fulfilled by the exporter before getting documentary clearances that allow them to hand off the goods to the carrier.

Simplified and modified processes

Our use case will follow a simplified version of the preceding process, with certain variations to demonstrate the value of blockchain in facilitating this trade. A payment promise is made by the importer's bank to the exporter's bank in two installments. The exporter obtains a clearance certificate from the regulatory authority, hands off the goods to the carrier, and then obtains a receipt. The production of the receipt triggers the first payment installment from the importer's bank to the exporter's bank. When the shipment has reached the destination port, the second and final payment installments are made, and the process concludes.

Terms used in trade finance and logistics

The following terms are used to refer to certain instruments and artifacts that are in play in our trade scenario. The application we will build in this chapter uses very simplified forms of these instruments:

- **Letter of credit**: As we have seen at the beginning of the chapter, this refers to a bank's promise to pay an exporter upon presentation of documentary proof of goods having been shipped. Called **L/C** for short, this document is issued by the importer's bank at the request of its client: the importer. The L/C states the list of documents that constitute proof of shipment, the amount to be paid, and the beneficiary (the exporter in our case) of that amount. A sample L/C is illustrated in the following screenshot:

Toy Bank, Ltd.

Issue Date: March 1, 2018
L/C Number: 23868

Toy Bank, Ltd. hereby issues this irrevocable documentary Letter of Credit to Lumber Inc. for US$500000 payable immediately upon sight by a draft drawn against Toy Bank, Ltd., in accordance with Letter of Credit number 23868.

The draft is to be accompanied by the following documents:

1. Order Bill of Lading
2. Packing List
3. Invoice

Authorized Signatory
Wood Bank Ltd.

We will introduce small variations in our use case to make this instrument comprehensible to the reader. Firstly, the L/C will be issued to the exporter's bank rather than directly to the exporter. Secondly, the L/C states that payment will be made in two identical installments, the first upon production of two documents and the second upon the goods reaching the destination.

- **Export license**: This refers to the approval given by the regulatory authority in the exporter's country for the shipment of the specified goods. In this book, we will refer to it as E/L for short. A sample E/L is illustrated in the following screenshot:

ABC Government

Department of Forestry: Inspection Services

License to Export Wood

LICENSE NUMBER: 76348

License Holder: Lumber Inc.

FOR THE PURPOSE OF EXPORTING WOOD BY SEA OR AIR

- **Bill of lading**: This is a document issued by the carrier to the exporter once it takes possession of the shipment. Called B/L for short, it simultaneously serves as a receipt, a contract obliging the carrier to transport the goods to a specified destination in return for a fee, and a title of ownership of the goods. This document is also listed in the L/C and serves as proof of shipment that will automatically trigger a payment clearance. A sample B/L is illustrated in the following screenshot:

Worldwide Shippers	BILL OF LADING FOR OCEAN TRANSPORT
Shipper *Lumber Inc.*	Booking ID *7625901*
Consignee *Toy Company*	Notify Party *Toy Bank, Ltd.*
Place of Receipt *Port ABC*	Place of Delivery *Port LMN*

PARTICULARS FURNISHED BY SHIPPER		
Description of Goods *Wood*	Weight *600 tons*	Measurement *1000m × 800 m*

Freight Charges   *US$40000*
Authorized Signatory, *Worldwide Shippers*

Shared process workflow

Every instance of a test case scenario presented in this chapter takes a long period of time to complete, involves interactions among different sets of entities at different times, and has many different moving parts that are difficult to keep track of. We hope to simplify this process using our workflow. Implemented on a blockchain, the sequences of transactions described in the following steps (and illustrated in the following diagram) can be carried out in an irrevocable and non-repudiable manner. In this sequence of events, we assume a straight, linear narrative where parties are in agreement with each other and nothing untoward happens; guards are built in the process only to catch errors.

The transactions in our workflow are as follows:

1. Importer requests goods from the exporter in exchange of money
2. Exporter accepts the trade deal
3. Importer asks its bank for an L/C in favor of the exporter
4. The importer's bank supplies an L/C in favor of the exporter, and payable to the latter's bank
5. The exporter's bank accepts the L/C on behalf of the exporter
6. Exporter applies for an E/L from the regulatory authority
7. Regulatory authority supplies an E/L to the exporter
8. Exporter prepares a shipment and hands it off to the carrier
9. The carrier accepts the goods after validating the E/L, and then supplies a B/L to the exporter
10. The exporter's bank claims half the payment from the importer's bank
11. The importer's bank transfers half the amount to the exporter's bank
12. The carrier ships the goods to the destination
13. The importer's bank pays the remaining amount to the exporter's bank

Here is a diagram to explain the transaction workflow:

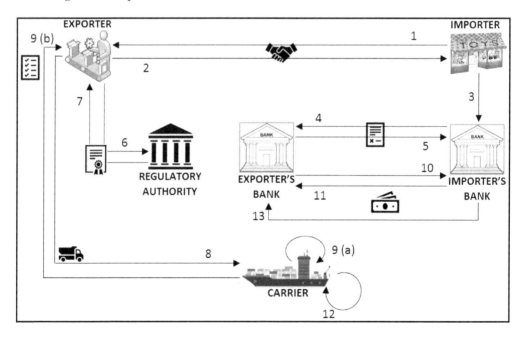

Shared assets and data

The participants in the previous workflow must have some information in common that gives them a view into the trade arrangement and its progress at any given moment.

The following is a table of the assets owned by the participants, which are shared with each other to drive the process from one stage to the next. This includes documentary and monetary assets:

Asset type	Asset attributes
Letter of credit	ID, issue date, expiration date, issuer, beneficiary, amount, and a list of documents
Bill of lading	ID, shipper (exporter), consignee (importer), party to notify (importer's bank), places of receipt and delivery, description of goods, and freight amount
Export license	ID, issue date, expiration date, beneficiary, license holder, and description of goods
Payment	Amount in standard currency units

The following are the data elements that circumscribe the options available to participants in each stage:

Data type	Data attributes
Trade agreement	Requested by importer and accepted by exporter
Letter of credit	Requested by importer, issued by importer's bank, and accepted by exporter's bank
Export license	Requested by exporter and issued by regulatory authority
Shipment	Prepared by exporter, accepted by carrier, and current position or location

Participants' roles and capabilities

There are six categories of participants in our scenario: which are exporter, importer, exporter's bank, importer's bank, carrier, and regulatory authority. The terms in this set refer to the roles an entity can assume in a trade deal; for example, a company exporting goods in one instance may be an importer in another. The capabilities and restrictions of each role are also detailed in the following list:

- Only an importer may apply for an L/C
- Only an importer's bank may supply an L/C

- Only an exporter's bank may accept an L/C
- Only an exporter may request an E/L
- Only a regulatory authority may supply an E/L
- Only an exporter may prepare a shipment
- Only a carrier may supply a B/L
- Only a carrier may update a shipment location
- Only an importer's bank may send money, and only an exporter's bank may receive money

Benefits of blockchain applications over current real-world processes

The risks inherent in transferring goods or making payments in the absence of safeguards (such as a trusted mediator) inspired the involvement of banks and led to the creation of the letter of credit and bill of lading. A consequence of these processes was not just additional cost (banks charge commission to issue letters of credit) or additional overhead. Applying and waiting for export licenses to be awarded also increases the turnaround time. In an ideal trade scenario, only the process of preparing and shipping the goods would take time. Recently, the adoption of SWIFT messaging over manual communication has made the document application and collection processes more efficient, but it has not fundamentally changed the game. A blockchain, on the other hand, with its (almost) instantaneous transaction commitments and assurance guarantees, opens possibilities that did not previously exist.

As an example, the one variation we introduced in our use case was payment by installments, which cannot be implemented in the legacy framework because there is no guaranteed way of knowing and sharing information about a shipment's progress. Such a variation would be deemed too risky in this case, which is why payments are linked purely to documentary evidence. By getting all participants in a trade agreement on a single blockchain implementing a common smart contract, we can provide a single shared source of truth that will minimize risk and simultaneously increase accountability.

In subsequent chapters, we will demonstrate in detail how our use case is implemented on the Hyperledger Fabric and Composer platforms. The reader will be able to appreciate both the simplicity and elegance of the implementation, which can then be used as a guide for other applications to revamp their archaic processes using this exciting new technology. However, before jumping into the code, we will look at the design of a Hyperledger network and we will set up our development environment.

Setting up the development environment

As you already know by now, an instance of a Hyperledger Fabric blockchain is referred to as a channel, which is a log of transactions linked to each other in a cryptographically secure manner. To design and run a blockchain application, the first step is to determine how many channels are required. For our trade application, we will use one channel, which will maintain the history of trades carried out among the different participants.

 A Fabric peer may belong to multiple channels, which from the application's perspective will be oblivious to each other, but which help a single peer run transactions in different applications on behalf of its owners (or clients). A channel may run multiple smart contracts, each of which may be an independent application or linked together in a multi-contract application. In this chapter, and in this book, we will walk the reader through the design of a single-channel, single-contract application for simplicity's sake. It is up to the reader to design more complex applications, relying on the information provided in this book as well as in the Fabric documentation.

Before we delve into the mechanics of setting up our system to install an application and run transactions on our smart contract, we will describe how to create and launch a network on which the application will be installed. A sample network structure will be used to illustrate trade operations throughout this chapter (in `Chapter 9`, *Life in a Blockchain Network*, you will see how this sample network can be modified as the requirements change and evolve).

Designing a network

The first step in determining a Hyperledger Fabric network structure for one's application is listing the participating organizations. Logically, an organization is a security domain and a unit of identity and credentials. It governs one or more network peers, and depends on a **membership service provider** (**MSP**) to issue identities and certificates for the peers as well as clients for smart contract access privileges. The ordering service, which is the cornerstone of a Fabric network, is typically assigned its own organization. The following diagram illustrates a typical peer network structure with clients, MSPs, and logical organization groupings.

The criterion for the approval of a transaction (or invocation) is an endorsement policy (which we will revisit later in this chapter). It is framed in terms of the organizations that are participating in the application network, and not the peers themselves:

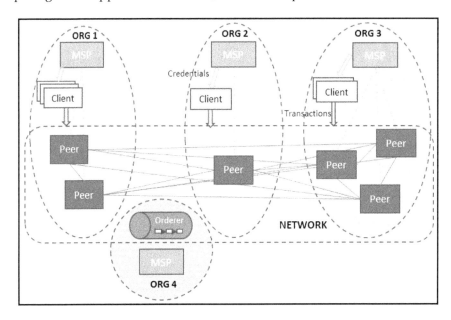

Figure 3.1: Blockchain network with peers distributed among organizations, and clients obtaining credentials from organizations to submit queries and invocations to the chaincode

The set of peers, the organizations they belong to, and the membership service providers serving each organization must be decided beforehand so that the appropriate services can be installed and run on those machines.

Our sample trade network will consist of four organizations, representing the exporter, importer, carrier, and regulator, respectively. The latter two represent the carrier and regulator entities, respectively. The exporter organization, however, represents both the exporting entity and its bank. Similarly, the importer organization represents the importing entity and its bank. Grouping entities with parties they trust into a single organization makes sense from both the perspective of security and cost. Running a Fabric peer is a heavy and costly business, so it is sufficient for a bank, which likely has more resources and a large clientele, to run such a peer on behalf of itself and its clients. A trading entity obtains the right to submit transactions or read the ledger state from its organizations in the role of a client. Our blockchain network therefore needs four peers, each belonging to a different organization. Apart from the peers, our network consists of one MSP for each of the four organizations, and an ordering service running in solo mode.

In a production application, the ordering service should be set up as a Kafka cluster on Zookeeper, but for the purpose of demonstrating how to build a blockchain application, the ordering service can be treated as a black box.

The ordering service belongs to its own separate organization with an MSP. The Organizations with their MSPs, peers, and clients of our trading network are illustrated in the following diagram:

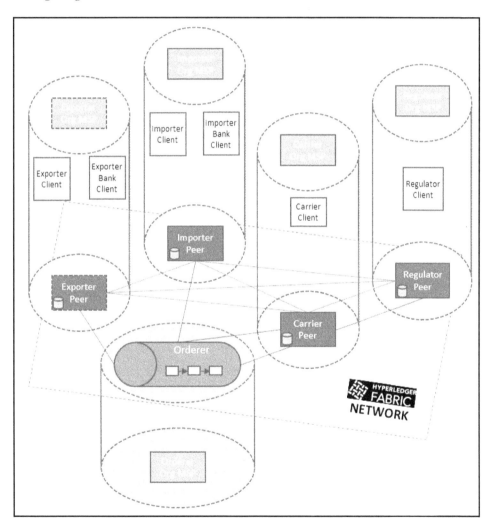

Figure 3.2: A trade network with peers, an orderer, and clients in their respective organizations

The reader may wonder how, if a trading party and its banker belong to the same organization, the application can distinguish the two (the exporter from the exporter's bank, and the importer from importer's bank) for the purpose of controlling access to the smart contract and ledger. Two ways of doing this are as follows:

- Embedding access control logic in the middleware and application layers (which we will describe later in this chapter), whereby users can be distinguished by their IDs (or login names) and an access control list mapping IDs to permitted chaincode functions is maintained.
- Having an organization's MSP, acting as a CA server, embed distinguishing attributes within the certificates it issues to members of an organization. The access control logic can be implemented in the middleware or even in the chaincode to parse the attributes and permit or disallow an operation as per application policy.

These mechanisms are not implemented in our application, in which bankers and clients are indistinguishable to the smart contract and the middleware layers. But the reader may treat this as an exercise, which should be straightforward for someone skilled at developing secure client-server applications.

Installing prerequisites

With the design of the network in hand, let's install the pre-requisite tools:

1. Ensure that you have the latest version of:
   - Docker using `https://docs.docker.com/install/`
   - Docker-Compose using: `https://docs.docker.com/compose/install/`

2. We will be using GitHub to share the source code of our tutorial. To access GitHub, the Git client needs to be installed and configured with authentication to GitHub. For more information, visit GitHub's official website at `https://help.github.com/articles/set-up-git/`.

3. Install the software required for the business network example: `https://hyperledger.github.io/composer/latest/installing/installing-prereqs`. The instructions above are for the Mac and Linux. Note that when using Windows, we recommend the use of a solution like Vagrant to run the development environment in a virtual machine.

4. Fabric is implemented in the Go language. Note that:
   - Go is syntactically similar to C++
   - We will also use Go to write chaincodes
   - Go can be installed from `https://golang.org/`

Note that the setup of Hyperledger Fabric and testing of the tutorial application in this book was done using Go 1.9, so the reader is advised to install and use 1.9 or a higher version

5. Next, we need to set up our environmental variables.

   `GOPATH` points to a workspace for the `go` source code, for example:

   ```
   $ export GOPATH=$HOME/go
   ```

   `PATH` needs to include the Go `bin` directory used to store libraries and executables, as we can see in the following snippet:

   ```
   $ export PATH=$PATH:$GOPATH/bin
   ```

6. Verify whether you have `make` installed on your system. On a Debian/Ubuntu system, you can install it using `sudo apt-get install make`.

Forking and cloning the trade-finance-logistics repository

Now we need to get our own copy of the original source code by forking the repository on GitHub. Then, we can clone the source code into a local machine directory with the following steps:

1. **In GitHub, navigate to the following repository**: `https://github.com/HyperledgerHandsOn/trade-finance-logistics`

2. **Fork the repository**: Use the Fork button at the top-right corner of the page to create a copy of the source code to your account

3. **Get the clone URL**: Navigate to your fork of the trade-finance-logistics repository. Click on the **Clone or download** button, and copy the URL

4. **Clone the repository**: In the Go workspace, clone the repository as follows:

```
$ cd $GOPATH/src
$ git clone
https://github.com/YOUR-USERNAME/trade-finance-logistics
```

We now have a local copy of all the trade-finance-logistics tutorial materials.

Creating and running a network configuration

The code to configure and launch our network can be found in the network folder in our repository (this is an adaptation of `fabric-samples/first-network`). For this exercise, we will run the entire network on a single physical or virtual machine, with the various network elements running in suitably configured Docker containers. It is assumed that the reader has a basic familiarity with containerization using Docker and configurations using Docker-compose. Once the prerequisites listed in the previous section are met, it is sufficient to run the commands in that section without any extra knowledge or configuration required of the reader.

Preparing the network

To build Fabric and Fabric-CA, you may need to install certain dependencies if they are missing. These include the `gcc`, `libtool`, and `ltdl` libraries. (On a Ubuntu Xenial system, all of the necessary prerequisites can be installed by running `sudo apt-get install libltdl-dev`. It is left to the reader to look for equivalents on other systems). We need to perform the following steps before generating network cryptographic material.

 The tutorial application was developed on Hyperledger Fabric version 1.1, so you will need to fetch and build components for that version.

1. Clone the Fabric (`https://github.com/hyperledger/fabric/tree/release-1.1`) source code repository. If you are using the `git clone` command, add the parameter `-b release-1.1`. Make sure the cloned `fabric` folder is either present, or symbolically linked, in `$GOPATH/src/github.com/hyperledger/`. When you attempt to build Fabric, it will look for libraries in this path.

2. Run `make docker` to build Docker images for the peers and orderers

3. Run `make configtxgen cryptogen` to generate the necessary tools to run the network creation commands described in this section

4. Clone the Fabric-CA (`https://github.com/hyperledger/fabric-ca/tree/release-1.1`) source code repository. (If you are using the `git clone` command, add the parameter `-b release-1.1`. Make sure the cloned `fabric-ca` folder is either present, or symbolically linked, in `$GOPATH/src/github.com/hyperledger/`. When you attempt to build Fabric-CA, it will look for libraries in this path.

5. Run `make docker` to build the Docker images for the MSPs

Generating network cryptographic material

The first step in the configuration of a network involves the creation of certificates and signing keys for the MSP of each peer and orderer organization, and for TLS-based communication. We also need to create certificates and keys for each peer and orderer node to be able to communicate with each other and with their respective MSPs. The configuration for this must be specified in a `crypto-config.yaml` file in the `network` folder in our code repository. This file contains the organization structure (see more details in the channel artifacts configuration section later), the number of peers in each organization, and the default number of users in an organization for whom certificates and keys must be created (note that an `admin` user is created by default). As an example, see the definition of the Importer's organization in the file as follows:

```
PeerOrgs:
- Name: ImporterOrg
  Domain: importerorg.trade.com
  EnableNodeOUs: true
  Template:
    Count: 1
  Users:
    Count: 2
```

This configuration indicates that the organization labeled `ImporterOrg` will contain one peer. Two non-admin users will also be created. The organization domain name to be used by the peer is also defined.

To generate cryptographic material for all the organizations, run the `cryptogen` command as follows:

```
cryptogen generate --config=./crypto-config.yaml
```

The output is saved to the `crypto-config` folder.

Generating channel artifacts

To create a network according to an organization's structure, and to bootstrap a channel, we will need to generate the following artifacts:

- A genesis block, containing organization-specific certificates that serve to initialize the Fabric blockchain.
- Channel configuration information.
- Anchor peer configurations for each organization. An anchor peer serves as a fulcrum within an organization, for cross-organization ledger syncing using the Fabric gossip protocol.

Like the `crypto-config.yaml` file, channel properties are specified in a file labeled `configtx.yaml`, which in our source code can be found in the `network` folder. The high-level organization of our trade network can be found in the `Profiles` section as follows:

```
Profiles:
  FourOrgsTradeOrdererGenesis:
    Capabilities:
      <<: *ChannelCapabilities
    Orderer:
      <<: *OrdererDefaults
      Organizations:
        - *TradeOrdererOrg
      Capabilities:
        <<: *OrdererCapabilities
    Consortiums:
      TradeConsortium:
        Organizations:
          - *ExporterOrg
          - *ImporterOrg
          - *CarrierOrg
          - *RegulatorOrg
  FourOrgsTradeChannel:
    Consortium: TradeConsortium
    Application:
```

```
    <<: *ApplicationDefaults
    Organizations:
      - *ExporterOrg
      - *ImporterOrg
      - *CarrierOrg
      - *RegulatorOrg
    Capabilities:
      <<: *ApplicationCapabilities
```

As we can see, the channel we are going to create is named `FourOrgsTradeChannel`, which is defined in the profile. The four organizations participating in this channel are labeled `ExporterOrg`, `ImporterOrg`, `CarrierOrg`, and `RegulatorOrg`, each of which refers to a subsection defined in the `Organizations` section. The orderer belongs to its own organization called `TradeOrdererOrg`. Each organization section contains information about its MSP (ID as well as the location of the cryptographic material, such as keys and certificates), and the hostname and port information for its anchor peers. As an example, the `ExporterOrg` section contains the following:

```
  - &ExporterOrg
    Name: ExporterOrgMSP
    ID: ExporterOrgMSP
    MSPDir: crypto-config/peerOrganizations/exporterorg.trade.com/msp
    AnchorPeers:
      - Host: peer0.exporterorg.trade.com
    Port: 7051
```

As you can see, the `MSPDir` variable (representing a folder) in this specification references the cryptographic material we generated earlier using the `cryptogen` tool.

To generate the channel artifacts, we use the `configtxgen` tool. To generate the genesis block (which will be sent to the orderer during network bootstrap), run the following command from the `network` folder:

```
configtxgen -profile FourOrgsTradeOrdererGenesis -outputBlock ./channel-
artifacts/genesis.block
```

The `FourOrgsTradeOrdererGenesis` keyword corresponds to the profile name in the `Profiles` section. The genesis block will be saved in the `genesis.block` file in the `channel-artifacts` folder. To generate the channel configuration, run the following code:

```
configtxgen -profile FourOrgsTradeChannel -outputCreateChannelTx ./channel-
artifacts/channel.tx -channelID tradechannel
```

The channel we will create is named `tradechannel`, and its configuration is stored in `channel-artifacts/channel.tx`. To generate the anchor peer configuration for the exporter organization, run:

```
configtxgen -profile FourOrgsTradeChannel -outputAnchorPeersUpdate
./channel-artifacts/ExporterOrgMSPanchors.tx -channelID tradechannel -asOrg
ExporterOrgMSP
```

The same process should be repeated for the other three organizations, while changing the organization names in the preceding command.

The environment variable `FABRIC_CFG_PATH` must be set to point to the folder that contains the `configtx.yaml` file in order for the `configtxgen` tool to work. The script file `trade.sh` (which we will use later) contains the following line to ensure that the `YAML` file is loaded from the folder in which the command is run:

```
export FABRIC_CFG_PATH=${PWD}
```

Generating the configuration in one operation

For convenience, the `trade.sh` script is configured to generate the channel artifacts as well as the cryptographic material using the commands and configuration files described previously. Just run the following command from within the `network` folder:

```
./trade.sh generate -c tradechannel
```

Although you can specify any channel name here, note that the configurations used to develop the middleware later in this chapter will depend on that name.

The `GOPATH` variable is set to `/opt/gopath` in the container that runs the peer.

Composing a sample trade network

The last command also has the effect of generating a network configuration file, `docker-compose-e2e.yaml`, which is used to start the network as a set of Docker containers using the docker-compose tool. The file itself depends on the statically configured files `base/peer-base.yaml` and `base/docker-compose-base.yaml`. These files collectively specify services and their attributes, and enable us to run them all in one go within Docker containers, rather than having to manually run instances of these services on one or more machines. The services we need to run are as follows:

- Four instances of a Fabric peer, one in each organization
- One instance of a Fabric orderer
- Five instances of a Fabric CA, corresponding to the MSPs of each organization

Docker images for each can be obtained from the Hyperledger project on Docker Hub (`https://hub.docker.com/u/hyperledger/`), with the images being `hyperledger/fabric-peer`, `hyperledger/fabric-orderer`, `hyperledger/fabric-ca for peers`, `orderers`, and MSPs, respectively.

The base configuration of a peer can be as follows (see `base/peer-base.yaml`):

```
peer-base:
image: hyperledger/fabric-peer:$IMAGE_TAG
environment:
  - CORE_VM_ENDPOINT=unix:///host/var/run/docker.sock
  - CORE_VM_DOCKER_HOSTCONFIG_NETWORKMODE=${COMPOSE_PROJECT_NAME}_trade
  - CORE_LOGGING_LEVEL=INFO
  - CORE_PEER_TLS_ENABLED=true
  - CORE_PEER_GOSSIP_USELEADERELECTION=true
  - CORE_PEER_GOSSIP_ORGLEADER=false
  - CORE_PEER_PROFILE_ENABLED=true
  - CORE_PEER_TLS_CERT_FILE=/etc/hyperledger/fabric/tls/server.crt
  - CORE_PEER_TLS_KEY_FILE=/etc/hyperledger/fabric/tls/server.key
  - CORE_PEER_TLS_ROOTCERT_FILE=/etc/hyperledger/fabric/tls/ca.crt
working_dir: /opt/gopath/src/github.com/hyperledger/fabric/peer
command: peer node start
```

Fabric configuration parameters can be set here, but if you use the pre-built Docker image for `fabric-peer`, the defaults are sufficient to get a peer service up and running. The command to run the peer service is specified in the last line of the configuration as `peer node start`; if you wish to run a peer by downloading the Fabric source and building it on your local machine, this is the command you will have to run (see *Chapter 4, Designing a Data and Transaction Model with Golang,* for examples). Also make sure you configure the logging level appropriately using the `CORE_LOGGING_LEVEL` variable. In our configuration, the variable is set to `INFO`, which means that only informational, warning, and error messages will be logged. If you wish to debug a peer and need more extensive logging, you can set this variable to `DEBUG`.

> The `IMAGE_TAG` variable is set to latest in the `.env` file in the `network` folder, though you can set a specific tag if you wish to pull older images.

Furthermore, we need to configure the hostnames and ports for each peer, and sync the cryptographic material generated (using `cryptogen`) to the container filesystem. The peer in the exporter organization is configured in `base/docker-compose-base.yaml` as follows:

```
peer0.exporterorg.trade.com:
  container_name: peer0.exporterorg.trade.com
  extends:
    file: peer-base.yaml
    service: peer-base
  environment:
    - CORE_PEER_ID=peer0.exporterorg.trade.com
    - CORE_PEER_ADDRESS=peer0.exporterorg.trade.com:7051
    - CORE_PEER_GOSSIP_BOOTSTRAP=peer0.exporterorg.trade.com:7051
    - CORE_PEER_GOSSIP_EXTERNALENDPOINT=peer0.exporterorg.trade.com:7051
    - CORE_PEER_LOCALMSPID=ExporterOrgMSP
  volumes:
    - /var/run/:/host/var/run/
    - ../crypto-
config/peerOrganizations/exporterorg.trade.com/peers/peer0.exporterorg.trad
e.com/msp:/etc/hyperledger/fabric/msp
    - ../crypto-
config/peerOrganizations/exporterorg.trade.com/peers/peer0.exporterorg.trad
e.com/tls:/etc/hyperledger/fabric/tls
    - peer0.exporterorg.trade.com:/var/hyperledger/production
  ports:
    - 7051:7051
    - 7053:7053
```

As indicated by the `extends` parameter, this extends the base configuration. Note that the ID (`CORE_PEER_ID`) matches that which is specified for this peer in `configtx.yaml`. This identity is the hostname for the peer running in the exporter organization, and will be used in the middleware code later in this chapter. The volumes section indicates the rules for copying the cryptographic material generated in the `crypto-config` folder to the container. The peer service itself listens on port `7051`, and the port that clients can use to subscribe to events is set to `7053`.

 In the file, you will see that the in-container ports are identical across peers, but are mapped to distinct ports on the host machine. Lastly, note that the MSP ID specified here also matches that specified in `configtx.yaml`.

The configuration of the orderer service is similar, as the following snippet from `base/docker-compose-base.yaml` indicates:

```
orderer.trade.com:
  container_name: orderer.trade.com
  image: hyperledger/fabric-orderer:$IMAGE_TAG
  environment:
    - ORDERER_GENERAL_LOGLEVEL=INFO
  ......
  command: orderer
  ......
```

The command to start the orderer is simply `orderer`, as the code indicates. The logging level can be configured using the `ORDERER_GENERAL_LOGLEVEL` variable, and is set to `INFO` in our configuration.

The actual network configuration that we will run is based on a file named `docker-compose-e2e.yaml`. This file does not exist in the repository but is rather created by the command `./trade.sh generate -c tradechannel`, which we ran earlier to generate channel and cryptographic material. This file depends on `base/docker-compose-base.yaml` (and indirectly `base/peer-base.yaml`) as you can see by examining the file contents. It is actually created from a template YAML file named `docker-compose-e2e-template.yaml`, which you can find in the `network` folder. The template file contains variables as stand-ins for key filenames that are generated using `cryptogen`. When `docker-compose-e2e.yaml` is generated, those variable names are replaced with actual filenames within the `crypto-config` folder.

For example, consider the `exporter-ca` section in `docker-compose-e2e-template.yaml`:

```
exporter-ca:
  image: hyperledger/fabric-ca:$IMAGE_TAG
  environment:
    ......
    - FABRIC_CA_SERVER_TLS_KEYFILE=/etc/hyperledger/fabric-ca-server-config/EXPORTER_CA_PRIVATE_KEY
    ......
  command: sh -c 'fabric-ca-server start --ca.certfile
/etc/hyperledger/fabric-ca-server-config/ca.exporterorg.trade.com-cert.pem
--ca.keyfile /etc/hyperledger/fabric-ca-server-
config/EXPORTER_CA_PRIVATE_KEY -b admin:adminpw -d'
```

Now, look at the same section in the generated file `docker-compose-e2e.yaml`:

```
exporter-ca:
  image: hyperledger/fabric-ca:$IMAGE_TAG
  environment:
    ......
    - FABRIC_CA_SERVER_TLS_KEYFILE=/etc/hyperledger/fabric-ca-server-config/ cc58284b6af2c33812cfaef9e40b8c911dbbefb83ca2e7564e8fbf5e7039c22e_sk
    ......
  command: sh -c 'fabric-ca-server start --ca.certfile
/etc/hyperledger/fabric-ca-server-config/ca.exporterorg.trade.com-cert.pem
--ca.keyfile /etc/hyperledger/fabric-ca-server-
config/cc58284b6af2c33812cfaef9e40b8c911dbbefb83ca2e7564e8fbf5e7039c22e_sk
-b admin:adminpw -d'
```

As you can see, the variable `EXPORTER_CA_PRIVATE_KEY` has been replaced with `cc58284b6af2c33812cfaef9e40b8c911dbbefb83ca2e7564e8fbf5e7039c22e_sk`, both in the environment variable and in the command. If you now examine the contents of the `crypto-config` folder, you will notice that there exists a file named `cc58284b6af2c33812cfaef9e40b8c911dbbefb83ca2e7564e8fbf5e7039c22e_sk` in the folder `crypto-config/peerOrganizations/exporterorg.trade.com/ca/`. This file contains the exporter organization's MSP's private (secret) signing key.

 The preceding code snippet contains the result of a sample run. The key filename will vary whenever you run the cryptographic material generation tool.

Let us now look at the configuration of an MSP in more detail, taking the example of the exporter organization MSP, as specified in `docker-compose-e2e.yaml`:

```
exporter-ca:
  image: hyperledger/fabric-ca:$IMAGE_TAG
  environment:
    - FABRIC_CA_HOME=/etc/hyperledger/fabric-ca-server
    - FABRIC_CA_SERVER_CA_NAME=ca-exporterorg
    - FABRIC_CA_SERVER_TLS_ENABLED=true
    - FABRIC_CA_SERVER_TLS_CERTFILE=/etc/hyperledger/fabric-ca-server-
config/ca.exporterorg.trade.com-cert.pem
    - FABRIC_CA_SERVER_TLS_KEYFILE=/etc/hyperledger/fabric-ca-server-
config/cc58284b6af2c33812cfaef9e40b8c911dbbefb83ca2e7564e8fbf5e7039c22e_sk
  ports:
    - "7054:7054"
  command: sh -c 'fabric-ca-server start --ca.certfile
/etc/hyperledger/fabric-ca-server-config/ca.exporterorg.trade.com-cert.pem
--ca.keyfile /etc/hyperledger/fabric-ca-server-
config/cc58284b6af2c33812cfaef9e40b8c911dbbefb83ca2e7564e8fbf5e7039c22e_sk
-b admin:adminpw -d'
  volumes:
    - ./crypto-
config/peerOrganizations/exporterorg.trade.com/ca/:/etc/hyperledger/fabric-
ca-server-config
  container_name: ca_peerExporterOrg
  networks:
    - trade
```

The service that will run in the MSP is the `fabric-ca-server`, listening on port `7054`, bootstrapped with the certificates and keys created using `cryptogen`, and using the default login and password (`admin` and `adminpw`, respectively) configured in the `fabric-ca` image. The command to start an instance of a Fabric CA server is `fabric-ca-server start` ..., as you can see in the preceding code.

Peers as well as CAs are configured for TLS-based communication, as indicated in the preceding configurations. The reader must note that if TLS is disabled in one, it must be disabled in the other too.

Also, as can be observed by examining `docker-compose-e2e.yaml`, we do not create a Fabric CA server (and container) for the orderer's organization. For the exercise we will go through in this book, statically created admin users and credentials for the orderer are sufficient; we will not be registering new orderer organization users dynamically, so a Fabric CA server is not needed.

Network components' configuration files

We have demonstrated how peers, orderers, and CAs can be configured in docker-compose YAML files. But such configurations are meant to override settings that have already been made by default in the components' respective images. Though a detailed description of these configurations is beyond the scope of this book, we will list the respective files and mention how a user may make changes to them.

For a peer, a `core.yaml` file (`https://github.com/hyperledger/fabric/blob/release-1.1/sampleconfig/core.yaml`) contains all of the important runtime settings, including but not limited to addresses, port numbers, security and privacy, and the gossip protocol. You can create your own file and sync it to the container using a custom `Dockerfile` instead of the one that is used by the `hyperledger/fabric-peer` image by default. If you log in to a running peer container (let's take the Exporter organization's peer's container from the network we just launched):

```
docker exec –it f86e50e6fc76 bash
```

Then you will find the `core.yaml` file in the folder `/etc/hyperledger/fabric/`.

Similarly, an orderer's default configuration lies in an `orderer.yaml` file (`https://github.com/hyperledger/fabric/blob/release-1.1/sampleconfig/orderer.yaml`), which is also synced to `/etc/hyperledger/fabric/` on the container running the `hyperledger/fabric-orderer` image. Keep in mind that both the `core.yaml` and `orderer.yaml` files are synced to the peer and orderer containers, so if you wish to create custom files, you will need to sync these YAML files to both these containers.

A Fabric CA server also has a configuration file called `fabric-ca-server-config.yaml` (`http://hyperledger-fabric-ca.readthedocs.io/en/latest/serverconfig.htm`), which is synced to `/etc/hyperledger/fabric-ca-server/` on the container running the `hyperledger/fabric-ca` image. You can create and sync custom configurations as you would for a peer or an orderer.

Launching a sample trade network

So, now that we have all the configuration for our network, and also the channel artifacts and cryptographic material required to run it, all we need to do is start the network using the `docker-compose` command, as follows:

```
docker-compose -f docker-compose-e2e.yaml up
```

You can run this as a background process and redirect the standard output to a `log` file if you so choose. Otherwise, you will see the various containers starting up and logs from each displayed on the console.

 Note that on some OS configurations, setting up Fabric can be tricky. If you run into problems, consult the documentation. A detailed description of how to install a Fabric network and examples is provided at `https://hyperledger-fabric.readthedocs.io/en/release-1.1/sampl es.html`.

The network can be launched in the background using our trade.sh script as well; just run:

```
./trade.sh up
```

From a different terminal window, if you run `docker ps -a`, you will see something as follows:

```
CONTAINER ID     IMAGE       COMMAND       CREATED       STATUS       PORTS       NAMES
4e636f0054fc     hyperledger/fabric-peer:latest       "peer node start"     3
minutes ago     Up 3 minutes     0.0.0.0:9051->7051/tcp,
0.0.0.0:9053->7053/tcp     peer0.carrierorg.trade.com
28c18b76dbe8     hyperledger/fabric-peer:latest       "peer node start"     3
minutes ago     Up 3 minutes     0.0.0.0:8051->7051/tcp,
0.0.0.0:8053->7053/tcp     peer0.importerorg.trade.com
9308ad203362     hyperledger/fabric-ca:latest       "sh -c 'fabric-ca-se...'"
3 minutes ago     Up 3 minutes     0.0.0.0:7054->7054/tcp
ca_peerExporterOrg
754018a3875e     hyperledger/fabric-ca:latest       "sh -c 'fabric-ca-se...'"
3 minutes ago     Up 3 minutes     0.0.0.0:8054->7054/tcp
ca_peerImporterOrg
09a45eca60d5     hyperledger/fabric-orderer:latest       "orderer"     3 minutes
ago     Up 3 minutes     0.0.0.0:7050->7050/tcp     orderer.trade.com
f86e50e6fc76     hyperledger/fabric-peer:latest       "peer node start"     3
minutes ago     Up 3 minutes     0.0.0.0:7051->7051/tcp,
0.0.0.0:7053->7053/tcp     peer0.exporterorg.trade.com
986c478a522a     hyperledger/fabric-ca:latest       "sh -c 'fabric-ca-se...'"
3 minutes ago     Up 3 minutes     0.0.0.0:9054->7054/tcp
ca_peerCarrierOrg
```

```
66f90036956a    hyperledger/fabric-peer:latest     "peer node start"    3
minutes ago    Up 3 minutes    0.0.0.0:10051->7051/tcp,
0.0.0.0:10053->7053/tcp    peer0.regulatororg.trade.com
a6478cd2ba6f    hyperledger/fabric-ca:latest    "sh -c 'fabric-ca-se...'"
3 minutes ago    Up 3 minutes 0.0.0.0:10054->7054/tcp
ca_peerRegulatorOrg
```

We have four peers, four MSPs, and an orderer running in separate containers. Our trade network is up and ready to run our application!

To view the running logs of a given container, note the container ID (first column in the preceding list) and simply run:

```
docker logs <container-ID>
```

To bring the network down, you can use either the docker-compose command:

```
docker-compose -f docker-compose-e2e.yaml down
```

Or our `trade.sh` script:

```
./trade.sh down
```

Summary

In this chapter, we introduced the business use case that our follow-on chapters will leverage to create a context around the code we will write. We have also deployed our first Hyperledger Fabric network and have now transitioned from theory to practice. Well done!

The next chapters will take you through the development of a blockchain application from two perspectives: (1) Foundation API using chaincode and the Fabric SDK (2) Business network implementation using Hyperledger Composer.

Through these two perspectives, we hope to give you an understanding of the flexibility of the solution and the ability to leverage each tool in the right context. To get ready for the next chapter, you should now stop your network using `./trade.sh` down.

4
Designing a Data and Transaction Model with Golang

In Hyperledger Fabric, chaincode is a form of a smart contract written by a developer. Chaincode implements a business logic agreed upon by stakeholders of the blockchain network. The functionality is exposed to client applications for them to invoke, provided they have the correct permissions.

Chaincode runs as an independent process in its own container, isolated from the other components of the Fabric network. An endorsing peer manages the lifetime of the chaincode and of the transaction invocations. In response to client invocations, the chaincode queries and updates the ledger and generates a transactions proposal.

In this chapter, we will learn how to develop chaincode in the Go language and we will implement the smart contract business logic of the scenario. Finally, we will explore the key concepts and libraries necessary for developing a fully functional chaincode.

While in the next sections we will explore snippets of code related to the concepts you can get a complete implementation of the chaincode at the following address:

```
https://github.com/HyperledgerHandsOn/trade-finance-logistics/tree/master/chain
code/src/github.com/trade_workflow_v1
```

Note that this is also available in the local git clone we created in the previous chapter.We have two versions of the chaincode, one in the `trade_workflow` folder and another in the `trade_workflow_v1` folder. We need two versions to demonstrate upgrades later in *Chapter 9*, *Life in a Blockchain Network*. In this chapter, we use the `v1` version to demonstrate how to write chaincode in Go.

In this chapter, we will be covering the following topics:

- Creating a chaincode
- Access control
- Implementing chaincode functions
- Testing chaincode
- Chaincode design topics
- Logging output

Starting the chaincode development

Before we can start coding our chaincode, we need to first start up our development environment.

The steps of setting up the development environment has been explained in *Chapter 3*, *Setting the Stage with a Business Scenario*. However, we now proceed with starting up the Fabric network in dev-mode. This mode allows us to control how we built and run the chaincode. We will use this network to run our chaincode in the development environment.

Here is how we start the Fabric network in dev mode:

```
$ cd $GOPATH/src/trade-finance-logistics/network
$ ./trade.sh up -d true
```

If you encounter any error while the network start, it could be caused by some left-over Docker container.
You can resolve this by stopping the network using ./trade.sh down -d true and running the following command: ./trade.sh clean -d true.
The -d true option tells our script to take action on the dev network.

Our development network is now running in five Docker containers. The network is composed of a single orderer, a single peer running in devmode, a chaincode container, a CA container, and a CLI container. The CLI container creates a blockchain channel named tradechannel at startup. We will use the CLI to interact with the chaincode.

Feel free to inspect the log messages in the logs directory. It lists the components and functions executed during network startup. We will keep the terminal open, as we will receive further log messages here once the chaincode has been installed and invoked.

Compiling and running chaincode

The cloned source code already includes all dependencies using Go vendoring. With that in mind, we can now begin to build the code and to run the chaincode with the following steps:

1. **Compile the chaincode**: In a new terminal, connect to the chaincode container and build the chaincode with the following command:

   ```
   $ docker exec -it chaincode bash
   $ cd trade_workflow_v1
   $ go build
   ```

2. Run the chaincode with the following command:

   ```
   $ CORE_PEER_ADDRESS=peer:7052 CORE_CHAINCODE_ID_NAME=tw:0
   ./trade_workflow_v1
   ```

We now have a running chaincode connected to the peer. The log messages here are indicating that the chaincode is up and running. You can also inspect log messages in the network terminal, which list the connections to the chaincode on the peer.

Installing and instantiating chaincode

We now need to install the chaincode on the channel before we initiate it, which will invoke the method `Init`:

1. **Installing the chaincode**: In a new terminal, connect to the CLI container and install the chaincode with the name `tw`, as follows:

   ```
   $ docker exec -it cli bash
   $ peer chaincode install -p
   chaincodedev/chaincode/trade_workflow_v1 -n tw -v 0
   ```

2. Now, instantiate the following `chaincode`:

```
$ peer chaincode instantiate -n tw -v 0 -c
'{"Args":["init","LumberInc","LumberBank","100000","WoodenToys","To
yBank","200000","UniversalFreight","ForestryDepartment"]}' -C
tradechannel
```

The CLI-connected terminal now contains a list of log messages of the interaction with the chaincode. The `chaincode` terminal shows messages from the `chaincode` method invocation and the network terminal show messages from communication between the peer and the orderer.

Invoking chaincode

Now we have a running chaincode, we can start to invoke some functions. Our chaincode has several methods that create and retrieve assets. For now, we will only invoke two of them; the first creates a new trade agreement and the second retrieves it from the ledger. To do this, complete the following steps:

1. Put a new trade agreement with a unique ID `trade-12` on the ledger with the following command:

```
$ peer chaincode invoke -n tw -c '{"Args":["requestTrade",
"trade-12", "50000", "Wood for Toys"]}' -C tradechannel
```

2. Retrieve the trade agreement with the ID `trade-12` from the ledger with the following command:

```
$ peer chaincode invoke -n tw -c '{"Args":["getTradeStatus",
"trade-12"]}' -C tradechannel
```

We now have a running network in `devmode` and we have tested our chaincode successfully. In the following section, we will learn how to create and test chaincode from scratch.

Dev Mode

In a production environment, the lifetime of the chaincode is managed by the peer. When we need to repeatedly modify and test the chaincode in a development environment, we can use `devmode`, which allows the developer to control the life cycle of the chaincode. Additionally, `devmode` directs the `stdout` and `stderr` standard files into the terminal; these are otherwise disabled in a production environment.

To use `devmode`, the peer must be connected to other network components, as in a production environment, and started with the argument `peer-chaincodedev=true`. The chaincode is then started separately and configured to connect to the peer. The chaincode can be repeatedly compiled, started, invoked, and stopped as needed from the terminal during development.

We will use the `devmode` enabled network in the following sections.

Creating a chaincode

We are now ready to start to implementing our chaincode, which we will program in the Go language. There are several IDEs available that provide support for Go. Some of the better IDEs include Atom, Visual Studio Code, and many more. Whatever environment you opt for will work with our example.

The chaincode interface

Every chaincode must implement the `Chaincode interface`, whose methods are called in response to the received transaction proposals. The `Chaincode interface` defined in the SHIM package is shown in the following listing:

```
type Chaincode interface {
    Init(stub ChaincodeStubInterface) pb.Response
    Invoke(stub ChaincodeStubInterface) pb.Response
}
```

As you can see, the `Chaincode` type defines two functions: `Init` and `Invoke`.

Both functions have a single argument, `stub`, of the type `ChaincodeStubInterface`.

The stub argument is the main object that we will use when implementing the chaincode functionality, as it provides functions for accessing and modifying the ledger, obtaining invocation arguments, and so on.

Additionally, the SHIM package provides other types and functions in order to build chaincodes; you can inspect the whole package at:
`https://godoc.org/github.com/hyperledger/fabric/core/chaincode/shim`.

Setting up the chaincode file

Let's now set up the `chaincode` file.

We will work with the folder structure cloned from GitHub. The chaincode files are located in the following folder:

```
$GOPATH/src/trade-finance-
logistics/chaincode/src/github.com/trade_workflow_v1
```

You can either follow the steps and inspect the code files in the folder, or you can create a new folder and create the code files as described.

1. First, we need to create the `chaincode` file

   In your favorite editor, create a file, `tradeWorkflow.go`, and include the following package and import statements:

   ```
   package main

   import (
       "fmt"
       "errors"
       "strconv"
       "strings"
       "encoding/json"
       "github.com/hyperledger/fabric/core/chaincode/shim"
       "github.com/hyperledger/fabric/core/chaincode/lib/cid"
       pb "github.com/hyperledger/fabric/protos/peer"
   )
   ```

In the preceding snippet, we can see that lines 4 to 8 import the Go language system packages, and lines 9 to 11 import the `shim`, `cid`, and `pb` Fabric packages. The `pb` package provides the definition of peer `protobuf` types and `cid` provides access control functions. We will take a closer look at CID in the section on access control.

2. Now we need to define the `Chaincode` type. Let's add the `TradeWorkflowChaincode` type that will implement the chaincode functions, as shown in the following snippet:

```
type TradeWorkflowChaincode struct {
    testMode bool
}
```

Make note of the `testMode` field in line 2. We will use this feld to circumvent access control checks during testing.

3. The `TradeWorkflowChaincode` is required in order to implement the `shim.Chaincode` interface. The methods of the interface must be implemented in order for `TradeWorkflowChaincode` to be a valid `Chaincode` type of the `shim` package.

4. The `Init` method is called once the chaincode has been installed onto the blockchain network. It is executed only once by each endorsement peer that deploys its own instance of the chaincode. This method can be used for initialization, bootstrapping, and in setting up the chaincode. A default implementation of the `Init` method is shown in the following snippet. Note that the method in line 3 writes a line into a standard output to report its invocation. In line 4, the method returns a result of the invocation of the function `shim`. Success with an argument value of `nil` signals a successful execution with an empty result, as shown as follows:

```
// TradeWorkflowChaincode implementation
func (t *TradeWorkflowChaincode) Init(stub
SHIM.ChaincodeStubInterface)           pb.Response {
    fmt.Println("Initializing Trade Workflow")
    return shim.Success(nil)
}
```

An invocation of a chaincode method must return an instance of the pb.Response object. The following snippet lists the two helper functions from the SHIM package to create the response object. The following functions serialize the response into a gRPC protobuf message:

```
// Creates a Response object with the Success status and with
argument of a 'payload' to return
// if there is no value to return, the argument 'payload' should be
set to 'nil'
func shim.Success(payload []byte)

// creates a Response object with the Error status and with an
argument of a message of the error
func shim.Error(msg string)
```

5. It's now time to move on to the invocation arguments. Here, the method will retrieve the arguments of the invocation using the stub.GetFunctionAndParameters function and validate that the expected number of arguments has been provided. The Init method expects to either receive no arguments and therefore leaves the ledger as it is. This happens when the Init function is invoked because the chaincode is upgraded on the ledger to a newer version. When the chaincode is installed for a first time, it expects to receive eight arguments that include details of the participants, which will be recorded as initial states. If an incorrect number of arguments is provided, the method will return an error. The codeblock validating arguments is as follows:

```
_, args := stub.GetFunctionAndParameters()
var err error

// Upgrade Mode 1: leave ledger state as it was
if len(args) == 0 {
  return shim.Success(nil)
}

// Upgrade mode 2: change all the names and account balances
if len(args) != 8 {
 err = errors.New(fmt.Sprintf("Incorrect number of arguments.
Expecting 8: {" +
            "Exporter, " +
            "Exporter's Bank, " +
            "Exporter's Account Balance, " +
            "Importer, " +
            "Importer's Bank, " +
            "Importer's Account Balance, " +
            "Carrier, " +
            "Regulatory Authority" +
```

```
            "}. Found %d", len(args)))
    return shim.Error(err.Error())
 }
```

As we can see in the preceding snippet, when the expected number of arguments containing the names and roles of the participants is provided, the method validates and casts the arguments into the correct data types and records them onto the ledger as an initial state.

In the following snippet, in lines 2 and 7, the method casts the arguments into an integer. If the cast fails, it returns an error. In line 14, a string array is constructed from string constants. Here, we refer to lexical constants as defined in the file constants.go, which is located in the chaincode folder. The constants represent keys under which the initial values will be recorded into the ledger. Finally, in line 16 for each of the constants one record (asset) is written onto the ledger. The function stub.PutState records a key and value pair onto the ledger.

Note, that data on the ledger is stored as an array of bytes; any data we want to store on the ledger must be first converted into a byte array, as you can see in the following snippet:

```
// Type checks
_, err = strconv.Atoi(string(args[2]))
if err != nil {
    fmt.Printf("Exporter's account balance must be an integer.
Found %s\n", args[2])
    return shim.Error(err.Error())
}
_, err = strconv.Atoi(string(args[5]))
if err != nil {
    fmt.Printf("Importer's account balance must be an integer.
Found %s\n", args[5])
    return shim.Error(err.Error())
}

// Map participant identities to their roles on the ledger
roleKeys := []string{ expKey, ebKey, expBalKey, impKey, ibKey,
impBalKey, carKey, raKey }
for i, roleKey := range roleKeys {
    err = stub.PutState(roleKey, []byte(args[i]))
    if err != nil {
        fmt.Errorf("Error recording key %s: %s\n", roleKey,
err.Error())
```

```
                    return shim.Error(err.Error())
        }
    }
```

The Invoke method

The `Invoke` method is invoked whenever the state of the blockchain is queried or modified.

All **create**, **read**, **update**, and **delete** (**CRUD**) operations on the assets held on the ledger are encapsulated by the `Invoke` method.

The invocation of this method happens when a transaction is created by the invoking client. When the ledger is queried for the state (that is, one or more assets are retrieved but the state of the ledger is not modified), the contextual transaction will be discarded by the client after receiving the response of `Invoke`. Once the ledger has been modified, the modifications will be recorded into the transaction. After receiving a response for the transaction to be recorded on the ledger, the client will submit that transaction to an ordering service. An empty `Invoke` method is shown in the following snippet:

```
func (t *TradeWorkflowChaincode) Invoke(stub shim.ChaincodeStubInterface)
pb.Response {
    fmt.Println("TradeWorkflow Invoke")
}
```

Typically, the implementation of chaincode will contain multiple queries and modification functions. If these functions are very simple, they can be directly implemented in the body of the `Invoke` method. However, a more elegant solution is to implement each function independently and then invoke them from the `Invoke` method.

The SHIM API provides several functions for retrieving the invocation arguments of the `Invoke` method. These are listed in the following snippet. It is up to the developer to choose the meaning and order of the arguments; however, it is customary for the first argument of the `Invoke` method to be the name of the function, with the following arguments the arguments of that function.

```
// Returns the first argument as the function name and the rest of the
arguments as parameters in a string array.
// The client must pass only arguments of the type string.
func GetFunctionAndParameters() (string, []string)

// Returns all arguments as a single string array.
// The client must pass only arguments of the type string.
func GetStringArgs() []string
```

```
// Returns the arguments as an array of byte arrays.
func GetArgs() [][]byte

// Returns the arguments as a single byte array.
func GetArgsSlice() ([]byte, error)
```

In the following snippet, the arguments of the invocation are retrieved in line 1 using the `stub.GetFunctionAndParameters` function. From line 3 onwards, a series of `if` conditions pass the execution, along with the arguments, into the requested function (`requestTrade`, `acceptTrade`, and so on). Each of these functions implement their functionality separately. If a non-existent function is requested, the method returns an error indicating that the requested function does not exist, as shown in line 18:

```
function, args := stub.GetFunctionAndParameters()

if function == "requestTrade" {
    // Importer requests a trade
    return t.requestTrade(stub, creatorOrg, creatorCertIssuer, args)
} else if function == "acceptTrade" {
    // Exporter accepts a trade
    return t.acceptTrade(stub, creatorOrg, creatorCertIssuer, args)
} else if function == "requestLC" {
    // Importer requests an L/C
    return t.requestLC(stub, creatorOrg, creatorCertIssuer, args)
} else if function == "issueLC" {
    // Importer's Bank issues an L/C
    return t.issueLC(stub, creatorOrg, creatorCertIssuer, args)
} else if function == "acceptLC" {
...

    return shim.Error("Invalid invoke function name")
```

As you can see, the `Invoke` method is a suitable place for any shared code that is needed for extracting and validating arguments that will be used by the requested functions. In the following section, we will look at the access control mechanism and place some of the shared access control code into the `Invoke` method.

Access control

Before we delve into the implementation of `Chaincode` functions, we need to first define our access control mechanism.

A key feature of a secure and permissioned blockchain is access control. In Fabric, the **Membership Services Provider** (**MSP**) plays a pivotal role in enabling access control. Each organization of a Fabric network can have one or more MSP providers. The MSP is implemented as a **Certificate Authority** (**Fabric CA**). More information on Fabric CA, including its documentation, is available at:
`https://hyperledger-fabric-ca.readthedocs.io/`.

Fabric CA issues **Enrollment Certificates** (**ecerts**) for network users. The ecert represents the identity of the user and is used as a signed transaction when a user submits to Fabric. Prior to invoking a transaction, the user must therefore first register and obtain an ecert from the Fabric CA.

Fabric supports an **Attribute-based Access Control** (**ABAC**) mechanism that can be used by the chaincode to control access to its functions and data. The ABAC allows the chaincode to make access control decisions based on attributes associated with user identity. Users with an ecert can also access a series of additional attributes (that is, name/value pairs).

During invocation, the chaincode will extract the attributes and make an access control decision. We will take a closer look at the ABAC mechanism in the upcoming chapters.

ABAC

In the following steps, we will show you how to register a user and create an ecert with attributes. We will then retrieve the user identity and the attributes in the chaincode to validate access control. We will then integrate this functionality into our tutorial chaincode.

First, we must register a new user with the Fabric CA. As part of the registration process, we have to define the attributes that will be used once the ecert is generated. A user is registered by running the command, `fabric-ca-client register`. The access control attributes are added by using the suffix `:ecert`.

Registering a user

 These steps are informational only and cannot be executed. For more information you can refer to the GitHub repository `https://github.com/HyperledgerHandsOn/trade-finance-logistics/blob/master/chaincode/abac.md`

Let's now register a user with a custom attribute named `importer` and the value `true`. Note that the value of the attribute can be of any type and is not limited to Boolean values, as shown in the following snippet:

```
fabric-ca-client register --id.name user1 --id.secret pwd1 --id.type user -
-id.affiliation ImporterOrgMSP --id.attrs 'importer=true:ecert'
```

The previous snippet shows us the command line when registering a user with the attribute `importer=true`. Note that the values of `id.secret` and other arguments depend on the Fabric CA configuration.

The preceding command can also define multiple default attributes at once, such as: `--id.attrs` and `importer=true:ecert,email=user1@gmail.com`.

The following table contains the default attributes used during user registration:

Attribute name	Command line argument	Attribute value
hf.EnrollmentID	(automatic)	The enrollment ID of the identity
hf.Type	id.type	The type of the identity
hf.Affiliation	id.affiliation	The affiliation of the identity

If any of the previous attributes are needed in ecert, they must be first defined in the user registration command. For example, the following command registers `user1` with the attribute `hf.Affiliation=ImporterOrgMSP`, which will be copied into ecert by default:

```
fabric-ca-client register --id.name user1 --id.secret pwd1 --id.type user -
-id.affiliation ImporterOrgMSP --id.attrs
'importer=true:ecert,hf.Affiliation=ImporterOrgMSP:ecert'
```

Enrolling a user

Here, we will enroll the user and create the ecert. `enrollment.attrs` defines which attributes will be copied into the ecert from user registration. The suffix opt defines which attributes of those copied from registration are optional. If one or more non-optional attributes are not defined on the user registration, the enrollment will fail. The following command will enroll a user with the attribute `importer`:

```
fabric-ca-client enroll -u http://user1:pwd1@localhost:7054 --
enrollment.attrs "importer,email:opt"
```

Retrieving user identities and attributes in chaincode

In this step, we will retrieve a user's identity during the execution of the chaincode. The ABAC functionality available to chaincode is provided by the **Client Identity Chaincode (CID)** library.

Every transaction proposal submitted to the chaincode carries along with it the ecert of the invoker –the user submitting the transaction. The chaincode has access to the ecert through importing the CID library and invoking the library functions with the argument `ChaincodeStubInterface`, that is, the argument `stub` received in both the `Init` and `Invoke` methods.

The chaincode can use the certificate to extract information about the invoker, including:

- The ID of the invoker
- The unique ID of the **Membership Service Provider** (**MSP**) which issued the invoker certificate
- The standard attributes of the certificate, such as its domain name, email, and so on
- The ecert attributes associated with the client identity, stored within the certificate

The functions provided by the CID library are listed in the following snippet:

```
// Returns the ID associated with the invoking identity.
// This ID is unique within the MSP (Fabric CA) which issued the
identity, however, it is not guaranteed to be unique across all
MSPs of the network.
func GetID() (string, error)

// Returns the unique ID of the MSP associated with the identity
that submitted the transaction.
// The combination of the MSPID and of the identity ID are
guaranteed to be unique across the network.
func GetMSPID() (string, error)

// Returns the value of the ecert attribute named `attrName`.
// If the ecert has the attribute, the `found` returns true and the
`value` returns the value of the attribute.
// If the ecert does not have the attribute, `found` returns false
and `value` returns empty string.
func GetAttributeValue(attrName string) (value string, found bool,
err error)

// The function verifies that the ecert has the attribute named
```

```
`attrName` and that the attribute value equals to `attrValue`.
// The function returns nil if there is a match, else, it returns
error.
func AssertAttributeValue(attrName, attrValue string) error

// Returns the X509 identity certificate.
// The certificate is an instance of a type Certificate from the
library "crypto/x509".
func GetX509Certificate() (*x509.Certificate, error)
```

In the following codeblock, we define a function, getTxCreatorInfo, which obtains basic identity information about the invoker. First, we must import the CID and x509 libraries, as seen in lines 3 and 4. The unique MSPID is retrieved in line 13 and the X509 certificate is obtained in line 19. In line 24, we then retrieve the CommonName of the certificate, which contains the unique string of the Fabric CA within the network. These two attributes are returned by the function and used in subsequent access control validation, as shown in the following snippet:

```
import (
    "fmt"
    "github.com/hyperledger/fabric/core/chaincode/shim"
    "github.com/hyperledger/fabric/core/chaincode/lib/cid"
    "crypto/x509"
)

func getTxCreatorInfo(stub shim.ChaincodeStubInterface) (string, string,
error) {
    var mspid string
    var err error
    var cert *x509.Certificate

    mspid, err = cid.GetMSPID(stub)
    if err != nil {
        fmt.Printf("Error getting MSP identity: %sn", err.Error())
        return "", "", err
    }

    cert, err = cid.GetX509Certificate(stub)
    if err != nil {
        fmt.Printf("Error getting client certificate: %sn", err.Error())
        return "", "", err
    }

    return mspid, cert.Issuer.CommonName, nil
}
```

We now need to define and implement the simple access control policy in our chaincode. Each function of the chaincode can only be invoked by members of a specific organization; each chaincode function will therefore validate whether the invoker is a member of the required organization. For example, the function `requestTrade` can be invoked only by members of the `Importer` organization. In the following snippet, the function `authenticateImporterOrg` validates whether the invoker is a member of `ImporterOrgMSP`. This function then will be invoked from the `requestTrade` function to enforce access control.

```
func authenticateExportingEntityOrg(mspID string, certCN string) bool {
    return (mspID == "ExportingEntityOrgMSP") && (certCN ==
"ca.exportingentityorg.trade.com")
}
func authenticateExporterOrg(mspID string, certCN string) bool {
return (mspID == "ExporterOrgMSP") && (certCN ==
"ca.exporterorg.trade.com")
}
func authenticateImporterOrg(mspID string, certCN string) bool {
    return (mspID == "ImporterOrgMSP") && (certCN ==
"ca.importerorg.trade.com")
}
func authenticateCarrierOrg(mspID string, certCN string) bool {
    return (mspID == "CarrierOrgMSP") && (certCN ==
"ca.carrierorg.trade.com")
}
func authenticateRegulatorOrg(mspID string, certCN string) bool {
    return (mspID == "RegulatorOrgMSP") && (certCN ==
"ca.regulatororg.trade.com")
}
```

In the following snippet is shown the invocation of access control validation, which has granted access only to members of `ImporterOrgMSP`. The function is invoked with the arguments obtained from the `getTxCreatorInfo` function.

```
creatorOrg, creatorCertIssuer, err = getTxCreatorInfo(stub)
if !authenticateImporterOrg(creatorOrg, creatorCertIssuer) {
    return shim.Error("Caller not a member of Importer Org. Access
denied.")
}
```

Now, we need to place our authentication functions into a separate file, `accessControlUtils.go`, which is located in the same directory as the main `tradeWorkflow.go` file. This file will be automatically imported into the main `chaincode` file during compilation so we can refer to the functions defined in it.

Implementing chaincode functions

At this point, we now have the basic building blocks of chaincode. We have the `Init` method, which initiates the chaincode and the `Invoke` method, which receives request from the client and the access control mechanism. Now, we need to define the functionality of the chaincode.

Based on our scenario, the following tables summarize the list of functions that record and retrieve data to and from the ledger to provide the business logic of the smart contract. The tables also define the access control definitions of organization member, which are needed in order to invoke the respective functions.

The following table illustrates the chaincode modification functions, that is, how to record transactions on the ledger:

Function name	Permission to invoke	Description
requestTrade	Importer	Requests a trade agreement
acceptTrade	Exporter	Accepts a trade agreement
requestLC	Importer	Requests a letter of credit
issueLC	Importer	Issues a letter of credit
acceptLC	Exporter	Accepts a letter of credit
requestEL	Exporter	Requests an export license
issueEL	Regulator	Issues an export license
prepareShipment	Exporter	Prepares a shipment
acceptShipmentAndIssueBL	Carrier	Accepts a shipment and issue a bill of lading
requestPayment	Exporter	Requests a payment
makePayment	Importer	Makes a payment
updateShipmentLocation	Carrier	Updates shipment location

The following table illustrates the chaincode query functions, that is, those needed to retrieve data from the ledger:

Function name	Permission to invoke	Description
`getTradeStatus`	Exporter/ExportingEntity/Importer	Gets current state of a trade agreement
`getLCStatus`	Exporter/ExportingEntity/Importer	Get current state of a Letter of Credit
`getELStatus`	ExportingEntity/Regulator	Get current state of an Export License
`getShipmentLocation`	Exporter/ExportingEntity/Importer/Carrier	Get current location of a shipment
`getBillOfLading`	Exporter/ExportingEntity/Importer	Get the bill of lading
`getAccountBalance`	Exporter/ExportingEntity/Importer	Get current account balance for a given participant

Defining chaincode assets

We are now going to define the structure of our assets, which will be recorded onto the ledger. In Go, the assets are defined as struct types with a list of attribute names and types. The definitions also need to contain JSON attribute names, which will be used to serialize the assets into the JSON objects. In the following snippet, you will see definitions for four assets in our application. Note that, the attributes of structs can encapsulate other structs and thus allow to create multi-level trees.

```go
type TradeAgreement struct {
    Amount              int         `json:"amount"`
    DescriptionOfGoods  string      `json:"descriptionOfGoods"`
    Status              string      `json:"status"`
    Payment             int         `json:"payment"`
}

type LetterOfCredit struct {
    Id              string      `json:"id"`
    ExpirationDate  string      `json:"expirationDate"`
    Beneficiary     string      `json:"beneficiary"`
    Amount          int         `json:"amount"`
    Documents       []string    `json:"documents"`
    Status          string      `json:"status"`
}

type ExportLicense struct {
```

```
    Id                      string              `json:"id"`
    ExpirationDate          string              `json:"expirationDate"`
    Exporter                string              `json:"exporter"`
    Carrier                 string              `json:"carrier"`
    DescriptionOfGoods      string              `json:"descriptionOfGoods"`
    Approver                string              `json:"approver"`
    Status                  string              `json:"status"`
}

type BillOfLading struct {
    Id                      string              `json:"id"`
    ExpirationDate          string              `json:"expirationDate"`
    Exporter                string              `json:"exporter"`
    Carrier                 string              `json:"carrier"`
    DescriptionOfGoods      string              `json:"descriptionOfGoods"`
    Amount                  int                 `json:"amount"`
    Beneficiary             string              `json:"beneficiary"`
    SourcePort              string              `json:"sourcePort"`
    DestinationPort         string              `json:"destinationPort"`
}
```

Coding chaincode functions

In this section, we will implement the chaincode functions we looked at previously. To implement the chaincode functions, we will use three SHIM API functions that will read assets from the Worldstate and record changes. As we have already learned, reads and writes of these functions are recorded into `ReadSet` and `WriteSet` respectively, and the changes do not affect the state of the ledger immediately. Only after the transaction has passed through validation and has been committed into the ledger will the changes take effect.

The following snippet shows a list of asset API functions:

```
// Returns the value of the `key` from the Worldstate.
// If the key does not exist in the Worldstate the function returns (nil,
nil).
// The function does not read data from the WriteSet and hence uncommitted
values modified by PutState are not returned.
func GetState(key string) ([]byte, error)

// Records the specified `key` and `value` into the WriteSet.
// The function does not affect the ledger until the transaction is
committed into the ledger.
func PutState(key string, value []byte) error
```

```
// Marks the the specified `key` as deleted in the WriteSet.
// The key will be marked as deleted and removed from Worldstate once the
transaction is committed into the ledger.
func DelState(key string) error
```

Creating an asset

Now that we can implement our first chaincode function, we will move on and implement a `requestTrade` function, which will create a new trade agreement with the status `REQUESTED` and then record that agreement on the ledger.

The implementation of the function is shown in the following snippet. As you will see, in line 9 we verify that the invoker is a member of `ImporterOrg` and has permission to invoke the function. From lines 13 to 21 we validate and extract the arguments. In line 23, we create a new instance of `TradeAgreement` initiated with the received arguments. As we learned earlier, the ledger stores values in the form of arrays of bytes. Thus, in line 24 we serialize `TradeAgreement` with JSON into an array of bytes. In line 32, we create a unique key, under which we will store `TradeAgreement`. Finally, in line 37, we use the key and serialized `TradeAgreement` alongside the function `PutState` to store the value into the `WriteSet`.

The following snippet illustrates the `requestTrade` function:

```
func (t *TradeWorkflowChaincode) requestTrade(stub
shim.ChaincodeStubInterface, creatorOrg string, creatorCertIssuer string,
args []string) pb.Response {
    var tradeKey string
    var tradeAgreement *TradeAgreement
    var tradeAgreementBytes []byte
    var amount int
    var err error

    // Access control: Only an Importer Org member can invoke this
transaction
    if !t.testMode && !authenticateImporterOrg(creatorOrg,
creatorCertIssuer) {
        return shim.Error("Caller not a member of Importer Org. Access
denied.")
    }

    if len(args) != 3 {
        err = errors.New(fmt.Sprintf("Incorrect number of arguments.
Expecting 3: {ID, Amount, Description of Goods}. Found %d", len(args)))
        return shim.Error(err.Error())
```

```
        }

    amount, err = strconv.Atoi(string(args[1]))
    if err != nil {
            return shim.Error(err.Error())
    }

    tradeAgreement = &TradeAgreement{amount, args[2], REQUESTED, 0}
    tradeAgreementBytes, err = json.Marshal(tradeAgreement)
    if err != nil {
            return shim.Error("Error marshaling trade agreement structure")
    }

    // Write the state to the ledger
    tradeKey, err = getTradeKey(stub, args[0])
    if err != nil {
            return shim.Error(err.Error())
    }
    err = stub.PutState(tradeKey, tradeAgreementBytes)
    if err != nil {
            return shim.Error(err.Error())
    }
    fmt.Printf("Trade %s request recorded", args[0])

    return shim.Success(nil)
}
```

Reading and modifying an asset

After we have implemented the function to create a trade agreement, we need to implement a function to accept the trade agreement. This function will retrieve the agreement, modify its status to ACCEPTED, and put it back on the ledger.

The implementation of this function is shown in the following snippet. In the code, we construct the unique composite key of the trade agreement we want to retrieve. In line 22, we retrieve the value with the function GetState. In line 33, we deserialize the array of bytes into the instance of the TradeAgreement struct. In line 41, we modify the status so it reads ACCEPTED; finally, in line 47, we store the updated value on the ledger, as follows:

```
func (t *TradeWorkflowChaincode) acceptTrade(stub
shim.ChaincodeStubInterface, creatorOrg string, creatorCertIssuer string,
args []string) pb.Response {
    var tradeKey string
    var tradeAgreement *TradeAgreement
    var tradeAgreementBytes []byte
```

```
    var err error

    // Access control: Only an Exporting Entity Org member can invoke this
transaction
    if !t.testMode && !authenticateExportingEntityOrg(creatorOrg,
creatorCertIssuer) {
        return shim.Error("Caller not a member of Exporting Entity Org.
Access denied.")
    }

    if len(args) != 1 {
        err = errors.New(fmt.Sprintf("Incorrect number of arguments.
Expecting 1: {ID}. Found %d", len(args)))
        return shim.Error(err.Error())
    }

    // Get the state from the ledger
    tradeKey, err = getTradeKey(stub, args[0])
    if err != nil {
        return shim.Error(err.Error())
    }
    tradeAgreementBytes, err = stub.GetState(tradeKey)
    if err != nil {
        return shim.Error(err.Error())
    }

    if len(tradeAgreementBytes) == 0 {
        err = errors.New(fmt.Sprintf("No record found for trade ID %s",
args[0]))
        return shim.Error(err.Error())
    }

    // Unmarshal the JSON
    err = json.Unmarshal(tradeAgreementBytes, &tradeAgreement)
    if err != nil {
        return shim.Error(err.Error())
    }

    if tradeAgreement.Status == ACCEPTED {
        fmt.Printf("Trade %s already accepted", args[0])
    } else {
        tradeAgreement.Status = ACCEPTED
        tradeAgreementBytes, err = json.Marshal(tradeAgreement)
        if err != nil {
            return shim.Error("Error marshaling trade agreement
structure")
        }
        // Write the state to the ledger
```

```
        err = stub.PutState(tradeKey, tradeAgreementBytes)
        if err != nil {
                return shim.Error(err.Error())
        }
    }
    fmt.Printf("Trade %s acceptance recordedn", args[0])

    return shim.Success(nil)
}
```

Main function

Last but not least, we will add the `main` function: the initial point of a Go program. When an instance of the chaincode is deployed on a peer, the `main` function is executed to start the chaincode.

In line 2 of the following snippet, the chaincode is instantiated. The function `shim.Start` starts the chaincode in line 4 and registers it with the peer, as follows:

```
func main() {
    twc := new(TradeWorkflowChaincode)
    twc.testMode = false
    err := shim.Start(twc)
    if err != nil {
            fmt.Printf("Error starting Trade Workflow chaincode: %s", err)
    }
}
```

Testing chaincode

Now we can write unit tests for our chaincode functions, we will use the in-built automated Go testing framework. For more information and documentation, visit Go's official website at: https://golang.org/pkg/testing/

The framework automatically seeks and executes functions with the following signature:

```
func TestFname(*testing.T)
```

The function name `Fname` is an arbitrary name that must start with an uppercase letter.

Note that the test suite file containing unit tests must end with the suffix, _test.go; therefore, our test suite file will be named `tradeWorkflow_test.go` and placed in the same directory as our `chaincode` file. The first argument of the `test` function is of the type `T`, which provides functions for managing test states and supporting formatted test logs. The output of the test is written into the standard output, it can be inspected in the terminal.

SHIM mocking

The SHIM package provides a comprehensive mocking model that can be used to test chaincodes. In our unit tests, we will use the `MockStub` type, which provides an implementation of `ChaincodeStubInterface` for unit-testing chaincodes.

Testing the Init method

First, we need to define the function needed to invoke the `Init` method. The function will receive references to `MockStub`, as well as to an array of arguments to pass to the `Init` method. In line 2 of the following code, the chaincode function `Init` is invoked with the received arguments, which is then verified in line 3.

The following snippet illustrates the invocation of the `Init` method:

```
func checkInit(t *testing.T, stub *shim.MockStub, args [][]byte) {
   res := stub.MockInit("1", args)
   if res.Status != shim.OK {
        fmt.Println("Init failed", string(res.Message))
        t.FailNow()
   }
}
```

We will now define the function needed to prepare a default array of values of the `Init` function arguments, shown as follows:

```
func getInitArguments() [][]byte {
   return [][]byte{[]byte("init"),
                []byte("LumberInc"),
                []byte("LumberBank"),
                []byte("100000"),
                []byte("WoodenToys"),
                []byte("ToyBank"),
                []byte("200000"),
```

```
                []byte("UniversalFreight"),
                []byte("ForestryDepartment")}
    }
```

We will now define the test of the `Init` function, as shown in the following snippet. The test first creates an instance of the chaincode, then sets the mode to test, and finally creates a new `MockStub` for the chaincode. In line 7, the `checkInit` function is invoked and the `Init` function is executed. Finally, from line 9 onwards, we will verify the state of the ledger, as follows:

```
func TestTradeWorkflow_Init(t *testing.T) {
    scc := new(TradeWorkflowChaincode)
    scc.testMode = true
    stub := shim.NewMockStub("Trade Workflow", scc)

    // Init
    checkInit(t, stub, getInitArguments())

    checkState(t, stub, "Exporter", EXPORTER)
    checkState(t, stub, "ExportersBank", EXPBANK)
    checkState(t, stub, "ExportersAccountBalance", strconv.Itoa(EXPBALANCE))
    checkState(t, stub, "Importer", IMPORTER)
    checkState(t, stub, "ImportersBank", IMPBANK)
    checkState(t, stub, "ImportersAccountBalance", strconv.Itoa(IMPBALANCE))
    checkState(t, stub, "Carrier", CARRIER)
    checkState(t, stub, "RegulatoryAuthority", REGAUTH)
}
```

Next, we verify whether each key's state is as expected with the `checkState` function, as shown in the following codeblock:

```
func checkState(t *testing.T, stub *shim.MockStub, name string, value
string) {
  bytes := stub.State[name]
  if bytes == nil {
    fmt.Println("State", name, "failed to get value")
    t.FailNow()
  }
  if string(bytes) != value {
    fmt.Println("State value", name, "was", string(bytes), "and not",
value, "as expected")
    t.FailNow()
  }
}
```

Testing the Invoke method

It's now time to define the test for the `Invoke` function. In line 7 of the following codeblock, `checkInit` is called to initialize the ledger, followed by `checkInvoke` in line 13, which invokes the `requestTrade` function. The `requestTrade` function creates a new trade asset and stores it on the ledger. To verify that the ledger contains the correct state, a new `TradeAgreement` is created and serialized in lines 15 and 16, before a new composite key is calculated in line 17. Finally, in line 18, the state of the key is verified against the serialized value.

Additionally, as previously outlined, our chaincode contains a series of functions that together define the trade workflow. We will chain the invocations of these functions into a sequence in the test to verify the whole workflow. The code of the whole function is available in the test file located in the `chaincode` folder.

```
func TestTradeWorkflow_Agreement(t *testing.T) {
    scc := new(TradeWorkflowChaincode)
    scc.testMode = true
    stub := shim.NewMockStub("Trade Workflow", scc)

    // Init
    checkInit(t, stub, getInitArguments())

    // Invoke 'requestTrade'
    tradeID := "2ks89j9"
    amount := 50000
    descGoods := "Wood for Toys"
    checkInvoke(t, stub, [][]byte{[]byte("requestTrade"), []byte(tradeID),
    []byte(strconv.Itoa(amount)), []byte(descGoods)})

    tradeAgreement := &TradeAgreement{amount, descGoods, REQUESTED, 0}
    tradeAgreementBytes, _ := json.Marshal(tradeAgreement)
    tradeKey, _ := stub.CreateCompositeKey("Trade", []string{tradeID})
    checkState(t, stub, tradeKey, string(tradeAgreementBytes))
    ...
}
```

Following snippet shows the function `checkInvoke`.

```
func checkInvoke(t *testing.T, stub *shim.MockStub, args [][]byte) {
    res := stub.MockInvoke("1", args)
    if res.Status != shim.OK {
        fmt.Println("Invoke", args, "failed", string(res.Message))
        t.FailNow()
    }
}
```

Running tests

We are now ready to run our tests! The `go test` command will execute all tests found in the `tradeWorkflow_test.go` file. The file contains a long series of tests that verify the functions defined in our workflow.

Let's now run the tests in the terminal with the following command:

```
$ cd $GOPATH/src/trade-finance-
logistics/chaincode/src/github.com/trade_workflow_v1
$ go test
```

The preceding command should generate the following output:

```
Initializing Trade Workflow
Exporter: LumberInc
Exporter's Bank: LumberBank
Exporter's Account Balance: 100000
Importer: WoodenToys
Importer's Bank: ToyBank
Importer's Account Balance: 200000
Carrier: UniversalFreight
Regulatory Authority: ForestryDepartment
...
Amount paid thus far for trade 2ks89j9 = 25000; total required = 50000
Payment request for trade 2ks89j9 recorded
TradeWorkflow Invoke
TradeWorkflow Invoke
Query Response:{"Balance":"150000"}
TradeWorkflow Invoke
Query Response:{"Balance":"150000"}
PASS
ok        trade-finance-logistics/chaincode/src/github.com/trade_workflow_v1
0.036s
```

Chaincode design topics

Composite keys

We often need to store multiple instances of one type on the ledger, such as multiple trade agreements, letters of credit, and so on. In this case, the keys of those instances will be typically constructed from a combination of attributes—for example, `"Trade"` + `ID`, yielding `["Trade1","Trade2", ...]`. The key of an instance can be customized in the code, or API functions can be provided in SHIM to construct a composite key (in other words, a unique key) of an instance based on a combination of several attributes. These functions simplify composite key construction. Composite keys can then be used just as a normal string key is used to record and retrieve values using the `PutState()` and `GetState()` functions.

The following snippet shows a list of functions that create and work with composite keys:

```
// The function creates a key by combining the attributes into a single
string.
// The arguments must be valid utf8 strings and must not contain U+0000
(nil byte) and U+10FFFF charactres.
func CreateCompositeKey(objectType string, attributes []string) (string,
error)

// The function splits the compositeKey into attributes from which the key
was formed.
// This function is useful for extracting attributes from keys returned by
range queries.
func SplitCompositeKey(compositeKey string) (string, []string, error)
```

In the following snippet we can see a function `getTradeKey`, which constructs a unique composite key of a trade agreement by combining the keyword `Trade` with an ID of the trade:

```
func getTradeKey(stub shim.ChaincodeStubInterface, tradeID string) (string,
error) {
    tradeKey, err := stub.CreateCompositeKey("Trade", []string{tradeID})
    if err != nil {
        return "", err
    } else {
        return tradeKey, nil
    }
}
```

In more complex scenarios, keys can be constructed from multiple attributes. Composite keys also allow you to search for assets based on components of the key in range queries. We will explore searching in more detail in the upcoming sections.

Range queries

As well as retrieving assets with a unique key, SHIM offers API functions the opportunity to retrieve sets of assets based on a range criteria. Moreover, composite keys can be modeled to enable queries against multiple components of the key.

The range functions return an iterator (`StateQueryIteratorInterface`) over a set of keys matching the query criteria. The returned keys are in lexical order. The iterator must be closed with a call to the function `Close()`. Additionally, when a composite key has multiple attributes, the range query function, `GetStateByPartialCompositeKey()`, can be used to search for keys matching a subset of the attributes.

For example, the key of a payment composed of `TradeId` and `PaymentId` can be searched for across all payments associated with a specific `TradeId`, as shown in the following snippet:

```
// Returns an iterator over all keys between the startKey (inclusive) and
endKey (exclusive).
// To query from start or end of the range, the startKey and endKey can be
an empty.
func GetStateByRange(startKey, endKey string) (StateQueryIteratorInterface,
error)

// Returns an iterator over all composite keys whose prefix matches the
given partial composite key.
// Same rules as for arguments of CreateCompositeKey function apply.
func GetStateByPartialCompositeKey(objectType string, keys []string)
(StateQueryIteratorInterface, error)
```

We can also search for all trade agreements with an ID within the range of 1-100 with the following query:

```
startKey, err = getTradeKey(stub, "1")
endKey, err = getTradeKey(stub, "100")

keysIterator, err := stub.GetStateByRange(startKey, endKey)
if err != nil {
    return shim.Error(fmt.Printf("Error accessing state: %s", err))
}
```

```
defer keysIterator.Close()

var keys []string
for keysIterator.HasNext() {
    key, _, err := keysIterator.Next()
    if err != nil {
        return shim.Error(fmt.Printf("keys operation failed. Error
accessing state: %s", err))
    }
    keys = append(keys, key)
}
```

State queries and CouchDB

By default, Fabric uses LevelDB as storage for the Worldstate. Fabric also offers the option to configure peers to store Worldstate in CouchDB. When assets are stored in the form of JSON documents, CouchDB allows you to perform complex queries for assets based on the asset state.

The queries are formatted in the native CouchDB declarative JSON querying syntax. The current version of this syntax is available at: http://docs.couchdb.org/en/2.1.1/api/database/find.html.

Fabric forwards queries to CouchDB and returns an iterator (StateQueryIteratorInterface()), which can be used to iterate over the result set. The declaration of the state based query function is as follows:

```
func GetQueryResult(query string) (StateQueryIteratorInterface, error)
```

In the following snippet, we can see a state-based query for all trade agreements that have the status ACCEPTED and a received payment of over 1000. The query is then executed and the found documents are written to the terminal, shown as follows:

```
// CouchDB query definition
queryString :=
`{
    "selector": {
            "status": "ACCEPTED"
            "payment": {
                    "$gt": 1000
            }
    }
}`

fmt.Printf("queryString:\n%s\n", queryString)
```

```
// Invoke query
resultsIterator, err := stub.GetQueryResult(queryString)
if err != nil {
    return nil, err
}
defer resultsIterator.Close()

var buffer bytes.Buffer
buffer.WriteString("[")

// Iterate through all returned assets
bArrayMemberAlreadyWritten := false
for resultsIterator.HasNext() {
    queryResponse, err := resultsIterator.Next()
    if err != nil {
        return nil, err
    }
    if bArrayMemberAlreadyWritten == true {
        buffer.WriteString(",")
    }
    buffer.WriteString("{\"Key\":")
    buffer.WriteString("\"")
    buffer.WriteString(queryResponse.Key)
    buffer.WriteString("\"")

    buffer.WriteString(", \"Record\":")
    buffer.WriteString(string(queryResponse.Value))
    buffer.WriteString("}")
    bArrayMemberAlreadyWritten = true
}
buffer.WriteString("]")

fmt.Printf("queryResult:\n%s\n", buffer.String())
```

Note that unlike queries over keys, the queries over state are not recorded into the `ReadSet` of the transaction. Thus, the validation of the transaction cannot actually verify whether changes to the Worldstate occurred between the execution and commitment of the transaction. The chaincode design must therefore take that into consideration; if a query is based on an expected invocation sequence, an invalid transaction may appear.

Indexes

Performing queries on large datasets is a computationally complex task. Fabric provides a mechanism for defining indexes on the CouchDB hosted Worldstate to increase efficiency. Note that indexes are also required for sorting operations in queries.

An index is defined in JSON in a separate file with the extension `*.json`. The full definition of the format is available at: `http://docs.couchdb.org/en/2.1.1/api/database/find.html#db-index`.

The following snippet illustrates an index that matches our query for the trade agreements we looked at earlier:

```
{
  "index": {
    "fields": [
      "status",
      "payment"
    ]
  },
  "name": "index_sp",
  "type": "json"
}
```

Here, the index files are placed into the folder `/META-INF/statedb/couchdb/indexes`. During compilation, the indexes are packaged along with the chaincode. Upon installation and instantiation of the chaincode on the peer, the indexes are automatically deployed onto the Worldstate and used by queries.

ReadSet and WriteSet

On receipt of a transaction invocation message from a client, the endorsing peer executes a transaction. The execution invokes the chaincode in the context of the peer's Worldstate and records all reads and writes of its data on the ledger into a `ReadSet` and `WriteSet`.

The transaction's `WriteSet` contains a list of key and value pairs that were modified during the execution by the chaincode. When the value of a key is modified (that is, a new key and value are recorded or an existing key is updated with a new value), the `WriteSet` will contain the updated key and value pair.

When a key is deleted, the `WriteSet` will contain the key with an attribute marking the key as deleted. If a single key is modified multiple times during chaincode execution, the `WriteSet` will contain the latest modified value.

The transaction's `ReadSet` contains a list of keys and their versions that were accessed during execution by the chaincode. The version number of a key is derived from a combination of the block number and the transaction number within the block. This design enables the efficient searching and processing of data. Another section of the transaction contains information about range queries and their outcome. Remember that when a chaincode reads the value of a key, the latest committed value in the ledger is returned.

If modifications introduced during chaincode execution are stored in the `WriteSet`, when a chaincode is reading a key modified during execution, the committed—not modified—value will be returned. Therefore, if a modified value is needed later during the same execution, the chaincode must be implemented such that it retains and uses the correct values.

An example of a transaction's `ReadSet` and `WriteSet` is as follows:

```
{
  "rwset": {
    "reads": [
      {
        "key": "key1",
        "version": {
          "block_num": {
            "low": 9546,
            "high": 0,
            "unsigned": true
          },
          "tx_num": {
            "low": 0,
            "high": 0,
            "unsigned": true
          }
        }
      }
    ],
    "range_queries_info": [],
    "writes": [
      {
        "key": "key1",
        "is_delete": false,
        "value": "value1"
      },
      {
        "key": "key2",
        "is_delete": true
      }
    ]
```

```
        }
    }
```

Multiversion concurrency control

Fabric uses a **multiversion concurrency control** (**MVCC**) mechanism to ensure consistency in the ledger and to prevent double spending. Double spending attacks aim to exploit flaws in systems by introducing transactions that use or modify the same resource multiple times, such as spending the same coin multiple times in a cryptocurrency network. A key collision is another type of problems that can occur while processing transactions submitted by parallel clients, and which may attempt to modify the same key/value pairs at the same time.

In addition, due to Fabric's decentralized architecture, the sequence of transaction execution can be ordered and committed differently on the different Fabric components (including endorsers, orderers, and committers), which in turn introduces a delay between the calculation and commitment of the transaction, within which key collision can occur. Decentralization also leaves the network vulnerable to potential problems and attacks by intentionally or unintentionally modifying the sequence of transactions by clients.

To ensure consistency, computer systems such as databases typically use a locking mechanism. However, locking requires a centralized approach, which is unavailable in Fabric. It's also worth noting that locking can sometimes introduce a performance penalty.

To combat this, Fabric uses a versioning system of keys stored on the ledger. The aim of the versioning system is to ensure that transactions are ordered and committed into the ledger in a sequence that does not introduce inconsistencies. When a block is received on a committing peer, each transaction of the block is validated. The algorithm inspects the `ReadSet` for keys and their versions; if the version of each key in the `ReadSet` matches the version of the same key in the Worldstate, or of the preceding transactions in the same block, the transaction is considered valid. In other words, the algorithm verifies that none of the data read from the Worldstate during transaction execution has been changed.

If a transaction contains range queries, these will be validated as well. For each range query, the algorithm checks whether the result of executing the query is exactly the same as it was during chaincode execution, or if any modification has taken place.

Transactions that do not pass this validation are marked as invalid in the ledger and the changes they introduce are not projected onto the Worldstate. Note that since the ledger is immutable, the transactions stay on the ledger.

If a transaction passes the validation, the `WriteSet` is projected onto the Worldstate. Each key modified by the transaction is set in the Worldstate to the new value specified in the `WriteSet`, and the version of the key in the Worldstate is set to a version derived from the transaction. In this way, any inconsistencies such as double spending are prevented. At the same time, in situations when key collisions may occur, the chaincode design must take the behavior of MVCC into consideration. There are multiple well-known strategies for addressing key collisions and MVCC, such as splitting assets, using multiple keys, transaction queuing, and more.

Logging output

Logging is a vital part of system code, enabling the analysis and detection of runtime problems.

Logging in Fabric is based on the standard Go logging package, `github.com/op/go-logging`. The logging mechanism provides severity-based control of logs and pretty-printing decoration of messages. The logging levels are defined in decreasing order of severity, as follows:

```
CRITICAL | ERROR | WARNING | NOTICE | INFO | DEBUG
```

The log messages are combined from all components and written into the standard error file (`stderr`). Logging can be controlled by the configuration of peers and modules, as well as in the code of the chaincode.

Configuration

The default configuration of peer logging is set to the level INFO, but this level can be controlled in the following ways:

1. A command line option logging level. This option overrides default configurations, shown as follows:

   ```
   peer node start --logging-level=error
   ```

   Note that any module or chaincode can be configured through the command line option, as shown in the following snippet:

   ```
   peer node start --logging-level=chaincode=error:main=info
   ```

2. The default logging level can also be defined with an `environment` variable `CORE_LOGGING_LEVEL`, as shown in the following snippet:

```
peer0.org1.example.com:
    environment:
        - CORE_LOGGING_LEVEL=error
```

3. A configuration attribute in the `core.yml` file, defining the configuration of a network can also be used with the following code:

```
logging:
    level: info
```

4. The `core.yml` file also allows you to configure logging levels for specific modules, such as for the `chaincode` or the format of messages, as shown in the following snippet:

```
chaincode:
  logging:
        level:  error
        shim:   warning
```

More detail on the various configuration options are provided in the comments of the `core.yml` file.

Logging API

The SHIM package provides APIs for the chaincode to create and manage logging objects. The logs generated by these objects are integrated with peer logs.

The chaincode can create and use an arbitrary number of logging objects. Each logging object must have a unique name, which is used to prefix log records in the output and to distinguish the records of different logging objects and the SHIM. (Remember that the logging object name SHIM API is reserved and should not be used in chaincode.) Each logging object has set a logging severity level at which the log records will be sent to the output. Log records with the severity level `CRITICAL` always appear in the output. The following snippet lists the API functions to create and manage logging objects in the chaincode.

```
// Creates a new logging object.
func NewLogger(name string) *ChaincodeLogger

// Converts a case-insensitive string representing a logging level into an
element of LoggingLevel enumeration type.
```

```
// This function is used to convert constants of standard GO logging levels
(i.e. CRITICAL, ERROR, WARNING, NOTICE, INFO or DEBUG) into the shim's
enumeration LoggingLevel type (i.e. LogDebug, LogInfo, LogNotice,
LogWarning, LogError, LogCritical).
func LogLevel(levelString string) (LoggingLevel, error)

// Sets the logging level of the logging object.
func (c *ChaincodeLogger) SetLevel(level LoggingLevel)

// Returns true if the logging object will generate logs at the given
level.
func (c *ChaincodeLogger) IsEnabledFor(level LoggingLevel) bool
```

The logging object `ChaincodeLogger` provides functions for logging records for each of the severity levels. The following shippet lists the functions of the `ChaincodeLogger`.

```
func (c *ChaincodeLogger) Debug(args ...interface{})
func (c *ChaincodeLogger) Debugf(format string, args ...interface{})
func (c *ChaincodeLogger) Info(args ...interface{})
func (c *ChaincodeLogger) Infof(format string, args ...interface{})
func (c *ChaincodeLogger) Notice(args ...interface{})
func (c *ChaincodeLogger) Noticef(format string, args ...interface{})
func (c *ChaincodeLogger) Warning(args ...interface{})
func (c *ChaincodeLogger) Warningf(format string, args ...interface{})
func (c *ChaincodeLogger) Error(args ...interface{})
func (c *ChaincodeLogger) Errorf(format string, args ...interface{})
func (c *ChaincodeLogger) Critical(args ...interface{})
func (c *ChaincodeLogger) Criticalf(format string, args ...interface{})
```

The default formatting of the records is defined by the configuration of SHIM, which places a space between the printed representations of the input arguments. For each severity level, the logging objects provide an additional function with the suffix `f`. These functions allow you to control the formatting of the output with the argument `format`.

The template of an output generated by the logging objects is as follows:

```
[timestamp] [logger name] [severity level] printed arguments
```

The output of all logging objects and of SHIM is combined and sent into the standard error (`stderr`).

The following code block illustrates an example of creating and using a logging object:

```
var logger = shim.NewLogger("tradeWorkflow")
logger.SetLevel(shim.LogDebug)

_, args := stub.GetFunctionAndParameters()
```

```
logger.Debugf("Function: %s(%s)", "requestTrade", strings.Join(args, ","))

if !authenticateImporterOrg(creatorOrg, creatorCertIssuer) {
    logger.Info("Caller not a member of Importer Org. Access denied:",
creatorOrg, creatorCertIssuer)
}
```

SHIM logging levels

The chaincode can also directly control the logging severity level of its SHIM by using the API function `SetLoggingLevel` as follows:

```
logLevel, _ := shim.LogLevel(os.Getenv("TW_SHIM_LOGGING_LEVEL"))
shim.SetLoggingLevel(logLevel)
```

Stdout and stderr

As well as the logging mechanisms provided by the SHIM API and integrated with the peer, during the development phase, the chaincode can use the standard output files. The chaincode is executed as an independent process and can therefore use the standard output (`stdout`) and standard error (`stderr`) files to record output using standard Go printing functions (for example, `fmt.Printf(...)` and `os.Stdout`). By default, the standard outputs are available in `Dev` mode, when the chaincode process is started independently.

In a production environment when the chaincode process is managed by the peer, the standard output is disabled for security reasons. When required, it can be enabled by setting the configuration variable `CORE_VM_DOCKER_ATTACHSTDOUT` of the peer. The outputs of the chaincode are then combined with the outputs of the peer. Keep in mind that these outputs should only be used for debugging purposes and should not be enabled in a production environment.

The following snippet illustrates additional SHIM API functions:

```
peer0.org1.example.com:
    environment:
            - CORE_VM_DOCKER_ATTACHSTDOUT=true
```

Listing 4.1: Enabling chaincode standard output files on a peer in docker-compose file.

Additional SHIM API functions

In this section, we provide an overview of the remaining API functions of shim available to chaincode.

```
// Returns an unique Id of the transaction proposal.
func GetTxID() string

// Returns an Id of the channel the transaction proposal was sent to.
func GetChannelID() string

// Calls an Invoke function on a specified chaincode, in the context of the
current transaction.
// If the invoked chaincode is on the same channel, the ReadSet and
WriteSet will be added into the same transaction.
// If the invoked chaincode is on a different channel, the invocation can
be used only as a query.
func InvokeChaincode(chaincodeName string, args [][]byte, channel string)
pb.Response

// Returns a list of historical states, timestamps and transactions ids.
func GetHistoryForKey(key string) (HistoryQueryIteratorInterface, error)

// Returns the identity of the user submitting the transaction proposal.
func GetCreator() ([]byte, error)

// Returns a map of fields containing cryptographic material which may be
used to implement custom privacy layer in the chaincode.
func GetTransient() (map[string][]byte, error)

// Returns data which can be used to enforce a link between application
data and the transaction proposal.
func GetBinding() ([]byte, error)

// Returns data produced by peer decorators which modified the chaincode
input.
func GetDecorations() map[string][]byte

// Returns data elements of a transaction proposal.
func GetSignedProposal() (*pb.SignedProposal, error)

// Returns a timestamp of the transaction creation by the client. The
timestamp is consistent across all endorsers.
func GetTxTimestamp() (*timestamp.Timestamp, error)

// Sets an event attached to the transaction proposal response. This event
will be be included in the block and ledger.
func SetEvent(name string, payload []byte) error
```

Summary

Design and implementation a well-functioning chaincode is a complex software engineering task which requires both the knowledge of the Fabric architecture, API functions and of GO language as well as the correct implementation of the business requirements.

In this chapter, we have learned step-by-step how to start a blockchain network in dev mode suitable for implementation and testing of the chaincode and how to use CLI to deploy and invoke chaincode. We have then learned how to implement the chaincode of our scenario. We explored the `Init` and `Invoke` functions through which Chaincode receives requests from clients, explored access control mechanism and the various APIs available to developer to implement chaincode functionality.

Finally, we learned how to test chaincode and how to integrate logging functionality into the code. To get ready for the next chapter, you should now stop your network using `./trade.sh` down -d true.

5
Exposing Network Assets and Transactions

If you have reached this far, congratulations! You have built the core of your blockchain application and the smart contract that directly reads, and more importantly, manipulates, the ledger that is the System-of-Record for your network. But, you are not close to finishing yet. As you can imagine, the contract is a sensitive piece of code that must be protected from misuse or tampering.

To produce a robust and secure application that is safe to release to business users, you must wrap the smart contract with one or more layers of protection and engineer it as a service that clients can access remotely through appropriate safeguards. In addition, the various stakeholders that wish to share a ledger and a smart contract may have unique and specific business logic needs that only they, and not the others, need to implement over and above the contract. For this reason, one blockchain application running one smart contract may end up offering different views and capabilities to different stakeholders.

In this chapter, you will first learn how to build a complete blockchain application from the ground up using our trade application as a guide and example. Later, you will learn about the various considerations that go into designing this application for a scenario of your choice and how to integrate that application with existing systems and processes.

The topics that will be covered in this chapter are as follows:

- Building a complete application
- Integrating the application with existing systems and processes

Building a complete application

In this section, you will learn how to build a complete application around the core smart contract that can be readily used by the business entities that have joined together to form a network. We will begin with a recap of the Hyperledger Fabric transaction pipeline to remind the reader what (and how) a blockchain application does from the perspective of the user (or client). Using code samples, we will show you how to build, design, and organize a network around the needs of business entities, create appropriate configurations, and effect the different stages of a blockchain transaction from start to finish. At the end of this process, the reader will understand how to engineer a Fabric application and expose its capabilities through a simple web interface. The only asset we need to possess in the beginning of this chapter is the contract, or chaincode, which was developed using either hands-on Go programming (see `Chapter 4`, *Designing a data and transaction model with Golang*).

In the back-end of this chapter, we will guide the experienced enterprise developer through more advanced topics, such as service design patterns, reliability, and other common engineering concerns. Although these concerns apply to every distributed application, we will discuss the special needs and issues of blockchain-based applications.

The nature of a Hyperledger Fabric application

In earlier chapters, we saw how Hyperledger Fabric can be viewed as a distributed transaction processing system, with a staged pipeline of operations that may eventually result in a change to the state of the shared replicated ledger maintained by the network peers. To the developer, a blockchain application is a collection of processes through which a user may submit transactions to, or read state from, a smart contract. Under the cover, the developer must channel a user request into the different stages of the transaction pipeline and extract results to provide feedback at the end of the process. Essentially, it is the application developer's job to implement one or more layers of wrappers around the smart contract, regardless of whether the contract was implemented by hand (see `Chapter 4`, *Designing a data and transaction model with Golang*) or using Hyperledger Composer (see `Chapter 6`, *Business Networks*).

An application developed with the smart contract (or the asset-entity model) at its core can be viewed as a transaction-processing database application with a set of views or a service API. However, the developer must keep in mind that every Hyperledger Fabric transaction is asynchronous, that is, the result of the transaction will not be available in the same communication session that it was submitted in. This is because, as we have seen in previous chapters, a transaction must be collectively approved by the peers in the network through consensus. As such, consensus may potentially take an unbounded amount of time, and the communication of a transaction result is designed as a publish/subscribe mechanism. The following diagram illustrates the blockchain application and transaction pipeline from the perspective of the developer:

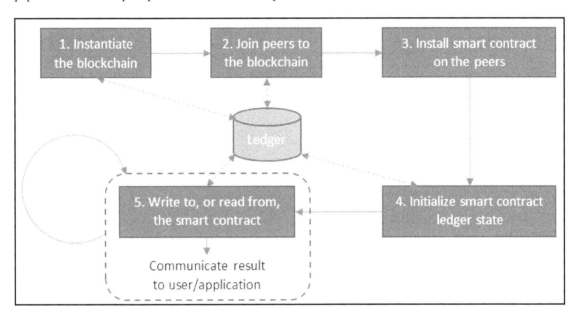

Figure 5.1: The stages in the creation and operation of a blockchain application

In the next section, the operations mentioned in this diagram will be described in more detail and mapped to specific Fabric mechanisms.

Application and transaction stages

The first step in the creation of an application is the instantiation of the blockchain, or the shared ledger itself. In Fabric parlance, an instance of a blockchain is referred to as a channel, and therefore the first step in a blockchain application is the creation of a channel and the bootstrapping of the network ordering service with the channel's genesis block.

The next step is the initialization of the peer network, whereby all the peer nodes selected to run the application must be joined to the channel, a process that allows each peer to maintain a copy of the ledger, which is initialized to a blank key-value store. Every peer that's joined to the channel will possess ledger commitment privileges and may participate in a gossip protocol in order to sync ledger state with each other.

After the creation of the peer network comes the installation of the smart contract on that network. A subset of the peers joined to the channel preceding it will be selected to run the smart contract; in other words, they will possess endorsement privileges. The contract code will be deployed to these peers and built for subsequent operation. As you know, by this point, the contract is referred to as chaincode in Fabric parlance, and that is the term that will be used for the rest of this chapter.

Once the chaincode has been installed on the endorsing peers, it will be initialized as per the logic that has been embedded in it (see `Chapter 4`, *Designing a Data and Transaction Model with Golang*, for examples).

At this point, unless something has gone wrong in one or more of the preceding steps, the application is up and running. Now, transactions may be sent to the chaincode to either update the state of the ledger (invocations) or to read the ledger state (queries) for the lifetime of the application.

 The application may change or evolve over time, requiring special operations to be carried out that are not captured in *Figure 5.1: The stages in the creation and operation of a blockchain application*. Those will be described in `Chapter 9`, *Life In A Blockchain Network*.

In the section titled *Building the Application* and onward, we will show how a trade application can be built around the chaincodes developed in `Chapter 4`, *Designing a Data and Transaction Model with Golang*, using suitable code and instructions.

Application model and architecture

The process of writing a Fabric application begins with chaincode, but ultimately the developer must make judicious decisions about how an end user or a software agent must interface with that chaincode. How the assets of the chaincode, and the operations of the blockchain network running that chaincode, ought to be exposed to the user is a question that ought to be dealt with carefully. Significant damage is possible if these capabilities are exposed without restriction, especially the ones involving blockchain bootstrapping and configurations. Proper operation of the chaincode itself relies not just on its internal logic, but suitable access controls being built above it. As we saw in the previous section, setting up an application and preparing it for use is a complex process. In addition, the asynchronous nature of ledger-update transactions requires an arbitration layer between the chaincode and the user. To allow the user to focus on transactions that impact the application rather than the details of the network modules, all this complexity ought to be hidden as much as possible. It is for this reason that a three-layer architecture has evolved as the standard for a Fabric application, as illustrated in the following diagram:

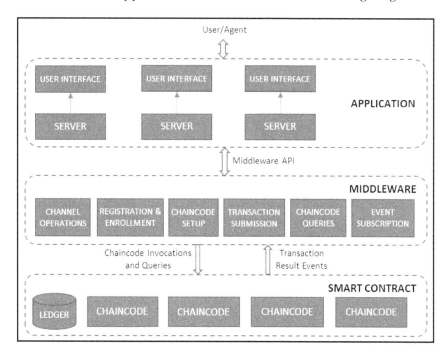

Figure 5.2 Typical three-layer architecture of a Hyperledger Fabric application

At the lowest layer lies the smart contract that operates directly on the shared ledger, which may be written using one or more chaincode units. These chaincodes run on the network peers, exposing a service API for invocations and queries, and publishing event notifications of transaction results, as well as configuration changes occurring on the channel.

In the middle layer lies the functions to orchestrate the various stages of a blockchain application (see *Figure 5.1: The stages in the creation and operation of a blockchain application*). Hyperledger Fabric provides an SDK (currently available in `Node.js` as well as in Java) to perform functions such as channel creation and joining, registration, and enrollment of users, as well as chaincode operations. In addition, the SDK offers mechanisms to subscribe to transaction and configuration-related events emanating from the network. Depending on application needs, an off-chain database may be maintained for convenience, or as a cache of ledger state.

At the topmost layer lies a user-facing application that exports a service API consisting mostly of application-specific capabilities, though administrative operations such as channel and chaincode operations may also be exposed for system administrators. Typically, a user interface should also be provided for ease of use, though a well-defined API may suffice if the user is a software agent. We refer to this layer simply as the application, as this is what the end user (or agent) will see. Also, given that any blockchain application and network is an agglomeration of diverse participants, this layer will often consist of multiple application stacks tailored to the different participants.

This architecture should not be set in stone; it is meant to serve purely as a guideline for developers. Depending on the complexity of the application, both the number of layers and the verticals (or distinct applications) may vary. For a very simple application that has a small number of capabilities, the developer may even choose to compress the middleware and application layers into one. More generally though, this decoupling enables different sets of capabilities to be exposed to different network participants. For example, in our trade use case, a regulator and an exporter would view the blockchain in different ways and have diverging needs, and therefore it would be useful to build distinct service sets for them rather than force-fit all capabilities into one monolithic application with a uniform interface. Yet both these applications ought to hide the complexities of network operations, such as the creation and joining of channels, or privileged operations such as the installation of chaincode onto peers in similar ways, which would therefore benefit from a common middleware layer.

The ways in which the application layers the users directly interact with can be designed present many choices and complexities, and we will delve into those in the latter part of this chapter. First, though, we will describe how to implement the guts of a Fabric application, focusing on the essential elements. For instructive purposes, our topmost layer will be a simple web server exposing a *RESTful* service API.

 The thinking behind this architecture and the principles driving it are independent of the underlying blockchain technology. To implement an identical application on a different blockchain platform than Hyperledger Fabric, only the smart contract and some parts of the middleware have to be reimplemented. The rest of the application can remain untouched with the end user not noticing any difference.

Building the application

Now that we have understood not just the methodology of designing a layered Fabric application but also the philosophy behind it, we can dive into the implementation. In the previous two chapters, we discussed how to implement and test the lowest layer, or the chaincode. Therfore, we can assume that the reader is now ready to add the middleware and application layers, which is what we will demonstrate in the following sections.

A prerequisite for the testing of middleware and application code is a running network. Before proceeding to the next section, please ensure that the sample four-organization network we configured and launched in the *Setting up the development environment section* in `Chapter 3`, *Setting the stage with a business scenario,* is still up and running.

Middleware – wrapping and driving the chaincode

The following diagram maps the transaction stages discussed in the *Application and Transaction Stages* section and illustrated in *Figure 5.1: The stages in the creation and operation of a blockchain application,* to Fabric terms and using Fabric terminology:

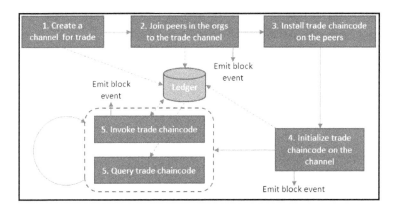

Figure 5.3: The stages in the creation and operation of a blockchain application

Fabric peers, orderers, and CAs (or MSPs) communicate using gRPC (`https://grpc.io/`), as well as the process spawned by the peer to run the chaincode (the process is really a Docker container). This process exports a service endpoint implementing the JSON RPC 2.0 specification (`http://www.jsonrpc.org/specification`) for channel and chaincode operations. We can write a wrapper application that communicates directly with chaincode using the service specification, but then we would have to write logic to parse and interpret the payload as well. With the Fabric platform and its specification likely to change in the future, this is not necessarily the best and most maintainable way to write an application, especially for production purposes. Fortunately, Hyperledger Fabric provides the means to run chaincode operations while hiding the details of the interface specifications and the communication protocol, in two different ways:

- **Command-Line Interface (CLI)**: Fabric provides commands that can be run from a Terminal to perform the various operations indicated in *Figure 5.3: The stages in the creation and operation of a blockchain application*. The tool to run these commands is `peer`, which is generated upon downloading the Fabric source code and building it (using `make`, or just `make peer`). Different switches can be used with this command to perform different channel and chaincode operations, and you will see some examples in this section.

- **Software Development Kit** (**SDK**): Hyperledger provides a toolkit and set of libraries for the easy development of applications to wrap the channel and chaincode operations in multiple languages, such as Node.js, Java, Go, and Python. These SDKs also provide functions to interact with MSPs, or instances of the Fabric CA.

Although CLI tools can be used for testing and demonstration purposes, they are inadequate for application development. The SDK libraries, in addition to the functions mentioned previously, provide the ability to subscribe to events emanating from the network, communicating information about state changes that are needed to drive the application logic. We will use the Node.js SDK to demonstrate how to build both our middleware and the higher-layer application. It is left to the reader to build equivalent applications in other languages of their choice using one of the other SDKs.

Installation of tools and dependencies

The functions that we will show how to build as part of our middleware can be found in the middleware folder in the code repository.

Prerequisites for creating and running the middleware

The reader is expected to be familiar with Node.js/JavaScript programming (especially the `Promise` pattern) and with the usage of the Node.js and `npm` tools:

1. Install Node.js (`https://nodejs.org/en/download/`) and npm (`https://www.npmjs.com/get-npm`).
2. Install the `fabric-client` and `fabric-ca-client` npm libraries:
   - You can install these packages from the `npm` registry, either manually by running `npm install <package-name>` or by setting the names and versions in your `package.json` file. As an example, the `package.json` in the middleware folder contains the following entries in the dependencies section:
     - `fabric-ca-client`: ^1.1.0
     - `fabric-client`: ^1.1.0

2. This instructs `npm` to install versions 1.1.0 of both of these packages:
   - Alternatively, you can clone the Fabric SDK node (`https://github.com/hyperledger/fabric-sdk-node/`) source code repository and import the two libraries locally as follows:
     - Run `npm` install in the `fabric-client` and `fabric-ca-client` folders
     - Install these packages as dependencies, either manually by specifying the path to the preceding folders in middleware/`package.json`, or by using the `npm` link command to add symbolic links to the packages in middleware/`node_modules`

In the following sections, we will use the `fabric-client` library to perform channel and chaincode operations involving the peer and the orderer, and the `fabric-ca-client` library to perform user registration and enrolment operations involving the CA (or MSP).

Installation of dependencies

Run `npm` install in the middleware folder to install the packages (libraries) specified in the `package.json` and their dependencies. You should see the packages downloaded to the `node_modules` folder.

A cleaner way of installing dependencies and configuring the middleware for regular operation is automated building using `Makefile`. You can simply run `make` in the `middleware` folder; see *Chapter 8, Agility In A Blockchain Network*, for more details on setting up and building your development and testing environment.

Creating and running the middleware

We will now write functions to execute and orchestrate the stages illustrated in *Figure 5.3: The stages in the creation and operation of a blockchain application*. But first, we will give an overview of the various configuration parameters that must be set for the application to work as intended

Network configuration

The first step in writing middleware is collecting all the configuration information necessary to identify and connect to the various elements of the network we created and launched in the previous section. It is useful, especially when writing code in JavaScript, to express such configurations in JSON format. In our sample code, the `config.json` file serves this purpose. This file contains the description of a network, whose attributes are contained in the trade-network object. Each property of this object describes the configuration of each unique organization that is part of the network, except for a property called the orderer, which simply refers to the orderer node. (Note: this is sufficient for our simple network containing just one orderer node.) Let's examine what must be specified in each organization's description by taking the `Exporterorg` property as an example:

```
"exporterorg": {
  "name": "peerExporterOrg",
  "mspid": "ExporterOrgMSP",
  "ca": {
    "url": "https://localhost:7054",
    "name": "ca-exporterorg"
  },
  "peer1": {
    "requests": "grpcs://localhost:7051",
    "events": "grpcs://localhost:7053",
    "server-hostname": "peer0.exporterorg.trade.com",
    "tls_cacerts": "../network/crypto-
config/peerOrganizations/exporterorg.trade.com/peers/peer0.exporterorg.trad
e.com/msp/tlscacerts/tlsca.exporterorg.trade.com-cert.pem"
  }
},
```

The `mspid` value must match the one specified in `network/configtx.yaml` for our middleware to be compatible with the channel artefacts and cryptographic material created for the network. The name and port information for the CA must match what was specified in `network/docker-compose-e2e.yaml`. Since we have just one peer in each organization, we name it peer for convenience, though one can easily define a different schema for a multi-peer organization setup. Note that the peer exports services for peer requests as well as for event subscriptions, and the ports match those exposed in `network/base/docker-compose-base.yaml`. The `server-hostname` must also match that specified in both `configtx.yaml` and the docker-compose configurations. As our network elements connect using TLS, the path to the peer's TLS certificate must also be specified here.

Lastly, if you compare the preceding schema snippet with the configurations of the other organizations, you will notice that the ports listed exactly matches those exposed in the docker-compose configurations. For example, the peers in the exporter, importer, carrier, and regulator organizations listen for requests on ports 7051, 8051, 9051, and 10051, respectively. The hostnames in the URLs simply refer to localhost, as that is where all our network element's containers are running.

Endorsement policy

The next step is to frame an endorsement policy for our chaincode that will be committed to the ledger during the instantiation. This endorsement policy dictates how many peers, belonging to what roles and organizations, need to endorse a ledger commitment transaction (or invocation). In the sample code, different endorsement policies are listed in constants.js, which contains various settings and keywords used by our middleware. The one that we will employ is ALL_FOUR_ORG_MEMBERS:

```
var FOUR_ORG_MEMBERS_AND_ADMIN = [
  { role: { name: 'member', mspId: 'ExporterOrgMSP' } },
  { role: { name: 'member', mspId: 'ImporterOrgMSP' } },
  { role: { name: 'member', mspId: 'CarrierOrgMSP' } },
  { role: { name: 'member', mspId: 'RegulatorOrgMSP' } },
  { role: { name: 'admin', mspId: 'TradeOrdererMSP' } }
];
var ALL_FOUR_ORG_MEMBERS = {
  identities: FOUR_ORG_MEMBERS_AND_ADMIN,
  policy: {
    '4-of': [{ 'signed-by': 0 }, { 'signed-by': 1 }, { 'signed-by': 2 }, {
'signed-by': 3 }]
  }
};
```

The list of principals is specified in the identities attribute of the policy and refers to member (or ordinary) users of the four peer organizations, as well as administrator users of the orderer organization. The policy attribute here states that an endorsement is required from a member of each of the four peer organizations; in all, four signatures will be required.

The variable TRANSACTION_ENDORSEMENT_POLICY is set to ALL_FOUR_ORG_MEMBERS in constants.js by default, and will be used to configure the channel endorsement policy later in this section.

User records

For both the channel world state and the user keys and certificates for the respective organizations, we will use a file-based store, as specified in `clientUtils.js`:

```
var Constants = require('./constants.js');
var tempdir = Constants.tempdir;
module.exports.KVS = path.join(tempdir, 'hfc-test-kvs');
module.exports.storePathForOrg = function(org) {
  return module.exports.KVS + '_' + org;
};
```

In `constants.js`, `tempdir` is initialized as follows:

```
var tempdir = "../network/client-certs";
```

Alternatively, you can also set the storage location to lie in the temporary folder designated by your operating system using the `os.tmpdir()` function; you will just need to create a subfolder there(say `<folder-name>`.) On a typical Linux, system, this storage location will default to `/tmp/<folder-name>/`, and folders will be created there for each organization. As we run the various operations, we will see these folders getting generated and files getting added to them.

Client registration and enrollment

Although cryptographic material for organization users can be created statically using the cryptogen tool, we must build capabilities in the middleware to dynamically create user identities and credentials, and enable those users to sign in to the network to submit transactions and query the ledger state. These operations require the mediation of users with privileged access (or administrators), who must be created when `fabric-ca-server` is started. By default, an administrative user is given the ID admin and the password `adminpw`, which is what we will use for our exercise in this section. The network that we created and launched uses these defaults, and it is left to the reader to modify them in `fabric-ca-server` and start commands in `network/docker-compose-e2e.yaml` (the following is from the `exporter-ca` section):

```
fabric-ca-server start --ca.certfile /etc/hyperledger/fabric-ca-server-
config/ca.exporterorg.trade.com-cert.pem --ca.keyfile
/etc/hyperledger/fabric-ca-server-
config/cc58284b6af2c33812cfaef9e40b8c911dbbefb83ca2e7564e8fbf5e7039c22e_sk
-b admin:adminpw -d
```

The steps to create a user through an administrator are as follows:

1. Load administrative user credentials from the local storage
2. If thee credentials don't exist, enroll, or sign in, the administrator to the Fabric CA server and obtain their credentials (private key and enrollment certificate)
3. Have the administrative user register another user with a given ID, specifying roles and affiliations, with the Fabric CA server
4. Using a secret returned upon registration, enroll the new user and obtain credentials for that user
5. Save the credentials to the local storage

Sample code for this can be found in `clientUtils.js`, with the following code snippets mostly being from the `getUserMember` function, which takes administrator credentials, the name of the organization to which the user must be enrolled, and the name/ID of the user to enroll. A handle to a client (an instance of `fabric-client`, or a client object (`https://fabric-sdk-node.github.io/Client.html`) must also be passed to the function:

```
var cryptoSuite = client.getCryptoSuite();
if (!cryptoSuite) {
  cryptoSuite = Client.newCryptoSuite();
  if (userOrg) {
    cryptoSuite.setCryptoKeyStore(Client.newCryptoKeyStore({path:
module.exports.storePathForOrg(ORGS[userOrg].name)}));
    client.setCryptoSuite(cryptoSuite);
  }
}
```

The preceding code associates the client handle with the local store, partitioned by organization, to store the credentials of the administrator and other users created on the fly:

```
var member = new User(adminUser);
member.setCryptoSuite(cryptoSuite);
```

This code ensures that the administrator user handle will be associated with our store:

```
var copService = require('fabric-ca-client/lib/FabricCAClientImpl.js');
var caUrl = ORGS[userOrg].ca.url;
var cop = new copService(caUrl, tlsOptions, ORGS[userOrg].ca.name,
cryptoSuite);
return cop.enroll({
  enrollmentID: adminUser,
  enrollmentSecret: adminPassword
}).then((enrollment) => {
  console.log('Successfully enrolled admin user');
```

```
    return member.setEnrollment(enrollment.key, enrollment.certificate,
  ORGS[userOrg].mspid);
  })
```

Here, we use the `fabric-ca-client` library to connect to the `fabric-ca-server`
instance associated with a given organization (whose URL can be obtained from our
`config.json`; for example, the `caUrl` for the exporter organization will be
`https://localhost:7054`). The enroll function allows the administrator to log in with
the MSP, and obtain the enrollment key and certificate.

Now that we have a handle to the administrator user in the form of the member object, we
can use it to enroll a new user with the user ID, which is represented by their username, as
follows:

```
var enrollUser = new User(username);
return cop.register({
  enrollmentID: username,
  role: 'client',
  affiliation: 'org1.department1'
}, member).then((userSecret) => {
  userPassword = userSecret;
  return cop.enroll({
    enrollmentID: username,
    enrollmentSecret: userSecret
  });
}).then((enrollment) => {
  return enrollUser.setEnrollment(enrollment.key, enrollment.certificate,
ORGS[userOrg].mspid);
}).then(() => {
  return client.setUserContext(enrollUser, false);
}).then(() => {
  return client.saveUserToStateStore();
})
```

During registration, we can specify what the user's roles will be, which in the preceding
code is client, allowing the username to submit invocations and queries to the chaincode.
The affiliation specified here is one of the subdivisions within an organization that are
specified in a Fabric CA server's configuration (`http://hyperledger-fabric-ca.`
`readthedocs.io/en/latest/serverconfig.html`) (updating this configuration is left as an
exercise to the reader; here, we will use the default affiliation). Using the returned secret,
the username is now enrolled with the server, and its key and enrollment certificate are
saved.

The call to `client.setUserContext` associates this user with the client handle, and `client.saveUserToStateStore` saves the user's credentials to our local store on the file system.

Similar functions to get handles to administrator users are `getAdmin` and `getMember`, also defined in `clientUtils.js`. The former retrieves an administrator user whose credentials were created using `cryptogen`, whereas the latter creates a new `admin` member dynamically.

Creating a channel

To create our trade channel, we first need to instantiate a `fabric-client` instance and a handle to the orderer using the configuration in `config.json` (see the `createChannel` function in `create-channel.js`):

```
var client = new Client();
var orderer = client.newOrderer(
  ORGS.orderer.url,
  {
    'pem': caroots,
    'ssl-target-name-override': ORGS.orderer['server-hostname']
  }
);
```

We use a file-based key-value store to save the ledger world state as follows (it is left as an exercise to the reader to try out other types of store, such as CouchDB, using `CouchDBKeyValueStore.js`):

```
utils.setConfigSetting('key-value-store', 'fabric-
client/lib/impl/FileKeyValueStore.js');
```

Next, we must enroll an administrator user for the orderer (using the mechanisms discussed in the previous segment). After a successful enrollment, the channel configuration that we created using the `configtxgen` tool (see `network/channel-artifacts/channel.tx`) must be extracted. The path to this configuration file is set in `constants.js`:

```
let envelope_bytes = fs.readFileSync(path.join(__dirname,
Constants.networkLocation, Constants.channelConfig));
config = client.extractChannelConfig(envelope_bytes);
```

We now need to enroll an administrator user for each of our four organizations. Each of these four admins, as well as the orderer admin, must sign the channel configuration, and the signatures collected as follows:

```
ClientUtils.getSubmitter(client, true /*get the org admin*/, org)
.then((admin) => {
  var signature = client.signChannelConfig(config);
  signatures.push(signature);
});
```

The `getSubmitter` function is defined in `clientUtils.js`, and is an indirect way of associating a member (either ordinary or administrator) of a given organization with the client object. In other words, it associates the client object with the *signing identity* (credentials and MSP identifications) of a user. Underneath, `getSubmitter` uses the functions `getAdmin`, `getUserMember`, and `getMember`, which we described in an earlier section.

 `getOrderAdminSubmitter` is analogous to `getSubmitter` and returns a handle to an `admin` user of the orderer's organization.

Finally, we are ready to build a channel creation request and submit it to the orderer:

```
let tx_id = client.newTransactionID();
var request = {
  config: config,
  signatures : signatures,
  name : channel_name,
  orderer : orderer,
  txId : tx_id
};
return client.createChannel(request);
```

The actual creation of the channel may take a few seconds, so the application logic should wait for a while before returning a successful result. The `channel_name` parameter is set in `clientUtils.js` to `tradechannel`, which is what we set it to when we launched our network (see `network/trade.sh`).

The channel creation step involves initializing the blockchain with the genesis block we created earlier in this chapter using `configtxgen`. The genesis block is just the first *configuration block* that is appended to the chain. A configuration block consists a specification of the channel and the organizations that are part of it, among other things; such a block contains no chaincode transactions. We will deal with configuration blocks again in *Chapter 9, Life in a Blockchain Network*, when we discuss how to augment networks.

Now, all we need to do to create a channel is call the
`createChannel('tradechannel')` function and wait for the result. This is the first step
in our test code, `createTradeApp.js`, which executes the basic sequence of operations
illustrated in *Figure 5.3: The stages in the creation and operation of a blockchain application*:

```
var Constants = require('./constants.js');
var createChannel = require('./create-channel.js');
createChannel.createChannel(Constants.CHANNEL_NAME).then(() => { ...... })
```

The code we use to associate different signing identities with a common
client object, and then sign a channel configuration, all in a single process,
is purely for demonstrative purposes. In a real-life production application,
the signing identities of different users belonging to different
organizations are private and must be guarded; hence there is no question
of pooling them together in a common location. Instead, the channel
configuration must be signed independently by different organizations'
administrators and passed around using some out-of-band mechanism to
accumulate the signatures (and also verify them.) Similar mechanisms
must be employed when a configuration is updated (see `Chapter 9`, *Life in
a Blockchain Network*) Independent, decentralized procedures must also be
followed for channel joining and chaincode installation, though we
demonstrate the basic mechanisms using centralized processes for
convenience.

Joining a channel

Now that `tradechannel` has been created, our four peers, one in each organization, must
be joined to the channel, a step that initializes the ledger on each node and prepares the
peer to run chaincode and transactions on it. For this, we will need to reuse the client
handle created in the previous step or instantiate one using a similar sequence of
operations. In addition, we must instantiate a handle to the channel, register the orderer,
and obtain the genesis block (implicitly sent to the orderer in the creation step using the
channel configuration), as indicated by the following code snippets from the `joinChannel`
function in `join-channel.js`:

```
var channel = client.newChannel(channel_name);
channel.addOrderer(
  client.newOrderer(
    ORGS.orderer.url,
    {
      'pem': caroots,
      'ssl-target-name-override': ORGS.orderer['server-hostname']
    }
```

```
    )
);
tx_id = client.newTransactionID();
let request = { txId : tx_id };
return channel.getGenesisBlock(request);
```

The transaction ID argument is optional in the preceding `getGenesisBlock` call. Now, for each organization, we must obtain a handle to an administrator user who will then submit a channel joining request for the peer belonging to that organization:

```
return ClientUtils.getSubmitter(client, true /* get peer org admin */,
org);
for (let key in ORGS[org])
  if (ORGS[org].hasOwnProperty(key)) {
    if (key.indexOf('peer') === 0) {
      data = fs.readFileSync(path.join(__dirname,
ORGS[org][key]['tls_cacerts']));
      targets.push(
        client.newPeer(
          ORGS[org][key].requests,
          {
            pem: Buffer.from(data).toString(),
            'ssl-target-name-override': ORGS[org][key]['server-hostname']
          }
        )
      );
    }
  }
}
tx_id = client.newTransactionID();
let request = {
  targets : targets,
  block : genesis_block,
  txId : tx_id
};
let sendPromise = channel.joinChannel(request, 40000);
```

As in the channel creation process, the `getSubmitter` function associates the signing identity of an administrator of a particular organization with the client object before submitting the channel join request. This request contains the genesis block as well as the configuration of every peer in that organization (loaded from the attributes containing the `peer` prefix within each organization in `config.json`, as you can see in the above code.)

A generous wait time of 40 seconds is indicated above as this process can take a while to complete. This join process needs to be executed independently by an administrator in each organization; hence, the function `joinChannel(<org-name>)` is called 4 times in sequence the main function `processJoinChannel`, which is called in our test script in `createTradeApp.js` as follows:

```
var joinChannel = require('./join-channel.js');
joinChannel.processJoinChannel();
```

 In a typical production network, each organization will independently run the join process, but only for its peers. The orchestration code (`processJoinChannel` in `join-channel.js`) that we use in our repository is meant for convenience and testing.

Installation of chaincode

Installation of chaincode results in the copying of source code to the peers we have selected to be endorsers, and every installation is associated with a user-defined version. The main function `installChaincode` is implemented in `install-chaincode.js`. This function in turn calls the `installChaincodeInOrgPeers` function for each of the 4 organizations in sequence; the latter function installs chaincode on the peers of a given organization. As in the case of a channel join, we create both client and channel handles for a given organization, enroll an administrator user for that organization, and associate that user with the client handle. This next step is to create an installation proposal and submit it to the orderer as follows:

```
var request = {
  targets: targets,
  chaincodePath: chaincode_path,
  chaincodeId: Constants.CHAINCODE_ID,
  chaincodeVersion: chaincode_version
};
client.installChaincode(request);
```

The targets refer to the configurations of the endorsing peers in the organization, and are loaded from `config.json`. `chaincodeId` and `chaincodeVersion` can be set by the caller (and defaults are set in `constants.js` as `tradecc` and `v0`, respectively), but the `chaincodePath` must refer to a location that contains the source code. In our scenario, the location refers to a path on the local file system: `github.com/trade_workflow`.

Internally in the SDK, the installation request packages the chaincode's source code into a prescribed format called `ChaincodeDeploymentSpec` (CDS)(https://github.com/ hyperledger/fabric/blob/release-1.1/protos/peer/chaincode.proto). This package is then signed (by the organization administrator associated with the client object) to create a `SignedChaincodeDeploymentSpec`(https://github.com/hyperledger/fabric/blob/ release-1.1/protos/peer/signed_cc_dep_spec.proto), which is then sent to the *lifecycle system chaincode* (LSCC) for installation.

The above procedure describes the *simple* case where each instance of a Signed CDS has only the signature of the identity associated with the client that issues the installation request. A more *complex* scenario is supported by Fabric whereby a CDS can be passed (out-of-band) to different clients (of the various organizations) and signed by each before the installation requests are received. The reader is encouraged to try out this variation using the available API functions and Fabric data structures(http://hyperledger-fabric. readthedocs.io/en/latest/chaincode4noah.html).

The success of an installation request is determined by checking the proposal response from each target peer as follows:

```
if (proposalResponses && proposalResponses[i].response &&
proposalResponses[i].response.status === 200) {
  one_good = true;
  logger.info('install proposal was good');
}
```

Finally, to orchestrate the installation on the entire network, we call the `installChaincode` function defined in `install-chaincode.js`. For the `fabric-client` to know where to load the `chaincode` source from, we temporarily set the `GOPATH` in the process to point to the right location in our project, which is the `chaincode` folder:

 This only works for `chaincode` written in Go

```
process.env.GOPATH = path.join(__dirname,Constants.chaincodeLocation);
```

For a successful installation, the `chaincode` folder must contain a subfolder named `src`, within which the `chaincode` path sent in the installation proposal must point to the actual code. As you can see, this finally resolves to `chaincode/src/github.com/trade_workflow` in our code repository, which indeed contains the source code we developed in `Chapter 4`, *Designing a Data and Transaction Model with Golang*.

In our `createTradeApp.js` script, we can now simply call:

```
var installCC = require('./install-chaincode.js');
installCC.installChaincode(Constants.CHAINCODE_PATH,
Constants.CHAINCODE_VERSION);
```

In a typical production network, each organization will independently run the installation process (defined in the `installChaincodeInOrgPeers` function), but only for its endorsing peers. The orchestration code (`installChaincode` in `install-chaincode.js`) that we use in our repository is meant for convenience and testing.

Instantiation of chaincode

Now that the endorsing peers in the network have the chaincode, we must instantiate that chaincode across our channel to ensure that all copies of the ledger are initialized with the right dataset (or key-value pairs). This is the final step in the setup of our smart contract before we can open it up for regular operation. Instantiation is a transaction that invokes the LSCC to initialize a chaincode on a channel, thereby binding the two and isolating the former's state to the latter.

This operation should be triggered centrally by any of the organizations authorized to initialize the chaincode (in our sample code, we use the administrator of the Importer's organization). Again, this follows the simple scenario (described in the installation section earlier) where the chaincode package is signed by a single organization administrator.

The default channel instantiation policy requires any channel MSP administrator to trigger the operation, but a different policy can be set in the Signed CDS structure if required.) In addition, the entity that triggers the instantiation operation must also be configured as a writer on the channel. Our procedure to create a channel configuration using `configtxgen` implicitly gave write permissions to administrators of the 4 organizations. (A detailed discussion of channel configuration policy is beyond the scope of this book.)

The main function to implement chaincode instantiation is implemented in `instantiate-chaincode.js` as `instantiateOrUpgradeChaincode`. This function can be used both to instantiate a newly deployed chaincode or update one that has already been running on the channel (see *Chapter 9, Life in a Blockchain Network*) As in the previous stages, we must create client and channel handles, and associate the channel handle with the client. In addition, all the endorsing peers in the network must be added to the channel, and then the channel object must be initialized with the MSPs associated with the channel (from each of the four organizations):

```
channel.initialize();
```

This sets up the channel to verify certificates and signatures, for example, from endorsements received from the peers. Next, we build a proposal for instantiation and submit it to all of the endorsing peers on the channel (snippet from the `buildChaincodeProposal` function):

```
var tx_id = client.newTransactionID();
var request = {
  chaincodePath: chaincode_path,
  chaincodeId: Constants.CHAINCODE_ID,
  chaincodeVersion: version,
  fcn: funcName,
  args: argList,
  txId: tx_id,
  'endorsement-policy': Constants.TRANSACTION_ENDORSEMENT_POLICY
};
channel.sendInstantiateProposal(request, 300000);
```

The path to the chaincode, and the ID and version, must match what was supplied in the installation proposal. In addition, we must supply the function name and argument list that will be sent to the chaincode and executed. (In our chaincode, this will execute the `Init` function.) Also note that the proposal contains the endorsement policy (`Constants.TRANSACTION_ENDORSEMENT_POLICY`) we set earlier, which requires a member from each of the four organizations to endorse a chaincode invocation. The proposal responses (one for each endorsing peer) returned by the orderer must be validated in the same way as in the installation stage. Using the result of the preceding `channel.sendInstantiateProposal` call, we must now build an instantiation transaction request and submit it to the orderer:

```
var proposalResponses = results[0];
var proposal = results[1];
var request = {
  proposalResponses: proposalResponses,
  proposal: proposal
};
```

```
channel.sendTransaction(request);
```

A successful response to `channel.sendTransaction` will allow our middleware to proceed on the basis that the instantiation was successfully submitted. This does not indicate, though, that the instantiation will successfully conclude with a commitment to the shared ledger; for that, our code will have to subscribe to events, and we will see how to do that later in this section.

Our script in `createTradeApp.js` triggers chaincode instantiation as follows:

```
var instantiateCC = require('./instantiate-chaincode.js');
instantiateCC.instantiateOrUpgradeChaincode(
  Constants.IMPORTER_ORG,
  Constants.CHAINCODE_PATH,
  Constants.CHAINCODE_VERSION,
  'init',
  ['LumberInc', 'LumberBank', '100000', 'WoodenToys', 'ToyBank', '200000',
'UniversalFrieght', 'ForestryDepartment'],
  false
);
```

The last parameter is set to `false`, indicating that an instantiation must be performed and not an upgrade. The first parameter (`Constants.IMPORTER_ORG`) indicates that the instantiation request must be submitted by a member (administrator in this context) of the importer's organization.

If the instantiation was successful, the chaincode will be built in Docker containers, one corresponding to each endorsing peer, and deployed to receive requests on behalf of their peers. If you run `docker ps -a`, you should see something like this in addition to the ones created upon launching the network:

```
CONTAINER ID    IMAGE     COMMAND    CREATED     STATUS    PORTS     NAMES
b5fb71241f6d    dev-peer0.regulatororg.trade.com-tradecc-v0-
cbbb0581fb2b9f86d1fbd159e90f7448b256d2f7cc0e8ee68f90813b59d81bf5
"chaincode -peer.add..."    About a minute ago    Up About a minute
dev-peer0.regulatororg.trade.com-tradecc-v0
077304fc60d8    dev-peer0.importerorg.trade.com-tradecc-
v0-49020d3db2f1c0e3c00cf16d623eb1dddf7b649fee2e305c4d2c3eb5603a2a9f
"chaincode -peer.add..."    About a minute ago    Up About a minute
dev-peer0.importerorg.trade.com-tradecc-v0
8793002062d7    dev-peer0.carrierorg.trade.com-tradecc-v0-
ec83c1904f90a76404e9218742a0fc3985f74e8961976c1898e0ea9a7a640ed2
"chaincode -peer.add..."    About a minute ago    Up About a minute
dev-peer0.carrierorg.trade.com-tradecc-v0
9e5164bd8da1    dev-peer0.exporterorg.trade.com-tradecc-v0-
dc2ed9ea732a90d6c5ffb0cd578dfb614e1ba14c2936b0ae785f30ea0f37da56
```

```
"chaincode -peer.add..."     About a minute ago     Up About a minute
dev-peer0.exporterorg.trade.com-tradecc-v0
```

Invoking the chaincode

Now that we have finished setting up our channel and installing chaincode for trade, we need to implement functions to execute chaincode invocations. Our code for this lies in the `invokeChaincode` function in `invoke-chaincode.js`.

The procedure to invoke the `chaincode` is the same as we did for instantiation, and the code is similar as well. The caller must build a transaction proposal consisting of the name of the `chaincode` function to be invoked and the arguments to be passed to it. Just providing the `chaincode` ID (`tradecc` in our implementation) is sufficient to identify the `chaincode` process to guide the request to:

```
tx_id = client.newTransactionID();
var request = {
  chaincodeId : Constants.CHAINCODE_ID,
  fcn: funcName,
  args: argList,
  txId: tx_id,
};
channel.sendTransactionProposal(request);
```

One difference with the instantiation proposal is that this operation does not typically require an administrative user in the organization; any ordinary member may suffice. This proposal must be sent to enough endorsing peers to collect the right set of signatures to satisfy our endorsement policy. This is done by adding all four peers in our network to the channel object (which must be created and initialized in the same way as in the previous stages). Once the proposal responses have been collected and validated in the same way as the instantiation proposals were, a transaction request must be built and sent to the orderer:

```
var request = {
  proposalResponses: proposalResponses,
  proposal: proposal
};
channel.sendTransaction(request);
```

We call `invokeChaincode` from our test script in `createTradeApp.js`. The chaincode function we would like to execute is `requestTrade`, which chronologically is the first function that ought to be invoked by a user in an importer's role (recall that we built access control logic within our `chaincode` to ensure that only a member of the Importer's organization may submit a `requestTrade`):

```
var invokeCC = require('./invoke-chaincode.js');
invokeCC.invokeChaincode(Constants.IMPORTER_ORG,
Constants.CHAINCODE_VERSION, 'requestTrade', ['2ks89j9', '50000','Wood for
Toys', 'Importer']);
```

The last parameter (`'Importer'`) simply indicates the ID of the user in the importer's organization who is to submit this transaction request. In the code, the credentials for this user are loaded if the user has already enrolled with the CA, otherwise a new user with that ID is registered using the `clientUtils.getUserMember` function.

As in the instantiation case, a successful `channel.sendTransaction` call simply indicates that the orderer accepted the transaction. Only subscribing to an event will tell us whether the transaction was successfully committed to the ledger.

Querying the chaincode

A chaincode query is somewhat simpler to implement as it involves the entire network, but simply requires communication from client to peer.

Client and channel handles should be created as in the previous stages, but this time, we will select just one or more peers from the caller's (or client's) organization to associate with the channel object. Then, we must create a query request (identical to an invocation proposal request) and submit it to the selected peers:

```
var request = {
  chaincodeId : Constants.CHAINCODE_ID,
  fcn: funcName,
  args: argList
};
channel.queryByChaincode(request);
```

The responses to the query can be collected and compared before being returned to the caller. The complete implementation can be found in the `queryChaincode` function in `query-chaincode.js`. We test this function by running a `getTradeStatus` chaincode query in our `createTradeApp.js` script:

```
var queryCC = require('./query-chaincode.js');
queryCC.queryChaincode(Constants.EXPORTER_ORG, Constants.CHAINCODE_VERSION,
'getTradeStatus', ['2ks89j9'], 'Exporter');
```

As with an invocation, we specify a user ID ('Exporter') and organization: here we want a member of the exporter's organization to check the status of a trade request.

Since a query is local to the client and its associated peers, the response is returned immediately to the client and does not have to be subscribed to (as in the case of invocation).

Completing the loop – subscribing to blockchain events

As we have seen in previous chapters, commitments to the shared ledger on a permissioned blockchain require a consensus among the network peers. Hyperledger Fabric in its v1 incarnation has an even more unique process to commit to the ledger: the transaction execution, ordering, and commitment processes are all decoupled from each other and framed as stages in a pipeline where endorsers, orderers, and committers carry out their tasks independent of each other. Therefore, any operation that results in a commitment of a block to the ledger is asynchronous in the Fabric scheme of things. Three of the operations we have implemented in our middleware fall into that category:

- Channel join
- Chaincode instantiation
- Chaincode invoke

In our description of these operations, we stopped at the point where a request is successfully sent to the orderer. But to complete the operation loop, any application that uses our middleware needs to know the final result of the request to drive the application logic forward. Fortunately, Fabric provides a publish/subscribe mechanism for the communication of results of asynchronous operations. This includes events for the commitment of a block, the completion of a transaction (successfully or otherwise), as well as custom events that can be defined and emitted by a chaincode. Here, we will examine block and transaction events, which cover the operations we are interested in.

Fabric offers a mechanism for event subscription in the SDK through an EventHub class, with the relevant subscription methods being registerBlockEvent, registerTxEvent, and registerChaincodeEvent, respectively, to which callback functions can be passed for actions to perform at the middleware layer (or higher) whenever an event is available.

Let's see how we can catch the event of a successful join in our middleware code. Going back to the `joinChannel` function in `join-channel.js`, the following code instantiates an `EventHub` object for a given peer, whose configuration is loaded from `config.json`. For example, to subscribe to events from the exporter organization's sole peer, the URL our `fabric-client` instance will listen to (under the covers) is `grpcs://localhost:7053`:

```
let eh = client.newEventHub();
eh.setPeerAddr(
  ORGS[org][key].events,
  {
    pem: Buffer.from(data).toString(),
    'ssl-target-name-override': ORGS[org][key]['server-hostname']
  }
);
eh.connect();
eventhubs.push(eh);
```

The listener, or callback, for each block event is defined as follows:

```
var eventPromises = [];
eventhubs.forEach((eh) => {
  let txPromise = new Promise((resolve, reject) => {
    let handle = setTimeout(reject, 40000);
    eh.registerBlockEvent((block) => {
      clearTimeout(handle);
      if(block.data.data.length === 1) {
        var channel_header =
block.data.data[0].payload.header.channel_header;
        if (channel_header.channel_id === channel_name) {
          console.log('The new channel has been successfully joined on peer
'+ eh.getPeerAddr());
          resolve();
        }
        else {
          console.log('The new channel has not been succesfully joined');
          reject();
        }
      }
    });
  });
  eventPromises.push(txPromise);
});
```

Whenever a block event is received, the code matches the expected channel name (`tradechannel` in our scenario) with the one extracted from the block. (The block payloads are constructed using standard schemas available in the Fabric source code, in the `protos` folder. Understanding and playing with these formats is left as an exercise to the reader.) We will set a timeout in the code (40 seconds here) to prevent our event subscription logic from waiting indefinitely and holding up the application. Finally, the outcome of a channel join is made contingent, not just on the success of a `channel.joinChannel` call, but also on the availability of block events, as follows:

```
let sendPromise = channel.joinChannel(request, 40000);
return Promise.all([sendPromise].concat(eventPromises));
```

For instantiation and invocation, we register callbacks not for blocks but for specific transactions, which are identified by IDs set during the transaction proposal creation. Code for the subscription can be found in the `instantiateChaincode` and `invokeChaincode` functions, in `instantiate-chaincode.js` and `invoke-chaincode.js` respectively. A code snippet from the latter illustrates the basic working of transaction event handling:

```
eh.registerTxEvent(deployId.toString(),
  (tx, code) => {
    eh.unregisterTxEvent(deployId);
    if (code !== 'VALID') {
      console.log('The transaction was invalid, code = ' + code);
      reject();
    } else {
      console.log('The transaction has been committed on peer '+
eh.getPeerAddr());
      resolve();
    }
  }
);
```

The parameters passed to the callback include a handle to the transaction and a status code, which can be checked to see whether the chaincode invocation result was successfully committed to the ledger. Once the event has been received, the event listener is unregistered to free up system resources (our code may also listen to block events in lieu of specific transaction events, but it will then have to parse the block payload and find and interpret information about the transaction that was submitted).

Putting it all together

The sequence of steps described previously can be run in one go through a suitably coded script. As mentioned earlier, `createTradeApp.js` contains such a script, which results in the creation of `tradechannel`, the joining of the four peers to that channel, the installation of the `trade_workflow` chaincode on all four peers, and its subsequent instantiation on the channel, which finally concludes with the creation of a trade request from the importer to the exporter and a follow-up querying the request status. You can run the following command and see the various steps being conducted on your console:

```
node createTradeApp.js
```

Just as an exercise, and to test out both the middleware library functions and the chaincode, you can complete the trade scenario that the createTradeApp.js script began by starting with a trade request acceptance by an exporter and culminating with full payment made to the exporter by the importer for a successfully delivered shipment. To view this in operation, run the following:

```
node runTradeScenarioApp.js
```

User application – exporting the service and API

The exercise in creating a set of functions for our middleware lays down the plumbing for a user-facing application we can build on top. Although we can architect the application in different ways, the set of capabilities it should offer will remain the same. Before demonstrating an approach to building an application for a blockchain user, we will discuss the salient features such an application should possess.

Applications

Referring to *Figure 5.2: Typical three-layer architecture of a Hyperledger Fabric application*, and our discussion in the *Application Model and Architecture* section of this chapter, different users of a Hyperledger Fabric application may need different and distinct applications. Our trade scenario is an example of this: users representing trading parties, banks, shippers, and governmental authorities may need different things from our application, even while they are collectively participating in the trade network and endorsing smart contract operations.

There are common operations that administrators of the different organizations must have the capability to perform. This includes the stages from the creation of a channel up to the instantiation of chaincode. Therefore, if we need to build different applications for each network participant, we should expose these capabilities to every instance of those applications. Once we get to the application itself, which consists of the set of invoke and query functions offered by the chaincode, we must create space for differentiation. An application designed for the trading parties and their banks must expose trade and Letter of Credit operations to the users. However, there is no need to expose these operations to a carrier, and therefore an application designed for the latter can and ought to limit the capabilities offered to those that impact the carrier's role, such as the functions to create Bills of Lading and to record the location of a shipment.

Here, for simplicity, we will amalgamate all the applications into one and demonstrate how to make it work. Diversification based on user roles and requirements is left as an exercise for the reader. Our amalgamated application will be implemented as a web server, loosely connecting the smart contract and the middleware, sounding it from the end users.

User and session management

The design of any service-oriented application requires the determination of users who will be allowed to access the application and perform various actions. For a Hyperledger Fabric application, special consideration ought to be given to the differentiation between user classes. Every Fabric network has a set of privileged users (who we have been referring to as administrators of organizations) and ordinary members. This differentiation of roles must be reflected in the design of the user-facing application, too.

The application must have an authentication layer as well as a mechanism for session management, allowing an already-authenticated user to exercise the application, limited by their role. In our example application, we will use **JSON Web Tokens** (**JWT**) for this purpose.

Designing an API

Before building our application, we must design a service API to cover the capabilities exposed by our middleware. We will design our API to be RESTful, as follows:

1. POST/login: Register a new user (administrative or ordinary) or log in as an existing one
2. POST/channel/create: Create a channel

3. `POST/channel/join`: Join the network peers to the channel created in this user's session

4. `POST/chaincode/install`: Install the `chaincode` on the peers

5. `POST/chaincode/instantiate`: Instantiate the `chaincode` on the channel

6. `POST/chaincode/:fcn`: Invoke the `chaincode` function `fcn` with passed arguments (in the body); examples for `fcn` are `requestTrade`, `acceptLC`, and so on

7. `GET/chaincode/:fcn`: Query the `chaincode` function `fcn` with passed arguments (in the body); examples for `fcn` are `getTradeStatus`, `getLCStatus`, and so on

Collectively, these API functions cover the transaction stages in *Figure 5.3: The stages in the creation and operation of a blockchain application.*

Creating and launching a service

We will implement an express (`https://expressjs.com/`) web application in Node.js to expose the preceding API. The code lies in the application folder in our repository, with the source code in `app.js` and the dependencies defined in `package.json`. As a prerequisite to running the web application, the dependencies must be installed either by running `npm install` or `make` (see *Chapter 8, Agility In A blockchain network*) within that folder.

The following code snippet shows how to instantiate and run the *express* server:

```
var express = require('express');
var bodyParser = require('body-parser');
var app = express();
var port = process.env.PORT || 4000;
app.options('*', cors());
app.use(cors());
app.use(bodyParser.json());
app.use(bodyParser.urlencoded({
  extended: false
}));
var server = http.createServer(app).listen(port, function() {});
```

To summarize, a web server is launched to listen for HTTP requests on port 4000. Middleware is configured to enable CORS, automatically parsing both JSON payloads and forming data in POST requests.

Our web server listens to requests over an insecure HTTP. In a production application, we would start an HTTPS server for secure, confidential communication with clients.

Now, let's see how to configure the various express routes to implement our service API functions.

User and session management

Before performing a network (channel) or chaincode operation, a user must establish an authenticated session. We will implement the /login API function as follows:

1. Create a JWT token for a user with an expiration time of 60 seconds
2. Register or log the user in
3. If successful, return the token to the client

The server expects the name of a user and an organization name for registration or login to be provided as form data in the request body. An administrative user is simply identified by the admin username. The request body format is:

```
username=<username>&orgName=<orgname>[&password=<password>]
```

A password must be supplied, but only if the <username> is admin. In that case, the middleware will simply check whether the supplied password matches the one that was used to start the fabric-ca-server for the organization's MSP. As mentioned earlier in this chapter, our MSP administrator passwords were set to the default adminpw.

 This is a naïve implementation, but as web application security is not the focus of this tutorial, this will suffice to show how a server and frontend can be implemented over a smart contract and middleware.

The code for JWT token creation and user registration/login can be found in the following express route configured in app.js:

```
app.post('/login', async function(req, res) { ... });
```

The reader may experiment with other mechanisms of session management, such as session cookies, in lieu of JWT tokens.

Our web application can now be tested. First, bring up the Fabric network using docker-compose (or trade.sh), as shown earlier in this chapter.

If you created fresh cryptographic keys and certificates for the organizations using `cryptogen` (or the `trade.sh` script), you MUST clear the temporary folder used by the middleware to save world state and user info, otherwise you may see errors if you try to register users with IDs that were used in a previous run of your application. For example: if the temporary folder is `network/client-certs` on your machine, you can simply run `rm -rf client-certs` from the `network` folder to clear the contents.

In a different terminal window, start the web application by running the following command:

```
node app.js
```

In a third terminal window, send a request to the web server using the `curl` command to create an ordinary user named `Jim` in the `importerorg` organization (this is the organization name specified in `middleware/config.json`):

```
curl -s -X POST http://localhost:4000/login -H "content-type:
application/x-www-form-urlencoded" -d 'username=Jim&orgName=importerorg'
```

You should see an output like the following:

```
{"token":"eyJhbGciOiJIUzI1NiIsInR5cCI6IkpXVCJ9.eyJleHAiOjE1MjUwMDU4NTQsInVz
ZXJuYW1lIjoiSmltIiwib3JnTmFtZSI6ImltcG9ydGVyb3JnIiwiaWF0IjoxNTI1MDAxNzE0fQ.
yDX1PyKnpQAFC0mbo1uT1Vxgig0gXN9WNCwgp-1vj2g","success":true,"secret":"LNHaV
EXHuwUf","message":"Registration successful"}
```

In the middleware, the function that gets executed here is `getUserMember` in `clientUtils.js`, which was discussed earlier in this chapter.

To create an administrative user in the same organization, run:

```
curl -s -X POST http://localhost:4000/login -H "content-type:
application/x-www-form-urlencoded" -d
'username=admin&orgName=importerorg&password=adminpw'
```

You should see an output as follows (the admin user was already registered, so this ended up being a login call):

```
{"token":"eyJhbGciOiJIUzI1NiIsInR5cCI6IkpXVCJ9.eyJleHAiOjE1MjUwMDQ4OTEsInVz
ZXJuYW1lIjoiYWRtaW4iLCJvcmdOYW1lIjoiaW1wb3J0ZXJvcmciLCJpYXQiOjE1MjUwMDE3NTF
9.BYIEBO_MZzQa52_LW2AKVhLVag9OpSiZsI3cYHI9_oA","success":true,"message":"Lo
gin successful"}
```

In the middleware, the function that gets executed here is `getMember` in `clientUtils.js`.

Network administration

As you can see in `app.js`, the API functions from channel creation to chaincode instantiation are implemented as express routes:

```
app.post('/channel/create', async function(req, res) { ... });
app.post('/channel/join', async function(req, res) { ... });
app.post('/chaincode/install', async function(req, res) { ... });
app.post('/chaincode/instantiate', async function(req, res) { ... });
```

To exercise these routes, the end user must log in as an administrator and use the returned token. Taking the output from the previous call, we can request channel creation as follows:

```
curl -s -X POST http://localhost:4000/channel/create -H "authorization:
Bearer
eyJhbGciOiJIUzI1NiIsInR5cCI6IkpXVCJ9.eyJleHAiOjE1MjUwMDU4OTEsInVzZXJuYW1lIj
oiYWRtaW4iLCJvcmdOYW1lIjoiaW1wb3J0ZXJvcmciLCJpYXQiOjE1MjUwMDE3NTF9.BYIEBO_M
ZzQa52_LW2AKVhLVag9OpSiZsI3cYHI9_oA"
```

Note that the format for the authorization header is `Bearer <JWT token value>`. The web server implicitly assumes that the channel name is `tradechannel`, which is set in `middleware/constants.js`. (You may augment the server API to accept a channel name in the request body if you wish.) The output ought to be as follows if everything goes well:

```
{"success":true,"message":"Channel created"}
```

Similar queries can be run by an administrator for channel join, chaincode installation, and chaincode instantiation. As an example, the instantiation API endpoint expects the chaincode path, chaincode version, and a list of arguments for the chaincode as follows:

```
curl -s -X POST http://localhost:4000/chaincode/instantiate -H
"authorization: Bearer
eyJhbGciOiJIUzI1NiIsInR5cCI6IkpXVCJ9.eyJleHAiOjE1MjUwMDU4OTEsInVzZXJuYW1lIj
oiYWRtaW4iLCJvcmdOYW1lIjoiaW1wb3J0ZXJvcmciLCJpYXQiOjE1MjUwMDE3NTF9.BYIEBO_M
ZzQa52_LW2AKVhLVag9OpSiZsI3cYHI9_oA" -H "content-type: application/json" -d
'{ "ccpath": "github.com/trade_workflow", "ccversion": "v0", "args":
["LumberInc", "LumberBank", "100000", "WoodenToys", "ToyBank", "200000",
"UniversalFreight", "ForestryDepartment"] }'
```

The output, if everything goes well, will be:

```
{"success":true,"message":"Chaincode instantiated"}
```

In the implementation of each of these routes, a check is made to ensure that the user (identified by the JWT token) is an administrative user, as follows:

```
if (req.username !== 'admin') {
  res.statusCode = 403;
  res.send('Not an admin user: ' + req.username);
  return;
}
```

If we were to use the token for the user registered as Jim, the web server would return a 403 error code to the client.

Exercising the application

Once the chaincode has been initialized by an administrative user, our application is open for business. Now, any ordinary user (such as Jim in the importer's organization) may request a chaincode invocation or query. For example, a trade request can be made as follows:

```
curl -s -X POST http://localhost:4000/chaincode/requestTrade -H
"authorization: Bearer
eyJhbGciOiJIUzI1NiIsInR5cCI6IkpXVCJ9.eyJleHAiOjE1MjUwMDU4NTQsInVzZXJuYW1lIj
oiSmltIiwib3JnTmFtZSI6ImltcG9ydGVyb3JnIiwiaWF0IjoxNTI1MDAxNzE0fQ.yDX1PyKnpQ
AFC0mbo1uT1Vxgig0gXN9WNCwgp-1vj2g" -H "content-type: application/json" -d
'{ "ccversion": "v0", "args": ["2ks89j9", "50000","Wood for Toys"] }'
```

Note that the chaincode version must be supplied in the request body. The output, if all goes well, will be:

```
{"success":true,"message":"Chaincode invoked"}
```

Subsequently, the status of the trade can be queried (again by `Jim`):

```
curl -s -X GET http://localhost:4000/chaincode/getTradeStatus -H
"authorization: Bearer
eyJhbGciOiJIUzI1NiIsInR5cCI6IkpXVCJ9.eyJleHAiOjE1MjUwMDU4NTQsInVzZXJuYW1lIj
oiSmltIiwib3JnTmFtZSI6ImltcG9ydGVyb3JnIiwiaWF0IjoxNTI1MDAxNzE0fQ.yDX1PyKnpQ
AFC0mbo1uT1Vxgig0gXN9WNCwgp-1vj2g" -H "content-type: application/json" -d
'{ "ccversion": "v0", "args": ["2ks89j9"] }'
```

Now, the output ought to contain the chaincode response:

```
{"success":true,"message":"{\"Status\":\"REQUESTED\"}"}
```

User/client interaction modes

Although running curl commands is sufficient to test our web application, the proper way to expose the application to the user would be through one or more web pages, with widgets for the user to trigger those commands.

As we saw in the middleware implementation section, various operations, including chaincode invocations, are asynchronous. In our implementation, we masked this asynchronous behavior by making the wrapper function return to the caller, but only when the request had been successfully sent to the orderer and the events subscribed for had been received and validated. We can also choose to expose this asynchronous behavior to the web application client. Using Web Sockets (`https://developer.mozilla.org/en-US/docs/Web/API/WebSockets_API`), the contents of a web interface presented to the end user may be dynamically updated whenever the event notification arrives at the callback registered with the event hub.

Designing good web interfaces is beyond the scope of this book, and it is left to the reader to leverage other sources of knowledge to build ones suitable for their applications.

Testing the Middleware and Application

We have shown how to exercise the Node JS-based middleware and application capabilities using sample scripts and `curl` commands. By observing the console output, you can find out if the application works as expected. For a production application, you will need a more robust and maintainable testing methodology that can evaluate correctness of the library functions and API endpoints on an ongoing basis. Both unit tests and integration tests should be part of your evaluation process. A hands-on demonstration of such testing is beyond the scope of this chapter, and writing unit and integration tests is left as an exercise to the reader. Mocha, which is a feature-rich JavaScript framework for asynchronous testing(`https://mochajs.org/`), can be used for this purpose.

Integration with existing systems and processes

When discussing end-to-end solutions with customers, we often explain that blockchain-related components represent a very small percentage of the overall footprint. This is still a very important set of components, but nonetheless they represent a small footprint.

This section will focus on the touch point between our traditional systems and the Hyperledger Fabric and Composer API.

We will explore the various patterns of integration we have leveraged and see how some of the non-functional requirements can influence the integration deployment. Finally, we will explore some additional considerations that integrators will need to keep in mind when designing their integration layer.

In short, in this section, you will:

- Understand the design consideration of the integration layer
- Review the integration design patterns
- Explore the impact of non-functional requirements on the integration

Design considerations

By now, you have experience with Fabric SDK and by the end of `Chapter 7`, *A Business Network Example*, you will have experienced using the `Composer REST` gateway. While those are certainly the main tools of the trade when it comes to integration, they are part of an ecosystem, and there needs to be an alignment of the business processes of the enterprise to make sure the integration makes sense.

As per the design considerations, we will look at the following aspects:

- Impact of decentralization
- Process alignment
- Message affinity
- Service discovery
- Identity mapping

Decentralization

Many attempts have been made to standardize IT functions and capabilities, but the reality is that no two organizations have the same IT landscape. Even for those who have selected the same ERP vendor, the systems will have been customized to meet the organization processes and needs.

This means that when planning your integration design, you should keep in mind that each organization may have their own way of invoking smart contracts and may not have the same IT capabilities or policies.

As an example, exposing events through Web Socket may make sense for an organization who is familiar with cloud-based technologies, but other organizations may not have the skills, or their IT security policies may not allow them to use the protocol.

While it may seem surprising to some, keep in mind that a network can be a mix of Fortune 500 organizations and start-ups. Consider the supply-chain industry for a moment; you will find some trucking company with little to no IT infrastructure, all the way to industry behemoths. Clearly, one size may not fit all.

Having said that, from a network perspective, you should consider the degree of support the network wants to provide to joining organizations. There are two possible approaches:

- **The network provides an integration asset**: This can take the form of a gateway that each participant deploys in their own infrastructure. The gateway is standard for everyone and manages the invocation of the smart contracts in a consistent manner.
  This can provide the benefit of accelerating the on-boarding process, but requires consideration about who owns, manages, and supports this IT component. Furthermore, some organizations may not want to deploy this piece of infrastructure due to trust issues.
- **Each participant builds their own integration layer**: The obvious downside of this approach is the recreation of the wheel by all participants, but it reduces the potential support issues created by deploying a common component in every organization.
  This may also be the preferred approach for use cases requiring deep system integration to achieve the benefit of process optimizations.

Process alignment

The integration layer will have to deal with two different viewpoints:

- **Organization IT system and business process viewpoint**: An organization business process may be hosted in an ERP such as SAP. In such a situation, when a specific business event warrants the invocation of a smart contract, this may be issued through a **Business API** (**BAPI**) call from the SAP system. The API call from the ERP may contain a variety of data structures, some of which will be completely irrelevant to the blockchain network.

- **Smart contract viewpoint**: This viewpoint has the particularity of having a data representation that is application agnostic. This means that all participants of the network will understand the nature of the data being processed.

It is up to the integration layer to reconcile the two and ensure that the proper semantic of the transaction is maintained in both systems. This may imply:

- **Mapping**: Moving data from one field name to the another
- **Transformation**: Aggregating, splitting, or computing a new value based on input
- **Cross-referencing**: Leveraging a reference table to map application-specific codes to values recognized by the network

The point here is that even if your network agrees to use the Hyperledger Composer REST gateway presented in Chapter 7, *A Business Network Example*, there is still work that needs to be done by each participant to ensure that the integration fits into the overall business processes of the organization.

Message affinity

While this is not an issue often discussed, ignoring it can lead to serious issues that will typically surface during integration or performance testing.

We refer to message affinity as a situation that occurs when a system issues a series of inter-dependent transactions, which are issued in a short period of time. Because each transaction is issued separately, they are subject to be processed in a different order than when they are issued by the client.

The result may be unpredictable, as the following example shows. To make it concrete, let's look at an **Order** process that would issue three separate transactions, as shown in the following diagram:

Figure 5.4: Processing service requests in order

Because the **Service Provider** is multi-threaded, the order of processing can vary depending on the load at the time. A potential result is illustrated in the following diagram:

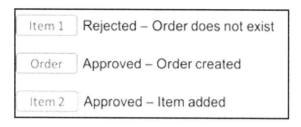

Figure 5.5: Potential service processing result

The first item being processed out of order would be rejected because the order object hasn't been created yet. However, the two subsequent objects would succeed and leave the system in a state where the order is recorded as having a single item instead of two.

The challenge with this situation is that it is hard to troubleshoot. An unaware developer may not be able to reproduce this behavior on his/her development platform.

Now, you may be wondering, how does that relate to blockchain and Hyperledger Fabric? Considering that Fabric transactions are asynchronously processed and that they are validated against every world state, this situation can arise. The client will issue the transaction and may asynchronously receive a message saying that the transaction was invalid because it did not correspond to the world state.

The moral of the story here is that when designing an API, make sure that they are at a granularity level that completely describes a business event. Too many fine-grained transactions only leads to message affinity, increased latency, and the potential for issues, as described here.

Service discovery

In the context of the integration to Hyperledger Fabric and Composer, the concept of service discovery is focussed on documenting and exposing the artifacts from Fabric: CA, peers, and orderers to the calling application.

As we now have experienced, in order for the application to get a transaction endorsed and added to the ledger, it needs to be able to interact with numerous components of these types. Having a way to maintain this information as a service configuration element will enable teams to quickly adapt to the evolving nature of the network.

Currently, when developing client applications using the Fabric SDK, the developer is responsible for managing and applying this service configuration.

Part of the roadmap of Hyperledger Fabric is the intent to facilitate this configuration.

One of the benefits of relying on a component such as the `Composer REST` gateway is that service discovery is provided by the gateway. Concretely, as you will soon discover, it provides the concept of a business card which contains both the identity information along with a connection profile, which has the list of Hyperledger Fabric services that can be used to execute transactions.

Identity mapping

Identity mapping is the process of converting the identity of an individual or an organization to an identity that is recognized on the network.

When looking at the solution from a business network perspective, what is the granularity of the identity that needs to be recognized? Will other organizations care whether Bob or Ann from ACME issued the transaction? In most cases, the answer will be no. Knowing that the transaction was issued by ACME will be sufficient.

Why is that, you may wonder. It is directly related to the concept of trust. Remember the concepts presented in *Chapter 1*, *Blockchain – Enterprise and Industry Perspective*; blockchain solves the problem of time and trust. Understanding where the trust issues come from helps us rationalize what identities should be used to transact on the network. In most cases, our experience has been that trust issues occur between organizations.

If you think about a use case where a bank customer transacts through their bank portal, the customer will not care about the backend systems; they trust their bank's security system.

Having said that, there are situations where an identity will need to be mapped:

- Business partners transacting through the integration layer of the organization
- Different departments with varying levels of privilege
- Users with different roles that drive different access privileges

In this case, the integration layer will need to convert the inbound credentials (API Key, User ID and Password, JTW token, and so on) into a Hyperledger Fabric identity.

When working with the Hyperledger `Composer REST` gateway, you can configure it to support multiple users. The server leverages the node passport framework to manage this authentication. This provides the flexibility of supporting different models (for example, user ID/password, JWT, and OAUTH).

Once the client is authenticated to the server, there is an additional step that consists of loading the Hyperledger Composer business card into the server's user repository. There needs to be implicit trust between the client and the server, as the business card contains the private key.

Integration design pattern

We will now look at some of the viable integration patterns we have seen in the industry. The list is by no means exhaustive, and given that we are still in the early days of the Hyperledger Fabric and Composer solutions, we expect that new patterns will emerge as people and organizations become more comfortable with the technology.

Enterprise system integration

In this category, we consider any organization's pre-existing systems that predate the joining of the network. As such, these systems have their own concepts and paradigms, and we will require a form of abstraction to reconcile the two worlds.

Integrating with an existing system of record

Following is a diagram to illustrate the blockchain network to an existing system of record:

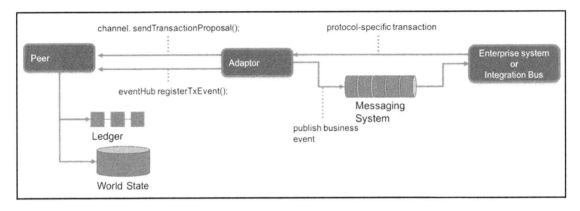

Figure 5.6: Integrating the blockchain network to an existing system of record

Most large enterprises looking at joining with a business network will eventually aim at integrating their system of record to make sure that they benefit from the real-time transparent distribution of transactions. In these circumstances, the process alignment we previously mentioned will be tremendously important.

As depicted in the preceding diagram, the approach will consist of leveraging an adaptor pattern to act as a data mapper between the two worlds. The adaptor will adopt the enterprise system application protocol and data structure to receive transaction requests. Optionally, it can also leverage existing foundations such as messaging services to propagate ledger events.

The important thing to note here is that this type of integration will be specific to an organization, and very little reuse will be possible.

As a variant of this pattern, some organizations will break the adaptor into two parts:

- **REST gateway**: Exposing a REST interface aligned with the Fabric smart contract
- **Integration bus**: Mapping the fields and connecting the enterprise systems

While in this variant reuse is higher, the same considerations only get moved one layer down.

Integrating with an operational data store

Here is a diagram that illustrates integrating the blockchain network to an operational data store:

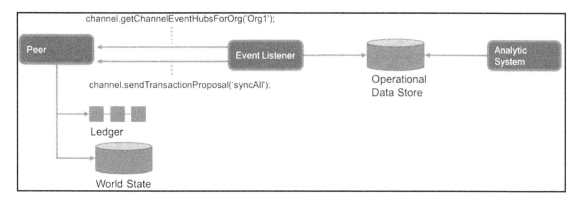

Figure 5.7: Integrating the blockchain network to an operational data store

Oftentimes, organizations are looking at ways of running analytics on the information from their ledgers. However, issuing multiple/large queries against the organization's peers will only impact the online performance of the system. Generally, the recognized approach in enterprise system design is to move the data to an operational data store. The data can then be easily queried. Additional views on the data can be created by enriching the data using different data sources.

In this pattern, the event listener subscribes to the Fabric organization events. As such, it can receive transactions from all channels the organization is entitled to. If the preservation of the data's integrity is important, the event listener can calculate a hash of every record and store them alongside the records.

You will notice that the pattern also accounts for a `syncAll` function that would allow the event listener to re-synchronize the data store with the latest view of the world state. Keep in mind that the implementation of this `syncAll` function will need to be done carefully and will most likely require that the function supports the pagination of the resultsets.

Microservice and event-driven architecture

The following diagram illlustrates microservice and event-driven architecture for a blockchain application:

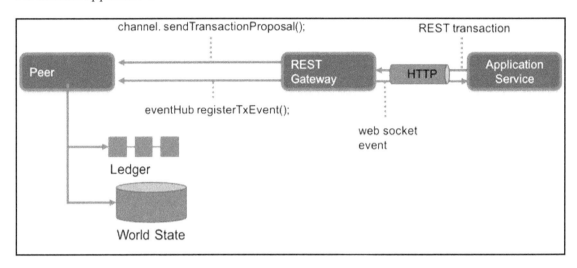

Figure 5.8: Microservice and event-driven architecture for a blockchain application

We've labeled this pattern as microservice and event-driven because this is the pattern most often seen for those types of architectures. However, the particularity of this pattern comes from the gateway. Such a system will not perform any data mapping; it will leverage a common communication protocol (HTTP) and data format (typically JSON, but it could be XML). There is also an expectation that the services will already be designed to understand the semantics of the data being transacted. Events are also propagated through the same protocol and data format.

Again, microservice applications tend to be newer applications, and they benefit from a more fine-grained interface. As such, they tend to evolve more quickly and be in a position to adapt and adhere to the transactions from the network. Similarly, event-driven applications will benefit from their low coupling to the other components of the system, and so are good candidates for this pattern.

Considering reliability, availability, and serviceability

The failure of software or hardware components is a fact of life for any industrial application, so you must design your application to be robust to failures and minimize the probability of downtime. We will discuss three key guidelines that are widely used in the industry to build and maintain systems, and briefly examine how they apply to an application built using Fabric or Composer tools.

Reliability

A reliable system is one that ensures correct operation in the face of failure, with high probability. This entails the following things:

- Continuous self-monitoring of the system
- Detection of failure or corruption in a component
- Fixing the problem and/or failing over to a working component

Although various practices have evolved in the industry to ensure reliability, redundancy and failover are commonly (or even universally) used.

In the context of a Fabric application of the kind we built in Section I, this has certain implications. Recall that Fabric has many different components that must work in concert (though in a loosely-coupled manner) to ensure successful operation. The ordering service is one such key component that, if it were to fail, would completely stall the transaction pipeline. Therefore, when building a production version of, say, our trade application, you must ensure that the orderer has enough redundancy built in. In practice, if your orderer is a Kafka cluster, this means ensuring that there are enough Kafka nodes (brokers) to take up the slack should one or more fail.

Similarly, the reliability of peers for endorsement and commitment is key to ensuring transaction integrity. Although blockchains, being shared replicated ledgers, are designed to be somewhat robust to peer failures, their vulnerabilities may vary depending on the application. If an endorsing peer fails, and if its signature is necessary to satisfy the transaction endorsement policy, transaction requests cannot be created. If an endorsing peer misbehaves, and produces incorrect execution results, the transaction will fail to get committed. In either case, the throughput of the system will reduce or fall to zero. To prevent this from happening, you should ensure that there is adequate redundancy built into the set of peers within each organization, especially the ones that are key to satisfying an endorsement policy. The following diagram illustrates a possible mechanism whereby transaction proposals are made to multiple peers, and absent or incorrect responses are discarded using a majority rule:

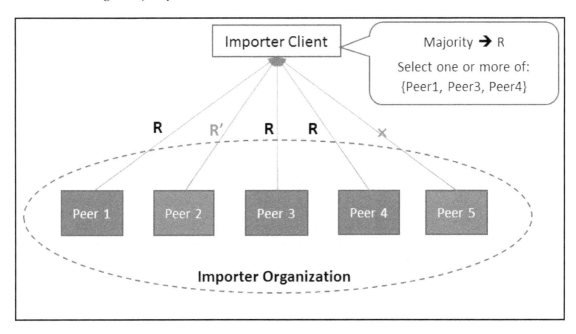

Figure 5.9 Redundant peers for reliable transaction endorsement

The level of reliability one gets from a system depends on the amount of resources devoted to monitoring and failover. For example, five peers in the preceding diagram are sufficient to counter two peer failures, but this now requires four more peers in the organization than what we used in our example network. To determine and ensure that your network yields the expected level of reliability, you will need to run integration tests on your complete system over a period of time.

Availability

The availability criterion is closely related to reliability, but it is more about ensuring system uptime with high probability, or as a corollary, minimizing the probability of system downtime. As with reliability, detection of failed nodes and ensuring adequate failover is the key to ensuring that your application will remain operational, even when one or more components fails. Determination of the desired availability level, allocating an adequate number of resources in the form of redundant and self-correcting components, and testing in a production environment are necessary to ensure that you get the desired performance from your application.

Serviceability

Serviceability or **maintainability** is the ease with which you can replace or upgrade parts of your system without impacting the system as a whole.

Consider a situation where you must upgrade the operating system on one or more of your ordering service nodes, or if you need to replace a faulty peer within an organization. As with reliability or availability, having redundant (or parallel) resources to which application operations can be switched seamlessly is the way to handle this in an industrial-scale system. So-called Blue-Green deployment is one of the popular mechanisms used for this purpose. In a nutshell, you have two parallel environments (let's say, for the ordering service), one called Blue and one called Green, where the Blue environment is receiving live traffic. You can upgrade the operating systems on the Green machines, test them adequately, and then switch the traffic from Blue to Green. Now, while Green is serving requests, you can upgrade Blue in the same manner.

In a blockchain application with loosely coupled components, it is advisable to have Blue and Green environments for each of the components (orderers, peers, and MSPs) and carry out the upgrades and testing in stages, or one component cluster at a time, to minimize the chances of a mishap.

Summary

Building a complete blockchain application is an ambitious and challenging project, not just because of the range of skills it requires—systems, networking, security, and web application development, to name a few—but because it requires concerted development, testing, and deployment by multiple organizations spanning multiple security domains.

In this chapter, we began with a simple smart contract and ended with a four-peer blockchain network that was ready to drive trade scenarios and store records in a tamper-resistant, shared, replicated ledger. In the process, we learned how to design an organization structure and configure a Fabric network. We learned how to build a channel, or an instance of a Fabric blockchain, get peers in a network to join the channel, and install and instantiate a smart contract on that channel, using the Fabric SDK. We learned how to expose the capabilities of our network and smart contract to end users through web applications, exposing service APIs. We also learned how a Hyperledger Fabric transaction pipeline works, and how the asynchronous nature of block commit operations must be factored into the implementation of the end-to-end application.

In the latter part of the chapter, we learned about various design patterns and best practices that can be used to build industry-scale blockchain applications. We also learned about the considerations to keep in mind while integrating these applications with existing systems and processes. Finally, we explored the performance aspects of running operational Fabric network and learned about the CAP theorem and how Fabric achieves data consistency in distributed environment.

The Hyperledger platforms and tools will, no doubt, evolve over time to serve industry and developer needs, but the architecture and methodology we described in our application-building exercise, as well as the design and integration patterns, should continue to serve as an educational guide in the long term.

Our journey so far has taken us to the foundation of the Hyperledger Fabric framework. We have worked with chaincode and integrated an application using the Fabric SDK API. These are essential skills.

In the next two chapters, we will now explore a different approach to modeling and implementing a business network.

6
Business Networks

This chapter introduces and explores a new concept—**a business network.** By understanding what business networks are and how they function, you'll be able to understand how blockchain technology can radically improve them. A blockchain, and in particular a Hyperledger Fabric blockchain, provides significant benefits for business networks because it radically simplifies the information and processes that knit businesses together, both reducing cost and creating new opportunities for the businesses within the network.

We'll see how the concept of a business network allows you to analyze a business by looking at the counterparties with which it interacts. And although business networks are industry specific, a single network can be used to support multiple use cases, and linked to other business networks to form networks of networks.

We'll spend some time introducing the vocabulary of business network, introducing key terms such as **participants**, **assets**, **transactions** and **events.** These elements are then combined to define the behaviour of the business problem being analyzed. We're able to use business requirement to create a technology blueprint that can be used to implement the solution. By the end of this chapter, you'll be ready to use Hyperledger Fabric and Hyperledger Composer to implement these ideas, which you will do in the following chapter.

While the idea of a business network is necessary to understand before you implement a blockchain network, you'll find it a helpful concept for wider issues such as performing blockchain analytics, integrating with existing systems, and how to structure your application and enterprise architectures. In this sense, this chapter can be read stand-alone without implementing a network afterwards.

We will be covering the following topics in this chapter:

- A language for business networks
- The concept of a business network
- Defining business networks

- Introducing participants
- Introducing assets
- Introducing transactions
- Introducing events
- Implementing a business network

A busy world of purposeful activity

Imagine for a moment that we're flying in a plane over a large city. We can see factories, banks, schools, hospitals, retail stores, car showrooms, ships and boats at the port, and so on. These are the structures that define the city.

If we look carefully, we'll see things happening within and between these structures. Lorries might be delivering iron ore to the factory, customers might be withdrawing money from banks, students might be sitting exams—it's a busy world down there!

And, if we could look a little closer, we would see that all these people and organizations are involved in meaningful activity with each other. Students receiving assessments from their teachers that will subsequently help them get into college. Banks giving loans to clients who can then move home. Factories making components from raw materials, which are assembled into complex objects by their customers. People buying used cars from dealerships that they use to get them to work every day, or go on vacation!

We might marvel at the diversity of all these structures and the processes between them. We might even wonder how it all manages to work together so effortlessly!

We might then reflect upon all these diverse activities, and wonder whether they all have something in common? Are there repeatable patterns that allow us to make sense of all this complexity? Is there a resolution at which all this activity looks the same? Are all these people and organizations, in some sense, doing the same thing?

The answer, of course, is yes! The following section gives us a better explanation.

Why a language for business networks?

A business network is a way of thinking that allows us to look at all these activities and describe it in a very simple language. And, because we're trying to formulate the world in a language that makes sense to a blockchain, and since blockchain is a simple technology, we expect the vocabulary of that language to be simple. In the next section, you'll see that it is!

But before we dive in, let's ask ourselves *why* we want to create a language that a blockchain can understand? Well, if we can, then we can bring all the benefits of the blockchain to the world described by that language. And, we can summarize these benefits neatly—increased trust.

Increased trust means that the student can show their high school certificates to their college, who can be confident about the veracity of the qualifications. It means that the bank can provide a loan to its customer at the lowest rates because it can be confident about the financial well-being of its client. It means that the component manufacturer can charge a higher price for their output because their customers in turn can be sure of the quality of the raw materials, knowing their provenance. And finally, the the buyer of the used car can be confident about their purchase because they can prove that it previously only had one, careful, owner!

Defining business networks

We can summarize all these idea using the concept of a business network:

> *A business network is a collection of participants and assets than undergo a life cycle described by transactions. Events occur when transactions complete.*

You may wonder what this means. After all that build-up, we're telling you that a couple of apparently simple sentences describe all this complexity?

The simple answer is yes—and we'll soon explain by describing in more detail what we mean by **participants**, **assets**, **transactions**, and **events**. Then, you'll see that all this rich behavior can be described by a relatively simple language vocabulary.

A deeper idea

In fact, there is a deeper idea behind business networks—that the language and vocabulary of technology should closely match that of the business domain, removing the need for significant translation between business concepts, and technology concepts. Business networks move away from the idea of disconnected technology by describing the underlying technology in the same language as the business. It makes it easier to reason about the world and more accurately translate ideas into a fully operational system.

Practically speaking, it means that while our initial vocabulary for business networks is simple, it is the beginning of a language that can become very rich in structure over time, so long as it describes the details and nuances of what happens in the real world. We'll come back to this idea later, but for now let's start by understanding participants.

Introducing participants

William Shakespeare said that the world is a stage on which men and women are the actors. In a similar way, a business network has a cast—a set of actors who are interacting with each other for some form of mutual benefit. We call these actors the participants in a business network. For example, the participants in an education network might be students, teachers, schools, colleges, examiners, or government inspectors. The participants in an insurance network might be policyholders, brokers, underwriters, insurers, insurance syndicates, regulators, or banks.

The idea of a participant is crucial to understanding business networks. You might find the term a little daunting at first, but there's really nothing to worry about. The key to understanding is in the name— participants *take part* in a business network. It's their actions that we are interested in. Different forms of the word are used to emphasize different aspects of their interactions: participant, party, and counter-party, for example. All these forms have their roots in the idea of action. As usual, we find that the bard knew a thing or two about how the world works!

Learn to love this word, because it's a door-opener! It's shorthand that you understand the founding principle of business—that who you do business with is of paramount importance. It's more important than this though; identifying the participants in a business network is the first thing that you do when determining whether there's an opportunity to benefit from the use of a blockchain. You need to understand the cast before you can really understand what's going on. And, as you learn more about the interactions between the participants, you'll be able to improve your understanding of what it means to be a particular participant.

Types of participant

There are different *types* of participants in a business network, and we group them into three broad categories. Surprisingly, we're not going to describe the most important category first!

Individual participants

Hopefully, this category is a fairly obvious one—the teacher, student or bank customer are all examples of individual participants. Whether you call them individuals, people, or even humans, this first category is what we would intuitively think of as a participant because we associate them with ourselves.

You might think that individuals are the most important participants in a network. After all, businesses exist to serve individuals, don't they? Well, yes they do, but it's a little more subtle than that. While a business network usually exists to serve the needs of individual end-consumers, blockchain is a technology that is more valuable for the businesses in the network. That's because it allows them to better coordinate their activities with each other, resulting in lower costs, and the opportunity for new goods and services for end-consumers. That's why you'll hear people utter sentences such as Blockchain is more important for B2B than B2C, or C2C—they're trying to communicate that the big win for business networks is to use blockchain as a pervasive fabric for efficient and creative business-to-business interactions.

Of course, individual participants are important. Businesses need to know their end-consumers, and often end-consumers are interacting with each other using the services provided by the business network. For example, if I wish to transfer money to you via a banking network, our respective banks need to know who we both are, so that the transaction can be properly validated and routed.

Finally, it's a fair rule of thumb that there are more individuals known to a business network than there are businesses in the network. Nothing too surprising here—it's just worth pointing this out so that your understanding of what it means to be an individual participant is complete!

Organizational participants

Organizational participants are the most important actors in a business network. The car dealership, the bank, the school, and the insurance company are all examples of organizational participants. When we first think about a particular business network, we identify these participants, followed by the goods and services they provide to each other and end-consumers. These organizational participants provide the infrastructure for the business network—the people, processes, and technology that make it work.

While organizations are made up of individuals, they are conceptually quite separate to them. An organization has its own identity, and its own purpose. It exists in a very real sense, independently to the individuals which belong to it. Organizations provide business networks with a sense of permanence. While individuals within an organization may change over time, and the number of individuals within the organization may grow or shrink, and even different roles within the organization may come and go, the organization remains constant; it is a structure with a much longer lifetime than any individual's membership of it.

The final point to note about the nature of the relationship between individuals and their organization is that it is individuals who perform the functions of the organization, as defined by the individual's organizational role. When a bank makes a loan to a customer, it is performed by a bank employee on behalf of the bank. In this way, the individuals are the agents of the organization, and an individual's role determines the set of tasks it can perform. For example, a school teacher can set a homework assignment for a student, but it requires a school principal to hire a new teacher. In a nutshell, individuals act on behalf of the organization, and with the authority of that organization.

System or device participants

System or device participants represent the technology components in the business network. They are really a special kind of individual participant, and if you find it helpful, you can just think of them that way. There are however, two reasons why we call them out separately.

Firstly, there are a lot of technology components in today's business networks! For example, there are ERP systems, payment engines, reservation systems, transaction processors, and much, much more. In fact, most of the heavy-lifting inside today's business networks is done by these systems. These systems are associated with organizations that own them, and just like the individuals we discussed earlier, these systems act on behalf of their owning organizations—they too are its agents.

The incorporation of a blockchain into a business network is going to add more system participants with whom the other participants (individual, organizational, and system/device) can interact. It's important to be aware of these blockchain system participants because they are going to provide very useful services to the business network!

Secondly, devices are becoming a more important part of the business world. And, while many devices today are relatively simple, there's no doubt that devices are acquiring more characteristics of being autonomous. We've all heard of the expected emergence of self-driving vehicles, and it's in this spirit that we introduce the concept of **device participants**. It may be increasingly important to think of these devices playing a larger role in business networks. So, while we don't expect cars to become intelligent anytime soon (whatever that might mean!), it's helpful to call out these increasingly autonomous devices as active rather than passive entities in a network.

Participants are agents

Our examination of participant types shows us that they all have one thing in common—they have a significant degrees of agency—they actively do things. Although systems and devices have a level of autonomy that is limited by their programming and algorithms, it is nonetheless helpful to think of them this way. And, the interactions between these relatively autonomous actors serves as a prompt to the next concept in a business network, namely **assets**. We'll see later that the entities that move between participants—assets—have none of this autonomy. These are subject to the forces placed upon them by participants. More on this later.

Participants and identity

Finally, and very importantly, participants have **identity**. For example, a student has a student ID, a driver has a driving license, and a citizen has a social security number. It's obvious that there is a difference between a participant and what's used to identify a participant. And, it's really important to hold these two concepts as closely related, but separate to each other.

For example, a participant might have different identities to participate in different business networks—it might be the *same* bank which participates in an insurance network, and a mortgage network, but it will have different identities in these two networks. Moreover, even within a single network, a participant might have their current identity compromised, allowing them to be impersonated. In this case, their compromised identity will be revoked and a replacement issued for use by the true participant, denying the impersonator, allowing trust to be restored. Different identities, but the same participant—that's the take-away message.

It's because of this concern over impersonation that certain identities are deliberately expired periodically. For example, X.509 digital certificates have an expiry date, after which they are no longer valid. However, just because the certificate has expired, it cannot be assumed that the participant is no longer present.

In fact, it's quite the opposite. The relative permanence of a participant compared to its identity means that it can be used to provide a long-term historical reference of who does what in a business network. The consistency of identity provided by a participant over time helps us reason about the history of interactions in a business network. We could do this without the concept of a participant—just using identities, and keeping a clear head about how and when they changed in relation to each other, but it would be less intuitive.

That's just about it on the topic of participants; you're now an expert! As you can tell, participants are probably the most important thing about a business network, which is why we spent quite a bit of time discussing them. Let's now turn our attention to the objects that move between participants, namely assets.

Introducing assets

We've seen how a business network is defined by the participants who operate within it. These participants are the active agents who perform meaningful interactions within the network, and its their transactions which are of paramount importance. We now ask ourselves the question, *What flows between participants?* To which the simple answer is assets.

To understand what we mean by an asset, let's look at some examples. We notice that a student receives coursework from their tutor. That same student may subsequently show their educational certificate to a university. A car dealer sells a car to a buyer. An insurance company insures that same car for a policyholder, issuing a policy. A policyholder makes a claim. These examples all contains assets: coursework, education certificate, car, policy, and claim.

Assets flow between participants

We can see that assets are the objects that flow between participants. Whereas participants have a significant degree of autonomy, assets are quite passive. This property of assets is foundational—assets tend to have the most meaning to the counter-parties who exchange them. That's not to say that other participants aren't interested in these assets, but it does emphasize the passive nature of assets. So what makes assets so important? Why are we bothering to talk about these passive objects?

The answer lies in our choice of word—asset. An asset is a thing of *value*. Even though assets are relatively passive, they represent the value that is exchanged between participants. Look at these example assets again with this value-based lens: coursework, education certificate, car, policy, and claim. Coursework is valuable to the teacher and student; an education certificate is valuable to the student and university; a car is valuable to the dealership and buyer; a policy is valuable to the insurance company and policy holder; a claim is valuable to the claimant and insurance company. Hopefully, it's now clear why assets are important, and why they are called assets!

As a minor note, don't think that because we have assets, we must have liabilities—we're not quite using the term this way. It's absolutely true that if we were to measure objects as counting for us, or counting against us, we would term them assets or liabilities, but that's not quite what's happening here—we're using asset as a concrete noun, rather than as a quality or abstract noun.

Tangible and intangible assets

Let's continue our understanding of assets by considering tangible and intangible assets. Tangible assets are things we can touch and feel—cars, paper money, or coursework. Intangible assets are things such as mortgages, intellectual property rights, insurance policies, and music files. In an increasingly digital world, we're going to see a lot more intangible assets. You'll hear people say that objects are becoming *de-materialized*, and the idea of an intangible assets nicely captures this concept.

A couple of small points should be noted to avoid confusion on our usage of the word intangible. Firstly, as we're dealing with a digital ledger, in some trivial sense, everything on a blockchain is intangible. What's interesting is the nature of the object itself—using the word intangible helps you to remember to look out for things that you cannot see in the physical world.

Secondly, the use of intangible is not intended as a statement of value. Often, in accounting systems, we use this term when we have trouble defining something, such as goodwill. Again, we're not using the word in this sense; our intangible assets have a more concrete, definite, and exchangeable form than this, because they are things of value, even if you cannot touch them.

The structure of assets

Let's now re-focus to look at the structure of assets. An asset has a set of attributes called **properties** and a set of attributes called **relationships**. Property attributes are easy to understand—they are the characteristics of an object. For example, a car has a date of manufacture, a color, and an engine size. Or, a mortgage has a value, lifetime, and repayment schedule. A particular asset is identified by a particular set of property **values**. For example, my car might be manufactured in 2015, be white in color and have a 1.8-litre engine. Another example—your mortgage might be worth 100,000 USD, have a lifetime of 25 years, and be payable monthly. It's important to distinguish this difference—between the structure of an asset *in general,* its **type,** and *particular* **instance** of an asset.

Secondly, an asset also has a set of attributes called **relationships**. A relationship is a special kind of property—it's a reference to another asset! You can see instantly why this is important. For example, a car has an insurance document. The car is an object of value, and the insurance document is an object of value. Moreover, an insurance document names a policy holder. In our examples, both the subject and the object are assets, and they relate to each other in a way that provides essential meaning.

We'll see later that describing or **modeling** these relationships is an extremely important activity, because we're describing how the world works. In the previous example, we made a deliberate mistake—yes, really! That's because in the real world, it's actually the policy document that is central, as it names the car and the policy holder. In modeling, we call this an associative relationship, and we'll see why it's really important to get this kind of thing right. For example, nowhere in the nature of a car will you find an insurance document—a car is insured by virtue of the fact that it is named in a valid policy document. Moreover, if I want to insure more people to drive the car, I add their name to the policy document, not to the car! Much more on this later—for now, it's enough to remember that assets have properties and references, and particular objects have concrete values for these attributes.

It's also worth a brief mention on the nature of what makes an asset attribute a property rather than a reference to another asset. A simple answer is: when properties get too *big*, break them out into an asset reference! Of course, that's a very unsatisfactory answer! Why? Because I didn't tell you what defines big! A better answer is that a reference is required when a property satisfies a separate concern. This principle—**separation of concerns**—is a key design principle in any system. For example, the policy validity date is not a separate concern for an insurance policy, but the car and named drivers are separate concerns. This principle helps us to reason about insurance policies, cars, and drivers independently of each other, which in turn allows us to model the real world more realistically. Finally, on this aspect of assets, property and relationship attributes are **domain-specific**—they relate to the nature of the problem at hand. So, for a car manufacturer, color might be an attribute of a car—but for a paint manufacturer color is most definitely an asset type!

Ownership is a special relationship

There's one particular kind of relationship that's particularly important in a business network, and that's the concept of **ownership**. Ownership is an associative relationship such as the insurance policy document we discussed earlier. Let's think about a specific example—a person owns a car. Is the owner an attribute of the car? Is the car an attribute of the person? After a little thinking, we might realize that neither statement captures what it means to *own* something. Ownership is a mapping between the person and the car. Ownership is a concept that's quite separate to the car and its owner.

It's important to understand this way of thinking about ownership, because in many cases we model the ownership relationship via the car, or via the owner, and that's sufficient for many purposes. But, the *nature* of an ownership relationship is an associative one, and it's important to realize this—because blockchains are often used to record ownership and transfer of ownership in a business network. For example, governments often hold ownership records—for land or vehicles. In these cases, the primary assets under consideration are ownership relationships. When a vehicle or land is transferred between participants, it's this ownership record that changes rather than the assets. That's important because we're often interested in the the history of a vehicle or piece of land, and while the vehicle or land itself may not change, it's ownership most definitely does. It's important, therefore, to be clear whether we're talking about the history of the asset, or the history of ownership. These kinds of history are often called **provenance**—they tell us who has owned an asset, and how it has changed over time. Both aspects are important because knowing the provenance of an asset increases our confidence in it.

Asset life cycles

This idea of provenance leads us very naturally to the concept of an **asset life cycle**. If we consider the history of an asset, then in some very meaningful sense, an asset is created, changed over time, and eventually ceases to exist. For example, consider a mortgage. It comes into existence when a bank agrees to lend a sum of money to a customer. It remains in existence for the term of the mortgage. As the interest rate changes, it determines the monthly repayment amount according to a fixed or a variable rate of interest. The term of the mortgage may be changed with the agreement of both the bank and the mortgage holder. Finally, at the end of the mortgage, it ceases to exist, although a historic record of it may be kept. The mortgage may be terminated early if the customer wishes to pay it off early (maybe they move home), or less fortunately if they default on the loan. In some sense, we see that the mortgage was created, the term was periodically changed, and then the mortgage was completed either normally or unexpectedly. This concept of a life cycle is incredibly important in a business network, and we'll discuss it in detail later, when we discuss **transactions**.

Returning to assets, we can see that during their life cycle, assets can also be **transformed**. This is a very important idea, and we consider two aspects of asset transformation—namely whether the the transformation involves **division** or **aggregation**, and whether it is a **homogeneous** or **heterogeneous** transformation. These terms sound a little intimidating, but they are very simple to understand, and best described using an example of each.

In the first example, we consider a precious gemstone that has been mined. In general, a mined gemstone is too large for any jeweler to use in a single piece of jewellery. It must be broken into smaller stones, each of which may be used for single item of jewellery. If we were to look at the history of a large, mined gemstone, we would see that it underwent a process of division. The initial asset was a gemstone, and it was transformed into a set of smaller gemstones, each of which was related to the original gemstone. We can see that the asset transformation is homogeneous, because although the smaller gemstones are most definitely different assets, they are the **same type** as the original asset. A similar process of homogeneous transformation often occurs with intangible assets, for example, when a large commercial loan or insurance request is syndicated among several companies to diversify risk, or when a stock is split.

In our next example, we consider the jeweler using a smaller gemstone. We imagine they use the gemstone to create a fine ring for a customer. To make the ring, they use all their skills to set the gemstone in a mounting on a bezel connected to a hoop via a shoulder. A jeweler's craft is to be admired—they transform a small block of silver and a gemstone into a valuable piece of jewellery. Let us consider for a moment the assets under consideration. We can see that the metal block and gemstone have been combined, or **aggregated**, to form the ring. We also note that the ring is a different asset to the gemstone or silver block, which served as inputs. We can see that these inputs have undergone a **heterogeneous transformation** because the output asset is of a different type.

These processes of aggregation and division are seen in many asset life cycles. It's very popular in manufacturing life cycles, but with intangible assets. For example, we see it in **mergers**, where companies can be combined together, or **acquisitions**, where one company ceases to exist by being incorporated into another company. The reverse processes of **de-merger** or **spin-off** is neatly described as asset division.

Describing asset's life cycles in detail with transactions

Let's consider *how* assets move through their life cycle. We have learned that assets are created, transformed, and eventually cease to exist. Although life cycle is a very useful concept, these steps seems somewhat limited. Surely there are richer descriptions for the set of steps an asset goes through in its life cycle? The answer is yes! **Transactions** define a rich, domain-specific vocabulary for describing how assets evolve over time. For example, an insurance policy is requested, refined, signed, delivered, claimed-against, paid-out against, invalidated, or renewed. Each step of this life cycle is a transaction—we're going to talk a lot more about transactions in the next section.

Finally, as with assets, participants can go through a life cycle, described by transactions. So, you might wonder, what is the difference between assets and participants? Well, it really comes down to thinking about form versus function. Just because assets can have a life cycle described by transactions, and likewise participants, does not make them the same thing. In the same way that birds, insects, and bats can fly, they are definitely not related. In a general sense, we think of participants and assets as as resources—they are related only in the most general sense.

That ends our discussion on assets! As we saw towards the end of the topic, **transactions** are of paramount importance in describing the asset and participant life cycles, so let's now turn to this subject!

Introducing transactions

Our journey so far has involved understanding the fundamental nature of a business network—that it is comprised of participants involved in the meaningful exchange of assets. Let's now focus on the most important concept in business networks—exchange.

Change as a fundamental concept

Why is exchange the most important idea? Well, without it, participants and assets have no purpose!

This seems like an excessively hyperbolic statement! However, if you think about it for a moment, participants only meaningfully exist in the sense that they exchange goods and services (collectively known as assets) with each other. If a participant does not exchange with another participant, they don't exist in any meaningful way. It's the same with assets—if they aren't exchanged between participants, then they don't exist in any meaningful way either. There's no point in an asset having a life cycle if it doesn't move between different participants, because the asset is private to a participant and serves no purpose in the business network outside the participant's private context.

Change, therefore, is the fundamental principle in business networks. When we think about exchange, transfers, commerce, buying, selling, agreement, and contracts, all of these motivational ideas are concerned with the business and the effects of change. Change gives the world of business motion and direction. The way we capture change is via a transaction. That's why transaction is the most important concept in a business network—it defines and records change—change of asset; change of asset ownership; change of participants. Whenever anything changes in a business network, there's a transaction to account for it.

Transaction definition and instance

The term transaction is often used in two closely related, but different ways, and it's important to be conscious of this difference. We sometimes use the term transaction to describe in general terms what happens in a transaction. For example, we might define that a property transaction involves a buyer paying an agreed amount to the owner of the property in exchange for possession of the property, and exchange of the deeds of title. (Almost always, the buyer also acquires the rights to subsequently sell the property.) In this sense, the term transaction is used to describe in general the process of exchange in the terms of the participants and assets involved.

The other sense in which the word transaction is used is as a description of a particular transaction. For example, we might say that on 10 May 2018, Daisy bought a bicycle from the Winchester bicycle shop for 300 GBP. We're using the term transaction here to describe a particular instance of a transaction. These two usages are very closely related, and the context almost always makes it clear which one we're talking about.

The fundamental difference between the two usages is that the former defines what it means to be a transaction, and the latter captures a particular instance of a transaction. In the real world, we see examples of transaction instances all the time—whenever we go into a shop to buy some goods, we are offered a receipt! In our previous example, Daisy probably got a receipt for her bicycle. The receipt might be made of paper, though nowadays it is often sent to our phone or email address. This receipt is a copy of the transaction—it's Daisy's personal record of what happened. The bicycle shop also keeps a copy of the transaction record themselves for their own accounting purposes.

Implicit and explicit transactions

Note that you don't often see an explicit transaction definition for a transaction like this; the definition is encoded in the people, processes, and technology that you interact with. For low-consequence transactions such as Daisy's, the transaction definition is implicit. Only if there's a dispute do we get to find out how the transaction is defined. For example, if Daisy's bicycle chain snaps after a couple of days, she might reasonably expect that the chain would be fixed free of charge, or the bicycle replaced, or she would get her money back. This is the point at which Daisy determines the true nature of her transaction with the Winchester bicycle shop.

It looks like this kind of implicit transaction definition only has downsides—but in fact that's not the case. Firstly, every country's laws have explicit notions of a fair transaction that would give Daisy reasonable expectations as she entered the transaction. In most countries this is called something such as a Sale of Goods Act, and it specifies the rights and responsibilities of all counter-parties involved in any commercial transaction. Secondly, the lack of an explicit contract simplifies the interaction between Daisy and the bicycle shop. Given that, in most cases, bicycles perform well for an extended period after purchase, a receipt is sufficient for most practical purposes. It would be both costly and timely to re-state what everyone knows to be true every time a simple purchase was made. This kind of simplification is an example of what people often call **reducing friction**.

For high-consequence transactions, or those with special conditions, the situation is very different—it is vital that the transaction definition is made explicit, in advance. If we look at Daisy's transaction again, we can see that if there was a dispute, there would have been other follow-up transactions—for example, the bicycle might have had its chain replaced, or in an extreme circumstance she might have got her money back. We can see that, in general, we would require several conditional transactions to describe a satisfactory interaction between participants for such a transaction. It means that if Daisy had been getting a mortgage, rather than a bicycle, it would have been necessary to specify several transactions and the conditions under which they could be executed. You've probably heard of a term for such a collection of transactions and conditions—a **contract**.

The importance of contracts

For high value assets, it's important to have a contract. It defines a related set of transactions and conditions under which they occur. A contract normally centers around a particular asset type and involves a well-defined set of participant types. If you look at a real-world contract, it includes a combination of statements about instances and statements about definitions. At the top of the contract, all the assets and participants will be laid out with particular values—namely Daisy (the buyer), Winchester bicycles (the seller), 300 GBP (the price), 10 May 2018 (the date of purchase) and so on. It's only after all these type-to-instance mappings have been laid out, that the contract is then defined in terms of these types, transactions, and conditions under which they occur, without reference to the particular instance values. This is what makes contracts a little strange to read at first—but once you can see the structure in terms of participants, assets, and transactions, and their respective values, they are actually quite easy to understand, and all the more powerful for this structure.

Signatures

The final thing we see in a contract is at the bottom of it—the signatures! In many ways, signatures are the most important part of a contract because they represent the fact that all counter-parties have agreed to the information contained within it. And of course, we see lots of signatures in the real world. Daisy's shop receipt normally has her signature on it—either physical or digital, via a private key. In simple transactions, the store's signature is actually implicit—they put a transaction code on a branded receipt, and keep a copy for their purposes—this satisfies the purposes of a signature.

However, for higher-consequence transactions, all counter-parties will be required to explicitly sign a contract. Even more pointedly, to ensure that every party is entering the contract with their *eyes open*, an independent third-party such as a solicitor, notary, or regulator, may be required to sign the contract to verify the willing, and free, participation of those counter-parties explicitly involved in the transaction.

Smart contracts for multi-party transaction processing

It's absolutely vital to understand these ideas. They are not particularly complicated, especially if you relate them to things you do every day! When it comes to understanding how a blockchain helps multiple counter-parties create and agree low-friction transactions related to high-value assets, we need to understand these terms, and their importance, both stand-alone and in relationship to each other.

Now, when we look at a business network, we can see that it is full of multi-party transactions governed by contracts! It's why transactions are the most important concept in a business network; they define and capture the agreed exchanges of valuable assets between different counter-parties.

Now, let's use a term you've probably heard many times when it comes to blockchains—**smart contracts**. They are simply a digital manifestation of these ideas. Smart contracts are a digital form of a contract—meaning that they can be easily interpreted and executed by a computer system. In reality, all computer systems that implement high- or low-consequence transactions implement contracts. But, unlike blockchains, these systems do not have a technology with a built-in vocabulary that makes the translation of these ideas into a technology platform a straightforward exercise.

Digital transaction processing

As we mentioned at the beginning of this chapter, that's the big idea of business networks implemented on blockchains. They make the translation from the real-world into a computer system as simple as possible. Hyperledger Fabric, in particular, makes all these ideas quite explicit, so that we can easily model and implement a business network. It keeps all the existing ideas intact, but implements them in a fundamentally **digital** manner—using computer processes, networks, and storage.

Transactions are at the center of a business network because they act on assets and participants. However, it's more than this. Even if we add more concepts to the business network, they must always be subject to transactions. Transactionality is the universal property that relates to all aspects of the business network. It's like the ability to fly that we mentioned earlier in the chapter—every object in the business network is subject to, and must be the subject of, transactions.

Initiating transactions

Coming up for air for a moment, we can see that transactions are usually initiated by one participant in a business network. This participant is usually the consumer of a service available from a particular service provider. For example, Daisy wishes to consume the services provided by Winchester bicycles, when it comes to buying a bicycle.

Most transactions initiated by participants are concerned with the change in state of an asset, but in some cases transactions can involve the change in state of a participant. For example, if I change my name by deed poll, then in some sense the asset being transformed is me—the participant. This reinforces the central nature of transactions—that they capture change no matter what the object.

Transaction history

When we previously discussed the provenance of assets, we saw that the history of an asset was important—it provided confidence to participants in a network—and this increased trust. Likewise, transaction history is important, because it too increases trust. Why? Well, it comes back to those signatures. Any change must agreed by all the participants involved in the transaction, and the signatures in each transaction provide confidence that every counter-party consented to the exchange. A history of transactions is even better—it shows that all all points in time, every participant in the network has agreed with every change described by every transaction!

A blockchain history contains a sequenced order of transactions. Although, an order seems to imply that transactions occur in a time-defined sequence, this is only partially true. For example, if I pay money into my bank account at 11.00 a.m., and then make a payment from my bank account at 11.30 a.m., there is a very real sense in which the first transaction happened before the second.

Likewise, if you pay money into your bank account at 11.00 a.m., and then you make a payment at 11.30 a.m., there is a definite ordering of your transactions. However, let's now ask whether our 11.00 a.m. transactions happened before or after each other? Or, our 11.30 a.m. transactions? Does it matter whether my 11.00 a.m. transaction is recorded after your 11.30 a.m. transaction, even though it may have occurred, in some sense, before it?

Transaction streams

This example shows us that it's the dependency of transactions that matters when discussing transaction history; transactions that are dependent on previous transactions are recorded after them. For **independent transaction streams**, this ordering is much less important. We have to be a little bit careful, because transactions have a nasty habit of becoming entangled with each other. For example, if your 11.30 a.m. transaction made its payment into my bank account, then two seemingly independent transaction streams have started to interfere with each other. This means that we cannot arbitrarily delay the recording of transactions.

Notice that we're not talking about the actual occurrence of the transaction—at a particular time, or in a particular place—but rather the recording of that transaction in a transaction history. It's a bit like a strange, but comprehensive history book that records Napoleon's excursion to Italy in 1800, at the same time as noting the United States Library of Congress founding in 1800, while also mentioning the completion of the literary work Kojiki-den by Motoori Norinaga in Japan in 1800. What's important is that these events are recorded—their east order in the book with respect to each other is not of crucial importance, as long as they appear at roughly the same time.

Separating transactions into different business networks

This seemingly contrived example of transaction history actually provides us with a deep insight into the design of business networks—that one record of all interactions in a network of complex interactions is not a good idea. The example starts to illustrate that it might be better design to associate a business network with a particular concern, rather than trying to combine all history into a single network. In our analogy, it would be better to have different history books for French, United States, and Japanese history and cross-reference them with each other!

This idea has concrete and important consequences for how you approach blockchain networks. It's not just good design, but essential design to separate business networks into those of separate concerns, and then link them together. It will lead to simpler, more comprehensible, more scalable, more extensible, and more resilient systems. You will be able to start small and grow, and be confident that no matter how things evolve you can cope with change. You'll see Hyperledger Fabric explicitly supports the idea of multiple business networks using concepts called networks and channels, and we'll discuss these in more detail later.

Transaction history and asset states

Examining business network history in more detail, we can see that there are two elements to the history of an asset (or participant), namely, its current value, and the sequenced set of transactions that led to this value. We can generate the value of the asset at all points in time if we sequentially apply from an arbitrary point in time all the transactions that affected it. Effectively, we think of transaction history as a set of transaction **events** that occur at different times and places in the business network, thereby determining its state at any given point in time.

We will see these two aspects of business networks explicitly expressed in Hyperledger Fabric via the concepts of a ledger **world state** and a ledger blockchain. The world state holds the latest value of an asset in a business network, whereas the blockchain holds the record of all transactions in the business network. This makes Hyperledger Fabric a little more powerful than other blockchains—like them, it records all the transactions in a blockchain. Additionally, it also calculates the current value of an asset, making it very easy to be confident that you're working with the the most up-to-date state. These most-recent values tend to be the most important because they represent the current state of the world. And, that's what most participants are interested in when it comes to initiating new transactions.

A business network as a history of transactions

In a very real sense, we can consider the business network as being a history of transactions. What do we mean by this? Well, we've seen that business networks are comprised of participants involved in multi-party transactional asset exchange defined by contracts. However, if we re-orient ourselves slightly, we see that the network is a product of its transaction history, which in turn cannot be separated from the assets and participants who initiated the transactions.

All these concepts are part of a whole, which supports and reinforces itself. Participants were just our first step to understanding—an entrance into the world of business networks. By learning more, we realize that transactions are in fact central, while at the same time being meaningless unless they refer to the assets and participants inside the network they both create, change, and describe! It's the transaction history that brings everything together into a coherent whole, and in this sense, it is the business network.

Regulators and business networks

A final word on a special kind of participant that is common to just about every kind of business network—the **regulator**. The nature of most business networks is that there is a participant whose role is to ensure that the transactions obey certain **rules**. For example, in the United States, the **Securities and Exchange Commission** (**SEC**) ensures that the participants performing transactions involving the securities assets do so according to agreed laws and rules, giving investors trust in the stock market. Or, in the United Kingdom, the **Driver and Vehicle Licensing Agency** (**DVLA**) ensures that vehicles are properly insured, taxed, and exchanged according to UK law. Another example is in South Africa, where the **Association for Food Science and Technology** (**SAAFoST**) ensure that transactions involving farming, food distribution, food processing, and food retail comply with appropriate South African law.

Every business network has a regulator of some kind to ensure proper oversight. Simply put, the regulator ensures that everyone plays the game according to the rules of the business network. We can see that a business network in which all the transactions are recorded digitally on a blockchain actually allows the regulator to do their job in a more efficient and timely manner.

Of course, one might ask why we need a regulator if all the transactions are available to the appropriately authorized participants who can prove correct or incorrect behavior? The answer is that regulators have the ability to sanction certain participants in the network—specifically to exclude them from the network, and confiscate their assets or those which they have illegally transacted upon. These sanctions are the most powerful transactions in the network as they provide ultimate power, and must accordingly be used only in extreme circumstances.

Congratulations! Given you've reached this far, you've really understood the fundamental nature of business networks. Even better, there's really only one more concept to cover in our discussion of business networks: events. Let's move on to the final aspect of business networks that you'll find empowering to understand.

Discussing events from the perspective of designing a business network using Composer

We've seen so far that the vocabulary of business networks contains a compact set of inextricably linked concepts—participants, assets, and transactions. Though small in number, these concepts are very expressive—they contain big ideas, with lots of aspects to them, which support and reinforce each other.

It's not that there's something *missing*, but by adding one extra concept, we're going to significantly increase the descriptive and design power of this vocabulary. This final concept is **event**—the last ingredient in the mix! The good news is that you've probably heard the term before, and many of the ideas that it supports are quite obvious. But make no mistake, events are a hugely powerful concept, and worth a little time to master—your investment in this topic will be handsomely rewarded.

A universal concept

We think of an event as denoting the occurrence or happening of a particular fact. For example, *The President arrived in Australia*, or *The stock market closed 100 points up today*, or *The truck arrived at the distribution center* are all examples of events. The fundamental idea seems quite simple—an event is a point in time when something significant happens. An event represents some kind of transition—moving the world from one state to a quite different state. This is the nature of events—history is transformed from a smooth line to a set of joined-up dots—where each dot represents a significant event.

In the domain of business networks, we can see events *everywhere*. Participants initiating transactions are events. Assets undergoing a series of transformations are events. Likewise, assets being exchanged between participants are events. An asset's life cycle is nothing but a series of events! We now see participants joining and leaving the business network as events. Think about transaction history, we see it as a set of events about participants and assets. Goodness, once we open our eyes, events really are everywhere! If we're not careful, were going to get overwhelmed by these little space invaders!

Messages carry event notifications

We think of messages as the carriers of event notifications. In the real world, we are notified of events via sent by text messages, or email, or maybe a newsfeed. We therefore make a distinction between an event and the communication of it. This is a very important distinction to make, because it illustrates that we are coupled to the event via a medium.

Let us now plant the idea—which we will return to later—that although there is a singular event, multiple participants can be notified via separate message notifications. We see that there is a loose coupling between event-producer and event-consumer. It all means events have a slightly intangible quality—their slightly abstract nature makes them hard to pin down except through the messages through which they are perceived.

A word of mild caution might be appropriate now—we can loose focus on what's important if we obsess about events. Firstly, it's obvious that we need to consider only significant events—events that will likely result in some kind of action. Everything other than the event is just noise—we don't need to consider it. And of course, what constitutes significant is going to be domain-, and problem-, specific—a stock market price rise is significant in a financial network, but not an educational network. So for now, let's use events as a tool for when significant things happen in a business network, when we need to understand what prompts participants to act. Let's see how that tool can be used.

An example to illustrate event structure

Take an example of a stock market event. Every time a stock goes up or down in price, we can represent this as an event. For example:

At UTC: 2018-11–05T13:15:30:34.123456+09:00
The stock MZK increased in price by 800 from 13000 JPY

We can see that this is a description of an event where the stock ABC increased by 800 Yen at a very specific time on 5 Nov 2018.

Just like assets and participants, we can see the term event can refer to the type or instance of an event. In our example, we've shown the type and instance information folded into one. The event has a type **Stock Market Tick** with a structure comprising **time**: 2018-11–05T13:15:30:34.123456+09:00, **symbol**: MZK, **currency**: JPY **previous**: 13000, **change**: +800. For each element in the structure, we've shown the particular instance for this event. We can see very clearly from this event what happened in a structured form.

Events and transactions

We can see that events are very closely related to transactions. Indeed, because an event often describes a transaction, it's not uncommon to see the terms used interchangeably. However, events describe a broader class of activity than transactions. Specifically, while events describe a change, transactions capture the recorded elements of the change. Transactions are often the result of an **external** event—one that does not happen as the result of the action of a particular participant or asset. In this case, a resulting transaction uses a subset of information from the external event as input. But, the event itself is not part of the transaction, other than in this limited sense. This requires a little thought—we're really picking apart some subtle, but important, differences.

In what might appear to be a contradiction, transactions can also generate events! Goodness, this appears to be getting complicated! But think for a moment—events simply describe something happening, and sometimes events are **explicitly** created by transactions, rather than happening due to a force outside any transaction. In our stock tick example, a transaction might generate an event to signal that the MZK stock has increased by over 5% in a single tick! This event might be **Rapid Stock Rise** with a structure **symbol**: MZK, **gain**: *6.1%*—it is *explicitly* generated by the transaction. The transaction embodies the part of a business process whereby a high percentage stock change is identified and communicated. The event is, in a very real sense, part of the transaction.

External versus explicit events

We can see, therefore, that events fall into two categories—**external events** and **explicit events**. We don't often think of these two terms as opposites, but they neatly describe the two different types of events in a business network. Our first event type is an **external event**—it is generated externally to the business network. This event will be processed by participants, and as such will likely result in a transaction—don't forget, only think about significant events—ones that will result in an action. With an external event, a significant amount of the event content is captured as transaction input, but nothing else about the event is remembered. If we want so save an external event, we generate an explicit transaction to do so.

Explicit events are different. Because they are generated within a transaction, they are automatically part of the transaction history. When the transaction is committed to the ledger, then these events will be set free into the network—where they will be consumed by any and all participants interested in them. In the case of explicit events, the ledger itself is the event producer.

Events cause participants to act

We can see, therefore, that events are important because they identify the change that causes participants to act! Just like in the real world, when an event happens, people and organizations hear about it, process the information in it, and generate actions because of that processing. We can see that events provide one of the primary motivational stimuli to participants to act—often by initiating new transactions and sometimes by generating new events.

Loosely coupled design

Let's now return to that idea of loose-coupling. Event producers and event consumers do not directly know about each other—they are said to be loosely coupled. For example, when a participant is added to a business network, existing participants do not need to contact the new joiner to introduce themselves. Instead, the existing participants listen for a new participant event if they are interested. Likewise, if a participant joins a network, it doesn't need to reach out to everyone and everything it is interested in, it just listens for events it thinks are significant—events that might cause it to act. We can see that the event producers and event consumers don't explicitly know about each other—they only know about events—and thus communication can wax and wane very easily—it's much more scalable.

We are now seeing that loose-coupling is a major difference between events and transactions. Transactions explicitly bind participants to each other—in a transaction, we name all the counter-parties. In an event, we have absolutely no idea of how, or even if, the producers and the consumers of the event are related. From a design perspective, it means that we can create a very flexible system. Participants can be coupled to each other in an almost infinitely flexible way via events, and this really does mirror the richness we see in the real world.

The utility of events

We now see why we've added events to our definition of a business network. Events allow the business network to be almost infinitely flexible. Revel in this little bit of chaos—it might be in some sense a little less analyzable, and that's OK. The real world isn't analyzable anyway—events provide a highly efficient coordination mechanism between participants so that important change gets agreed and recorded via multi-party transactions.

Congratulations! Remember that definition of a business network?

A business network is a collection of participants and assets than undergo a life cycle described by transactions. Events occur when transactions complete.

We've realized that those couple of sentences are maybe a little more powerful than might first appear—they describe a very rich world indeed. Let's do a worked example to see these ideas at work!

Implementing a business network

We've had a tour through the world of business networks, and we've seen the importance of multi-party transaction processing of assets between participants—it's the very lifeblood of these networks. Indeed, because of the importance of today's business networks, a significant amount of technology is already deployed in their pursuit. If you've worked in IT for a little while, you've probably heard of **Business-to-Business** (**B2B**), and maybe even **Electronic Data Interchange** (**EDI**) [protocols]. These terms describe the idea and technology of how businesses exchange information with each other. You might even have heard of, or have experience with, networking protocols such as AS1, AS2, AS3, and AS4. These define standard mechanisms about how to exchange business data between two organizations. Don't worry if you haven't heard these terms—the key take-away is that business networks exist today in a very really sense, and have lots of technology applied to them.

What does implementing a business network mean? Well, when it comes to the exchange of tangible assets such as cars or equipment or important documents, a blockchain captures representations of the assets, participants, transactions, and events in a business network. But, in the case of intangible assets it's a little different—in some meaningful sense, the increasing de-materialization of assets means that their representation inside a computer system is as real as the asset itself.

The importance of de-materialization

Consider the case of music. One hundred years ago, it would have been recorded on bakelite, and then through a series of technological innovations, it moved to vinyl, Compact Disc, digital mini-disc. Each step was cheaper than the previous, and of higher quality. But, about 25 years ago, something different happened! The first MP3 format was introduced to support high-fidelity audio capture.

This was the de-materialization step, and it was quite different to the other steps. Yes, it was cheaper, and of higher quality, but critically it stopped music having a physical representation. This de-materialization pattern is increasingly common—financial products such as bonds, securities, swaps, mortgages, and such are primarily represented digitally. More and more documents and forms are becoming digitized—from trivial examples such as airplane and train tickets, to more important education certificates, and employment and health records. This move towards digital means that the blockchain has more relevance than we might otherwise assume.

So, when we implement a business network on a blockchain, we are often close to processing the actual assets in a business network. And, it's arguable that even in the case of tangible assets, the information about assets is as important as the asset itself! This seems like hyperbole, but think about it for a moment. Let's say you own a car. The car needs to have petrol, it needs to be taxed, serviced, and insured. It needs an annual test to make sure it is roadworthy. There's a lot of economic activity centered around that car of yours! Which means that the information about the car is very valuable —indeed, over the lifetime of a car, the total running costs will usually be double the cost of the car. So, maybe the information about the car is more valuable than the car!?

Blockchain benefits for B2B and EDI

A blockchain can provide a simpler, more comprehensive, approach to **business-to-business (B2B)** information processing across multiple organizations. Whereas **Electronic Data Interchange (EDI)** protocols are only concerned with the exchange of information, a blockchain can store data in a ledger, process data with smart contracts, and **communicate and exchange** data via consensus. Blockchain provides a holistic approach to multi-party transaction processing. In a blockchain, all the processing, data, and communications in a business network are accessed from one coherent system. That's in contrast to a traditional B2B approach where data, processing, and exchange are managed by different systems. This separation directly results in significant amounts processing to join-up information across these systems, and a lack of overall transparency. This process is described as **reconciliation**—it ensures that that there are not significant differences between the information at different parts of the business network—it is timely and costly.

We now see the benefits of implementing a business network on a blockchain. Rather than a set of different systems that record assets, and different programs that operate on them, there is a shared view of the asset and its complete transactional life cycle. Blockchain provides an explicit shared understanding of the asset and its life cycle, of participants, transactions, and events. This shared nature of blockchain provides increased trust through increased transparency, and that radically simplifies and accelerates processing. For example, organizations don't have to perform periodic reconciliation with other counterparts to make sure that their systems tally—because everything tallies all the time, in a blockchain.

So, let's say we want to get the benefits of a blockchain for multi-party transaction processing—how do we do this? That's what we're going to be concerned with in the remainder of this chapter—the basic architectural approach, but mostly design tools, that you can use to implement a blockchain technology platform for a business network.

Participants that interact with the blockchain

Firstly, which participants interact with the blockchain? The first thing to say is that the primary beneficiaries of a blockchain in a business network are the participants that hold the most data, and typically that is organizations. It's not to say that individuals cannot host an instance of the blockchain ledger, but its more likely that they will be interacting with a organization that manages part of the blockchain. Indeed, they may not even know that they are consuming a blockchain. Within an organization, although it is individuals using applications that will be interacting with the blockchain, critically, they will be doing so on behalf of the organization—they are the agents of the organization.

Likewise, when it comes to system and device participants, it's unlikely that devices will host a copy of the blockchain ledger. In this way, devices are a little more like individual participants. In contrast, systems in the network can act either on behalf of an organization, or in some cases, actually represent the organization. What does this mean, that a system represents an organization? Well, if we think about a B2B system, then an organization really does appear to the network as its B2B gateway—for all intents and purposes, the gateway is the organization. It this way, we can see that it would make sense for a large system to be very closely allied to an instance of the blockchain ledger.

Accessing the business network with APIs

Organizations, individuals, systems, and devices interact with the blockchain via a set of business network APIs. We'll see in a moment how these APIs are created, but for now it's enough to know that a blockchain network is consumed like a regular IT system. The difference is internal—these APIs are implemented on a blockchain infrastructure, and this ultimately provides a simpler and richer set of APIs than would otherwise be practically possible. However, consumers of blockchain APIs don't need to worry about this—they just issue APIs, and the services they require just happen. The trade-off that's occurring is that the blockchain infrastructure requires more coordination between the organizations in the business network. They have to agree on participants, assets, transactions, and events in advance, and how they evolve. While they can, and should, process, store, and communicate information uniquely when outside the blockchain, they must agree when it's on the blockchain. That's the trade-off: up-front agreement for the promise of radical simplification of business processes in normal running.

At a high level, business network APIs are easy to understand. In a vehicle network, we might have APIs such as `buyVehicle()`, `insureVehicle()`, `transferVehicle()`, `registerVehicle()`, and so on. These APIs are domain-specific—the APIs just mentioned would be very different to those in a commercial paper network—`issuePaper()`, `movePaper()`, and `redeemPaper()`. It's important that APIs are domain-specific because it makes them meaningful to the participants in the network who are using them—such APIs speak the language of the participants.

A 3-tier systems architecture

These APIs work inside a very standard systems architecture. Typically, end users will have a presentation tier running on their web browser or mobile device. This will communicate with an application server tier, using an API that is defined by the application according to the overall solution being developed. This application tier might be running in the cloud or on an on-premise system. It's where all the application logic for the application resides, and it is the consumer of the business network APIs provided by the blockchain. This application may be doing other work, such as accessing a database, or performing analytics—but from our perspective, it's the interaction point with the blockchain network. It consumes the blockchain APIs, not the end-device. Summarized, these APIs operate within a typical 3-tier systems architecture structure of presentation, application, and resource management.

Alternatively, if we have a device or system interacting with the blockchain, then it will not have a presentation tier—it will either use the application API or blockchain APIs directly. In a very real sense, a device is the presentation tier, and the system is the application tier. Again, this is all very standard.

Hyperledger Fabric and Hyperledger Composer

The basic design approach is likewise very straightforward. We use Hyperledger Composer to model the participants, assets, transactions, and events in a particular business network. We then use that model to generate both blockchain—smart contracts and ledgers that implement these elements that are deployed to the blockchain network created using Hyperledger Fabric. We also use the Hyperledger Composer model to generate a set of domain-specific APIs to access the transactions that manipulate them in the Hyperledger Fabric blockchain. As we've seen, these APIs will be used by applications on behalf of individuals, organizations, systems, and devices.

Summary

In this chapter, we've been introduced to business networks and explored them in detail. By understanding the key components of participants, assets, transactions and events, we've seen that in some sense all business networks share the same concerns.

By classifying the different types of participants—individuals, organizations, systems and devices, we are able to properly describe who initiates transactions that capture change in the business network. By understanding the concept of an asset—a thing of value, whether tangible or intangible—we were able to describe and understand the resources that move between participants, and how they express the reason participants interact with each other. Understanding participants and assets allowed us to understand how changes to these are captured in transactions. And finally, concept of an event allowed us to understand when significant change to the network happened, and act upon it.

We spent a few moments discussing how these concepts are consumed using APIs, and in the next chapter, we're going focus much more on this aspect—how to demonstrate all these ideas in a real-world example of a business network. We're going to use Hyperledger Fabric and Hyperledger Composer in particular, so that you can see how to apply these ideas in practice.

A Business Network Example

In this chapter, we are going to bring together all the concepts we've discussed with a sample business network, involving a real-world example. Specifically, we're going to do a detailed walk-through of the Hyperledger Composer letter of credit sample, so that you can understand how participants, assets, transactions, and events are realized in code. We'll show how the business network is used, analyzed, defined, and how that definition is used to generate APIs, test them, and integrate them into a sample application. This is going to be a comprehensive tour that will get you from concepts right into implementation. We're going to use the letter of credit sample because it represents a well-known process that's often discussed in relation to blockchain. Let's discuss the process first, and then see why it's used as the poster child example.

The letter of credit sample

And so we get to our sample. Alice, the owner of QuickFix IT in the Italy, wishes to buy computers from Bob, who runs Conga computers in the USA. Alice is going to apply for a letter or credit from her bank, Dinero Bank, which will be accepted by Bob's bank, Eastwood Banks, as a form of payment.

We're going to try out the whole process using the letter of credit sample application found at `https://github.com/hyperledger/composer-sample-applications`. This repository contains a number of sample applications of business networks–we're going to use the letters of credit sample.

Installing the sample

If you've followed the steps in `Chapter 3`, *Setting the Stage with a Business Scenario,* you should have all of the prerequisites done. Now fork a copy of the sample application's repository (`https://github.com/hyperledger/composer-sample-applications`) to your GitHub account, and then clone it to your local machine using the following commands:

```
cd <your local git directory>
git clone git@github.com:<your github name>/composer-sample-
applications.git
```

Navigate the the appropriate directory and install the letter of credit sample application using the following commands. It will take a few minutes for the application to download and install:

```
cd composer-sample-applications
cd packages/letter-of-credit
./install.sh
```

The install script will also start the application presentation tier in your browser. Let's investigate.

Running the sample

You'll see that your browser has opened up tabs corresponding to the different participants in the network. Click on the different tabs to see the different participants in the network. We're going to inhabit each of these personae as we work through the sample. Let's walk through the process by trying out the application:

Step 1 – preparing to request a letter of credit

We start with preparing for our request:

1. Select the first tab on your browser–you will see the following page:

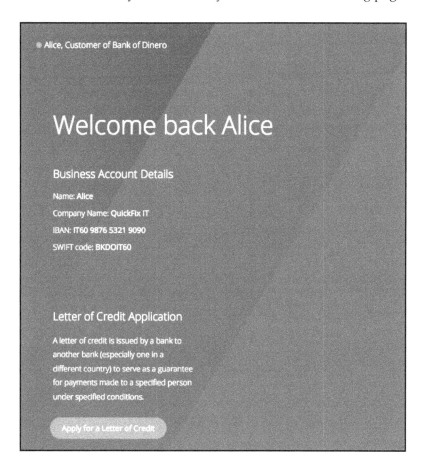

2. You are now Alice! You can see your bank and your account details. You can apply for a letter of credit by clicking on the **Apply** button. Try it!

3. You'll be presented with a page where you can request a letter of credit:

Letter of Credit

Contract Details

● ● ● ● ● ● ● ●

Application Request

NAME
Alice Hamilton

COMPANY NAME
QuickFix IT

IBAN
IT60 9876 5321 9090

SWIFT CODE
BKDOIT60

BANK NAME
Bank of Dinero

Supplier Request

NAME
Bob Appleton

COMPANY NAME
Conga Computers

IBAN
US22 1234 5678 0101

SWIFT CODE
EWBKUS22

BANK NAME
Eastwood Banking

Product Details

TYPE
None

QUANTITY
0

PRICE PER UNIT
€0.00

TOTAL
€0.00

Edit

Terms of Letter of Credit

• The correct quantity of product has been delivered.
• The product was received within 30 days of the placement of the order.
• The product is not damaged and functions as expected.

Edit

Step 2 – requesting a letter of credit

This is the first stage of the process you're going to request a letter of credit to buy computers from Bob! At the top of every screen, you'll see exactly where you are in the process, for example:

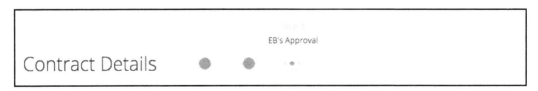

On the left-hand side of the page, you'll see the merchants' details—those of Alice and Bob. Notice the company names and account details:

Let's make an application as Alice. On the right-hand side of the screen, you can enter the details of the trade. Let's pretend that Alice requests 1,250 computers from Bob, at a unit price of 1,500. The application has a total value of 1.875M EUR:

Also note that Alice can chose (with her bank's permission) some of the terms and conditions on the application. These are important terms and conditions of the contract with Bob—unless they are satisfied, neither party will receive goods or payment:

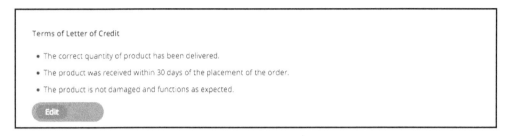

You can edit these if you wish, although the process is not affected by them.

Click on the **Start approval process** button when you're ready to move to the next stage of the process:

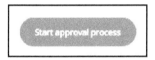

Congratulations, you've just applied for a letter of credit!

Step 3 – importing bank approval

This is next stage of the process. Click on the next tab in your browser. You are now Matias, an employee of Alice's bank, Dinero, who needs to process her application! Here's the page that Matias sees:

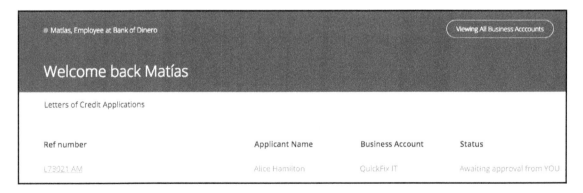

It shows the application from Alice, and that it is waiting for approval from Matias. He is acting on behalf of Dinero Bank, and applies whatever process is required to approve or reject the letter. We might imagine that in a sophisticated process, Matias would only have to approve exceptional letters that could not be automatically approved.

If Matias clicks on the application, he is presented with the details, which are essentially the same as Alice requested:

In our scenario, Matias will approve the letter of credit, and the process will continue! Select the **accept** button and we'll move to the next step:

Step 4 – exporting bank approval

Click on the next tab in your browser. You are now Ella, an employee of Bob's bank, Eastwood, who has been informed that Alice wishes to do business with Bob:

This sample has taken a little creative license with the process–normally, the letter would be presented to Bob by Alice. Bob would then present it Ella. However, we can see that because everyone can view the letter in advance, process innovations are possible. We'll elaborate on this point later.

We can see that Ella authorizes the next stage in the process–and we can see where the letter is in the process flow. When Ella selects the letter, she can see the following details:

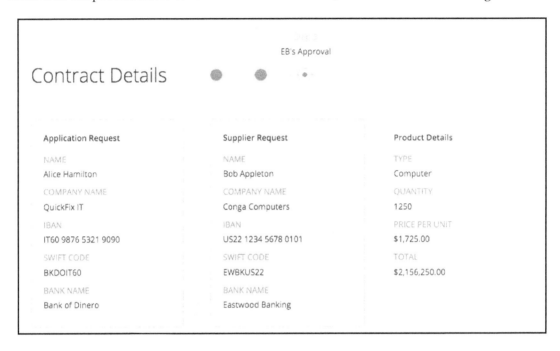

Notice that the currency has been changed. Alice had to make her payment in US dollars because that's what Bob wanted, but Ella and Matias have agreed on an exchange rate for Alice and Bob, so that each can use their own currency. Alice will be charged in euros, and Bob will be paid in dollars.

At the top of the screen, you'll see the following information that relates to the process. We can see where we are in the process; increased transparency is made possible due to the singular nature of a blockchain, even though different organizations each host and approve their stage of the process via their own systems:

Let's move the process forward again. Ella can approve the letter by clicking on the **accept** button:

Step 5 – letter received by exporter

Click on the next tab in your browser. You are now Bob, and you can see the letter of credit from Alice:

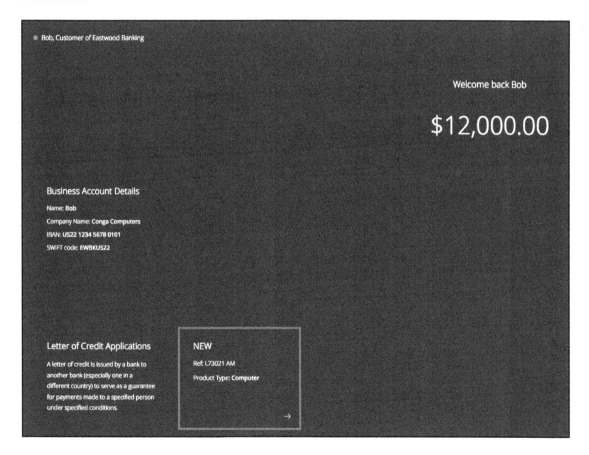

In this process example, Bob can be pretty sure that Alice is trustworthy because his bank has told him in advance. If Bob selects the letter, he will be shown its details:

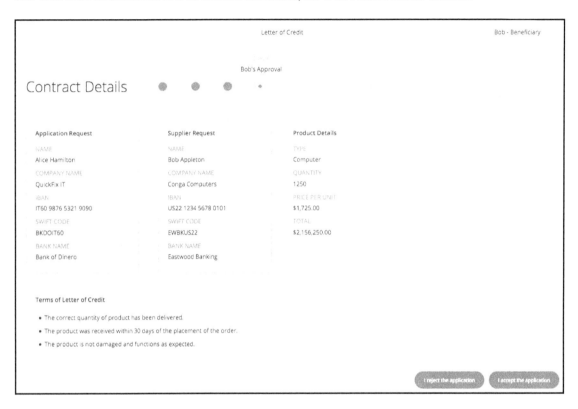

Hopefully, you're starting to understand the process now–so let's not spell out all the details again! Just note how Bob has increased trust because of the transparency available to him. Bob accepts letter as payment (Click **Accept**), and now has to ship the goods to Alice!

Step 6 – shipment

You will be returned to Bob's initial screen, but notice that now there's an option to ship the goods to Alice:

Click on **Ship Order** to indicate that the goods have been shipped to Alice:

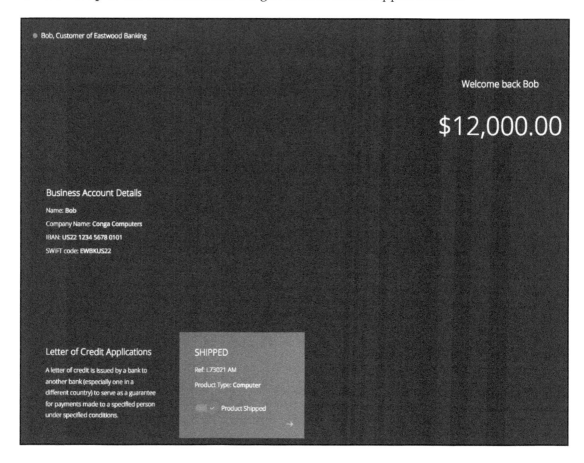

Bob can now see that as far as the letter of credit process is concerned, he is finished–the order has been shipped.

But Bob hasn't yet received payment—Alice must receive the goods first before this can happen. Note the history in the bottom right hand corner of Bob's web page. Bob can see where he is in the overall process, and that some steps need to be completed before he receives payment:

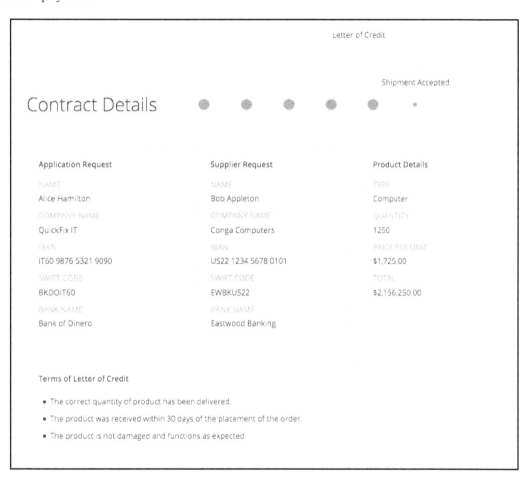

Let's return to Alice to continue with the next step in the process.

Step 7 – goods received

Go back to Alice's tab in your browser:

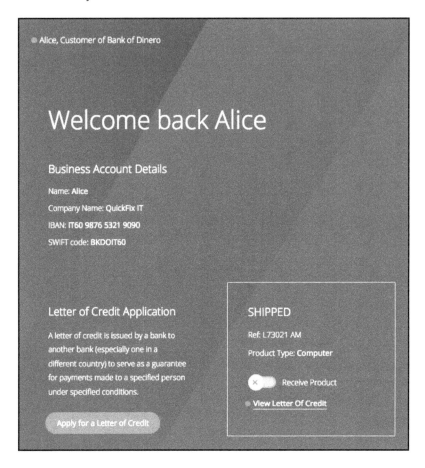

When Alice receives the computers from Bob, she can click on **Receive Order** to indicate this, and review the letter of credit. At this point, both banks are able to release payment. Let's move to Matias's web page to see this process step.

Step 8 – payment

Matias can see that Alice and Bob are happy and that payment can therefore be made. Click through Matias's initial page to see the details of the current letter:

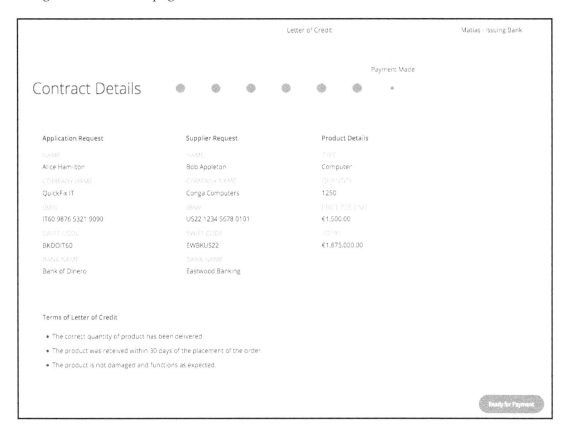

Matias can see that Alice has received the goods, and Matias can click on **Ready for Payment** to move to the next step of the process.

Step 9 – closing the letter

Ella can now close the letter and make the payment to Bob:

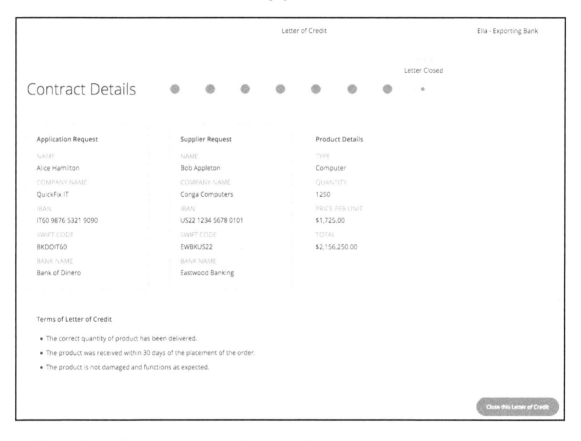

As Ella, click on **Close** to move to the final step of the process.

Step 10 – Bob receives payment

If we move back to Bob's web page and refresh it, we can see that Bob has some good news! Check out his increased balance:

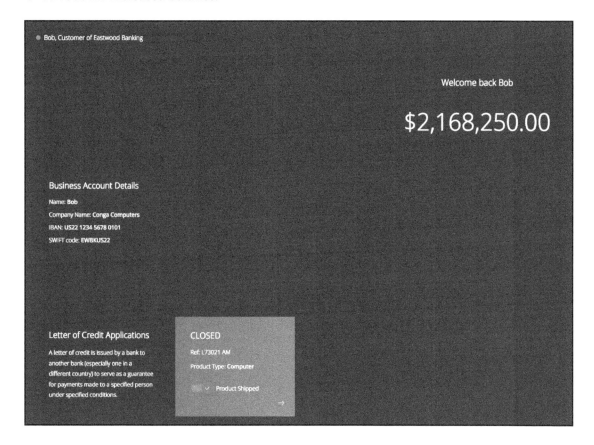

Bob has now received payment for the computers he shipped to Alice. The business process is complete.

Recapping the process

Alice wanted to buy computers from Bob, and used the letter of credit process to facilitate this exchange. She bought goods in dollars, but was charged in Euros. She was able to be confident that the goods met her terms and conditions before she paid for them.

Bob sold computers to Alice, an overseas customer he didn't previously know. The letter of credit process allowed him to be confident that he would receive payment for his goods in his local currency, US dollars, as long as Alice was happy with the goods.

Matias and Ella, representatives of Dinero Bank and Eastwood Bank, respectively, provided a system that allowed Alice and Bob to trust that each would fulfill mutually agreeable conditions in order to receive payment. They were able to charge Alice and Bob a fair price for their services. They were aware in near real-time of every step in the business process.

Let's now see how this process was implemented using Hyperledger Composer and Hyperledger Fabric.

Analyzing the letter of credit process

At the core of the business network is a **business network definition** that contains the formal description of assets, participants, transactions, and events. We're going to examine this for the letter of credit application. By the end of this chapter, you'll be able understand how the network is implemented and accessed by the application. Moreover, you'll have the knowledge to build your own network and applications that consume it.

The Playground

If you move to the next tab in the demo, you'll find the Hyperledger Composer Playground has been opened for you:

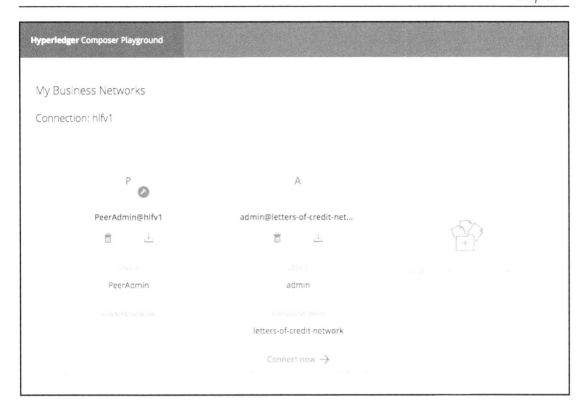

The Playground is a tool that will allow you to investigate the business network. The initial view of Playground contains a **wallet** full of **business network cards**. Just like a real wallet, these cards allow you to connect to different networks. When you use a particular card to connect to a network, you act as a different participant. This is useful for testing the network. Let's connect to the network as an administrator, and see what's in it! (We'll create our own network card later.)

Viewing the business network

On the business network card marked `admin@letters-credit-network`, click **Connect now**. You'll be presented with a web page:

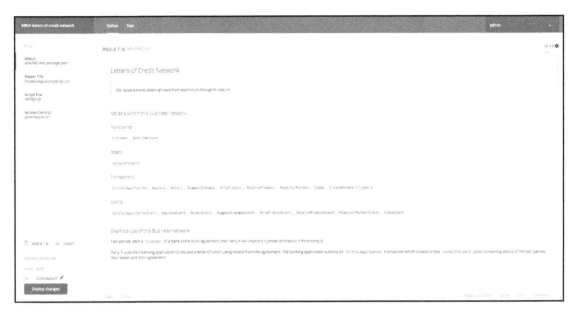

View of business network definition

This is a view of the business network definition. It contains definitions of the participants, assets, transactions, and events we discussed in `Business Networks` – for the letter of credit network. On the left-hand side of the page are a set of files that contain information relating to these concepts for the network we're connected to. We've selected **About**, and on the right-hand side, we can see a description of the business network. Let's investigate this description in a little detail–it's really important to understand.

A description of the business network

The `READ.ME` file contains a natural language description of the network in terms of its assets, participants, transactions, and events.

The participant descriptions

The participants are listed in the business network description:

```
Participants
  Customer, BankEmployee
```

In our example, there are four participant **instances**—Alice and Bob, Matias and Ella. But notice how there are only two participant **types**, namely `Customer` and `Employee`. In our network, Alice and Bob are participants of the `Customer` type, whereas Matias and Ella are participants of the `BankEmployee` type. We can see that these types are named from the perspective of a bank–that's because the network service is being provided by the Dinero and Eastwood banks, and used by Alice and Bob.

We're going to see more details about these participant types and the particular instances in the network soon. But for now, just think about how we've reduced the actors in the network to two very simple representations. Even though we saw a rich behavior in the application, in terms of participants, the network is quite simple. You'll see this in business networks–while there can be many instances of participants, the number of types is usually very limited, and rarely exceeds 10. Of course, rules are made to be broken, but you'll find it helpful to think of networks this way–it makes the analysis much more manageable.

The asset descriptions

If you were surprised that the number of participant types is small in this business network, then you're going to amazed when you see the number of asset types:

```
Assets
  LetterOfCredit
```

Now, this is a sample network–here to teach us about the concepts of business networks, rather than be an exhaustive representation of the world of letters of credit. However, if you think about our example, the whole flow was primarily concerned with just one asset type: the **letter**.

To be fair, we didn't focus on the goods being transferred–the computers, or the payment. In a real system, these would described as assets. Even so, notice how the number of asset **types** would still be relatively small. We can create limitless numbers of instances of letters of credit, computers, and payments, but there will remain only a few types.

We'll look at the details of this asset type a little later.

The transaction descriptions

Let's now move to the transaction types in the business network:

```
Transactions
  InitialApplication, Approve, Reject, SuggestChanges, ShipProduct,
ReceiveProduct, ReadyForPayment, Close, CreateDemoParticipants
```

At last, we can see quite a few types! This is typical–while the numbers of the types of participants and assets is quite limited, assets have rich life cycles. If you think about our application, the letter of credit goes through many **states**, as it interacts with the different participants in the network. These transactions correspond directly to those interactions. (Ignore CreateDemoParticipants, this is a transaction that sets up the demo!)

The transaction names are fairly straightforward to understand–these are closely related to the letter's life cycle. They are the steps you went through using the application, as different participants. Alice made the InitialApplication, and had the option to SuggestChanges to the terms and conditions of the letter. Mattias and Ella could Approve or Reject the letter. Bob invoked ShipProduct to indicate that he had performed his end of the bargain, and Alice used ReceiveProduct to likewise indicate she had received the computers. Finally, Matias indicated that the letter was ReadyForPayment, and Ella issued the Close transaction to end the process and trigger payment to Bob.

There's no reason why the number of transaction types has to be larger than the number of types of assets. One could easily imagine many different asset types that had the same, relatively simple, life cycle. Imagine a retailer's product inventory for example–goods could be sourced, delivered, sold, and returned. This is a relatively simple life cycle, but the number of different types of goods could be quite large. However, we might expect these different goods all to share this life cycle through some commonality of behavior; after all, they are all products. There will be more on this idea of inheritance later.

We'll look at the implementation of these transactions in more detail, but for now, it's most important to understand the conceptual picture of asset flow between the participants in the network, as described by transactions, rather than worrying about the exact logic behind these transactional changes.

The event descriptions

Finally, let's look at the list of events in the business network:

```
Events
  InitialApplicationEvent, ApproveEvent, RejectEvent, SuggestChangesEvent,
ShipProductEvent, ReceiveProductEvent, ReadyForPaymentEvent, CloseEvent
```

We can see that the events have names matching the transaction types, and this is typical. These are **explicit** events that are generated by transactions to indicate when certain events occur in the business network. In our scenario, they are used by the user interfaces to keep the web pages up to date, but of course could be used for much more sophisticated notification processing, for example, `CloseEvent` could be used to trigger payment to Bob.

When you first define a business network, you'll find that the events closely mirror the transactions. But, over time, you'll find that more sophisticated **explicit** events get added, for example, Matias or Ella might want to generate a specific event for a `HighValue` letter, or a `LowRisk` application.

We'll look at the details of these events later.

A model of the business network

Now that we've understood the types in the business network in natural language, let's see how they are defined technically. On the left-hand side of the Playground, select **Model File**.

 In this business network, there is only one model file that defines the participants, assets, transactions, and events. In a bigger application, we'd keep the information from different organizations in their own files, and often in their own namespace. It allows them to be kept separate but brought together when necessary. Let's see how namespaces work.

Namespaces

Our example uses a single namespace:

```
namespace org.acme.loc
```

This namespaces says that *the type definitions in this file have been defined by the Acme organization's letter of credit process.* All this is a short name! Use namespaces–they'll help you clearly separate, and more importantly, **communicate**, your ideas. It is recommended to use a hierarchical name so that it's clear which organizations in the network are defining the relevant types being used by the network.

Enumerations

Next, we see a set of enumerated types:

```
enum LetterStatus {
  o AWAITING_APPROVAL
  o APPROVED
  o SHIPPED
  o RECEIVED
  o READY_FOR_PAYMENT
  o CLOSED
  o REJECTED
}
```

These are the **states** through which the letter is going to transition. When we access a letter, we're going to be able to identify where the business process is using this enumeration. All the names are fairly self explanatory.

Asset definitions

We now come to the first really significant definition–the letter of credit asset:

```
asset LetterOfCredit identified by letterId {
  o String letterId
  --> Customer applicant
  --> Customer beneficiary
  --> Bank issuingBank
  --> Bank exportingBank
  o Rule[] rules
  o ProductDetails productDetails
  o String [] evidence
  --> Person [] approval
  o LetterStatus status
  o String closeReason optional
}
```

Let's spend a little time on this definition, as it's both central to understanding the business network, and Hyperledger Composer in particular.

First, note the **asset** keyword. It indicates that what follows is a data structure that describes an asset. It's just like a type definition in a normal programming language, but with some special characteristics that we'll see later.

We can see that the asset is of the `LetterOfCredit` type. In this example, we only have one asset type–in more sophisticated examples, we'd have more types of assets. For example, we could extend this model to include a `Shipment` asset, and a `Payment` asset:

```
asset Shipment
asset Payment
```

For now, let's skip the **identified by** clause, moving to the first element in the asset definition:

```
o String letterId
```

The letter `o` indicates that this field is a **simple attribute** of the asset. It's a slightly strange way of indicating this, so just think of it as a decoration. This first attribute is the `letterId`. Recall that when a letter is created in the business network, a unique ID is assigned to it. If you recall, in our example, we had `letterId L64516AM` or `L74812PM`. This is indicated by the field having the `String` type–lots of types are available, as we'll see. We can see that this definition allows us to associate a human-readable identifier with the asset. Note that this must be a unique identifier!

Let's now return to the `identified by` clause:

```
identified by letterId
```

Now we can understand that this indicates that the `letterId` attribute is the one by which the asset is uniquely identified. It's a simple but powerful idea that relates closely to the real-world. For example, a car might have a **Vehicle Identification Number** (**VIN**) that uniquely identifies it.

Let's move to the next attribute:

```
--> Customer applicant
```

The first thing we notice is the --> decorator! (Type it as two dashes and a greater than symbol on your keyboard). This is a **reference attribute**–it points to something! In the case of a letter, it points to a different type, Customer, and the name of this element is applicant. See how the reference concept is a little more complex than the simple attribute we saw earlier–that's because it does more work. This field is saying that the letter has an applicant which is of the Customer type, and that you need to look it up via this reference.

In our example, an instance of a letter will point to **Alice**, as she's a customer of Dinero Bank who makes an application. Notice that this a reference attribute refers to a *different* object in the business network. This idea of a reference is very powerful–it allows assets to point to other assets, as well as participants, and the same for participants. With references, we're able to represent the rich structures that we see in the world. It means that we can create assets that can be combined and divided, and the same is possible for participants. In our example, we use the reference to see who has applied for a letter by navigating the reference. Again, we can see that this model is very bank-centric. We'll see later that Customer is in fact a participant, and we'll see how participants, such as Alice, are defined. But for now, let's stay with the asset definition.

As we discussed in Business Networks, our application uses a simple way of modeling ownership–in the real-world, it is often an associative reference. We could most easily model this more sophisticated associative relationship as an OwnershipRecord, which pointed to an asset and pointed to a participant if we wished to do so:

```
asset OwnershipRecord identified by recordId {
    o String recordId
    --> LetterOfCredit letter
    --> Customer letterOwner
```

We can instantly see the power of this approach. We're able to model the relationships that exist in the real-world, making our applications more realistic and therefore easier to use. For our purposes, our current model is perfectly adequate.

Let's move to the next field:

```
--> Customer beneficiary
```

This is a very similar field to the previous one, and in our example, an instance of this element would be **Bob**. There's no need to spend time on this definition. It's important, of course, but it just points the letter at Bob. If you recall, our application always has the two counterparties associated with a letter.

The next two fields have a similar structure, but we're going to spend a little more time discussing them:

```
--> Bank issuingBank
--> Bank exportingBank
```

We can see that these fields are also references to other objects, and we might suspect they are participants, given their names–issuingBank and exportingBank! Examples instances of these types are **Dinero Bank** and **Eastwood Bank**, who act on behalf of Alice and Bob, respectively.

With these first four reference fields, we've modeled the very rich structure of the asset. We've shown that a letter of credit really has four participants involved in it. We've given them symbolic names and types, and shown how they relate to the asset. Moreover, we've done it without writing any code. We're going to have to do that a little later, but for now, notice how we've captured the fundamental nature of a letter of credit in our model. It's worth spending a little time really understanding this point.

We're only going to consider one more field in the asset definition because hopefully you're getting the hang of this! It's an important field:

```
o LetterStatus status
```

Remember those ENUMs that were defined right at the top of the file? Good! This is the field that's going to contain those different values, such as AWAITING_APPROVAL or READY_FOR_PAYMENT. You're often, if not always, going to have fields and enumerations like this in your business network, because they capture in a very simple form where you are in the business process you're modeling. If you're comfortable with workflows or finite state machines, you might like to think of these as **states**–they are a very important idea.

Participant definitions

We now move to the next set of definitions in the model file: the participants!

Let's have a look at the first participant definition:

```
participant Bank identified by bankID {
  o String bankID
  o String name
}
```

This is our first `participant` type definition, a bank. In the sample application, we have two instances of this type: **Dinero Bank** and **Eastwood Bank**.

We can see that participants are `identified by` the `participant` keyword, after which follows the type name–**Bank**. In this case, a participant type is an organization, rather than an individual. As with assets, every participant has a unique ID for identification, and we can see that for banks, it's the `bankID` field:

```
participant Bank identified by bankID
```

For our example, a bank has been modeled very simply–just a `bankID` and a `name`, both of which are strings:

```
String bankID
String name
```

We can see that banks really are much simpler than letters. It's not just that they have fewer fields with simpler types. More importantly, they don't refer to any other participants or assets–that's what makes them simple–a lack of references, a simple structure. Your models will be like this too–some assets and participants will have a relatively simple structure, whereas others will have much more, including references to other assets and participants.

Recall that these types were referred to from the asset definition. If you need to do so, look at the letter type definition again to see the references:

```
--> Bank issuingBank
--> Bank exportingBank
```

Can you see how the **letter asset** and **bank participants** are related now? Great!

Let's now look at the next type of participant. It's a little different to what we've seen before, and for now, ignore the **abstract** keyword:

```
abstract participant Person identified by personId {
  o String personId
  o String name
  o String lastName optional
  --> Bank bank
}
```

It feels like we have four instances of the `Person` type in our application–Alice and Bob, Matias and Ella! Let's have a look at how individual participants are defined:

```
abstract participant Person identified by personId
```

Again, ignore the **abstract** keyword. This statement defines the participant of the `Person` type that is `identified by` a unique field in its type definition. These types are going to be the individual participants in our application, rather than the organizations (that is, banks) that we defined earlier. (We might expect that `Bank` and `Person` will be structurally related–we'll see later!)

If we look at the definition in a little more detail, we can see their structure is a little more interesting than `bank`:

```
o String personId
o String name
o String lastName optional
--> Bank bank
```

We can see that `Person` also has a name and a last name. But notice that the last name is `optional`:

```
o String lastName optional
```

We can see that the `optional` keyword indicates that `lastName` may or not be present. You may recall in our example that Alice and Bob provided surnames (Hamilton and Appleton), but the banks' employees, Matias and Ella, did not. This optionality has been modeled–see how it helps us make our applications more like the real-world.

However, the most important field is the next one:

```
--> Bank bank
```

Why? It reveals **structure**. We can see that a person is related to a bank. In the case of Alice and Bob, it's the bank they have accounts with. In the case of Matias and Bob, it's their employer. We'll come back to whether this is actually the right place to model this relationship, but for the moment, what's important is that we have an individual participant that has a relationship with an organizational participant. You can see that it's not just assets that have complex structure–participants can have them too!

But hold on, it's not quite that simple. We skipped something in the definition, didn't we? See the following:

```
abstract participant Person identified by personId {
```

The `abstract` keyword almost totally destroys everything we've just said about `Person` types! The abstract types are special because they *cannot have instances*. Really? That's seems counter-intuitive, given we can see Alice and Bob, and Matias and Ella.

To understand what's happening, we need to move to the next participant definition:

```
participant Customer extends Person {
    o String companyName
}
```

Look carefully at the first line of this definition:

```
participant Customer extends Person {
```

We can see that we've defined a special type of `Person` called a `Customer`! That's better than before, because Alice and Bob are `Customers`. We don't actually have instances of `Person` participants in our application—we have instances of `Customer` types.

We can see now that the `extends` keyword in the `Customer` type definition is paired with the `abstract` keyword in the `Person` type definition. They are part of this bigger idea of the type specialization and inheritance that we referred to earlier:

```
abstract participant Person
participant Customer extends Person
```

It's the `abstract` keyword that stops us defining instances of `Person`! That's important, because in our example, it's actually correct—there are no instances of the `Person` type, only instances of the `Customer` type.

We can see that a `Customer` has one extra attribute when extending a `Person` type, their company name:

```
    o String companyName
```

In the case of Alice, this will be QuickFix IT, and for Bob, it will be Conga Computers.

Finally, let's look at the last participant type, `BankEmployee`:

```
participant BankEmployee extends Person {
}
```

We don't need to describe this in detail—you can see that, such as `Customer`, `BankEmployee` extends the `Person` type, but unlike it, it does not add any extra attributes. That's OK! In our application, Matias and Ella are instances of this type.

We can now see why the `Person` type is helpful. It's not just that it cannot be instantiated, it's also that it captures what's common between `Customer` and `BankEmployee`. It doesn't just save typing–it reveals an inner structure that improves and reflects our understanding of the business network.

Bearing this in mind, you might like to consider whether it might be slightly more realistic to model as follows:

```
abstract participant Person identified by personId {
    o String personId
    o String name
    o String lastName optional
}

participant Customer extends Person {
    o String companyName
    --> Bank customerBank
}

participant BankEmployee extends Person {
    --> Bank employeeBank
}
```

In real-life scenarios, the actual participant identity will be stored outside the model. This is due to the fact that personal identity and immutable ledgers are not a good combo. Storing Alice's personal information on the ledger means that it will be there forever.

Can you see how this model shows that the nature of the bank relationship is different for `Customer` than it is for `BankEmployee`?

There's an important point here–there is no such thing as a correct model. Models merely serve a purpose–they are either sufficient or insufficient. Both of our models are perfectly sufficient for our purposes because we don't need to make a distinction between `Customers` and `BankEmployees` in terms of their relationship to a bank.

OK, that's enough on participants. Let's move on to the next element in the model definition.

Concept definitions

Look at `ProductDetail` rather than `Rule`, as it's a little easier to understand, initially:

```
concept ProductDetails {
    o String productType
    o Integer quantity
    o Double pricePerUnit
}
```

Concepts are minor, but helpful elements, in the model. They are neither assets nor participants–they merely define the structural elements contained within them.

This preceding concept defines `ProductDetail`. We might argue that this is in fact an asset–for the purposes of our application, it's not something that gets transferred between participants! It's maybe a little clearer when we look at the `Rule` concept, which captures the terms and conditions of the letter of credit:

```
concept Rule {
    o String ruleId
    o String ruleText
}
```

This is something that is less like an asset or a participant, but it is helpful to have as a separate type, as it reveals an important structure.

Transaction definitions

Let's move on! The next section is really important–the transactions! Let's start by looking the first transaction definition:

```
transaction InitialApplication {
    o String letterId
    --> Customer applicant
    --> Customer beneficiary
    o Rule[] rules
    o ProductDetails productDetails
}
```

We can see that like assets and participants, transactions are defined with their own keyword:

```
transaction InitialApplication {
```

The `transaction` keyword identifies that what follows is a type definition for a transaction. It's just like the `asset` or `participant` keywords. Notice that there isn't an `identified by` clause in the transaction definition.

This transaction definition represents the initial application made by Alice for the letter of credit. It's quite obvious really, isn't it? A particular instance of a transaction would be created by the application that Alice uses, and we can see the information contained within it:

```
o String letterId
--> Customer applicant
--> Customer beneficiary
o Rule[] rules
o ProductDetails productDetails
```

If you look back at Alice's web page, then you'll see all this information: the `applicant` Alice, the `beneficiary` Bob, the **terms and conditions** (**rules**), and the **product details**. Notice that the applicant and beneficiary are references to participants, whereas the rules and product details are concepts.

We can see that the transaction has a relatively simple structure but powerfully captures the intention of an `applicant` (for example, Alice) to apply for a letter of credit to do business with a `beneficiary` (for example, Bob).

Event definitions

Look at the next definition in the model file:

```
event InitialApplicationEvent {
    --> LetterOfCredit loc
}
```

It's an event! You'll often see this–an event definition immediately next to a transaction of the same name. That's because this is really an **external** event–it's simply capturing the applicant applying for a letter of credit. It simply points to the letter that generated the event. In the application, it's simply used to keep the UI up-to-date, but in general, all kinds of processing could be triggered by this initial application.

Continue to look through the model file, and you'll see transactions and events defined for every step of the process, and sometimes extra attributes relevant to that transaction step. Spend a little time looking at these–they are interesting!

As we've seen, it's also possible to declare more explicit events, such as a high value letter, or a low-risk application. Imagine our application doing this with the following events:

```
event highValueLetterEvent {
   --> LetterOfCredit loc
}

 event lowRiskLetterEvent {
   --> LetterOfCredit loc
}
```

Which transactions in the model file do you think these would be associated with?

To determine this, we need to think about the process—a high-value letter is known about immediately after application, so it would be associated with the `InitialApplication` transaction. However, until the transaction has been initially processed by the both banks, and both applicant and beneficiary assessed, it's hard to say that the letter is low risk. It means that this event would be more closely associated with the `Approve` transaction.

Moreover, in this higher resolution scenario, we would consider creating separate transactions for importer bank approval and exporter bank approval, `ImportBankApproval` and `ExportBankApproval`.

Examining the live network

Great—now that we've seen how the types of participants, assets, transactions, and events are defined in the business network, let's see how instances of these types are created. The Playground tool has another feature that is very nice—it allows us to look inside the business network, while it's running, to see instances of these types, and select the **Test** tab at the top of the Playground page:

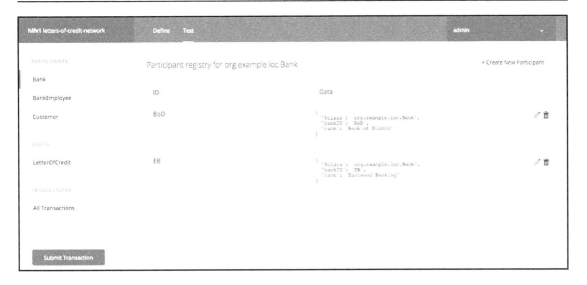

You'll see that the view has changed a little. On the left-hand side, we can see the participants, assets, and transactions that have been defined for this business network: `Bank`, `BankEmployee`, `Customer`, and `LetterOfCredit`, as well as transactions. You can select these, and as you do, you'll see that the right-hand pane changes. Try it!

Select the `LetterOfCredit` asset, and on the right-hand pane, you'll see the following (expand the view with **Show All**):

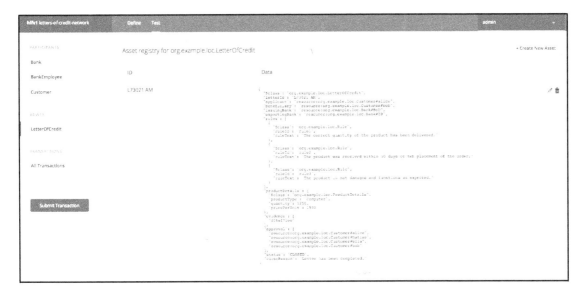

Wow—this is interesting! This is an actual letter of credit from our application. Let's have a look at the letter in detail, and how it maps to the type structure we examined earlier.

Examining a letter of credit instance

We can see the ID, L73021 AM, and the instance information. It's shown as a JSON document, and you can see that the structure mirrors that in the LetterOfCredit definition, but it has real instance data in it.

You can see that every asset and participant contained within the letter has a class ($class), which is formed from the namespace concatenated with the type name. For example:

```
"$class": "org.example.loc.LetterOfCredit"
"$class": "org.example.loc.ProductDetails"
```

Notice also how the information for this letter has been captured:

```
"letterId": "L73021 AM"
"productType": "Computer"
"quantity": "1250"
```

Finally, notice how the letter is in its final state:

```
"status": "CLOSED"
"closeReason": "Letter has been completed."
```

All of this data is incredibly powerful. Why? Because the type and instance information is kept together, just like in a real contract, it can be properly interpreted after it's been written. You can imagine how helpful that is for analytics tools who like to look for patterns in the data!

For reference attributes, we can see that the structure is a little different:

```
"applicant": "resource:org.example.loc.Customer#alice"
"beneficiary": "resource:org.example.loc.Customer#bob"
"issuingBank": "resource:org.example.loc.Bank#BOD"
"exportingBank": "resource:org.example.loc.Bank#ED"
```

We can see that these attributes are references to participants, and if we click on the **Participant** tab, we're able to see them! Click on the **Bank** tab:

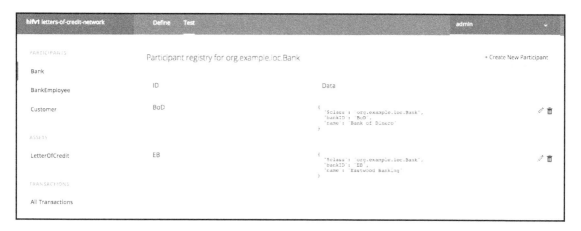

Examining participant instances

You can see the two banks in our network, their type, and instance information! Click on the different participant and asset tabs, and inspect the data to see how the types have become instantiated in the scenario. Spend time on this–it's important that you understand this information, link it to types, and really think about how it relates to the business network. Don't be deceived–the information looks simple–there are some powerful ideas in here that will take a little time to connect. However, we encourage you to do this–it's really worth understanding how everything links together, so that you can do the same!

Examining transaction instances

Now click on the **All Transactions** tab:

You can see the full transaction life cycle of our application run-through. (Your times may be a little different!) If you scroll through the transactions, you can see exactly what happened in our scenario–Alice applied for a letter, Matias approved it, and so on. If you click on **view record**, you'll be able to see the details of an individual transaction.

For example, let's look at the `InitialApplication` made by Alice:

We can see the transaction details (we've edited them slightly to fit the page):

```
"$class": "org.example.loc.InitialApplication",
"letterId": "L73021 AM",
"applicant": "resource:org.example.loc.Customer#alice",
"beneficiary": "resource:org.example.loc.Customer#bob",
"transactionId":
"c79247f7f713006a3b4bc762e262a916fa836d9f59740b5c28d9896de7ccd1bd",
"timestamp": "2018-06-02T06:30:21.544Z"
```

Notice how we can see the exact details of this transaction! Again, incredibly powerful! Spend some time looking at the transaction records in this view.

Submitting a new transaction to the network

There's a lot more we can do with the Playground; we're now going to interact with the business network dynamically!

Ensure that you've selected the `LetterOfCredit` asset type in the **Test** view. Notice the **Submit Transaction** button on the left-hand pane:

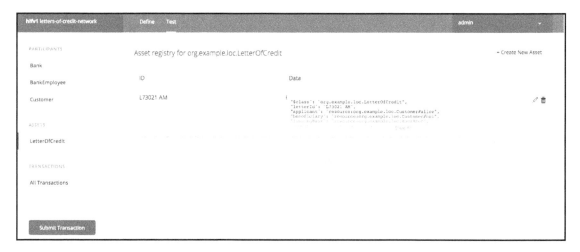

We're going to interact with the business network by submitting a new `LetterOfCredit` application. If you press **Submit Transaction**, you'll be presented with the following entry box:

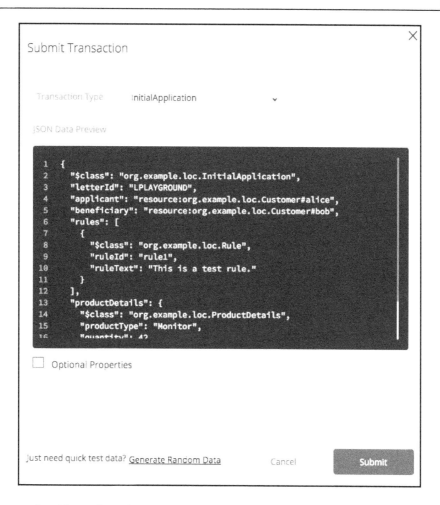

In the **Transaction Type** dropdown, you'll see all the possible transactions listed. Select `InitialApplication` and replace the JSON Data Preview with the following data:

```
{
    "$class": "org.example.loc.InitialApplication",
    "letterId": "LPLAYGROUND",
    "applicant": "resource:org.example.loc.Customer#alice",
    "beneficiary": "resource:org.example.loc.Customer#bob",
    "rules": [
      {
        "$class": "org.example.loc.Rule",
        "ruleId": "rule1",
        "ruleText": "This is a test rule."
      }
```

```
    ],
    "productDetails": {
      "$class": "org.example.loc.ProductDetails",
      "productType": "Monitor",
      "quantity": 42,
      "pricePerUnit": 500
    }
  }
```

Can you see what this transaction describes? Can you see the new `LetterId` between Alice and Bob as `Customer` and `Beneficiary`? Can you see the `ProductDetails`, `Quantity`, and `Price`?

If you press **Submit**, you'll see that you're returned to the main view, and that a new letter has been created:

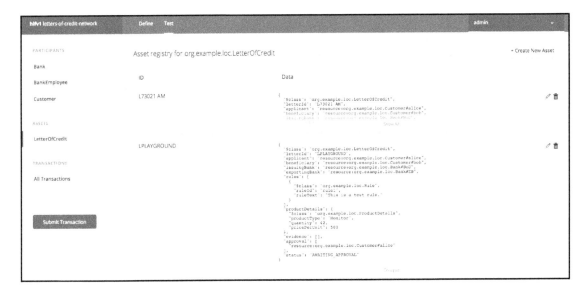

Congratulations, you've just submitted a new application for a letter of credit!
But wait! If we've interacted with the live network, then what happens if we return to our application view. If you got back to Alice's view, you'll notice that she has a new letter:

The Hyperledger Composer Playground has allowed us to interact with the live business network! Moreover, if we select Matias's page, we can see the letter is waiting for approval:

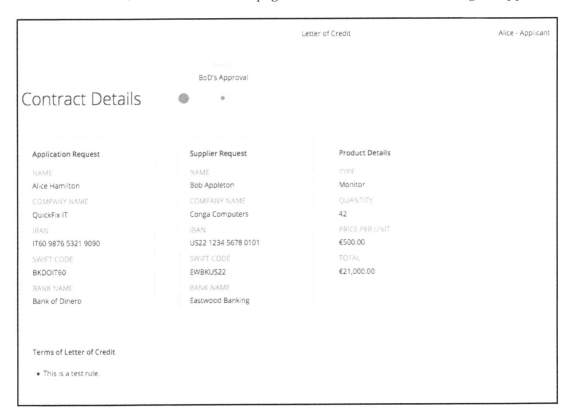

Notice all the attributes are those that you entered in the sample transaction! You can now use the Playground to move this letter through its full life cycle. We recommend that you spend some time doing this–it will help you solidify your knowledge.

Understanding how transactions are implemented

This is all very impressive, but how does it work–where's the logic that implements these transactions that manipulate participants and assets, and creates events? To understand this, we need to look at the transaction programs–the code that runs when transaction are submitted to the network that refer to these assets, participants, and events.

The transaction code is held in a **Script File**, and if you select **Script File** on the **Define** tab, you'll see the following:

This is the code that implements transactions! Today, Hyperledger Composer uses JavaScript to implement these functions, and that's what you're looking at on this page–JavaScript. If you page through the script file, you'll see that there's a function for every transaction defined in the model file.

Let's examine one of the transactions we've been playing with up to this point–the `InitialApplication` transaction. Notice how the function starts:

```
/**
 * Create the LOC asset
 * @param {org.example.loc.InitialApplication} initalAppliation - the
InitialApplication transaction
 * @transaction
 */
 async function initialApplication(application) {
```

The comments and the first line of program code are effectively saying the following function implements the `InitialApplication` transaction, which takes an `org.example.loc.InitialApplication` type, and assigns it to the locally-scoped `application` variable. In a nutshell, it connects program logic to the transaction definition we saw in the model file.

The first important line of code is the following:

```
const letter = factory.newResource(namespace, 'LetterOfCredit',
application.letterId);
```

`factory.newResource()` creates a new local `LetterOfCredit` in the `org.example.loc` namespace, using the identifier supplied by the caller of the function in the input `application.letterId` transaction variable. This statement assigns the result of this function to a local `letter` variable.

It's important to understand that this statement has not created a letter in the business network; `factory.newResource()` merely creates a correctly shaped JavaScript object that can now be manipulated by the following subsequent logic, and after it is properly formed using the input provided by the caller (for example, the application being used by Alice), it can be added to the business network!

Notice how `applicant` and `beneficiary` are assigned:

```
letter.applicant = factory.newRelationship(namespace, 'Customer',
application.applicant.getIdentifier());
letter.beneficiary = factory.newRelationship(namespace, 'Customer',
application.beneficiary.getIdentifier());
```

The transaction makes sure that Alice and Bob's identifiers are placed correctly in the letter. In our network, `application.applicant.getIdentifier()` would resolve to `resource:org.example.loc.Customer#alice` or `resource:org.example.loc.Customer#bob`. The transaction logic systematically constructs the letter of credit using the supplied input and information already stored in the business network.

Next, notice how `issuingBank` and `exportingBank` navigate via the participant to their bank. The program logic is navigating the references in the participant and asset definitions to do this:

```
letter.issuingBank = factory.newRelationship(namespace, 'Bank',
application.applicant.bank.getIdentifier());
letter.exportingBank = factory.newRelationship(namespace, 'Bank',
application.beneficiary.bank.getIdentifier());
```

We can see in these statements how the transaction has to use the structure that was defined in the model. It can add any proprietary business logic to do this, but it must conform to this structure. Examine each line that assigns to `letter` and see whether you can understand what's happening in these terms. It takes a little getting used to, but it's really important to understand this–the transaction is transforming the business network from one state to another using this logic.

Notice the last statement of the letter assignment:

```
letter.status = 'AWAITING_APPROVAL';
```

See how the enum types are being used to set the initial state of the letter.

The next really important statement in the function is the following:

```
await assetRegistry.add(letter);
```

This now adds the letter to the business network! At this point, we have created a new application for a letter of credit in the business network. The letter we created in local storage has been sent to the network, and is now a live asset that points to the participants and assets in the network.

Finally, we emit an event to signify that the transaction has taken place:

```
const applicationEvent = factory.newEvent(namespace,
'InitialApplicationEvent');
applicationEvent.loc = letter;
emit(applicationEvent);
```

As with the letter, we create a local event of the right shape–an `InitialApplicationEvent`, complete its details, and `emit()` it. Examine the different transactions and their logic to become comfortable with the precise processing of each transaction–you'll be richly rewarded for this effort.

Creating business network APIs

For the final part of this chapter, we're going to show you how your application can interact with these transaction functions in business networks using APIs. The sample application and the Playground both interact with the business network using APIs.

Indeed, you can see that from a service consumer's perspective, neither Alice, Bob, Matias, nor Ella were aware of the blockchain–they just interacted with some user interfaces that resulted in these transaction functions (or similar) being executed to manipulate the business network according to the business logic encoded in these transaction processing functions.

It's these user interfaces and applications that use APIs to interact with the business network. If you're new to APIs, then you can read about them here. Although more technically accurate, few people use the term **Web API**–it's just **API**:

Let's have a look at the APIs for our business network! If you select the final tab in the demo, you'll see the following page:

This is the **Hyperledger Composer REST server**. It is a server that's exposing the APIs in our business network. These APIs are described using a standard SWAGGER format.

SWAGGER API definitions

SWAGGER is an open standard for describing APIs–https://swagger.io/specification/ These APIs have been generated by Hyperledger Composer using the same vocabulary as defined in the model to describe the participants, applications, and transactions that were defined for this business network! It means that the SWAGGER APIs have obvious meaning to both the business and technical user.

For every type of participant, asset, and transaction in the business network, there is an API for it.

Querying the network using SWAGGER

Select one of these APIs LetterOfCredit:

Hyperledger Composer REST server

Approve : A transaction named Approve   Show/Hide   List Operations   Expand Operations

Bank : A participant named Bank   Show/Hide   List Operations   Expand Operations

BankEmployee : A participant named BankEmployee   Show/Hide   List Operations   Expand Operations

Close : A transaction named Close   Show/Hide   List Operations   Expand Operations

CreateDemoParticipants : A transaction named CreateDemoParticipants   Show/Hide   List Operations   Expand Operations

Customer : A participant named Customer   Show/Hide   List Operations   Expand Operations

InitialApplication : A transaction named InitialApplication   Show/Hide   List Operations   Expand Operations

LetterOfCredit : An asset named LetterOfCredit   Show/Hide   List Operations   Expand Operations

`GET`	/LetterOfCredit	Find all instances of the model matched by filter from the data source.
`POST`	/LetterOfCredit	Create a new instance of the model and persist it into the data source.
`GET`	/LetterOfCredit/{id}	Find a model instance by {{id}} from the data source.
`HEAD`	/LetterOfCredit/{id}	Check whether a model instance exists in the data source.
`PUT`	/LetterOfCredit/{id}	Replace attributes for a model instance and persist it into the data source.
`DELETE`	/LetterOfCredit/{id}	Delete a model instance by {{id}} from the data source.

ReadyForPayment : A transaction named ReadyForPayment   Show/Hide   List Operations   Expand Operations

ReceiveProduct : A transaction named ReceiveProduct   Show/Hide   List Operations   Expand Operations

Reject : A transaction named Reject   Show/Hide   List Operations   Expand Operations

ShipProduct : A transaction named ShipProduct   Show/Hide   List Operations   Expand Operations

SuggestChanges : A transaction named SuggestChanges   Show/Hide   List Operations   Expand Operations

System : General business network methods   Show/Hide   List Operations   Expand Operations

[BASE URL: /api , API VERSION: 1.0.0]

Notice the GET and POST verbs for this API. Most modern APIs are defined using REST and JSON, and that's what you see here. Practice expanding and collapsing the views to see all the different options.

When you're happy, select InitialApplication GET:

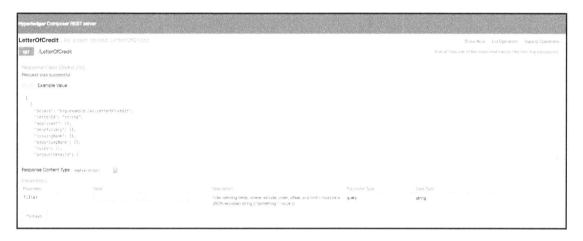

Just like with Playground, you're able to interact with the business network using the same APIs as applications. It's quite a bit more technical as a view, but that's OK–as a programmer, you should feel comfortable with this.

The API we've selected allows a program to query (GET) all the letters in a business network. If you select **Try it out!**, you'll see the following response:

```
Hyperledger Composer REST server

Curl

curl -X GET --header 'Accept: application/json' 'http://localhost:3000/api/LetterOfCredit'

Request URL

http://localhost:3000/api/LetterOfCredit

Response Body

  [
    {
      "$class": "org.example.loc.LetterOfCredit",
      "letterId": "L73021 AM",
      "applicant": "resource:org.example.loc.Customer#alice",
      "beneficiary": "resource:org.example.loc.Customer#bob",
      "issuingBank": "resource:org.example.loc.Bank#BoD",
      "exportingBank": "resource:org.example.loc.Bank#EB",
      "rules": [
        {
          "$class": "org.example.loc.Rule",
          "ruleId": "rule1",
          "ruleText": "The correct quantity of product has been delivered."
        },
        {
          "$class": "org.example.loc.Rule",
          "ruleId": "rule2",
          "ruleText": "The product was received within 30 days of the placement of the order."
        },
        ]

Response Code

  200
```

This details show you the exact API that was issued. It was a GET request on the `http://localhost:3000/api/LetterOfCredit` URL, and the response body shows the data that was returned. You should be able to see that it's very similar in structure to the Playground data, and if you scroll through the response, you'll see the two letters in the network.

Testing the network from the command line

You can also interact with the network from a terminal using the `curl` command, and the syntax is shown for you:

```
curl -X GET --header 'Accept: application/json'
'http://localhost:3000/api/LetterOfCredit'
```

Try this out in a terminal, and you'll see the data on the command line:

```
letters-of-credit — -bash — 119×35
$ curl -X GET --header 'Accept: application/json' 'http://localhost:3000/api/LetterOfCredit'
[{"$class":"org.example.loc.LetterOfCredit","letterId":"L73021 AM","applicant":"resource:org.example.loc.Customer#alice
","beneficiary":"resource:org.example.loc.Customer#bob","issuingBank":"resource:org.example.loc.Bank#BoD","exportingBan
k":"resource:org.example.loc.Bank#EB","rules":[{"$class":"org.example.loc.Rule","ruleId":"rule1","ruleText":"The correc
t quantity of product has been delivered."},{"$class":"org.example.loc.Rule","ruleId":"rule2","ruleText":"The product w
as received within 30 days of the placement of the order."},{"$class":"org.example.loc.Rule","ruleId":"rule3","ruleText
":"The product is not damaged and functions as expected."}],"productDetails":{"$class":"org.example.loc.ProductDetails"
,"productType":"Computer","quantity":1250,"pricePerUnit":1500},"evidence":["dl6af7lee"],"approval":["resource:org.examp
le.loc.Customer#alice","resource:org.example.loc.BankEmployee#matias","resource:org.example.loc.BankEmployee#ella","res
ource:org.example.loc.Customer#bob"],"status":"CLOSED","closeReason":"Letter has been completed."},{"$class":"org.examp
le.loc.LetterOfCredit","letterId":"LPLAYGROUND","applicant":"resource:org.example.loc.Customer#alice","beneficiary":"re
source:org.example.loc.Customer#bob","issuingBank":"resource:org.example.loc.Bank#BoD","exportingBank":"resource:org.ex
ample.loc.Bank#EB","rules":[{"$class":"org.example.loc.Rule","ruleId":"rule1","ruleText":"This is a test rule."}],"prod
uctDetails":{"$class":"org.example.loc.ProductDetails","productType":"Monitor","quantity":42,"pricePerUnit":500},"evide
nce":[],"approval":["resource:org.example.loc.Customer#alice"],"status":"AWAITING_APPROVAL"}]$ ▮
```

It's a lot less beautiful than the Playground or SWAGGER view, but if you're a programmer, you know how powerful this is! Think about how this can help with automated testing, for example.

Creating a new letter using SWAGGER

We can also create a new application for a letter of credit from the SWAGGER view. Select the `InitialApplication` API.

We're going to use the POST verb to create yet another application for Alice:

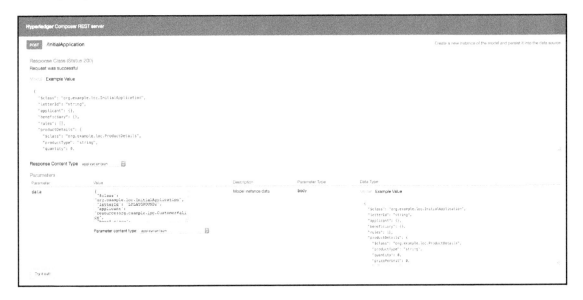

In the value box, paste the following data:

```
{
  "$class": "org.example.loc.InitialApplication",
  "letterId": "LPLAYGROUND2",
  "applicant": "resource:org.example.loc.Customer#alice",
  "beneficiary": "resource:org.example.loc.Customer#bob",
  "rules": [
   {
    "$class": "org.example.loc.Rule",
    "ruleId": "rule1",
    "ruleText": "This is a test rule."
   }
  ],
  "productDetails": {
    "$class": "org.example.loc.ProductDetails",
    "productType": "Mouse Mat",
    "quantity": 40000,
    "pricePerUnit": 5
  }
}
```

Can you see what this application is for? Can you see how Alice wants to apply for a letter to buy 40000 Mouse mats from Bob at 5 dollars each?

If you press **Try it out!**, a new letter will be created! You can now view this new letter using the SWAGGER console, the application, or the Playground. Let's try each:

This is the view using SWAGGER:

```
Hyperledger Composer REST server

  Request URL

    http://localhost:3000/api/InitialApplication

  Response Body


    {
      "$class": "org.example.loc.InitialApplication",
      "letterId": "LPLAYGROUND2",
      "applicant": "resource:org.example.loc.Customer#alice",
      "beneficiary": "resource:org.example.loc.Customer#bob",
      "rules": [
        {
          "$class": "org.example.loc.Rule",
          "ruleId": "rule1",
          "ruleText": "This is a test rule."
        }
      ],
      "productDetails": {
        "$class": "org.example.loc.ProductDetails",
        "productType": "Mouse Mat",
        "quantity": 40000,
        "pricePerUnit": 5
      },
      "transactionId": "ce8d71fade7f620e1b088115e506fe8829c9686a6991a950514084c47373a286"
    }

  Response Code

    200

  Response Headers

    {
      "access-control-allow-credentials": "true",
      "connection": "keep-alive",
      "content-length": "480",
      "content-type": "application/json; charset=utf-8",
      "date": "Sat, 09 Jun 2018 07:45:59 GMT",
      "etag": "W/\"1e0-9NS3iiX4JFBqDeXHSC5AYc1oous\"",
      "vary": "Origin, Accept-Encoding",
      "x-content-type-options": "nosniff",
      "x-download-options": "noopen",
      "x-frame-options": "DENY",
      "x-xss-protection": "1; mode=block"
    }
```

This is the view using the Playground:

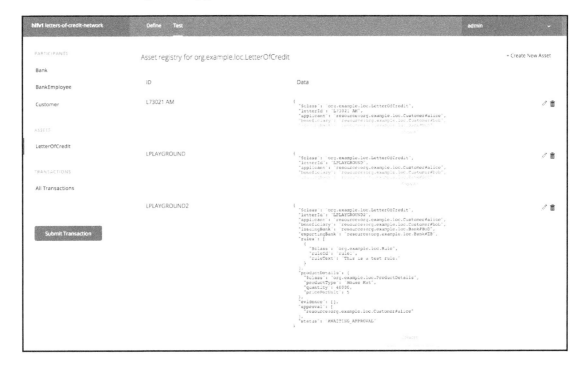

This is the view using the application (Matias's view):

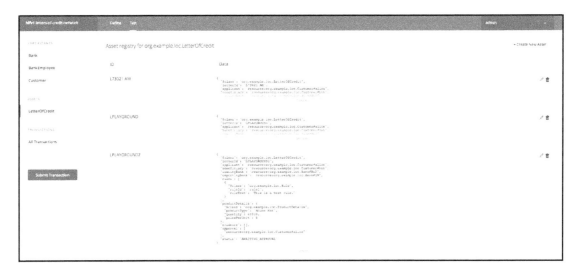

Network cards and wallets

Finally, before we finish this chapter, we're going to add **you** to this business network so that you can submit transactions! To do this, we're going to return to the **business network cards** and **wallet** that first allowed us to connect to the network. Recall that all applications, Playground included, have a wallet that contains business network cards that can be used to connect to different networks. When an application uses a particular card to connect a network, it is identified as a particular participant instance in the network.

1. Let's create a new participant! On the **Test** tab, select **Customer** participants:

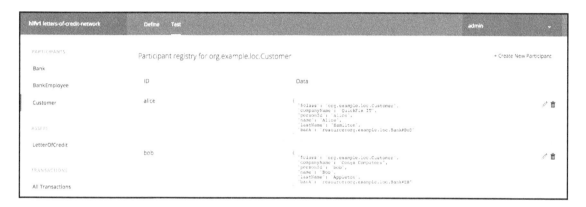

2. You'll see the participant information for Alice and Bob. Click on **Create New Participant**:

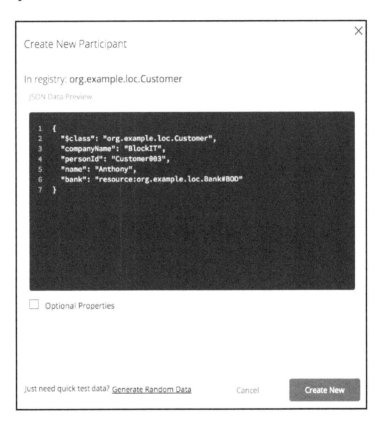

This page will allow you to issue the API to create a new participant. We've entered the following details for a new participant, called Anthony, who works for BlockIT:

```
{
    "$class": "org.example.loc.Customer",
    "companyName": "BlockIT",
    "personId": "Customer003",
    "name": "Anthony",
    "bank": "resource:org.example.loc.Bank#BOD"
}
```

Note his identifier, and a reference to Bank of Dinero. Click **Create New** and notice how the participant registry has been updated:

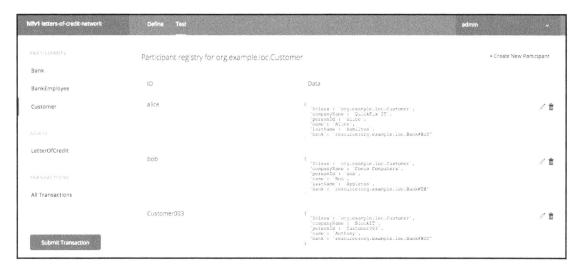

We've created a new participant in the network. (Feel free to use your own details, just ensure that your participant has valid data, specifically references to existing banks.)

Click on the **ID registry** under **admin**. You'll now be presented with a list of **identities** associated with the Playground.

Whereas Alice's and Bob's digital certificates are private to their application, here we can see the identities associated with the current playground user–the administrator of the business network:

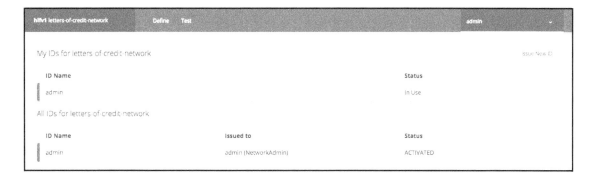

Click **Issue New ID**:

Enter ID003 for the ID Name and associate it with the new participant we created, `org.example.loc.Customer#Customer003`, and click **Create New**:

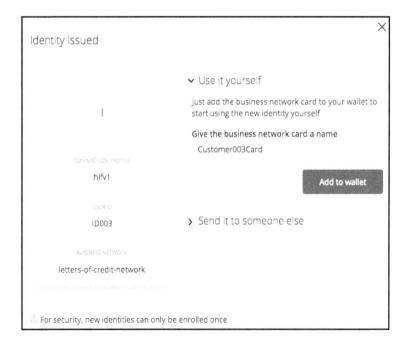

Give the business network card a name, and click **Add to wallet**.
You'll see that the list of IDs has been updated with ID003, associated with Customer003:

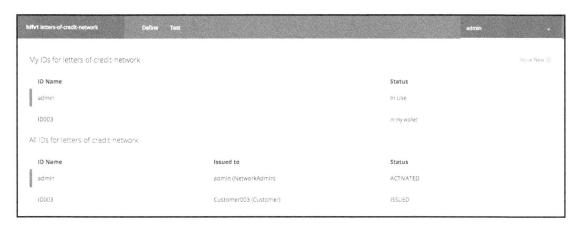

Click on the **My Business Networks** user in the **admin** tab to return to the Composer
Playground initial page:

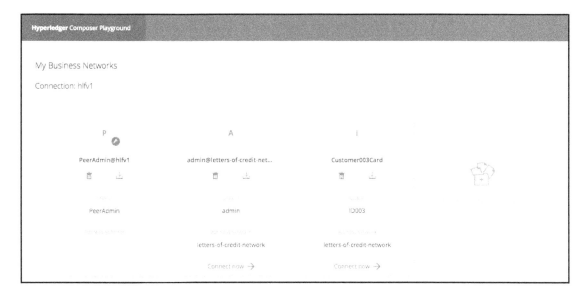

We can see that the Playground wallet now contains a new business network card that
allows you to connect to our network. Click on **Connect now** for Cusotmer003Card.
You're now connected to the network as Customer003, rather than the Admin.

Access-control lists

All applications, including the Composer Playground, use a business network card from their wallet (a file on the local file system) to connect to the network. The card contains the IP address of the network, the participant's name, and their X.509 public key. This information is used by the network to ensure that they can only have **rights** to perform certain operations against resources in the network. For example, only particular bank employees should be able to authorize a letter of credit.

You can see how these rights are defined for a business network by examining the Access Control List (ACL) for the network. Select **AccessControl** on the **Define** tab:

Scroll through the list to see what rights different users have over the different resources in the network. These rules can relate to types or instances, though the former is more common. Spend a little time investigating the ACL rules in this file.

Summary

You've learned how to make a real business network, using Hyperledger technology. You know how to interact with the business network as a user, as a designer, and as an application developer. You know how to define the participants, assets, transactions, and events, and how to implement their creation in the code. You know how to expose these as APIs so that external applications can consume them! You can learn a lot more about Hyperledger Composer and Hyperledger Fabric, consult the product documentation to do that. Armed with that information, and the knowledge in this chapter, you're in a great place to start building your own business network!

Let's now turn our attention to how we manage the development lifecycle in a blockchain network - how we achieve agility in a blockchain network. We'll look at the process and tools that help us set up and manage the day-to-day operations of getting blockchain software developed.

Agility in a Blockchain Network

8

At this point, if all went well, you should have a fully functional decentralized application, with the associated smart contracts running on Hyperledger Fabric. With this knowledge in hand, life is going to be good, right? Well, like anything, solutions evolve over time. It could be a change in regulation, the introduction of a new member in the consortium, or a simple bug in your smart contract—whatever the cause, the solution will grow, and without solid development and operational practices, changes will be slow and your life will be painful.

Considering that maintaining agility in the development processes of an IT organization is already very challenging, how can it be done in a consortium? How can companies of various cultures with different velocities come together to deliver and maintain the solution in a time frame that allows them to maintain the competitive edge that the network provides?

While a lot has already been written on the topic of IT agility and DevOps, this chapter will focus on applying some of these concepts to a blockchain network. We say *some* because our attention will be on those concepts that are specific/different to blockchains. Through automation and the deployment of a **continuous integration and delivery** (**CI and CD**) pipeline, we will discuss the impact that a blockchain network has on the people, the process, and the technology.

In this chapter, we will cover the following topics:

- Defining the promotion process
- Configuring the continuous integration pipeline
- Protecting the source control
- Updating the network
- Implication of the consortium on team structures

Defining the promotion process

As you may already be aware, the promotion process defines the key set of activities and gates that any system modification will need to go through. It typically encompasses the development, packaging, testing (for example, unit-testing, functional verification, and integration testing), versioning, and deployment. Usually, an organization will have a standardized approach that will be documented in order to describe what is expected of the project and its support teams. In the case of a Hyperledger Fabric network, there will be at least two different promotion processes for the following:

- **Smart contracts**: As these components are at the vital to business interaction between the participants of the systems, it is imperative that every participant agrees to the content of the contract
- **Integration layer**: As they sit on the boundary of the network, their promotion process will depend on who owns them (a consortium versus a specific organization)

Optionally, there might also be a process to control changes to the policies of the network; however, it will be closely aligned with the smart contract promotion process.

However, before jumping straight into the configuration of the pipeline, let's spend a bit of time to understand the considerations of these two promotion processes.

Smart contract considerations

As we mentioned, smart contracts are vital to business interaction between the participants of any blockchain network. As they essentially contain the rules and conditions under which a transaction is deemed valid, we need to ensure that every participant and organization agrees to its validity—otherwise, trust will be compromised.

Conditions for promoting a smart contract would include the following:

- **Traceability to an issue**: Is this a bug-fix or a new feature? Along with this element, there might be a need for organizations to approve the issue before it moves to implementation.
- **Successful execution of all tests**: This may be self-evident for some, but most tests should be automated and the results captured.

- **Code review from key parties**: Would you sign a contract without reviewing its terms and condition? Well, the code review serves a similar purpose.
- **Impact assessment**: Is the new version of the smart contract backwards-compatible? Changes that are not backwards-compatible will require additional planning.
- **Sign-off from key parties**: Preceding all the other points, do you have the blessing of all relevant parties? Where will you record this?

The definition of key parties will be something that will be left for the consortium to define. Key parties could be all organizations that currently use that smart contract, or perhaps the term could refer to a subset of technical leads or members of the founder organization.

Preceding the conditions for promoting a smart contract, promotion frequency could also be contentious. Some organizations are used to quarterly cycles while others are used to a weekly deployment. Friction is bound to occur if such a factor is not discussed upfront as this will have a direct impact on the operational expense an organization may need to account for to maintain their participation to the expected level of the consortium. It is also to be noted that smart contracts may be scoped to the entire network or the pair or set of participants. The scoping of these smart contracts and various permutation and combinations represents interesting system modifications needed for promotion.

The point is that the conditions and process of modifying a smart contract should be defined upfront by the consortium to avoid any misunderstanding and frustration. In a sense, this is no different than a traditional contract being modified; the terms for the conditions of a contract modification need to be agreed upfront to avoid conflicts.

Integration layer considerations

As we have seen in `Chapter 5`, *Exposing the Network Assets and Transactions*, there are a few patterns that an organization and a consortium can use to invoke transactions on the network. The selected pattern will help drive the management of the promotion process.

If the service layer of an application directly invokes the fabric SDK, then the owner of the application will have to manage its promotion process. If, instead, the consortium imposes the use of a REST gateway, then you can expect that its deployment will follow a process like the one for a smart contract.

No matter the owner, the abstraction provided by the integration layer should isolate the application from the smart contract and as such, it would be expected that they evolve independently. However, this does not remove the importance of the impact assessment.

Promotion process overview

With these concepts defined, let's turn our attention to the promotion process of our application. As we are using Git as our software configuration management tool, we will leverage its social coding features to support our promotion process:

- We can use Git issues to record new features or bug fixes
- We can use Git branches to isolate proposed modifications
- Git GPG is used to sign every commit and tag
- Pull requests are used to enforce governance

The following diagram summarizes the process we will use to configure our application:

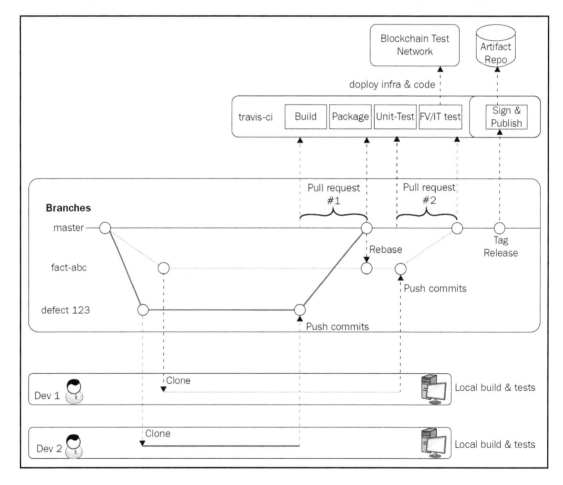

Wondering what a pull request is?
This chapter assumes that the reader is already familiar with many of the Git concepts. If this is not the case, it might be a good idea to pause and explore what Git has to offer.

As a quick summary, a pull request is the process by which people can submit code changes between forks (that is, different repositories) or branches (within a repository). It provides a controlled way to review, comment on, and ultimately approve all code changes.

We will now go through the process in detail and focus on the issue of trust and the provenance of the code. As we've been discussing, since smart contracts are at the heart of blockchain networks, we need to ensure that we closely track their evolution to avoid unfortunate events. From that perspective, we will want to have traceability from the requirements (Git issues) all the way to the deployment.

As such, every code modification should start with the creation of a Git issue. It should properly identify what its scope is—feature request or bug fix—and then describe precisely what work is expected.

We will cover the governance aspect in a few chapters, but for now we can assume that the issue will have been prioritized and work will be assigned according to the consortium's priority.

Once the developer is assigned to work on the issue, his first step will be to create a temporary Git branch to track all code changes related to this Git issue. Code modification should never be done on the master branch as it represents the stable version of the code, and new features and bug fixes should be reviewed before their integration into the stable stream.

It is expected that developers will run all the appropriate tests within their own local environments and only commit back to the branch when code is ready and all unit tests complete successfully.

When the time comes to commit the changes, Git provides a feature that allows you to sign all your work using **GPG**. What is GPG, you ask? It stands for **GNU Privacy Guard**, and it is an open implementation of the `openpgp` standard. It basically provides a tool that helps you sign and encrypt data using your own private key. Git has implemented GPG to allow developers to sign their work. Each commit or tag can be signed using the GPG key of the author, thereby providing nonrepudiation of commits.

Why sign code modification using GPG? Some may say this is an overhead, but consider that the code being modified represents a legal contract and is at the root of the trust of the network. From this point of view, it might be desirable to ensure that the identity of authors is proven beyond a doubt.

Using single-factor authentication for normal commits may not be sufficient to prove their authorship; consider all the reports on the internet of people spoofing the identities of others.

Without signed commits, we can imagine a situation where a rogue developer modifies a smart contract for their own benefit and gets away by claiming they were not the real author of the code change. Such an event would jeopardize the viability of the network and far outweigh the inconvenience of signing commits.

Now that the developer has signed the commits, they are ready to submit a pull request. The pull request has been configured to check the following criteria:

- The temporary branch is up to date with the content from the master
- Every commit is signed
- The code owners have reviewed and accepted the code changes
- The continuous integration pipeline has successfully completed

The pipeline will be automatically triggered when the pull request is created. Once all the conditions are met, then one of the code owners may merge the code with the master branch and commit those changes (while signing the commit, of course).

In a real-life scenario, the consortium would have additional environments (user acceptance environment, staging environment, and so on) where the complete solution stack would be tested.

The final step described in the diagram focuses on tagging the release. The idea here is that a single release may be built from a series of multiple pull requests. When the consortium is ready to release a new version, it should tag it to represent the official version being deployed.

It is on this event that the pipeline will be triggered again, but with a different objective: build, test, sign, and publish the smart contract to an artifact repository. This artifact repository could be one of many popular solutions out there, but in our case, for simplicity's sake, we will attach the smart contract to a Git release.

Some of you may wonder why we are not deploying directly on the network. Again, the intent is to maintain a clear delineation between the centralized build process and the decentralized nature of the network. Each organization can be notified of the new smart contract to deploy, pull the archive, validate against the signature, and deploy it.

In summary, here are a few points on the promotion process:

- Every code change is tied to a change request
- Developers sign their modification using GPG
- Master branch integrity is preserved by the pull request process
- The pipeline builds and tests the code for pull requests
- The pipeline publishes the smart contract to the artifact repository when changes are tagged
- Each organization receives a notification when a new version is available

In the next section, we will start configuring the continuous integration pipeline we have just defined.

Configuring a continuous integration pipeline

Not all languages are created equal, and while we could debate the benefits of strongly typed languages such as Java and Go versus untyped ones such as JavaScript, the fact is that we need to rely on unit tests to ensure that the code is working as intended. This is not a bad thing in itself—every code artifact should be supported by a set of tests with adequate coverage.

What does that have to do with a continuous delivery pipeline, you may be wondering? Well, it's all about the tests and, in the case of JavaScript code, this is very important. While pipeline will need to ensure the following:

- The code is meeting all quality rules
- All unit tests are successful
- All integration tests are successful

Once these steps are successful, then the process will be able to package and publish the result.

So, in the next sections, we will experiment with the deployment and configuration of our pipeline using one of the popular cloud-based continuous integration services: Travis CI. We will cover the following elements:

- Customizing the pipeline process
- Publishing our smart contract against a repository

Once this is all done, we will move on to configure our Git repository to control how changes are validated and integrated. So without further ado, let's get started.

Customizing the pipeline process

You may recall that in our promotion process, we identified two events within the life cycle that were meant to trigger the pipeline:

- Pull requests
- Tag release

Some may wonder why only these events were specifically chosen. If you recall the process, the developers are expected to manually run tests on their local environment, so there is not an absolute need to trigger the pipeline every time someone delivers code to their own branch. However, when initiating the process of delivering the code to the master branch, it is important to validate that the code can be built, deployed, and tested before accepting changes to the master branch. The same goes with tagging a release—this is an indication that a new version has been cut, and so it makes sense to rerun the pipeline one last time to publish the deployment unit (the smart contract package, in our case).

In any case, this is the guideline we have set for our pipeline, but other teams may choose different approaches. The reader should consider this a guideline and not a definitive approach to continuous delivery.

Local build

Before we dive into the configuration of the pipeline, let us quickly look at how the build process is organized. First thing to note is that our solution is now technology rich: Fabric, Composer, `go`, `node.js`. These technologies have quite a few dependencies that needs to be in place for the build to work; Think about the pre-requisites for Fabric and Composer, `go` and its libraries, `NVM`, `NPM`, `Node` and all the packages deployed.

To get a consistent build output between the local and remote environment we need to have a way to reduce and contain the dependencies.

This is where the approach of using `Docker` and `make` comes in:

- Docker provides us an environment that help contains the dependencies and `make` the execution consistent between environments.
- `make` helps us manage the dependencies and because it is built-in to most OS (except Windows unfortunately) it reduces the needs for extra tool deployment and configuration.

This combo allows developer to run the build on their system with minimum effort. No need to deploy additional packages, if the system has Docker and `make` then it is good to go.

 Windows users: While Windows does come with `make`, we would recommend that you look at GNU `Make`.
You can follow the installation instructions from this site: `http://gnuwin32.sourceforge.net/packages/make.htm`

As we mentioned, Docker provides a pre-built environment which exists within the container, thus avoiding the need to deploy the plethora of tools on the local workstation. Here is the composer task:

```
.PHONY: composer
composer:
  echo ">> Building composer package within Docker container"
  docker run --rm -v $(COMPOSER_PATH):/src -v $(DIST_DIR):/dist -w /src
node:8.11 sh -c "$(COMPOSER_BUILD_CMD)"
```

Breaking the docker run command:

- `--rm`: Remove the container at the end of the build
- `-v`: Mount the src and dist directory from the git clone folders
- `-w`: Make the container `/src` directory the working directory
- `node:8:11`: Container image with node 8.11 deployed and configured
- `sh -c "$(COMPOSER_BUILD_CMD)"`: The build command to run

As you can see, with minimal configuration the build is now taking place within the container but using the local git clone files and folders. The nice thing about it is that the container will behave the same whether running locally or in our build pipeline.

Why the .PHONY you ask? Makefile is a great but ancient tool. As such, it originally primarily focused on file dependencies.

If someone ever defined a file called build or test, make would consider that the task was up-to-date and do nothing.

.PHONY tells make to not consider those tags as file.

Feel free to explore the remainder of the tasks of the Makefile. Chaincode will be built using a different image (golang:1.9.6) but leverages the same approach.

From a Makefile tasks perspective the following dependencies are defined:

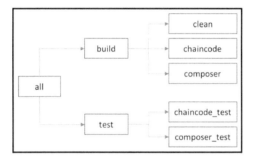

In the next section, we will make use of the make build and make test command to execute our pipeline.

Configuring Travis CI

Getting started with Travis CI is pretty straightforward. You basically need to point your browser to the www.travis-CI.org website, authenticate using your GitHub identity, and authorize Travis to access your GitHub account, and Travis CI will create a profile for you and sync it with your Git account. Once this is done, you will be presented with a list of Git projects. You only need to flick the switch next to our project and Travis CI will start tracking the events in your GitHub repository:

Customizing the pipeline using .travis.yml

While Travis CI is now tracking our Git repository, it is not yet smart enough to know what to do with it when an event occurs. To tell Travis CI what to do, we need to create a special file within the root of the repository. Whenever a Git event happens (for example, a Git pull request), the `.travis.yml` file will be processed and used to orchestrate the pipeline execution.

In the case of our smart contract, we have the following `.travis.yml` in the root of our Git repository:

```
sudo: required
services:
- docker
dist: trusty
cache:
   directories:
   - node_modules
script:
- make build
- make test
```

Since our `Makefile` is making use of Docker container to `make` the build independent of the environment in which it is run, we need to let Travis know about this. Hence, the first three lines of the file provide an indication that the build process will `make` use of Docker. The `dist: trusty` is fixing the Linux distribution to ensure consistency of the system behaviour.

The important lines represent the two major steps of the process:

- **Cache**: This is an optimization of of the build and ensures that the node_modules is not always re-loaded every time the build runs.
- **Script**: This is where the build commands are provided. In this case, the step includes the following:
    - `make build`: Builds the chaincode and the composer BNA
    - `make test`: Unit test execution

The details of the tasks for chaincode was covered in a previous chapter so we won't cover those details again. However we will focus on the Composer build and explore the stanza of the `package.json` file:

```
[...]
"scripts": {
  "prepare": "mkdirp ../dist && composer archive create --sourceType dir --
sourceName . -a ../dist/trade-finance-logistics.bna",
  "pretest": "npm run lint",
  "lint": "eslint .",
  "test": "nyc mocha -t 0 test/*.js && cucumber-js",
  "coverage": "nyc check-coverage",
  "posttest": "npm run coverage"
},
[...]
```

 You will find the `package.json` under the trade-finance-logistics repository in the composer folder.

Lets quickly review each of the default commands generated when the composer project was generated:

- `prepare`: This command will package our project into a BNA file. This script runs before the `install` and will use the Hyperledger composer command-line interface to create the archive. The only modification we have done to this task was to add the sub-directory `..` to the creation of the dist directoring and output of the BNA file.
- `lint`: Runs the `eslint` tool, which is a tool we use to analyse the code while searching patterns. The rules applied by this tool can be adjusted through the `.eslintrc.yml` file.

- test: The mocha unit test framework will run the tests that are located in the project test directory and will be invoked by the nyc tool. The nyc tool is used to measure the coverage of the mocha tests.

You will then need to add these two tasks to the package.json:

- posttest: This task is a trigger that gets activated once the test have run. In this case it will call the coverage task.
- coverage: Runs the nyc tool in reporting mode. This task will assess whether there are sufficient unit tests to cover the code. This task fails the build if the minimums defined in the nyc stanza of the package.json are not met. The following is a sample of this config:

```
"nyc": {
  "lines": 99,
  "statements": 99,
  "functions": 99,
  "branches": 99
},
```

By modifying the package.json we now have "gates" that run the verification of the test coverage and the code quality and fails if the minimum is not met.

Publishing our smart contract package

At this point, in traditional deployments, we could consider automating the deployment of our application to push it to production automatically. However, in the case of a blockchain network, allowing a single process to push production code to multiple organizations and locations could be the Achilles heel of the network.

Instead of trying to push production code to multiple organizations, we will publish the BNA file to a trusted store (in this case, the GitHub release) and let every organization pull the archive.

Fortunately for us, Travis CI has a function used within the deploy step that allows us to automatically attach the smart contract package to a tagged release. The function requires an OAUTH_TOKEN to be configured on our GitHub account, and it needs to be added to the Travis configuration to allow Travis to attach the smart contract to the release.

While that configuration could be done manually, there is a simple command-line interface for Travis that will automatically push the token to Git Hub and add the deploy section to the .travis.yml.

We can install `travis` CLI using the following command:

```
gem install travis
```

Once the CLI is installed, we run the following command:

```
$ travis setup releases
Username: ldesrosi
Password for ldesrosi: ********
File to Upload: ./dist/network.bna
Deploy only from HyperledgerHandsOn/trade-finance-logistics? |yes|
Encrypt API key? |yes| no
```

The tool will ask for a few pieces of information: our GitHub user ID, password, location of the file we want to upload (our BNA), whether we want to only `deploy` from our repository, and if we want to encrypt our API key. On this last question, it is important to say no. We will soon explain why.

The tool will add a section like the following at the end of the `.travis.yml` file:

```
deploy:
  provider: releases
  api_key: 3ce1ab5452e39af3ebb74582e9c57f101df46d60
  file_glob: true
  file: ./dist/*
  on:
    repo: HyperledgerHandsOn/trade-finance-logistics
```

The first thing we will do is copy the API key to our workstation clipboard and go back to the Travis CI site. On the main dashboard, you should see your repository, and on the right-hand side, you will see a button called **More Options**. By clicking it and selecting **Settings,** you will be presented with a panel, split into a few sections.

Scroll down a bit and you will find the **Environment Variables** section. Go through the following steps:

1. In the `name` field, type **OAUTH_TOKEN**
2. In the `value` field, paste the API key you copied in the `.travis.yml` file
3. Click **Save**

The results should be as follows:

Environment Variables

Notice that the values are not escaped when your builds are executed. Special characters (for bash) should be escaped accordingly.

OAUTH_TOKEN   🔒 ••••••••••••••••

                                                                                        OFF   Display value in
                                                                                               build log

You see, while we could have kept the **OAUTH_TOKEN** encrypted in our `.travis.yml` file, it would have been stored in our GitHub repository to be viewed by everyone. By moving the key to the environment, we avoid this.

We can now modify the configuration file to refer to the environment variable we just defined:

```
deploy:
 provider: releases
 api_key: ${OAUTH_TOKEN}
 file_glob: true
 file: ./dist/*
 on:
 repo: HyperledgerHandsOn/trade-finance-logistics
 tags: true
```

The `on:` section provides the ability to restrict the publication process to the `tag` event on your repository.

With the `package.json` and the `.travis.yml` modified, we just need to update our repository by committing and pushing our changes to the master branch. Our pipeline is now fully configured! In a few sections, we will see how network participants can be notified of the new release and retrieve the archive, but for now, let's look at what we need to configure in Git.

Configuring your Git repository

In this section, we will see how to properly protect our Git repository by doing the following:

- Setting the code owners of our smart contract
- Protecting the master branch

- Configuring Git for commit signing and validation
- Testing the process by submitting a pull request

Setting the code owners of our smart contract

We will start by defining the code owners for our smart contract.

Ideally, in a large consortium, the code owners should not be the same group as the one that modifies the code. Remember, these steps are meant to reinforce the trust in the network.

Code owners are defined in a file called CODEOWNERS, which can reside either in the root directory or the .Github directory. GitHub allows us to define different code owners depending on file patterns, so while we could get very creative, we will focus on a few artifacts from our Hyperledger composer project:

- `package.json`: As it controls the build and packaging process, this represents a key file to control.
- `header.txt`: This contains the license. As such, you may want a specific set of people who have oversight on this one (think lawyers).
- `JavaScript files`: This contains the core logic of the smart contracts. Depending on the complexity, this could be further broken down depending on the files, but we will keep it at a high level.
- `*.cto files`: This should be aligned to the owners of the JavaScript.
- `*.acl files`: This should be aligned to the owners of the JavaScript.
- `*.qry files`: This should be aligned to the owners of the JavaScript.
- `*.md files`: This represents the documentation of your smart contract. Depending on the scope, this could be aligned to the same owners as the JavaScript or a different set of people.

Sample content of the CODEOWNERS

The following represents a basic set of rules concerning the CODEOWNERS based on the authors of this book. Feel free to adjust it to your own team. The important point to note here is that the last pattern to match will be the one used to identify the owners who need to perform the review. As such, we must be careful as to the order of the rules:

```
# In this example, documentation and Header.txt are part # of the default
match. Default owners if nothing else
```

```
# matches.
*        @ldesrosi
# Code related should be validated by Rama.
# JavaScripts files could have been separated
# into tests versus logic by using folder's structure
*.qry    @rama
*.acl    @rama
*.cto    @rama
*.js     @rama
# Package.json should be reviewed by everyone
package.json    @ldesrosi @rama @ODOWDAIBM
```

Instead of listing each individual member of the team in the rules, we could have used the concept of GitHub teams to assign the code ownership.

With the CODEOWNERS defined, we can now focus on submitting it to the master branch. Using a command-line prompt, go through the following steps:

1. Navigate to the location of the clone of your repository
2. Create a new directory called .Github
3. Change directory to the newly created directory
4. Create the CODEOWNERS file according to the content defined in the previous section
5. Commit the new file and directory:

```
Git add -A
Git commit -m "Setting initial code ownership."
```

6. Push the commits to the master branch:

```
Git push
```

Protecting the master branch

As we previously discussed, since the master branch represents the stable version of our smart contract, we need to properly control how code changes are introduced.

We will now configure our repository to ensure that only pull requests can alter the content of the master branch. To achieve this, the first step is to open a browser and point it to your Git repository.

Once the web page has loaded, go through the following steps:

1. Looking at the top tabs of the Git pages, you should be able to locate the **Setting** tab
2. Once you click on it, a side menu should appear on the left-hand side of the page
3. Select the **Branches** menu item and you should be able to see the **Protected branches** section
4. Select the master branch from the dropdown

This will open the page that contains all the options we need to set to properly protect the master branch.

The content should be set to the following:

This first set of options, circled in red, ensures that every change to the master branch is done through pull requests and that the approval process can only be done on up-to-date code, and by the code owners only.

We have highlighted this section in red because, while these are very important when working in teams, it should be disabled for our exercise. Essentially, GitHub will not let you review your own pull requests and will prevent you from completing the steps later on.

The second set of options provides the ability to define `checks` to be performed before allowing the code to be merged. We will shortly be adding one of these checks in the next section.

The final option also ensures that even administrators of the repository need to follow the process of pull requests when modifying the code.

Configuring Git for commit signing and validation

At this point, we have a protected our Git branch and identified who should be reviewing code changes. We also know that signing commits is a good way for a developer to prove that they were the author of a code change. However, unless everyone signs their commits, how can you be certain that unsigned commits are valid?

Fortunately, there are some GitHub applications that are emerging to solve that problem. We will use one such application called `probot-gpg`, available at `https://probot.Github.io/apps/gpg/`.

By navigating to this page using your browser, you will be able to click the **Install** button. You will be brought to a page that will allow you to select which repository you want to allow the application to select. In our case, we will select the `yourID/trading-smart-contract/` repository. Click **Install** and the application will be granted access to your repository.

Configuring GPG on your local workstation

To make sure everything is working nicely, we will now set up GPG on our local workstation and test our repository by submitting a pull request. In this section, we will do the following:

- Install GPG and generate our set of `gpg` public and private keys
- Import our `gpg` public key in our GitHub profile
- Submit a pull request to the master branch with a signed commit

The client application for gpg can be found on the www.gnupg.org website. From the website, you may download either the source code or the precompiled binaries. Depending on your operating system and the option chosen (Source code or Binaries), follow the instructions provided on the website and install the client.

In order to configure the system to use gpg keys to sign our Git commits, we will need to do the following:

1. Generate a gpg key
2. Export the public key
3. Import the public key in our Git
4. Configure our Git client to make use of our gpg key

To get started, open a terminal and type the following command:

```
gpg --full-generate-key
```

The gpg tool will now ask a few questions on the characteristics of the key:

- **Kind of key**: Select the default (RSA and RSA)
- **Key size**: Select the maximum size (4,096)
- **Key validity period**: Make sure that the key does not expire

With the characteristics of the key provided, the gpg tool will ask about the identity associated with the key:

- **Real name**
- **Email**
- **Comment**: You may want to use the comment box to indicate the purpose of this identity (signing GitHub commits)

 Make sure that the email matches the entries of your GitHub profile, or else the system will not be able to reconcile the identity to the commit. Remember that case matters for GitHub: yourID@email.com is not the same email as yourID@email.com.

Finally, the tool will ask for a passphrase to protect the private key and ask you to generate entropy by moving the mouse around. After a few seconds, you should see an output such as the following:

```
gpg: key 3C27847E83EA997D marked as ultimately trusted
gpg: directory '/Users/yourID/.gnupg/openpgp-revocs.d' created
```

```
gpg: revocation certificate stored as '/Users/yourID/.gnupg/openpgp-
revocs.d/962F9129F27847E83EA997D.rev'
public and secret key created and signed.
pub    rsa4096 2018-02-03 [SC]
       962F9129FC0B77E83EA997D
uid     Your Name (GitHub Signing Identity) <yourID@email.com>
sub    rsa4096 2018-02-03 [E]
```

With the `gpg` created, we now need to export the key in a format that GitHub will be able to understand. To achieve this, we run the following command:

`gpg --armor --export <<email-you-use-to-generate-the-key>>`

The tool will output the public key directly in the console and should look as follows:

```
-----BEGIN PGP PUBLIC KEY BLOCK-----
mQINBFp1oSYBEACtkVI1fGR5ifhVuYUCruZ03NglnCmrlVp9Nc417qUxgigYcwYZ
[...]
vPF4Gvj2O/1+95LfI3QAH6pYOtU8ghe9a4E=
-----END PGP PUBLIC KEY BLOCK-----
```

Copy the whole key to the clipboard, including the header and, using your browser, go to your GitHub profile and select the **SSH and GPG keys** tab from the left-hand side menu.

You should see two sections—**SSH** and **GPG**. Click the **New GPG Key** button and paste the contents of your clipboard in the entry field that shows up. Finally, click the **Add GPG Key** button, and, if everything goes well, GitHub should show you a similar entry:

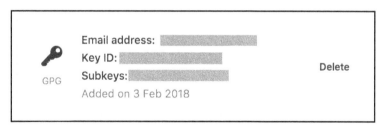

Take note and copy the **Key ID** to your clipboard. We will reuse that key to configure our Git client.

Back in the console, type the following command:

`git config --global user.signingkey 3C27847E83EA997D`

At this point, you should have a fully configured pipeline and protected Git repository. We're now ready to start testing our configuration.

 To facilitate the testing steps in the next section, we have not activated the gpg signing configuration in our Git client. We will activate it in the next section.

Testing the end-to-end process

With all of the configuration done, we will run through a simple scenario that will allow us to test our configuration and ensure that everything is working smoothly.

The scenario will consist of addressing the need to add a new transaction. In order to deliver this new feature, we will perform the following steps/tests:

1. Create a new transaction for our business network. Once we are done coding, we will then try to do the following:
    1. Push a commit to the master branch directly
    2. Submit a pull request with an unsigned commit

2. Add test cases to cover our new transaction:
    1. Amend our commit to be signed
    2. Add our test case and submit an additional signed commit

3. Release the new version of the business network
    1. Merge the pull request on the master branch
    2. Create a new release and check that the BNA is published

Creating a new transaction

For the purpose of our tests, we will keep the new transaction relatively simple: our transaction will merge two assets into one, adding their value in the process.

To declare the new transaction, we will edit the model file and add this new declaration:

```
transaction MergeAssets {
--> Asset mergeFrom
--> Asset mergeTo
}
```

With the definition created, let's add the logic in the `/lib/logic.js` file:

```
/**
 * Sample transaction
 * @param {org.example.biznet.MergeAssets} tx
 * @transaction
 */
function onMergeAssets(tx) {
  var assetRegistry;
  var mergeFromAsset = tx.mergeFrom;
  var mergeToAsset = tx.mergeTo;
  mergeToAsset.value += tx.mergeFrom.value;

  return getAssetRegistry('org.example.biznet.SampleAsset')
    .then(function(ar) {
      assetRegistry = ar;
      return assetRegistry.update(mergeToAsset);
    })
    .then(function() {
      return assetRegistry.remove(mergeFromAsset);
    });
}
```

That's all there is to it! Of course, some may remark that we are not following a good methodology—where are our unit tests for this code? Let's proceed. Don't worry, it's all part of the plan!

Pushing a commit to the master branch directly

With the code modification done, lets try to add the source code to our Git repository. To do so, we will go through the following steps:

1. Navigate to the location of the clone of your repository
2. Commit the new file and directory:

```
git add -A
git commit -m "Testing master branch protection."
```

3. Push the commits to the master branch:

```
git push
```

The `push` command should fail with an error message, such as the following:

```
$ git push
Counting objects: 3, done.
Delta compression using up to 8 threads.
Compressing objects: 100% (2/2), done.
Writing objects: 100% (3/3), 367 bytes | 367.00 KiB/s, done.
Total 3 (delta 0), reused 0 (delta 0)
remote: error: GH006: Protected branch update failed for refs/heads/master.
remote: error: Waiting on code owner review from ldesrosi.
To https://github.com/HyperledgerHandsOn/trade-finance-logistics.git
 ! [remote rejected] master -> master (protected branch hook declined)
error: failed to push some refs to
'https://Github.com/yourID/trading-smart-contract.Git'
```

If you get a similar message, you know you're on the right path. If the `push` command succeeds, you should probably go back to the *Protecting the master branch* section.

Submitting a pull request with an unsigned commit

Continuing from our previous attempt, we know that we need a separate branch to store our work before we can submit a pull request to the master branch. Now that we've committed a change, we need to be careful not to lose our work. The first thing we will do will be to *undo* our commit by running the following command:

```
git reset HEAD^
```

To save our work, we will use a nice function from Git that will temporarily store our work:

```
git stash
```

With our modification saved, we can then create the new branch locally by running the `Git checkout` command. For those who are less familiar with Git, the `-b` option specifies the name of the new branch and the last parameter indicates that the new branch is based on the master branch:

```
git checkout -b Feat-1 origin/master
```

With the new branch created locally, we can restore our modification using the following:

```
git stash pop
```

Finally, we can commit our code and push it to the Feat-1 branch:

```
git add -A
git commit -m "Testing commit signing."
git push
```

With these commands executed, our Feat-1 branch should now contain the additional transaction code. Let's switch to our browser and create the pull request on GitHub:

1. Select the Feat-1 branch and click the **New pull request** button
2. Make sure the branches can merge and click the **Create pull request** button

The result on the next screen will show that the pull request is failing the gpg check and the Travis build. The details for the build should show that the test coverage is not sufficient to meet the threshold we established previously:

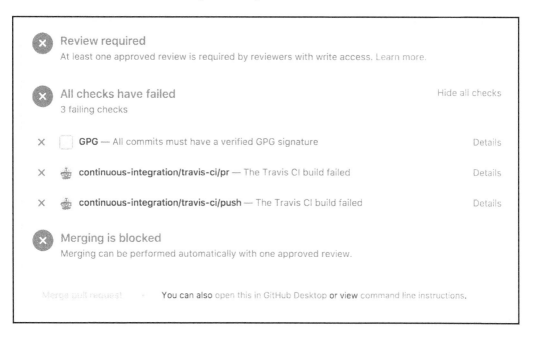

If you get the same results, then you are doing well! If your pull request has no such check failing, make sure that you look at the *Configuring Git for commit signing and validation* section.

We'll now correct our build and add the necessary tests!

Adding test cases

Before adding our test case, we will first enable gpg signing and amend our previous commit with a signature. This should get us on the right path to a healthy pull request.

Submitting a pull request with a signed commit

We can now finalize and activate our gpg signing. In the console, type in the following command:

```
git config --global commit.gpgsign true
```

Now, instead of having to create a separate branch and go through the same steps all over again, we will simply amend our commit and add our signature to it:

```
git commit --amend -S -m "Testing commit signing."
```

You may get the following error when trying to amend your commit:
error: gpg failed to sign the data
fatal: failed to write commit object
If you do, you may need to set the following environment variable:
export GPG_TTY=$(tty)

The command will delegate the signing to GPG, and you should be asked for your gpg passphrase. Once this is completed, we can push our changes to our test branch using the following command:

```
git push origin test --force
```

We need to --force our change as we are only amending our commit.

If you go back to the browser and look at the pull request, you should now have something like the following:

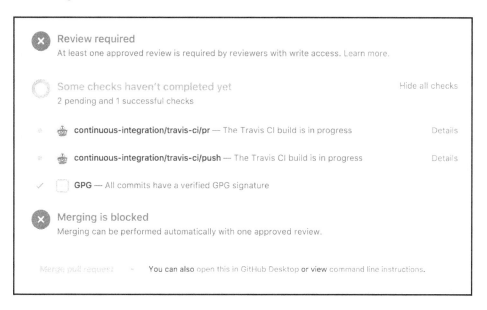

We should have solved one problem—the signing of commits. If you have the same results, you now know everything is configured properly. You can go ahead and focus on correcting the test coverage by adding a test for our new transaction.

Adding the mergeAssets unit test

Let's add the content of this additional test case to the test/logic.js file:

```
describe('MergeAssets()', () => {
  it('should change the value to ' + assetType + ' to 200', () => {
  const factory =
businessNetworkConnection.getBusinessNetwork().getFactory();
  // Create the asset 1
  const asset1 = factory.newResource(namespace, assetType, 'ASSET_001');
  asset1.value = 100;
  // Create the asset 2
  const asset2 = factory.newResource(namespace, assetType, 'ASSET_002');
  asset2.value = 100;

  // Create a transaction to change the asset's value property
  const mergeAssetTx = factory.newTransaction(namespace, 'MergeAssets');
  mergeAssetTx.mergeFrom = factory.newRelationship(namespace, assetType,
```

```
asset1.$identifier);
 mergeAssetTx.mergeTo = factory.newRelationship(namespace, assetType,
asset2.$identifier);

 let assetRegistry;
 return businessNetworkConnection.getAssetRegistry(namespace + '.' +
assetType).then(registry => {
   assetRegistry = registry;
   // Add the asset to the appropriate asset registry
   return assetRegistry.add(asset1);
 }).then(() => {
   return assetRegistry.add(asset2);
 }).then(() => {
   // Submit the transaction
   return businessNetworkConnection.submitTransaction(mergeAssetTx);
 }).then(() => {
  // Get the asset
  return assetRegistry.get(asset2.$identifier);
 }).then(newAsset => {
  // Assert that the asset has the new value property
  newAsset.value.should.equal(200);
 });
});
});
```

We won't cover the details of this test case, as it has been covered in previous chapters. However, if you want to see whether the test has completed successfully, run the following command:

```
npm test
```

Let's commit this new test to Git:

```
git add -A
git commit -S -m "Added new test case"
git push origin Feat-
```

This should automatically trigger our build pipeline, which should complete successfully and leave our pull request in the following state:

This should allow you to merge the pull request. Click the **Merge request** button, confirm the merge, and get ready to create your first release!

If your pull request is not green and asks for a code review, you may have forgotten to uncheck the **Require pull request reviews before merging** option, as mentioned in the *Protecting the master branch* section.

Releasing the new version

We are now ready to release our new business network archive. Go to your web browser and navigate to the **Code** tab of your Git repository. You should see an **x releases** option in the top navigation bar, as shown in the following screenshot:

Click on the releases and then click on the **Draft a new release** button. Fill in the form in a similar way to the following example:

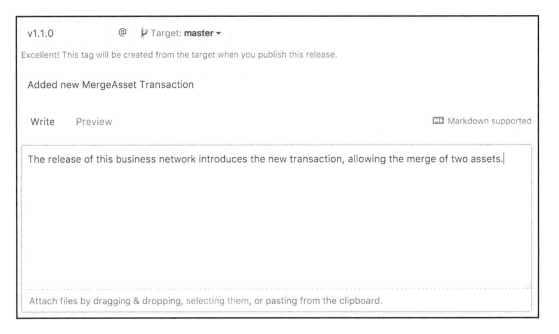

Click on the **Publish release** button at the bottom of the form. This should trigger your build pipeline one final time and, after a few minutes, you should have the BNA file attached to the list of assets associated with your release:

Well done! We've configured a complete pipeline using Travis CI and GitHub, and we've explored how to properly sign and protect our smart contracts.

Our last step will now be to see how the various network participants can automate the retrieval of the **business network archive** (**BNA**) and `deploy` smart contract updates.

Updating the network

With the BNA file published and tagged to a release, we will now look at the process to install/update the business network in our consortium. More specifically, we will look at the following steps:

- Release notification
- Business Network update

Notifying the consortium

There are a few ways and techniques that can be applied to ensure that every organization is notified that a business network is ready to be updated.

The one thing that is for certain is that manual notification is not an option; as the number of smart contracts and participants grows, you need a reliable notification process.

The following diagram depicts a potential process for deploying a business network following the delivery of a new release:

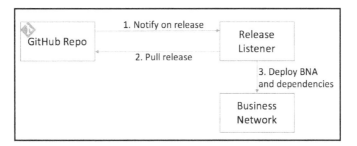

As we've previously discussed, we do not distribute the BNA as this would create the opportunity for someone to tamper with the archive. Instead, the notification only informs every organization of the existence of a new release and lets the consortium retrieve and `deploy` the archive.

This is effectively what the concept of the release listener is doing: listening for notification and then issuing a request to GitHub to retrieve the archive of the new release.

 The release listener is a concept that would need to be implemented by a consortium should they decide to adhere to this approach.
Do not look for the source code—it does not exist (yet).

The release listener could be implemented to listen for events coming from one of two sources:

- **GitHub webhooks**: By providing the URL of the release listener, GitHub webhooks can be configured to send a JSON message on specific events. In our case, it would be the `Release` event.
- **Travis CI notification**: There is also a concept similar to the webhook in Travis CI. There are also other mechanism, such as Atom feed and Slack integration, that may be more suitable to your team.

The choice of the mechanism really depends on your business requirements but, generally, the use of GitHub webhooks would be preferable as they are triggered by the actual event we are interested in: the release of a new version of the smart contract.

 Even if someone was to send a false notification to the release listener, because it only retrieves released binaries from GitHub, it would not be possible for a third party to inject a **bad** archive.

Upgrading the business network

At this point in time, we will assume that we have received a notification and that we are in charge of deploying the new version. Keep in mind that the business network could be deployed into multiple channels. So, while the BNA deployment is not required on every peer, it is required for every channel that expects to run those transactions.

Our deployment will consist of two simple steps:

1. Downloading the new version
2. Updating the business network

Downloading a new version

Given that we have just released the new version and that the pipeline has added the binary to the release, we can simply download the archive using the `curl` command, as follows:

```
curl
https://Github.com/HyperledgerHandsOn/trade-finance-logistics/releases/down
load/v1.1.0/network.bna -L -o network.bna
```

The `-L` option is used to tell `curl` to follow any redirect command. Following the execution of this command, the BNA file should be on your local filesystem.

Updating the business network

Since the BNA content is actually stored in the world state, submitting a business network update can be done from any client that has access to the administrative certificates.

Thus, to update the network, you submit the following command:

```
composer network install -a ./network.bna -c <card-name>
composer network upgrade -n trade-finance-logistics -v 0.0.1 -c <card-name>
```

> In order to test the deployment of an updated BNA, please refer to:
> `https://github.com/HyperledgerHandsOn/trade-finance-logistics/`
> `tree/master/composer.`

Note that the other dependent components, such as the REST gateway and the application, would also need to be considered in a production deployment.

Summary

Hopefully, this chapter will have given you a good overview of the challenges and considerations required to align a consortium around the promotion process.

Continuous delivery pipelines are an essential part of providing the velocity to a consortium, removing manual processes, and ensuring that every organization can review and approve code changes before they go live. We've looked at some of the key events such as the pull request and the tag release.

Over the course of this chapter, you have completed the configuration of a complete continuous integration pipeline, including testing and publication of the business network archive. Furthermore, we have seen how we can protect the production-ready code by protecting the master branch and ensuring that every change is subject to a code review by key participants from organizations. We have also looked at how we can ensure we maintain the provenance of each Git commit using gpg signature. Finally we have reviewed a process to deploy updates in a trusted manner.

One thing is sure: automation is the key to agility—by eliminating repetitive manual tasks and providing a structure to how we modify the code, we enable organizations to be more agile and respond quickly, whether to defects or new requirements. This chapter was, of course, only a small introduction to this approach and its associated concepts; some of these topics could warrant their own books.

Life in a Blockchain Network

9

Your Fabric network should now be set up and running your application connecting different entities through a smart contract and serving users through a web interface. In addition, to help your developers and system administrators maintain code, push updates, and manage network configuration, you should have instituted a process whereby system testing and maintenance can be done with safeguards in place and no interruption to service.

Yet, this will not be the terminal state of your application. Needs and expectations evolve, and this is especially true for an application that involves multiple collaborating entities, all of whom will have differing requirements at different points in time. In addition, it is expected that software itself will continually change and evolve even if the nature and function of an application are kept intact. Finally, any distributed service-oriented application (a description that can be applied to any Hyperledger Fabric application) must be prepared for the nature and numbers of end-users to increase or decrease over time, necessitating changes in both hardware and software resource allocation.

Over the lifetime of your blockchain application, you will therefore see many changes that necessitate updates to code and configuration. The kinds of changes listed previously are not unique to Fabric networks, or even blockchains in general, but the mechanisms we will need to use and the considerations in selecting those mechanisms are quite specific to the platform. These, then, will be the main, though not sole, focus of this chapter. We will first examine the different ways in which your Fabric application may need to be modified, with specific scenarios illustrated through sample code and configurations and guidelines to plan for system upgrades. We will then discuss application and network membership changes and the relevant considerations that apply to industry-scale blockchain applications. In the backend of the chapter, we will delve into system maintenance: monitoring the health of your application and system resources and designing or upgrading your system to ensure high performance.

The following topics will be covered in this chapter:

- Modifying or upgrading a Hyperledger Fabric application
- Fabric blockchain and application life cycle
- Adding the new organization to the network
- Modification in chaincode logic
- Dependency upgrades in chaincode
- Endorsement policy update
- System monitoring and performance
- Profiling containers and applications
- Measuring application performance

Modifying or upgrading a Hyperledger Fabric application

The design of a generic Hyperledger Fabric application presented in `Chapter 5`, *Exposing Network Assets and Transactions*, offers hints about the types of upgrades that may be required during its lifetime. Let us examine the various ways in which the requirements of a Fabric network and its users change over time:

- **Software updates**: Changes and upgrades are an integral part of software maintenance. More frequently, modifications are required to fix bugs, performance inefficiencies, and security flaws (for example, think of the Windows Update Service). Less frequently, though almost equally inevitably, major design changes must be made to software to handle unanticipated challenges. Also, given that most applications depend on other (third-party) software, any upgrades in the latter trigger corresponding changes in the former. Think of Windows Service Packs as an analogy.
In the Hyperledger Fabric world, you as an application developer or system administrator must support both application-level upgrades and platform-level upgrades. The former involves bug fixes and changes in application logic and bug fixes, and the latter involves changes to the underlying Fabric software. Software update processes are well known, and some of the techniques are discussed in `Chapter 5`, *Exposing Network Assets and Transactions*; for testing and reliable failover apply to bug fixing and general maintenance as well.

If you recall the 3-layer architecture of our canonical Fabric application, the upper layers, which consist of the middleware (exercising the Fabric SDK), the web servers, and user interfaces, are typically under the control of a single organization, and they can therefore be updated through processes instituted within that organization. But, as we have seen in *Chapter 8*, *Agility in a Blockchain Network*, the smart contract, or the chaincode, is a special case as it is a piece of software that is collectively agreed upon and developed by all the participating organizations. Therefore, any update to chaincode must also be consensus-driven, and it is not as straightforward as just pushing through an update after testing. We will describe the chaincode upgrade process through examples later in this section.

Finally, upgrades to the Fabric software have the potential to impact functionality and data and therefore must be done with care. We will describe the mechanisms and the pitfalls later in this section.

- **Changing resource requirements**: The resources you allocate to run an application in the beginning of its life cycle, just like the application code, are unlikely to satisfy changing user requirements. It is very likely that your application receives increasing user traffic as time goes by, and no software improvement can make up for limits in hardware. Similarly, if we recall the requirements for RAS (see *Chapter 5*, *Exposing Network Assets and Transactions*), proper functioning of a distributed application requires redundancy, failover, and load balancing across your system resources.

  In Fabric terms, what this translates to is that you may have to add more nodes to your network. You may need more peers to serve transaction endorsement requests, and the network as a whole may need more orderer nodes to handle and balance the load of a currently bottlenecked ordering service (on the flipside, nodes can be removed to save on cost if traffic is too light). Otherwise, you may need extra peer nodes in an organization just for endorsement corroboration or extra orderer nodes for more reliable distributed consensus (though this may come at a performance cost). Regardless of the reason for additions and removals of nodes in your network, you as a Fabric developer or administrator must support upgrades of this nature, and we will see how this can be done later in this section.

- **Changing user memberships**: Besides variations in user traffic, one must be prepared for changes in user memberships for system access over time. In Fabric terms, this implies adding or removing users or clients who are permitted to send requests to the application and view application state. Within an organization, there will always be a need to add or remove users who are permitted to access the blockchain and to elevate or decrease privileges granted to existing users. We have already discussed examples of membership creations and authorizations in *Chapter 5*, *Exposing Network Assets and Transactions*, and later in this section, we will see how channel policies can be updated using runtime configurations.

- **Changing application policies**: Transactions (chaincode invocations) in a Hyperledger Fabric application must satisfy endorsement policies, which are collectively decided on by the participants. It is possible, and even expected, that such policies will change over time for a variety of different reasons, including performance (which we will discuss in the latter part of this chapter.) For example, an endorsement policy for the approval of a member of every organization may be relaxed to a requirement that requires just two organizational endorsements. On the flipside, the policy can be made more stringent to overcome the lack of trust among the blockchain participants. The mechanisms Fabric offer to modify endorsement policies will be discussed through examples later in this section.

- **Changing network configurations**: Finally, there will always be a need to modify the blockchain network itself to meet enhanced expectations. More organizations may want to participate in the application as time goes by, especially if the initial versions of the application prove their worth. Some organizations may want to leave too, for several reasons. Even within a given organization, there may be a need to expand or rebalance the resources devoted to the application in question. Now, even though most distributed applications face these situations requiring enhancements and resource reconfigurations, blockchain applications have special needs because of their unique nature. Recall that a blockchain is a shared ledger that must be validated and accepted by every participating network peer using common, agreed-upon rules. Therefore, the structure and properties of the network themselves must be commonly agreed upon and recorded on the ledger.

- In Hyperledger Fabric terms, an application is built on one or more channels (blockchain instance) whose rules and contents are private to application participants. Therefore, any changes in the network requires configuration changes being applied to a channel. The addition of a new organization with its own peer set or the removal of an organization will require a channel reconfiguration, as would changes in peer or orderer addresses, and the selection of anchor peers within organizations. Other examples include core properties of the channel, such as block size and timeouts; channel access policies for reads, writes, and administration operations; hashing mechanisms; and consensus mode for ordering service. Although a comprehensive coverage of channel configuration use cases is beyond the scope of this chapter, we will see how to push a reconfiguration in a Fabric network through examples later in this section.

To summarize, changes to a Fabric application require not just the usual software maintenance procedures of code and configuration changes, tests and updates, but consensus-driven operations that are specific to blockchains. In the remainder of this section, we will focus on the two main modes of application updates supported by Hyperledger Fabric.

- **Channel configuration updates**: This covers addition and removal of organizations, resource changes (addition, removal, or modifications to peer and orderer nodes), changes in channel properties (policy and block creation rules, hashing, and consensus mechanisms).
- **Smart contract updates**: This covers changes to chaincode and transaction endorsement policy.

Later, we will briefly touch on upgrades to the Fabric platform software.

To implement such upgrades, we will need to augment the application and set of tools that we created from chapters 3 to 7, with suitable mechanisms. Fortunately, the designers of the Fabric platform anticipated the kinds of evolutions we have discussed in this chapter, and the SDK we used to build the initial version of our trade application (see *Chapter 5, Exposing Network Assets and Transactions*) offers the capabilities necessary to build these mechanisms. Before we turn to implementation details, let us revisit the Fabric transaction pipeline and modify it to incorporate updates.

Fabric blockchain and application life cycle

Consider the trade scenario that we have realized as a Fabric application, with the stages illustrated in *Figure 5.3: The stages in the creation and operation of a blockchain application* (see `Chapter 5`, *Exposing Network Assets and Transactions*), when modified to incorporate channel and chaincode updates, is illustrated in *Figure 9.1: The stages in the lifecycle of a blockchain application* (we omit the ledger and event emissions in the diagram for convenience, as they are not required to explain the application stages):

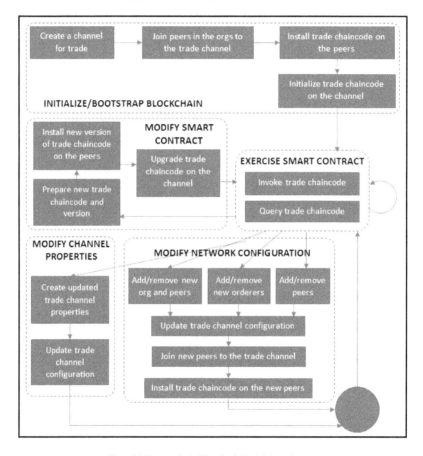

Figure 9.1: The stages in the life cycle of a blockchain application

 This diagram is not meant to be an exhaustive representation of all possible stages of a Fabric application, but rather of the most salient ones.

As we can see, some types of updates require many more operations than others. Any additions of endorsing peer nodes, either within existing organizations or in newly added ones, requires the explicit joining of those peers to the channel and the subsequent installation of the current version of chaincode on those peers. No explicit instantiation is needed on those peers; the gossip protocol among the network peers will eventually sync the latest copy of the shared ledger on the newly added ones. The smart contract modification process though will require an explicit channel-wide upgrade following the installation of the new version of the chaincode on the peers. This upgrade step is equivalent to the original instantiation though it acts on the current state rather than on a blank ledger. In some scenarios, the upgrade of chaincode and endorsement policies may immediately follow a channel reconfiguration for the addition of a new organization; in this case, the installation of the current version of chaincode on the new peers may be skipped and the upgraded chaincode version will be installed directly. We will describe how to augment our trade application to implement such a system upgrade in the next subsection.

Before we proceed, let us understand what the blockchain looks like when the system undergoes different kinds of changes. *Figure 9.2* illustrates the sections of a blockchain with different kinds of blocks added for different application operations:

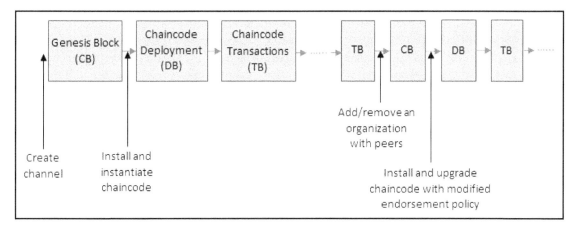

Figure 9.2: A section of a blockchain with configuration blocks, blocks containing deployment transactions, and regular chaincode transactions

As we can see, our blockchain (or in other words, the shared ledger transaction log) begins with a genesis block (the first configuration block on the channel), which contains the initial configuration of the channel. The next step is the deployment and instantiation of the initial version of the chaincode and subsequently regular operation (chaincode invocations) ensues. At some point, a new organization with peers can be added, which results in another configuration block being added to the chain, overriding the previous configuration block. Similarly, a new version of chaincode can be created and upgraded, with the upgrade being recorded in a block. In between these configuration and deployment blocks, regular chaincode transactions can occur, and depending on the configured block size, one or more transactions can be bundled in a block and appended to the chain. Let us now see how to augment our trade application to implement the features we have discussed in this chapter thus far.

Channel configuration updates

As mentioned earlier in this chapter, there are many reasons why a channel configuration may have to be changed. As channel behavior is completely dictated by its configuration, and any update is recorded on the blockchain, hence overriding the earlier configuration, this is a very sensitive operation that must be restricted to privileged users, just like the initial portions of our application creation steps such as channel creation and joining (see *Chapter 5*, *Exposing Network Assets and Transactions*) were. An exhaustive discussion and demonstration of channel configuration changes is beyond the scope of this book, but we will show the mechanism of updates and a way to wrap those mechanisms in our application; this mechanism and process can be applied to any configuration change.

For demonstration, we will use the common situation where a new organization and peers must be added to the application. Consider our trade scenario where thus far, an exporter and its bank have shared an organization whose MSP and peer is maintained by the latter. The importer and its bank belong to a single organization as well, the logic being that banks have more incentive as well as resources to maintain peers and MSPs. But this logic may not hold forever. Let's say our exporter, who started out as a small-scale operator, gains higher profit and a higher reputation for honesty as well as quality over time. Now a large-scale exporter of raw material with huge cash reserves and clout in the market, it has an incentive to join a trade network on blockchain as a peer rather than a dependent of a bank. It also maintains bank accounts with different banks and therefore has the need and potential to participate in multiple blockchains (channels) simultaneously. It would like to continue to participate in the trade channel and wrapping application, but in its own organization, running its own MSP and its own network peer, independent of the bank.

The resulting network that we must create is illustrated in *Figure 9.3: The augmented trade network with an organization, MSP, and peer for an exporter (or exporting entity)*:

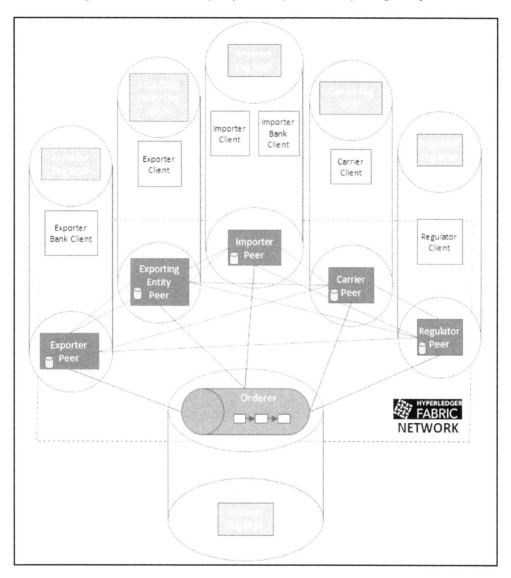

Figure 9.3: The augmented trade network with an organization, MSP, and peer for an exporter (or exporting entity)

We'll call the new organization `ExportingEntityOrg`, its MSP `ExportingEntityOrgMSP`, and the peer exporting entity. This is because the names exporter, `ExporterOrg`, and `ExporterOrgMSP` have already been taken in our network to represent the exporter's bank; new organizations and peers must have unique names.

Prerequisites for adding a new organization to the network

The tools you need to upgrade your network are similar to the ones that were used in `Chapter 3`, *Setting the Stage with a Business Scenario*:

1. Clone the Fabric source code repository:
    1. Run `make docker` to build Docker images for the peers and orderers.
    2. Run `make configtxlator` to generate tools necessary to run the network creation commands described in this section (we will use `configtxlator` when we turn our attention to the middleware code)

2. In addition, we assume that the reader followed the procedures described in `Chapter 3`, *Setting the Stage with a Business Scenario*, and has already created the channel configuration and crypto material files for the earlier 4-organization network.

If you recall, in `Chapter 3`, *Setting the Stage with a Business Scenario*, we created channel artifacts and crypto material for the four organizations, consisting of the genesis block, the initial channel configuration, the anchor peer configuration for each organization, and certificates and signing keys for all network operations involving the peers, clients, and MSPs. The configurations were defined in `configtx.yaml` and `crypto-config.yaml`, respectively in the network folder, and processed using the `configtxgen` and `cryptogen` tools. Clearly, these configurations must be modified to add a new organization, but changing configurations can be messy. The good news is that we can increment our network by creating additional configuration files and keeping the original ones intact. That way, it'll be easy for an administrator to track the evolution of the organization structure and resources. Our incremental configuration files are defined in the `network/add_org/` folder.

Generating network cryptographic material

The `crypto-config.yaml` file contains information only about the new organization, sufficient to generate certificates and signing keys:

```
PeerOrgs:
  # ExportingEntityOrg
  - Name: ExportingEntityOrg
    Domain: exportingentityorg.trade.com
    EnableNodeOUs: true
    Template:
      Count: 1
    Users:
      Count: 1
```

As we can see, the specification is identical to the ones we defined for our initial four organizations, except that the MSP name and organization domain reflect the nature of the exporting entity organization. To generate the crypto material just for this organization, run the `cryptogen` command as in *Chapter 5*, *Exposing Network Assets and Transactions*, but this time using the configuration file defined in the `add_orgs` folder:

```
cryptogen generate --config=./add_org/crypto-config.yaml
```

The output is saved to `crypto-config/peerOrganizations`, where you will see a folder named `exportingentityorg.trade.com` in addition to the existing organization's folders. This folder contains the keys and certificates for our new organization.

Generating channel artifacts

Similarly, the `configtx.yaml` contains only the specification of the exporting entity's organization in the organizations section, as follows:

```
Organizations:
  - &ExportingEntityOrg
    Name: ExportingEntityOrgMSP
    ID: ExportingEntityOrgMSP
    MSPDir: ../crypto-
config/peerOrganizations/exportingentityorg.trade.com/msp
    AnchorPeers:
      - Host: peer0.exportingentityorg.trade.com
        Port: 7051
```

This specification essentially replicates that of every other organization and peer; only the names and paths are modified to identify and set up the new organization (that this assumes a `crypto-config` folder to have already been generated in the current directory). To build the incremental channel configuration, run the following command:

```
FABRIC_CFG_PATH=$PWD/add_org && configtxgen -printOrg ExportingEntityOrgMSP
> ./channel-artifacts/exportingEntityOrg.json
```

Here, we encounter our first difference from the procedure followed in *Chapter 3*, *Setting the Stage with a Business Scenario;* instead of building separate files for configuration blocks, anchor peers, and so on, we just build a JSON spec that contains all the relevant information, including policy specification and certificates for an admin user, the CA root, and the TLS root for the exporting entity's organization, and save it to the `channel-artifacts` folder. Later in this section, we will use this JSON in our channel configuration update procedure.

 To ensure that `configtxgen` looks for the `configtx.yaml` in the `add_org` directory, we must temporarily change the `FABRIC_CFG_PATH` environment variable.

Generating the configuration and network components in one operation

You can also carry out all the preceding operations using the trade.sh script. Just run the following command from within the `network` folder:

```
./trade.sh createneworg
```

 The channel name is implicitly assumed to be `tradechannel`.

This command, in addition to creating cryptographic material and channel configuration, generates a docker-compose configuration for just for the new organization in `add_org/docker-compose-exportingEntityOrg.yaml`. It runs the following services:

- One instance of a Fabric peer for the exporting entity's organization
- One instance of a Fabric CA for the exporting entity's organization

The specification and the dependencies are like those we encountered in `docker-compose-e2e.yaml` in *Chapter 3*, *Setting the Stage with a Business Scenario*, as follows:

```
services:
  exportingentity-ca:
    image: hyperledger/fabric-ca:$IMAGE_TAG
    environment:
      - FABRIC_CA_HOME=/etc/hyperledger/fabric-ca-server
      - FABRIC_CA_SERVER_CA_NAME=ca-exportingentityorg
      - FABRIC_CA_SERVER_TLS_ENABLED=true
      - FABRIC_CA_SERVER_TLS_CERTFILE=/etc/hyperledger/fabric-ca-server-
config/ca.exportingentityorg.trade.com-cert.pem
      - FABRIC_CA_SERVER_TLS_KEYFILE=/etc/hyperledger/fabric-ca-server-
config/fc435ccfdaf5d67251bd850a8620cde6d97a7732f89170167a02970c754e5450_sk
    ports:
      - "11054:7054"
    command: sh -c 'fabric-ca-server start --ca.certfile
/etc/hyperledger/fabric-ca-server-config/ca.exportingentityorg.trade.com-
cert.pem --ca.keyfile /etc/hyperledger/fabric-ca-server-
config/fc435ccfdaf5d67251bd850a8620cde6d97a7732f89170167a02970c754e5450_sk
-b admin:adminpw -d'
    volumes:
      - ../crypto-
config/peerOrganizations/exportingentityorg.trade.com/ca/:/etc/hyperledger/
fabric-ca-server-config
    container_name: ca_peerExportingEntityOrg
    networks:
      - trade

  peer0.exportingentityorg.trade.com:
    container_name: peer0.exportingentityorg.trade.com
    extends:
      file: ../base/peer-base.yaml
      service: peer-base
    environment:
      - CORE_PEER_ID=peer0.exportingentityorg.trade.com
      - CORE_PEER_ADDRESS=peer0.exportingentityorg.trade.com:7051
      - CORE_PEER_GOSSIP_BOOTSTRAP=peer0.exportingentityorg.trade.com:7051
      -
CORE_PEER_GOSSIP_EXTERNALENDPOINT=peer0.exportingentityorg.trade.com:7051
      - CORE_PEER_LOCALMSPID=ExportingEntityOrgMSP
    volumes:
      - /var/run/:/host/var/run/
      - ../crypto-
config/peerOrganizations/exportingentityorg.trade.com/peers/peer0.exporting
entityorg.trade.com/msp:/etc/hyperledger/fabric/msp
      - ../crypto-
config/peerOrganizations/exportingentityorg.trade.com/peers/peer0.exporting
```

```
entityorg.trade.com/tls:/etc/hyperledger/fabric/tls
        - peer0.exportingentityorg.trade.com:/var/hyperledger/production
    ports:
      - 11051:7051
      - 11053:7053
      - 11055:6060
    networks:
      - trade
```

This file is generated using the template YAML `add_org/docker-compose-exportingEntityOrg-template.yaml`, with the CA key filename (denoted by the variable `EXPORTINGENTITY_CA_PRIVATE_KEY`) in both the `FABRIC_CA_SERVER_TLS_KEYFILE` and in the command replaced with the secret key filename in `crypto-config/peerOrganizations/exportingentityorg.trade.com/ca/`, which in our example preceding is `fc435ccfdaf5d67251bd850a8620cde6d97a7732f89170167a02970c754e5450_sk`.

 This key filename will vary with every instance of execution of the `cryptogen` tool.

In addition, note that the certificate filename in the environment variables `exportingentity-ca:FABRIC_CA_SERVER_TLS_CERTFILE` and the paths specified in the volumes section match what was generated using `cryptogen`. The IDs, hostnames, and port values match what was specified in the `congfigtx.yaml` file. Finally, we ensure that the container ports are mapped to unique ports (in the 11,000s range) to avoid conflicts with the ports exposed by the containers of the peers and MSPs of the older organizations.

Launching the network components for the new organization

To start the peer and MSP for our new organization, just run the following command:

```
docker-compose -f add_org/docker-compose-exportingEntityOrg.yaml up
```

You can run this as a background process and redirect the standard output to a log file if you choose. Otherwise, you will see the various containers starting up and logs from each displayed on the console. From a different terminal window, if you run `docker ps -a`, you will see the following two additional containers:

```
CONTAINER ID      IMAGE      COMMAND      CREATED      STATUS      PORTS      NAMES
02343f585218     hyperledger/fabric-ca:latest      "sh -c 'fabric-ca-se..."
16 seconds ago     Up 16 seconds      0.0.0.0:11054->7054/tcp
ca_peerExportingEntityOrg
a439ea7364a8     hyperledger/fabric-peer:latest      "peer node start"      16
seconds ago     Up 16 seconds      0.0.0.0:11055->6060/tcp,
0.0.0.0:11051->7051/tcp, 0.0.0.0:11053->7053/tcp
peer0.exportingentityorg.trade.com
```

You can launch the network using the script file in the repository as follows:

```
./trade.sh startneworg
```

 The channel name is implicitly assumed to be `tradechannel`.

This will start the containers in the background, and you can view the logs in `logs/network-neworg.log`. Now our network has 5 peers, 5 MSPs, and an orderer running in separate containers. We are now ready to begin the process of reconfiguring the channel to accept the new organization.

 To stop the containers associated with the exporting entity's organization, you can just run `./trade.sh stopneworg`.

This will not clear out all the volumes (run docker volume is to check) as the containers of the initial 4-org network are still running. Only after you bring the own entire network, you will be able to clear out the remaining active volumes.)

Updating the channel configuration

Now we will turn our attention to the middleware. In *Chapter 5*, *Exposing Network Assets and Transactions*, when we created `tradechannel`, the blockchain was initialized with the genesis block created using the `configtxgen` tool. The genesis block happens to be the first configuration block of a channel. Subsequent channel configuration changes involve appending new configuration blocks to the channel, each uniquely versioned, and the latest overriding the previous ones. In the upgrade scenario, it's the configuration in the genesis block that will be overridden, as we assume that no other changes have been made since our channel was created and made ready for use in *Chapter 5*, *Exposing Network Assets and Transactions*.

The logic to upgrade channel configurations lies in `upgrade-channel.js` in the `middleware` folder in our code repository, and it is based on the Fabric SDK Node API. The following prerequisites are also required:

- `configtxlator`: This was built from the Fabric source code earlier in this chapter. Please ensure that it lies in your system path.
- `jq`: This is a command-line JSON processor, for creating and parsing JSON objects. On an Ubuntu system, you can install this using `apt-get install jq`. Please ensure that it lies in your system path too.

In the `upgradeChannel` function, there is boilerplate code to create client and channel objects, which the reader should already be familiar with. The channel upgrade procedure requires the collection of signatures over the new configuration from an administrative user of every existing organization (4 in our network) just as in the channel creation procedure. But many additional steps are required before signatures can be generated and collected. First, we will need to fetch the latest configuration block from the orderer. We do this in the code using the following function call:

```
channel.getChannelConfigFromOrderer();
```

This returns a block `configuration_block`, whose config field contains the current channel configuration. The version of this configuration can be extracted from the sequence field of the configuration as follows: `configuration_block.config.sequence`. The full configuration spec is defined in the Fabric source code as a protobuf (`common.Config`), and its examination is left as an exercise to the reader.

In the code, we now create a folder to store temporary files that will be created in the subsequent steps. These files are created using the `configtxlator` tool, which we use in the absence of equivalent API functions in the Fabric SDK Node API:

```
if(!fs.existsSync('./tmp/')) {
  fs.mkdirSync('./tmp');
}
```

Having obtained the configuration, we need to dump it in the protobuf format to a file:

```
fs.writeFileSync('./tmp/config.pb', configuration_block.config.toBuffer());
```

Next, we need to decode this configuration into JSON format using `configtxlator`. We do this purely for convenience because it is easier to parse a JSON and apply our intended configuration changes to it:

```
cproc.execSync('configtxlator proto_decode --input ./tmp/config.pb --type
common.Config | jq . > ./tmp/config.json');
```

This results in the creation of a file named `config.json` in the `temporary` folder. If you view the contents of this file, you will see the underlying configuration structure of the channel and the various properties that can be updated.

Now we need to append the configuration of the new (exporting entity) organization to it. The latter is contained in the file `exportingEntityOrg.json`, created using the `configtxgen` tool earlier in this section and saved to `network/channel-artifacts`. We create the new appended configuration `modified_config.json` using the `jq` tool as follows:

```
cproc.execSync('jq -s \'.[0] *
{"channel_group":{"groups":{"Application":{"groups":
{"ExportingEntityOrgMSP":.[1]}}}}}\' ./tmp/config.json ../network/channel-
artifacts/exportingEntityOrg.json > ./tmp/modified_config.json');
```

If you view the contents of `modified_config.json`, you will see that it is very similar in structure to `config.json`; the difference is that it contains the definitions of 5 organizations where the latter contains only 4. We now convert this new configuration to protobuf format (`modified_config.pb`) so `configtxlator` can process it:

```
cproc.execSync('configtxlator proto_encode --input
./tmp/modified_config.json --type common.Config --output
./tmp/modified_config.pb');
```

Note that we use the same protobuf schema (common.Config) that we used to decode the configuration obtained from the orderer.

Finally, we will use `configtxlator` to compute the delta (or difference) between the original and the new configuration protobufs:

```
cproc.execSync('configtxlator compute_update --channel_id ' + channel_name
+ ' --original ./tmp/config.pb --updated ./tmp/modified_config.pb --output
./tmp/exportingEntityOrg_update.pb');
```

The generated protobuf `exportingEntityOrg_update.pb` contains full definitions of the `exportingentityOrg` and pointers to the existing 4 organizations. This is sufficient for a channel configuration update as the full definitions of the other organizations are already contained in the previous configuration block (in our example, the genesis block).

Now all we have to do is read the delta configuration and get admin signatures from each of the existing four organizations. The code for this is similar to the code we examined in the channel creation stage:

```
config = fs.readFileSync('./tmp/exportingEntityOrg_update.pb');
var signature = client.signChannelConfig(config);
signatures.push(signature);
```

All we need to do now is create an update request and send it to the orderer:

```
let tx_id = client.newTransactionID();
var request = {
  config: config,
  signatures : signatures,
  name : channel_name,
  orderer : orderer,
  txId  : tx_id
};
client.updateChannel(request);
```

The request structure can contain either a config or an envelope field. The latter has the common.Envelope protobuf format and is a wrapper around the configuration we just created. The Fabric orderer will accept either. Using envelope instead of config is left as an exercise to the reader.

To push the channel configuration update, just run:

```
node run-upgrade-channel.js
```

Please ensure that the original 4-org network from Chapter 5, *Exposing Network Assets and Transactions* is up and running, and that the channel creation step (see middleware/createTradeApp.js for an example) has already been performed.

Adding the new organization to the network

The new organization is logically added to the channel through a configuration update. To physically add it to our trade network and make it participate in shared ledger transactions, we need to:

- Join the exporting entity organization's peers to tradechannel
- Install the current version of the chaincode on the newly added peers

The good news is that there is nothing new to be done here. We have already implemented functions for both these procedures (`joinChannel` in `join-channel.js` and `installChaincode` in `install-chaincode.js`, respectively), and we just need to exercise them on behalf of the new organization's resources.

Before running these steps, we must augment the network configuration used by the middleware. Earlier, we used `config.json` in the `middleware` folder to represent the 4-organization network. We will now replace that with `config_upgrade.json` in the same folder. All this file contains is one extra property in trade-network called `exportingentityorg` (which is how the middleware code will recognize our new organization) as follows:

```
"exportingentityorg": {
  "name": "peerExportingEntityOrg",
  "mspid": "ExportingEntityOrgMSP",
  "ca": {
    "url": "https://localhost:11054",
      "name": "ca-exportingentityorg"
  },
  "peer1": {
    "requests": "grpcs://localhost:11051",
    "events": "grpcs://localhost:11053",
    "server-hostname": "peer0.exportingentityorg.trade.com",
    "tls_cacerts": "../network/crypto-
config/peerOrganizations/exportingentityorg.trade.com/peers/peer0.exporting
entityorg.trade.com/msp/tlscacerts/tlsca.exportingentityorg.trade.com-
cert.pem"
  }
}
```

Note that the ports indicated previously match those specified in the docker-compose-exportingEntityOrg.yaml file we used to start the MSP and peer for this organization. The path to the certificate matches what was generated using `cryptogen` earlier in this section, and the names match what was specified in the `configtx.yaml`. The organization has just one peer, which is exactly what we specified in the latter file.

To ensure that the middleware functions load the right configuration, we need to change the value of the `networkConfig` variable in `constants.js` from `config.json` to `config_upgrade.json`. We do that in the file `new-org-join-channel.js` as follows:

```
var Constants = require('./constants.js');
Constants.networkConfig = './config_upgrade.json';
```

Now we are ready to run the channel join procedure for the single peer belonging to the exporting entity's organization. The code for this in `new-org-join-channel.js` is as follows:

```
var joinChannel = require('./join-channel.js');
Client.addConfigFile(path.join(__dirname, Constants.networkConfig));
var ORGS = Client.getConfigSetting(Constants.networkId);
joinChannel.joinChannel('exportingentityorg', ORGS, Constants);
```

The call to `joinChannel` has the effect of joining the peer whose details are specified in the `trade-network:exportingentityorg:peer1` section in `config_upgrade.js` to `tradechannel`. To execute this operation, just run the following:

```
node new-org-join-channel.js
```

The new peer is now part of the channel and will eventually sync the contents of the shared ledger for the channel through the gossip protocol from the existing network peers.

Similarly, we can install the chaincode on this peer by calling the `installChaincode` function in `install-chaincode.js`. But as it happens, we would like to demonstrate the chaincode upgrade capability at this time. So instead of running the installation procedure twice, we can straightaway install the new version on all 5 peers. We will describe that procedure in the next section.

Smart contract and policy updates

As we observed in the early part of this chapter, the smart contract binding peers on a shared channel is subject to change for a variety of reasons ranging from code fixes to evolving needs of the participants. Regardless of the reason, the mechanism offered by Hyperledger Fabric and the semantics of the change remain constant. The mechanism is what we we'll demonstrate in this section.

Closely associated with the smart contract, at least in the Fabric view of a blockchain, is the endorsement policy that must be satisfied for the result of a transaction to be committed to the shared ledger. As we will see, the same mechanism that can upgrade a smart contract can be used to modify the endorsement policy too.

Modification in chaincode logic

Let us first consider a scenario that requires us to update (or upgrade) our trade chaincode. The addition of a new organization, which we just carried out in the previous section, necessitates certain changes in chaincode. As an example, let us consider the following code snippet in the `acceptTrade` function in `chaincode/src/github.com/trade_workflow/tradeWorkflow.go`:

```
// Accept a trade agreement
func (t *TradeWorkflowChaincode) acceptTrade(stub
shim.ChaincodeStubInterface, creatorOrg string, creatorCertIssuer string,
args []string) pb.Response {
  // Access control: Only an Exporter Org member can invoke this
transaction
  if !t.testMode && !authenticateExporterOrg(creatorOrg, creatorCertIssuer)
{
    return shim.Error("Caller not a member of Exporter Org. Access
denied.")
  }
```

The preceding access control logic dictates that only a member of the exporter's organization may accept a trade. In our earlier 4-organization network, this made sense because both the exporter and the exporter's bank were part of one organization, and we relied on further access control at higher layers to distinguish bankers from their clients for the purpose of executing chaincode operations. But now that we have added an organization to serve the exporter's needs independent of its bank (referring to the exporter now as an exporting entity), we ought to change the access control logic accordingly. And this is not the only function that requires such a modification in access control logic.

Therefore, we need to produce a new version of the chaincode. In our code repository, this can be found in `chaincode/src/github.com/trade_workflow_v1/`. The contents of the code, it will look almost identical to the original version except for some of these access control filter rules. Let's look at a similar code snippet in the `acceptTrade` function in `chaincode/src/github.com/trade_workflow_v1/tradeWorkflow.go`:

```
// Accept a trade agreement
func (t *TradeWorkflowChaincode) acceptTrade(stub
shim.ChaincodeStubInterface, creatorOrg string, creatorCertIssuer string,
args []string) pb.Response {
  // Access control: Only an Exporting Entity Org member can invoke this
transaction
  if !t.testMode && !authenticateExportingEntityOrg(creatorOrg,
creatorCertIssuer) {
    return shim.Error("Caller not a member of Exporting Entity Org. Access
denied.")
```

```
        }
```

Note that the function `authenticateExporterOrg` has been replaced with `authenticateExportingEntityOrg`. If you view the contents of the `accessControlUtils.go` file, you will notice that the definition for the latter function has been added.

 In a real-world application involving various organizations, changes in chaincode would have to be made through collaboration and consultation, passed around to the different stakeholders though an out-of-band mechanism, examined, vetted, and tested, before they are deemed to be ready for deployment to the network.

Dependency upgrades in chaincode

Access control logic is not the only thing we will need to change in the chaincode. We use a somewhat contrived scenario where the initial version of the chaincode was created when only an early version of Fabric (say v1.0) was available. If you examine the logic to extract the MSP identity of the organization from which the transaction was issued as well as the common name in the certificate issued to the submitter of the chaincode transaction, it is done manually using the standard Go libraries. This is illustrated in the following code snippet in the `getTxCreatorInfo` function in `chaincode/src/github.com/trade_workflow/accessControlUtils.go`:

```
    creatorSerializedId := &msp.SerializedIdentity{}
    err = proto.Unmarshal(creator, creatorSerializedId)
    ......
    certASN1, _ = pem.Decode(creatorSerializedId.IdBytes)
    cert, err = x509.ParseCertificate(certASN1.Bytes)
    ......
    return creatorSerializedId.Mspid, cert.Issuer.CommonName, nil
```

When the Fabric platform was upgraded to v1.1, a new package called **cid** was implemented to perform the preceding operations and hide details of the protobuf structure and the certificate parsing. To make our chaincode cleaner and more aligned with Fabric changes, it is necessary to upgrade our preceding logic to use the new package. This is what we do in our upgraded version of chaincode in `chaincode/src/github.com/trade_workflow_v1/accessControlUtils.go`:

```
    import (
      ......
      "github.com/hyperledger/fabric/core/chaincode/lib/cid"
      ......
    )
```

```
......
func getTxCreatorInfo(stub shim.ChaincodeStubInterface) (string, string,
error) {
  ......
  mspid, err = cid.GetMSPID(stub)
  ......
  cert, err = cid.GetX509Certificate(stub)
  ......
  return mspid, cert.Issuer.CommonName, nil
}
```

Ledger resetting

A chaincode upgrade is like instantiation, and both result in the execution of the Init function. In the initial version of the chaincode, many ledger values were initialized, but unless we change that logic, those initial values will overwrite the current state of the ledger. Therefore, we add code to the Init function in chaincode/src/github.com/trade_workflow_v1/tradeWorkflow.go to emulate a no-op, but we also leave the original logic intact to ensure that values can be overwritten during an upgrade if there is a business need to do so, as the following code snippet illustrates:

```
func (t *TradeWorkflowChaincode) Init(stub shim.ChaincodeStubInterface)
pb.Response {
  ......
  // Upgrade Mode 1: leave ledger state as it was
  if len(args) == 0 {
    return shim.Success(nil)
  }
  // Upgrade mode 2: change all the names and account balances
  if len(args) != 8 {
    ......
```

Endorsement policy update

Our original transaction endorsement policy required a member of each of the 4 organizations to endorse (sign) a chaincode invocation transaction. Now that we have added a new organization, we must update that policy to require a signature from a member of each of the 5 organizations. In the middleware folder, this new policy is defined in constants.js as follows:

```
var FIVE_ORG_MEMBERS_AND_ADMIN = [{
  role: {
    name: 'member',
```

```
        mspId: 'ExporterOrgMSP'
      }
    }, {
      role: {
        name: 'member',
        mspId: 'ExportingEntityOrgMSP'
      }
    }, {
      role: {
        name: 'member',
        mspId: 'ImporterOrgMSP'
      }
    }, {
      role: {
        name: 'member',
        mspId: 'CarrierOrgMSP'
      }
    }, {
      role: {
        name: 'member',
        mspId: 'RegulatorOrgMSP'
      }
    }, {
      role: {
        name: 'admin',
        mspId: 'TradeOrdererMSP'
      }
    }];

var ALL_FIVE_ORG_MEMBERS = {
  identities: FIVE_ORG_MEMBERS_AND_ADMIN,
  policy: {
    '5-of': [{ 'signed-by': 0 }, { 'signed-by': 1 }, { 'signed-by': 2 }, {
'signed-by': 3 }, { 'signed-by': 4 }]
  }
};
```

To switch the endorsement policy in our middleware, we just need to change the value of
the TRANSACTION_ENDORSEMENT_POLICY variable in constants.js from
ALL_FOUR_ORG_MEMBERS to ALL_FIVE_ORG_MEMBERS.

Upgrading chaincode and endorsement policy on the trade channel

Now we are ready to carry out the upgrade process, which will require two steps:

1. The installation of the new version of chaincode on the network peers
2. The upgrade of the chaincode and endorsement policy on the channel

The code to perform these steps can be found in `middleware/upgrade-chaincode.js` and simply involves calling functions we have already implemented (see *Chapter 5, Exposing Network Assets and Transactions*). The following code snippet shows what we need to do for installation:

```
var Constants = require('./constants.js');
var installCC = require('./install-chaincode.js');
Constants.networkConfig = './config_upgrade.json';
Constants.TRANSACTION_ENDORSEMENT_POLICY = Constants.ALL_FIVE_ORG_MEMBERS;
installCC.installChaincode(Constants.CHAINCODE_UPGRADE_PATH,
Constants.CHAINCODE_UPGRADE_VERSION, Constants);
```

Note in the preceding code that the 5-organization network configuration is used and so is the 5-organization endorsement policy. The new path and version of the chaincode are set in `constants.js` as follows:

```
var CHAINCODE_UPGRADE_PATH = 'github.com/trade_workflow_v1';
var CHAINCODE_UPGRADE_VERSION = 'v1';
```

The path is relative to the chaincode/src folder in the repository, as the GOPATH is temporarily set to wherever the `chaincode/` folder has been copied to (see `constants.js` and `install-chaincode.js`). The version is set to v1 as opposed to the initiation version, which was v0.

 The chaincode version ID you choose MUST be unique in the lifetime of the chaincode; that is, it must not have been used for any previous version.

Triggering the upgrade is the next step, which is almost identical to the instantiation step from the developer's perspective:

```
var instantiateCC = require('./instantiate-chaincode.js');
instantiateCC.instantiateOrUpgradeChaincode(
  Constants.IMPORTER_ORG,
  Constants.CHAINCODE_UPGRADE_PATH,
  Constants.CHAINCODE_UPGRADE_VERSION,
```

```
    'init',
    [],
    true,
    Constants
);
```

As we can see preceding, we exercise the option of leaving the ledger state as it currently stands by passing an empty argument's list. In the function `instantiateOrUpgradeChaincode` in `instantiate-chaincode.js`, after a proposal is built, `channel.sendUpgradeProposal(request, 300000)` is called instead of `channel.sendInstantiateProposal(request, 300000)` to send the request to the orderer. As in the case of instantiation, we register event listeners to tell us whether the request succeeded.

To push the chaincode upgrade, run:

```
node upgrade-chaincode.js
```

To test the new chaincode, run:

```
node five-org-trade-scenario.js
```

This will run a sequence of trade operations (invocations and queries on the chaincode) involving the various parties from the request of a trade to the final payment for delivery of a shipment.

Platform upgrades

Your distributed blockchain application must anticipate and support changes made to the platform components. Focusing on the components we have created and launched in our sample trade network, these include the Fabric peer, orderer, and CA (or MSP.) Just like the application chaincode is subject to change to account for bugs and new requirements, so can the platform change over time. Fabric, since its genesis in late 2015, has changed many times, each change being pushed as an upgrade with a new version, and the current version is 1.1. Whenever a platform component gets upgraded, you need to replace those components in your running system without disrupting the life cycle of your application. In this section, we will demonstrate how to do that.

You can run your network components in different configuration, one way using docker containers, which is the approach we have demonstrated in this book. To upgrade platform components running in docker containers, the first thing you need to do is generate new images for the various components. This can be done either by downloading the relevant images from Docker Hub or downloading the source and building the images natively using make docker; the latter approach is what we have followed in this book. To see the entire list of Hyperledger Fabric images downloaded to your system, you can run something as follows:

```
docker images | grep hyperledger/fabric
```

You will see a long list of image entries, most of them duplicated, with the latest tag being a pointer to one of the images with a specific tag name. Since our docker-compose YAML files in the network folder (`docker-compose-e2e.yaml`, `base/docker-compose-base.yaml`, and `base/peer-base.yaml`) depend only on the images for fabric-peer, fabric-orderer, and fabric-ca, let us examine just those:

```
hyperledger/fabric-peer     latest    f9224936c8c3    2 weeks ago     187MB
hyperledger/fabric-peer     x86_64-1.1.1-snapshot-c257bb3    f9224936c8c3
2 weeks ago    187MB
hyperledger/fabric-orderer    latest    5de53fad366a    2 weeks ago
180MB
hyperledger/fabric-orderer    x86_64-1.1.1-snapshot-c257bb3    5de53fad366a
2 weeks ago    180MB
hyperledger/fabric-ca    latest    39fdba61db00    2 weeks ago    299MB
hyperledger/fabric-ca    x86_64-1.1.1-snapshot-e656889    39fdba61db00    2
weeks ago    299MB
```

You will see something like the preceding when you run the `docker images` command. The Docker images listed here were built natively from the release-1.1 branches of the Fabric and Fabric CA source code. If you download a different version of the source code and build the images using make docker, you will see a third image entry for each of the preceding components, and your latest image tag will be linked to the one that you just created.

We will go through an following example where the trade network's orderer and peers are upgraded. We will leave upgrading fabric-ca as an exercise to the user. To do this in a running application, you will need to perform the following sequence of steps:

1. Download or build new versions of platform component images
2. Stop the components
3. (Optional) make a backup of your ledger contents for safety
4. Stop the running chaincode containers

5. Remove the chaincode container images from your system
6. Ensure that the image tags referenced in the docker-compose YAML files are linked to the new versions of the components
7. Start the components

You can also choose to stop, upgrade, and start each component in turn rather than all at once. You will need to stop all incoming requests to the system while this upgrade is going on, which should be a simple matter of shutting down your application web servers.

There is sample code to upgrade our trade network in this manner in the upgradeNetwork function in network/trade.sh in the code repository. Here, we assume that the user will either:

- Pass the new image tag (such as x86_64-1.1.1-snapshot-c257bb3 in the preceding list) as a command-line parameter using the -i switch, or
- Link the latest tag to the new image

Before calling the function. Now we must stop the orderer and peers:

```
COMPOSE_FILE=docker-compose-e2e.yaml
......
COMPOSE_FILES="-f $COMPOSE_FILE"
......
docker-compose $COMPOSE_FILES stop orderer.trade.com
......
for PEER in peer0.exporterorg.trade.com peer0.importerorg.trade.com
peer0.carrierorg.trade.com peer0.regulatororg.trade.com; do
  ......
  docker-compose $COMPOSE_FILES stop $PEER
  ......
done
```

As we can see preceding code, the docker-compose YAML file used to start the network must be used to stop individual components too.

 The preceding example assumes that only the first 4 organizations are part of the network.

Once the containers are stopped, we can choose to backup the ledger data as follows:

```
LEDGERS_BACKUP=./ledgers-backup
mkdir -p $LEDGERS_BACKUP
......
```

```
docker cp -a orderer.trade.com:/var/hyperledger/production/orderer
$LEDGERS_BACKUP/orderer.trade.com
......
for PEER in peer0.exporterorg.trade.com peer0.importerorg.trade.com
peer0.carrierorg.trade.com peer0.regulatororg.trade.com; do
   ......
   docker cp -a $PEER:/var/hyperledger/production $LEDGERS_BACKUP/$PEER/
   ......
done
```

The contents of the ledger on the peers as well as the orderer are now backed up to your local machine in the ledgers-backup folder.

Now we should remove all the chaincode images because new ones need to be created by the new fabric-peer images, and the presence of old images will block that creation:

```
for PEER in peer0.exporterorg.trade.com peer0.importerorg.trade.com
peer0.carrierorg.trade.com peer0.regulatororg.trade.com; do
   ......
   CC_CONTAINERS=$(docker ps | grep dev-$PEER | awk '{print $1}')
   if [ -n "$CC_CONTAINERS" ] ; then
     docker rm -f $CC_CONTAINERS
   fi
   CC_IMAGES=$(docker images | grep dev-$PEER | awk '{print $1}')
   if [ -n "$CC_IMAGES" ] ; then
     docker rmi -f $CC_IMAGES
   fi
   ......
done
```

 Note that we must first check to see if the chaincode containers are running, and stop them if they are, otherwise the images cannot be removed.

Now we can restart the stopped orderer and peer containers. When running docker-compose up, the orderer and peer containers will be started with the new image:

```
docker-compose $COMPOSE_FILES up --no-deps orderer.trade.com
......
for PEER in peer0.exporterorg.trade.com peer0.importerorg.trade.com
peer0.carrierorg.trade.com peer0.regulatororg.trade.com; do
   ......
   docker-compose $COMPOSE_FILES up --no-deps $PEER
   ......
done
```

You can run the entire upgrade process in one shot by running the script in either of the following ways:

```
./trade.sh upgrade [-i <imagetag>]
```

If the `<imagetag>` is not specified, it will default to latest, as mentioned earlier.

You can now continue to run your distributed trade application. Note that platform changes may also be accompanied by changes in chaincode and SDK API, which may necessitate an upgrade to your chaincode or your middleware or both. As we have demonstrated examples of those in previous sections, the reader should not be fully equipped to upgrade both the application and the underlying blockchain platform at any point during the application's and network's life cycle.

System monitoring and performance

You have now built your application and instituted various processes and mechanisms in anticipation of changes over its lifetime. An additional, but no less essential, process that you must have in place and carry out from time to time is monitoring and performance measurement. Any production application you build for real-world users and institutions must meet certain performance goals to be useful to its users, and by implication, the application's stakeholders. Therefore, understanding how your application performs and trying to improve its performance is a key maintenance task; any dereliction in this task may result in your application having a short shelf life.

The art (and science) of system performance measurement and analytics is a broad and extensive set of topics, and it is not our intention to cover these topics deeply or exhaustively in this book. To obtain such a coverage, the interested reader is encouraged to read other canonical texts on the topic (for example, `https://www.amazon.com/Systems-Performance-Enterprise-Brendan-Gregg/dp/0133390098`.) Instead, we will offer a preview of what performance measurement and gaining insight into a blockchain application entails, and offer some hints and suggestions about the tools and techniques a developer or system administrator can utilize for these purposes.

Broadly speaking, systems maintenance for performance involves three, roughly sequential, categories of tasks, though these tasks can collectively repeat in cycles over the lifetime of a system:

- Observation and measurement
- Evaluation (or analysis) and gaining insight (or understanding)
- Restructuring, redesign, or reimplementation for improvement

In our discussion in this section, we will mainly focus on some aspects of the following:

- What is important to measure in a Fabric application
- The mechanisms a Fabric application developer or administrator can use for measurement
- The performance-inhibiting aspects of Fabric that an application designers and developers should be aware of

Measurement and analytics

Before discussing Hyperledger Fabric in particular, let's understand what measurement and analytics means for a distributed system, of which a blockchain application is an example. The process begins with a comprehensive understanding of the architecture of the system, its various components, and the degrees and natures of coupling among those components. The next step is to institute mechanisms to monitor the various components and collect data attributes that have any bearing on performance, either continuously or at periodic intervals. This data must be collected and communicated to a module that can then analyze it to generate meaningful representations of system performance, and possibly provide more insight into the workings of the applications and its existing inefficiencies. The analyzed data can also be used to ensure that the system is working at a desired level of performance, and to detect when it is not, something which is of high (if not critical) importance to user-facing systems.

Such techniques and processes are well known in the world of distributed systems analytics, and also in mobile analytics (which can be considered to be a special case of the former.) Agents can be configured to observe or monitor a system component, either actively or passively: in the former, systems can be instrumented (for example, by inserting special data collection code) to make them self-monitor their activities and gather information, whereas in the latter, data collection can be done by a piece of software that is external to the component being monitored. A pipeline exists to communicate this data on a continuous or periodic basis to a central repository, where the data can be accumulated for later processing, or is immediately processed and consumed. The pipeline may modify the data to make it read for analytics too. In data analytics parlance, this pipeline is typically referred to as **extract-transform-load** (**ETL**). If the volume and frequency of data generation is very high, and if the number of data sources is very large, such analytics is also referred to as **big data analytics**.

ETL processes or big data analytics are beyond the scope of this chapter and book, but the takeaway for a serious blockchain developer or administrator is that there exist frameworks to perform such analytics, either for distributed systems configured with servers and databases at their backends (and a Fabric blockchain application is an example of this) such as Splunk (`https://www.splunk.com/en_us/solutions/solution-areas/business-analytics.html`) or Apteligent (`http://www.apteligent.com/`), or for mobile applications such as Tealeaf (`https://www.ibm.com/in-en/marketplace/session-replay-and-interaction-analytics`) and Google Analytics (`https://developers.google.com/analytics/solutions/mobile`). The same frameworks can be used or adapted to monitor and analyze blockchain applications too.

What should we measure or understand in a Fabric application

An application built on Hyperledger Fabric and its associated tools is, in effect, a **distributed transaction processing system**.

Blockchain applications vis-à-vis traditional transaction processing applications

Think about what a traditional transaction processing system looks like. You will have a database at the backend to store, process, and serve data; this database may be centralized or distributed, and in the latter case, maintain replicas or partitions. In front of the database, you will have one or more web servers or application servers to manage and run your application logic; and further in front, you will have one or more interfaces for interaction with users.

Similarly, a Fabric blockchain application has peers maintaining a shared replicated ledger as the equivalent of a database. The smart contract code is analogous to stored procedures and views in a traditional database management system. The middleware and application server, whose architecture and workings we have demonstrated for our trade application, can be equivalents of or even hosted by traditional application servers. Finally, we can design web interfaces for user interaction just as we would for a traditional transaction processing application. Of course, we used `curl` as a substitute to test out our trade use case.

Metrics for performance analysis

Therefore, a blockchain application's performance is affected by similar factors to those affecting a traditional DBMS-based transaction processing application. First, we must constantly monitor the health of the hardware resources that are hosting the application components. For every machine that is running a peer or orderer or CA, we need to track basic health indicators, such as CPU usage, memory usage, disk I/O speeds, network bandwidth, latency, and jitter, and available storage space (this is not meant to be an exhaustive list). These factors, especially CPU usage for processing-heavy systems, determine whether the application is running at optimal performance levels.

As we have seen in this book, a Fabric network can be started in a variety of configurations, from a single dedicated machine (physical or virtual) for each peer and orderer to a single-machine setup running each component in an isolated `docker` container (like our trade network setup in this book). In the latter case, you will need to monitor the health of not only the machines but also each container. Also remember that each Fabric chaincode instance always runs in a docker container rather than on a dedicated machine. Plus, when it comes to understanding (or profiling) applications, the CPU, memory, and I/O usage of application components are of the most relevance. We will look at some tools to measure container and application performance later in this section.

Moving from the external factors to the application itself, the performance of a Fabric application (just like any other transaction processing application) is defined by two characteristic metrics:

- **Throughput**: This is the number of transactions per unit time that your system can yield. As Fabric is a loosely coupled system and a transaction has multiple stages (see `Chapter 5`, *Exposing Network Assets and Transactions*, for examples in our trade scenario), we can measure throughputs for the different stages. But the overall throughput, from the time a client constructs a transaction proposal for endorsement up to the time when an event indicating ledger commitment is received, provides the best overall picture of how your application performs. On the other hand, if we want to measure just the orderer throughput, we would need to collect statistics just for the part where the client sends an endorsed transaction envelope to the orderer and gets back a response.

- **Latency**: As most Fabric applications will ultimately be user-facing, it's not just the processing capacity or volume that will matter in a real-world scenario but also how long each transaction takes. As in the case of throughput, we can measure different latencies—chaincode execution and endorsement, ordering and block creation, transaction validation and ledger commitment, and even event publishing and subscription. We can also measure inter-component communication latency in an effort to understand the limitations of the communication infrastructure.

There are other important things to measure, such as the time taken to synchronize ledger states across peers (using the **gossip** protocol), but from a transaction processing perspective, the preceding two metrics are of prime importance. When we measure these factors, we get an understanding of how the overall application is performing, and also its constituent parts such as the ESCC and VSCC in a peer and the Kafka service in an orderer.

Measurement and data collection in a Fabric application

Now that we know what we ought to measure, let us look at some examples of hands-on measurement and data collection. We will use our single-VM (Linux), multiple-docker-container trade network for demonstrative purposes, and let the reader extrapolate those methods (with the help of more comprehensive texts on measurement) to other setups.

Collecting health and capacity information

A standard way to get information about CPU, memory, and other activity on your system is by examining info in /proc. In addition, an array of tools is available in Linux to obtain specific pieces of information. The sysstat package contains many of them, for example, iostat to collect CPU and I/O statistics, pidstat to collect health statistics for each process, and sar and sadc to collect similar statistics as cron jobs. Just as a sample, running iostat on a VM running the entire trade network and the chaincode yields the following CPU info and I/O statistics for the two virtual hard drives:

```
Linux 4.4.0-127-generic (ubuntu-xenial)    05/28/2018    _x86_64_    (2
CPU)

avg-cpu:  %user    %nice    %system    %iowait    %steal    %idle
          0.31     0.01       0.26       0.11      0.00     99.32

Device:            tps    kB_read/s    kB_wrtn/s    kB_read    kB_wrtn
```

```
sda                   1.11          16.71         11.00        688675       453396
sdb                   0.00           0.05          0.00          2014            0
```

The `vmstat` tool similarly presents a summary of the virtual-machine-wide information as follows:

```
procs -----------memory---------- ---swap-- -----io---- -system-- ------
cpu-----
 r  b   swpd   free   buff  cache   si   so    bi    bo    in    cs us sy id
wa st
 0  0      0 2811496 129856 779724    0    0     7     5   127   342  0  1 99
 0  0
```

For continuous per-process statistics, you can also use the well-known `top` command, and also `dstat`, which also generates output in CSV format for easy consumption. If you want to connect your measurement mechanisms to an ETL analytics pipeline, the `nmon` tool(`http://nmon.sourceforge.net/pmwiki.php`), which does comprehensive performance data collection and reporting in well-known formats, may be the ideal tool.

But we must also specifically profile the containers that are running the application components. The `perf` tool is very handy as a Linux performance counter and profiling tool. It can collect profiles on a per thread, per process, and per CPU (or processor) basis. Data collection is done by using the `perf report` command with different switches, which results in data being collected and stored in a file called `perf.data` in the folder the command was run in. This data can them be analyzed using the `perf report` command. In addition, `bindfs` (`https://bindfs.org/`) can be used to map symbols in a `perf` report to processes running inside docker containers. Lastly, `perf stat` can be used to collect system-wide statistics. The `perf` Wiki (`https://perf.wiki.kernel.org/index.php/Main_Page`) gives more information about how to use this tool.

Profiling containers and applications

Our application components must also be profiled to produce instruction-level information and call stacks for us to analyze, not just to track performance but also to debug application flaws. The strace tool can be used to record system calls made by a running docker container. As an example, get the process ID for our orderer container as follows:

```
docker inspect --format '{{ .State.Pid }}' orderer.trade.com
```

Recall that our container was named `orderer.trade.com` in our docker-compose YAML file. The output will be a process ID; let's call it `<pid>`. Now run `strace` on that process:

```
sudo strace -T -tt -p <pid>
```

You should see a continuous output, something like the following:

```
strace: Process 5221 attached
18:48:49.081842 restart_syscall(<... resuming interrupted futex ...>) = -1
ETIMEDOUT (Connection timed out) <0.089393>
18:48:49.171665 futex(0x13cd758, FUTEX_WAKE, 1) = 1 <0.000479>
18:48:49.172253 futex(0x13cd690, FUTEX_WAKE, 1) = 1 <0.000556>
18:48:49.174052 futex(0xc420184f10, FUTEX_WAKE, 1) = 1 <0.000035>
18:48:49.174698 futex(0xc42002c810, FUTEX_WAKE, 1) = 1 <0.000053>
18:48:49.175556 futex(0x13cd280, FUTEX_WAIT, 0, {1, 996752461}) = -1
ETIMEDOUT (Connection timed out) <1.999684>
```

To analyze the output, read the canonical `strace` documentation. Note that this tool is available only on Linux systems. Also, in your docker-compose YAML file, you can configure a container to run `strace` internally. As an example, take the container definition of `peer0.exporterorg.trade.com` in `network/base/docker-compose-base.yaml`. You can augment it to enable `strace` as follows (added configuration italicized):

```
peer0.exporterorg.trade.com:
  container_name: peer0.exporterorg.trade.com
  cap_add:
   - SYS_PTRACE
  security_opt:
    - seccomp:unconfined
```

Finally, for information more specific to the Fabric platform and the application you have developed on it, there is Go profiling to turn to. The Fabric components (peers, orderers, and CAs) are written in Golang, as is the chaincode, and finding out which parts of the program use more time and resources are of critical importance in improving the quality of your application. For such profiling, we can use `pprof` (`https://golang.org/pkg/net/http/pprof/`), Golang's built-in profiler (`https://blog.golang.org/profiling-go-programs`). (Please ensure you have `go` installed on the system in which you intend to run your profiler.) To capture an application profile consisting of call graphs and run frequency (equivalent to CPU usage) of various functions in the graph, `pprof` requires a Go application to run an HTTP server as follows:

```
import "net/http"
http.ListenAndServe("localhost:6060", nil)
```

To get a profile, we can use `go tool` to hit this server and fetch the data. As an example, if your application is running a server on port `6060`, you can get a heap profile by running:

```
go tool pprof http://localhost:6060/debug/pprof/heap
```

You can replace `localhost` with an appropriate host name or IP address in the preceding command. To get a 30-second CPU profile instead, run:

```
go tool pprof http://localhost:6060/debug/pprof/profile
```

Hyperledger Fabric provides built-in support for such profiling (`https://github.com/hyperledger-archives/fabric/wiki/Profiling-the-Hyperledger-Fabric`), at least on the Fabric peer. To enable profiling (or running the HTTP server), we need to configure the peer (or in our case, the `docker` container running the peer) suitably. Recall that the core configuration for each peer in our sample trade network is defined in `network/base/peer-base.yaml`. Notice the following lines:

```
services:
  peer-base:
    image: hyperledger/fabric-peer:$IMAGE_TAG
    environment:
      ......
      - CORE_PEER_PROFILE_ENABLED=true
      ......
```

Also recall that our peer's port mappings between the container and the host are defined in `network/base/docker-compose-base.yaml`. Examples of exporter and importer org peers are given as follows:

```
peer0.exporterorg.trade.com:
  ......
  ports:
    ......
    - 7055:6060
    ......
peer0.importerorg.trade.com:
  ......
  ports:
    ......
    - 8055:6060
    ......
```

Though within their containers, the profile server runs on port 6060, on the host machine, pprof will hit port 7055 to capture the exporter organization peer's profile and port 8055 to capture the importer organization peer's profile.

As an example, let us capture a 30-second CPU profile of the exporter organization's peer. We can start up the trade network and run the channel creation and chaincode installation steps using middleware/createTradeApp.js. In a different terminal window, we can run:

```
go tool pprof http://localhost:7055/debug/pprof/profile
```

This will eventually generate a file in ~/pprof, and spew something like the following on your console:

```
Fetching profile over HTTP from http://localhost:7055/debug/pprof/profile
Saved profile in /home/vagrant/pprof/pprof.peer.samples.cpu.006.pb.gz
File: peer
Build ID: 66c7be6d1f71cb816faabc48e4a498bf8052ba1b
Type: cpu
Time: May 29, 2018 at 5:09am (UTC)
Duration: 30s, Total samples = 530ms ( 1.77%)
Entering interactive mode (type "help" for commands, "o" for options)
(pprof)
```

Lastly, the tool leaves a pprof shell to run a variety of profiling commands from, to analyze the obtained dump. For example, to get the top five most active functions or goroutines:

```
(pprof) top5
Showing nodes accounting for 340ms, 64.15% of 530ms total
Showing top 5 nodes out of 200
      flat  flat%   sum%        cum   cum%
     230ms 43.40% 43.40%      230ms 43.40%  runtime.futex
/opt/go/src/runtime/sys_linux_amd64.s
      30ms  5.66% 49.06%       30ms  5.66%  crypto/sha256.block
/opt/go/src/crypto/sha256/sha256block_amd64.s
      30ms  5.66% 54.72%       30ms  5.66%  runtime.memmove
/opt/go/src/runtime/memmove_amd64.s
      30ms  5.66% 60.38%       30ms  5.66%  runtime.usleep
/opt/go/src/runtime/sys_linux_amd64.s
      20ms  3.77% 64.15%      110ms 20.75%  runtime.findrunnable
/opt/go/src/runtime/proc.go
```

The `tree` command displays the entire call graph in textual form, a section of which looks something like this:

```
(pprof) tree
Showing nodes accounting for 530ms, 100% of 530ms total
Showing top 80 nodes out of 200
                                                    ----------------+-------------
      flat  flat%   sum%       cum    cum%   calls calls% + context
                                                    ----------------+-------------
                                               70ms 30.43% |   runtime.stopm
/opt/go/src/runtime/proc.go
                                               50ms 21.74% |
runtime.notetsleep_internal /opt/go/src/runtime/lock_futex.go
                                               40ms 17.39% |   runtime.ready
/opt/go/src/runtime/proc.go
    230ms 43.40% 43.40%      230ms 43.40%                  | runtime.futex
/opt/go/src/runtime/sys_linux_amd64.s
                                                    ----------------+-------------
                                               30ms   100% |
crypto/sha256.(*digest).Write /opt/go/src/crypto/sha256/sha256.go
     30ms  5.66% 49.06%       30ms  5.66%                  |
crypto/sha256.block /opt/go/src/crypto/sha256/sha256block_amd64.s
                                                    ----------------+-------------
```

You can also view the graph pictorially, either on a web page or by generating a file:

```
(pprof) png
Generating report in profile001.png
```

The following example here shows the call graph generated as a PNG image:

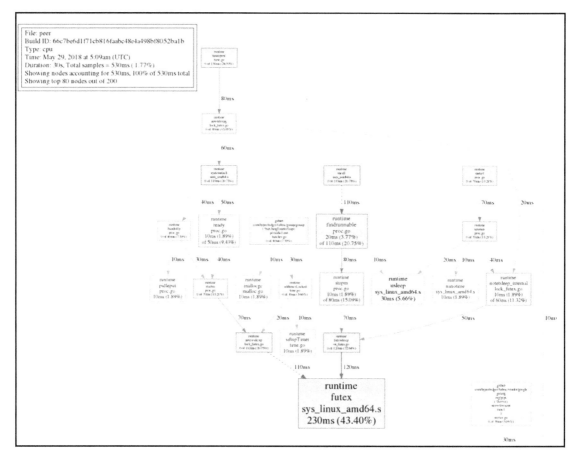

Figure 9.4: A section a call graph representing the functions executed in a peer node within a 30-second period

This is a section of the call graph image, which each box representing a function and the box's size indicating the frequency of that function (that is, the number of profile samples in which that function was running). Directed graph edges indicate calls made from one function to another, with the edges indicating the time spent in making such calls.

For more `pprof` options and analytical tools, the reader is encouraged to read the documentation.

Measuring application performance

Measuring throughput and latency of your application is somewhat less arcane than many of the tools described previously; it will involve instrumenting your code to collect and record timing information. In your code, you will need to either add logging (or communication, for remote reporting) instructions to record when a particular operation is being performed, or add appropriate hooks that can enable or disable data collection as per requirement.

Measuring latency is fairly straightforward; you can record the times of various operations such as client proposal submission, return of endorsement, orderer's acknowledgment of a request, ledger commitment time, and the time when the event was received. Collecting data for a large number of transactions will enable you to get overall transaction latency as well as the latency incurred in individual operations.

To get throughput information, you will need to generate transaction loads of different volumes and different frequencies. Then you can increase the load on your application up to the point when the observed frequency of transaction commitment (or receiving of an event) decreases below the transaction load generation frequency. Apart from that, you will need to instrument the code the way you did to measure transaction latencies. You can change different application parameters and characteristics and run such throughput measurements to determine application and resource characteristics for optimal performance.

Given all the information we can collect using the tools described in this section, an application or network designer can conduct advanced analytics to determine what parts of the system (for example, from a `pprof` call graph) are performing well, and what parts are bottlenecks. One can then try to remedy performance limitations by adding more resources to "bottlenecked" components or reimplement the system to make those components more efficient. Load balancing across different redundant resources is another widely used technique to maintain high performance levels. Bottleneck detection and analysis is a very important topic in its own right, and the reader is encouraged to study texts and academic papers to gain a better understanding.

Fabric engineering guidelines for performance

We will now move from the general to the specific. In this section, we will offer a commentary on Hyperledger Fabric performance, discuss the salient characteristics of the platform that impact performance, and lay out guidelines for developers to extract the best performance from their applications.

Platform performance characteristics

The Fabric architecture and transaction pipeline should be very familiar to the readers of this book by now. It is a complex distributed system and its performance depends on many factors, ranging from the architecture of the application interacting with Fabric to consensus implementation, transaction size, block size, Fabric network size, as well as capability of the underlying hardware and physical network medium.

At the time of writing this book, performance measurements reveal that Fabric can yield a throughput of several thousand transactions per second (`https://arxiv.org/abs/1801.10228.`). The caveat our readers need to keep in mind is that these measurements were carried out using chaincodes that performed very simple operations, and using application and network configurations that may not represent a typical production blockchain network. Fabric performance is bound to the specific use case and the underlying hardware. For example, performance on IBM Z systems exceeds other platforms due to optimized Go compilers leveraging hardware acceleration capabilities such as for cryptographic algorithms and others. Good performance depends on the availability of sufficient resources and proper configuration; we will discuss configuration at length later in this section.

System bottlenecks

A simple inspection of the Fabric architecture and transaction stages will reveal the possible bottleneck components. The ordering service is a prime and obvious example. Every transaction MUST pass through this service and get included in a block to have a chance at ledger commitment. But keep in mind that there is still no guarantee that a transaction will not be rejected at commitment time. Therefore, the performance of the ordering service, in a way, sets the baseline for your application's performance. Clearly, increasing orderer resources, either by adding more nodes or adding capacity to each individual node, may result in better performance. Other ordering mechanisms may also be used in place of the current Fabric default, which is Kafka. As the Fabric platform evolves, expect to see better and faster ordering algorithms.

Another system bottleneck lies at the ledger commitment stage when the transactions have to be evaluated both for authenticity of endorsements and to enforce database (ledger) consistency by managing read and write conflicts. Cryptographic operations are heavy by nature, and recent changes to Fabric (in *v1.1*, for example) have made signature validations more efficient. As a developer or a network engineer, you can streamline performance by minimizing the possibility of transaction failures because of invalid signatures or inter-transaction conflict. For the former, better validation at endorsement stage and during the request generation for the orderer should decrease the chances of failure.

To reduce conflicts, one needs to experiment with varying block sizes (remember that checks are made for conflicts among transactions within a block). Though larger blocks may result in higher throughput, conflicts may have the opposite effect. You can also design your chaincode in ways that will minimize the possibility of conflicts among different invoke transactions. For explanation of how Fabric detects and handles conflicts in blocks see `Chapter 4`, *Designing a Data and Transaction Model with Golang*, in the *Multiversion concurrency control* section.

Configuration and tuning

Continuing from our previous discussion, you can configure various parameters to optimize your application's performance. Many of these parameters are outcomes of the system requirements such as the network size. But a few parameters in your core Fabric configuration (see `Chapter 3`, *Setting the Stage with a Business Scenario*, in *Network Components' Configuration Files* section) can be adjusted to maximize performance. One of them is the block size. It's possible to determine the precise block size (both in bytes and in the number of transactions) that you should set for your application through experimentation (or adjustment of the parameter until you achieve optimal throughput and latency). For example, measurements on a crypto-currency application called Fabcoin revealed an optimal block size of 2 MB (`https://arxiv.org/abs/1801.10228`). But the reader must keep in mind the trade-off discussed in the previous section whereby a larger number of transactions in a block may also result in higher conflict rates and transaction rejections.

Your selection of transaction endorsement policy will also have a significant performance impact. The more the signatures that need to be collected from endorsing peers, the more time it will take to validate the signatures at commitment time. Also, the more complex your policy (namely the more clauses it has), the slower the validation will be. Now there is a trade-off to be made here. More endorsers and a more complex policy will usually provide higher assurance (reliability as well as trust), but it will come at a cost to performance (both throughput and latency). Therefore, a blockchain application administrator must determine what service level as well as trust level are required and tweak the parameters accordingly.

There are various other factors that could affect the performance of a Fabric application: this includes overhead due to the *gossip* protocol among the peers to sync the ledger contents, the number of channels you use in your application, and the transaction generation rates. At the hardware level, performance is determined by the number and performance of CPUs available to the components. Generally, it can be stated that increasing the number of CPUs yields an increase in the performance of the components and of the overall blockchain network. If you are interested in more details, a good paper to read on this topic is *Hyperledger Fabric: A Distributed Operating System for Permissioned Blockchains, EuroSys '18* (`https://dl.acm.org/citation.cfm?id=3190538`), also available at `https://arxiv.org/pdf/1801.10228v1.pdf`.

Ledger data availability and caching

You can further improve the performance of your distributed Fabric application by optimizing the availability of data (that is, retrieval time) stored in the ledger. There are several strategies to do this, and we will outline two of them here.

Redundant committing peer

To increase data availability to client applications, an additional committing peer (or multiple peers) may be deployed topologically closer to the client application or to middleware components accessing the data. The committing peer receives newly created blocks and maintains up to date ledger. It does not participate in the endorsement process and thus does not receive transaction proposal requests from clients. The performance of the peer is thus fully dedicated to maintaining ledger and responding to requests for data. An important considerations in terms of network performance and system security configuration is to choose and set up the location such that the committing peer can unobstructed connect to the channel and the network throughput allows to receive newly created blocks with a low delay.

Data caching

Data retrieved from a peer may be stored in an application cache so that future requests for that data can be served faster. To maintain the data in the cache up to date, the application must monitor changes in the underlying ledger and update the cached data with new state modifications. As discussed earlier, the peer emits event notifications about newly committed transactions into the ledger. The notification can be intercepted by the client and by inspecting the content of the transaction, the client can determine whether the cache should be updated with new values.

Fabric performance measurement and benchmarking

We hope this section of the book has given the reader an understanding of why performance measurement and analysis are important, and some clues about how to make his/her application provide adequate level of service. We will conclude by pointing the reader to tools that currently exist within the Hyperledger framework to measure performance (mainly throughout, latency, and resource utilization) using sample benchmark applications.

For an in-depth and comprehensive performance measurement tools suite, you should look at `fabric-test` (`https://github.com/hyperledger/fabric-test/`.) In particular, PTE (`https://github.com/hyperledger/fabric-test/tree/master/tools/PTE`) is a flexible tool that can be used to drive parameterized transaction load using sample chaincodes.

Hyperledger Cello (`https://www.hyperledger.org/projects/cello`) is not a performance measurement tool but rather a blockchain provisioning and management system that enables the launching of networks on different platforms (virtual machines, clouds, and container clusters). It can be used as an aid to launch, test, and measure sample networks before attempting a production deployment.

Hyperledger Caliper (`https://www.hyperledger.org/projects/caliper`) is another project that is currently developing a benchmarking framework to allow users to measure the performance of a specific blockchain implementation with a set of predefined use cases, and produce reports. The reader should keep in mind that these projects are works-in-progress, and should keep an eye on further developments driven by research in the areas of blockchain performance benchmarking.

Summary

Maintaining and augmenting a blockchain application is possibly even more challenging than creating and bootstrapping it, as one needs to be skilled in monitoring and analytics and also in assessing the impact of changes.

In this chapter, we described the various ways in which a Hyperledger Fabric application can and will inevitably change over its lifetime. We described in detail, using our canonical trade application as an example, how organizations and peers can be added to a running network, how channel configurations can be augmented, how platforms can be upgraded, and how the smart contract (chaincode) itself can be modified without adversely affecting the application state.

In a later part of the chapter, we gave an overview of the tools a developer of system administrator can use to measure, analyze, and improve the performance of a Fabric blockchain application. We also provided guidelines to engineering the system for better performance.

With further research and development, the Hyperledger suite will no doubt be augmented with more and better mechanisms for system changes and monitoring. This chapter should serve as a handy guide for the typical Fabric developer or administrator to maintaining their production application.

10
Governance, Necessary Evil of Regulated Industries

For those of you who have experienced projects without clear decision-making processes, you'll have felt the pain of the churns as decisions are constantly questioned and modified due to the influence of various stakeholders. Politics gets in the way and the objectives of the project end up getting challenged, budgets get cut, and the long-term vision is missing or confusing.

While this is something you can expect from a traditional IT project, a blockchain project has the characteristic of having a good deal more stakeholders. A typical business network will be composed of organizations that are sometimes competing and sometimes cooperating. In this context, it is not hard to see that there are high risks of finding conflicting perspectives, points of view, and interests.

Whether you are a developer or a CIO, understanding what you can expect from such projects and how a governance model can help alleviate some of the issues may be helpful in preparing you for what is to come.

This chapter will present a few of the patterns we have seen in various industries and explore how these blockchain business networks can be formed, as well as how the underlying governance model functions.

This chapter will provide a view on the following topics:

- What is governance?
- Various business models
- Role of governance in a business network
- Typical governance structure and phases
- Roles and processes to consider
- Impact of governance on the IT solution

Decentralization and governance

Some of you may be wondering why we are covering governance in a blockchain book. After all, aren't blockchain networks supposed to be decentralized, and thus guarded against the control of a single entity? While this is true from a technology perspective, the reality is that we are human, and for an enterprise-grade blockchain network to succeed, there are a lot of decisions that need to be made throughout the life cycle of the network.

Even bitcoin, the decentralized, anonymous, permissionless network, must deal with important and hard decisions. A case in point is the controversy around bitcoin block size. In the early days of bitcoin, a limit of 1 MB was set on the block size. As the network scaled up, this limit became problematic. Numerous proposals were issued, but the need for a consensus across the entirety of bitcoin nodes made the change difficult to agree on. This debate started in 2015, but the community had to wait until February 2018 for a partial solution, SegWit, to be partially adopted. We say partial because **SegWit**, which stands for **segregated witness**, only alleviates the problem by separating the signatures from the transaction payload, thereby allowing the inclusion of more transactions within a block—a lot of discussion and exchanges to reach a partial answer.

Furthermore, consider that blockchain business networks are meant to create trust in an environment where not all participants fully trust each other. How will they reach a consensus on how to manage a network?

Knowing there will be conflicts and disparate views, how can we address this? Well, we need a process that will involve the important decision makers of each key organization. There needs to be a basic agreement on a process that participants agree to follow and respect the outcome of. We need a way to *govern* the network—we need governance.

So, is governance about decision making? Not really. Governance is about providing a framework that guides the decision-making process. It does so by providing a clear delineation of roles and responsibilities, and ensures that there are agreed processes to reach and communicate decisions.

We've been talking about decisions in a generic fashion, but what types of decision need to be managed through the governance process? We will properly answer this question in the *Roles and processes* section, but for now, suffice it to say that everything that deals with funding, the functionality roadmap, system upgrades, and network expansion are certainly key topics that should be covered by a governance process.

Business and IT governance are topics that have been covered at length. As such, you will find many IT governance standards that aim at defining a proven structure to guide practices within the IT industry. A few examples of such standards are:

- **Information Technology Infrastructure Library** (**ITIL**): ITIL is primarily focused on how IT renders services to the business and aims at defining a process model that supports IT service management, essentially expressing an IT service as a function of the business benefits they bring instead of the underlying technical details.
- **Control Objectives for Information and Related Technologies** (**COBIT**): This standard is broken down into two parts: Governance and Management. The governance portion of COBIT focusses on ensuring that the enterprise objectives are met through a series of control objectives around the evaluation, direction, and monitoring processes.

In any case, standard approaches always need to be adjusted and adapted to the business model and context.

Exploring the business models

A business model focusses on creating a structure that describes the flow of how an organization creates and captures value in a market.

In the context of a business network, it is interesting to look at the value chain and understand where that value originates. What makes a blockchain network so appealing from a financial perspective? Well, as we have seen in `Chapter 1`, *Blockchain—Enterprise and Industry Perspective*, blockchain technologies offer an opportunity to solve the issues of time and trust, thereby reducing inefficiencies and operational costs.

Blockchain benefits

What types of benefit can come from addressing the issues of time and trust? Let's look at a few examples of where and how these benefits can be implemented in the following sections.

Supply chain management

The supply chain is made up of many actors, from the producer to the logistic service providers, port authority, manufacturer, and ultimately, the consumer. The industry must deal with a variety of regulations, and while there are many data exchanges in place between different organizations, getting a single version of the truth is not possible.

The lack of trust in a supply chain stems from the fact that many of the organizations involved fear that data might leak to competitors. This in turn translates to the following issues:

- **Visibility**: Where is my order? Where is my container? Without transparency, the manufacturer's forecasting is impacted, and can lead to production delays.
- **Administrative overhead**: Data needs to be keyed in multiple times, requiring human effort and the need for a reconciliation process to detect errors.
- **Disputes**: The lack of access to a common source of information leads to discrepancies in the perception of the different actors, turning these discrepancies into disputes.
- **Investigation**: As a consequence of the dispute, efforts have to be made by multiple parties to gather facts and resolve the issue.

In this context, a decentralized, permissioned ledger means that every order and every shipment could be tracked in real time, all while preventing competitors from accessing sensitive information. This model would contribute to eliminating duplicate data entries, reducing human error, and expediting investigation, as the provenance of each transaction could easily be demonstrated.

Given the worldwide economy, it is not hard to imagine the potential savings. Imagining a world where there is a single source of truth that is managed through a permissioned ledger, and where all relevant actors can get access to the information, we can see the immediate benefits that this would bring throughout the supply chain.

Healthcare

The healthcare industry has a wide range of use cases that can be explored, including the pharmaceutical supply chain, clinical trials, and electronic health records. We will focus on this last use case, as it is closer to our heart (literally).

The promise of electronic health records has always been appealing, and the benefits at first glance seem to be numerous:

- **Complete view of the patient's history**: By eliminating the inherent duplication of paper-based records, the patient should get more accurate diagnostics and receive more coherent long-term care, all in a timely fashion
- **Reduction in duplication**: Whether from duplicate tests being requested by different doctors or the fact that every clinic and hospital has to maintain its records, there is a potential waste of resources in the healthcare system
- **Prevention of fraudulent actions**: Whether it is double accounting by rogue clinics or the claiming of false prescriptions, there are many scenarios where the duplication of records creates the opportunity for abuse

While the benefits may seem obvious, the lessons from existing electronic health record projects would seem to hint at the fact that they are expensive and may not immediately deliver the expected benefits. Some research have found that:

- Digitally documenting patient/doctor session created additional work for the doctor
- Electronic health record systems were creating an increase in IT spending
- Additional effort had to be spent on change management and training

Since then, recent studies have shown that such solutions tend to have a positive return on investment in the long run (taking around five years to achieve a benefit).

Given that the value and benefits come from a wide/standardized adoption of the technology, and given the extent of the medical network of many countries, it is not hard to see how this type of endeavor is fraught with political complexities.

Can blockchain networks improve an area that has been long touted as a prime area of innovation for centralized technologies? While technically we can envision an elegant blockchain solution where clinics and hospitals join the network to get access to the patient's record, could the real challenge lie in governance?

Finance – letter of credit

At this point of the book, you should be familiar with the concept of the letter of credit. However, let's quickly recap the concept behind it, illustrated in the following diagram:

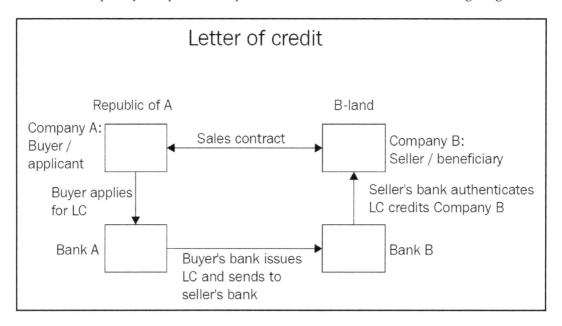

The letter of credit is a payment vehicle whereby, on request from a buyer, a bank will issue a letter of credit to a seller, stating that provided that the terms and conditions are met, payment will be issued. While this process is very much ingrained in international trade, the use of letters of credit is a very old process that has its root in the First Crusade, where the Knights Templar needed to find a way to allow pilgrims to travel to Jerusalem without the danger of carrying money around.

Today's letter of credit process is a complex one. While examples typically involve two banks, the reality is that there will be many more participants involved in such a network. This translates into a process that is costly and constrained by the time it takes to execute it.

A blockchain network can create an opportunity to optimize the process; with a blockchain network, the letter of credit is stored on the ledger, and this guards against a double-spending scenario, whereby the owner of the letter could attempt to cash it again.

The benefit is measured by the reduction in the time delay and the cost, but it also provides the major benefit of reducing the underlying risks associated with such a transaction. Finally, banks can also now consider introducing new services, such as the ability to make incremental payments to the seller.

The fact that transactions on the ledger are final is what makes this scenario appealing to banks. It also gives us the ability to start with a smaller network, get early value, and expand as the solution becomes proven, essentially reducing the amount of early coordination required to establish the network.

From benefits to profits

Whatever the market or the business model, there must be a return on the investment in such a way that the following formula holds true:

Value created by blockchain - Network operation cost > 0

Essentially, with a positive return, and out of common business interests, a network-level business model can emerge. Obviously, the objective will be to maximize the value and minimize the costs, thereby delivering higher margins. It is not hard to understand that when the network can deliver a high margin of benefits, organizations will flock to the network, eager to join. That is, unless the business model favors a few at the expense of many.

Thus, the selection of a business model that is fair and suitable for most of its members will be a deciding factor in the success or failure of the network.

Network business model

Let's now look at the various business models that have been used so far:

- Founder-led network
- Consortium-based network
- Community-based network
- Hybrid models

We will be discussing each of these models in the following sections.

Founder-led network

There are many valid situations where the founder-led network can be valuable, and we will cover those shortly. A normal founder-led network will have the following architecture:

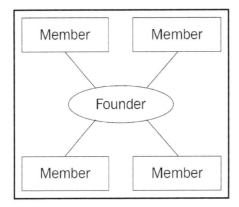

However, we will start with a warning: a founder-led network should not be a way to avoid hard business discussions with potential network participants.

From our time working in this field, we have come to interact with organizations that really believe in the value of blockchain networks, but are feeling overwhelmed at the idea of decentralizing control of the network. They end up creating a roadmap where their initial stage is to dive into the technology and postpone the business discussion until subsequent phases. The end result is typically a fabric network hosted within the founder infrastructure, exposing the network through an API gateway. In some cases, it goes as far as not providing a different identity (that is, a private key and certificate) to the participants. The risk here is that while the solution is technically viable, it fails to deliver value according to the tenets of blockchain networks.

This is not to say that organizations should not adopt a founder-led approach with a phased roadmap, but it is important to get buy-in from potential participants early in the establishment of the network to avoid either a lack of adoption or significant rework efforts.

The founder-led network is typically leveraged by the following types of organization:

- **Startups**: They tend to have a unique perspective on their industry and bring innovation and fresh ideas. Their business model is typically oriented toward providing an added value service to the industry. While innovation may propel them to industry recognition, their success hinges on credibility and funding.
- **Industry leaders**: From their industry perspective, they have enough influence to establish their network. They get the support of their suppliers and other organizations to define the agenda and use cases to support.
- **Interdepartmental blockchain projects**: This model may not initially qualify as a business model, given that it is meant to serve the purpose of internal coordination in an organization, but the reason for bringing it up here is that those projects are good candidates to evolve beyond the boundary of the organization.

As a founding member of the network, these organizations get the opportunity to define the policies and the focus of the network. Organizations that succeed with their network get a leadership position and can hope to capture the value of the network.

However, these advantages do come at the risk of the need to convince other organizations to join. They also bear the complete burden of investing capital to get the project started and to get the required expertise to deliver the solution. They are also exposed to the risk of significant rework if other industry leaders request changes before joining.

Consortium-based network

A consortium is a grouping of two or more organizations with a common business objective that is realized through the business network. The architecture of this network is as follows:

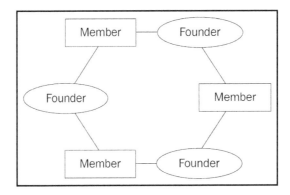

These organizations will often be in the same industry or in closely related industries. The point is that their association is derived from a level of synergy in their processes and a common/shared benefit in cooperating through the consortium.

A key feature of a consortium is that each member retains their legal entity and status. Through the creation of the consortium, they will typically enter contractual and legal agreements that will guide the governance, activities, and investments required to turn their vision into a reality.

We make a distinction between founders and members since the former will have typically faced a similar situation as the organization adopting a founder-led network model. They will have faced similar issues, risks, and benefits as the founder-led network, but they will offset the risks through expanded industry participation. Consortium founders may also choose to monetize the network as other organizations join.

Additionally, members of a consortium may have taxation benefits, contribute to improving the regulatory posture of the industry, and create a voice that has increased influence. However, they are also exposed to potential liability and nonperformance, where one founder may not be able to contribute to an equivalent level as the other founders.

Community-based network

The community-based network is, in essence, a more informal consortium of organizations that are like-minded. Together, they form a business ecosystem that aims to foster collaboration across different industries to create new business opportunities. The architecture of this network is as follows:

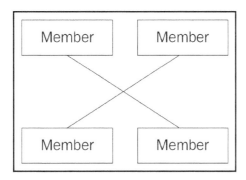

In this model, the solution may evolve into a marketplace where each member may work to offer added-value services. The power of this model comes from the implicit free structure and the freedom for the best idea to surface. This is the best model to naturally support the concept of a decentralized network and governance. It can, however, suffer from the same issues as the consortium if the contributions of its members are not well aligned and the potential liabilities are ignored.

Hybrid models

Business models are not static and will evolve over time. So, while a network may start as a community, it is conceivable that it could evolve into a consortium. Furthermore, any of these models can benefit from the two hybrid models that we will be discussing.

Joint venture

In the joint venture model, a few organizations agree to form a new legal entity that is jointly owned. Each organization can contribute to the funding and the equity, and the revenue and operational expense are shared across the parties. The control of the joint venture lies in the parties that form it, not with the joint venture itself.

New corporation

The new corporation model is essentially similar to the joint venture model, but is a complete spin-off from an enterprise or a consortium. This **new corporation** (**NewCo**) may provide a service to the parties that contributed to its creation; however, the profit and loss are completely owned by the NewCo.

Role of governance in a business network

Having reviewed the various business models, we can see that the control that each participant has will vary based on that model. By properly understanding the model and the interests of each party, we can create a decision process that makes sense to everyone.

So, while we understand that governance is about the process to reach a decision, should every single business, operational, and technical decision be managed and tracked by the governance process? Some would argue that only important topics should be covered by the governance process, but then what are the important topics? This is the role of a governance model: defining each decision domain and making sure everyone understands the level of ceremony (that is, the formalisms and official processes) to each category of decision. A bug fix to a smart contract may not require much attention, but an upgrade to the blockchain technology may require a heightened degree of focus. Agreeing upfront on how each of these categories should be handled will help current and future participants understand the expectations that will be placed on them.

Independent of the process complexity, another consideration that will need to be addressed will be the centralization versus decentralization of the decision making. Distributing the power of decision making may make the process seem fair, reduce the risk of undue control, and encourage free thinking, but in doing so, it may create delays in the achievement of a consensus.

While this makes sense in the context of a community-driven network, would it work with a founder-led network?

Probably not. If the founder is investing capital and resources, they may not want to share control over the network. Keep in mind that this is not an absolute rule. How critical the decision is will play a large role in the amount of control that is applied. Going back to our previous example of a bug fix on a smart contract, it could be expected that the decision as to when to deploy should be decentralized, but that the decision as to the next feature to implement should be centralized.

The following table shows the relationship between governance and business models, and (generally speaking) how the business model will drive the governance structure. Essentially, we can see that on both sides of the scale, we have the community-based network, which tends to be a completely decentralized business model, and thus can only survive in a decentralized governance:

	Business Model	
	Decentralized	Centralized
Decentralized	Community-based	Consortium-based
Centralized	Consortium-based	Founder-led Consortium-based

Governance (vertical label on left side)

An attempt at centralizing governance would probably compromise its very existence as the community members would either reject the control or push for the creation of a consortium. On the other end of the spectrum, we have the founder-led network, which by its very own nature tends to retain control in the founding organization. Consortium business models tend to be variable and depend very much on their own individual nature. A highly regulated industry may require an equivalent high degree of centralization to ensure that all parties adhere to the established standards. Then again, a consortium could achieve decentralized governance by imposing rules or adopting a consensus mechanism for decision making.

To conclude our examination of the role of governance in a business network, let's quickly look at the kinds of decisions that a business network will need to address:

- **Membership life cycle**: Decisions associated with the process of on-boarding and off-boarding participants to the network.
- **Funding and fees**: Decisions focused around how the network will be funded. This may cover areas such as centralized infrastructure, common services, staffing, and so on.
- **Regulation**: Most industries need to meet specific regulations that are often geographically bound. This category focuses on key decisions to ensure that these regulations are met and enforced.
- **Education**: Decisions on the level of training to provide to members and external organizations regarding the use of and integration into the network.

- **Service life cycle**: All decisions related to the IT components, covering aspects such as the deployment of new smart contracts all the way to system updates.
- **Disputes**: Because disputes are almost always unavoidable, these decisions deal with the resolution process.

In the next section, we will dive into each of these areas and explore some of their intricacies. However, it is worth noting that in every category of decision, there will be a balancing act between the following:

- Cost versus risk
- Competition versus cooperation
- Formalism versus agility

Business domains and processes

In this section, we will look at the scope of processes that a governance model should aim to address. Each of these areas of decisions should be considered by any network to avoid bad surprises. Not every decision needs to be bound by a formal process, but considering these elements will avoid bad surprises down the road.

Membership life cycle

As we know, a blockchain network is meant to be fully decentralized. Thus, the expansion of participants is a normal thing that we would expect to see in a healthy network.

However, since this is an enterprise-grade network that is subject to rules and regulations, there are things that need to be established upfront during network formation and the on-boarding of new participants:

- **Who owns the privilege to invite organizations to the network?**
  This should include considerations as to who can submit a proposal to create a new organization, but should also include considerations for channel-level invitation. Are there privacy and confidentiality constraints that will need to be accounted for during the on-boarding?

- **What are the minimum security requirements that the organization needs to meet?**
  An organization that cannot properly secure their peers would risk exposing their ledger data and compromising their private keys. Dealing with fraudulent transactions would lead to chaos and painful investigation. Clearly articulating the security requirements will help a new participant understand the level of investment they need to make.
- **What are the standard contractual agreements that participants should accept?**
  As we mentioned in previous chapters, the smart contract should be accepted as the law within the network, but this needs to be bounded by contractual agreements that not only recognize this fact, but also state the expectation of the participant and the dispute processes.
- **What are the IT service-level agreements that the participant will need to adhere to?**
  As we have seen in `Chapter 8`, *Agility in a Blockchain Network*, getting an agreement on the frequency of promotion to smart contracts and the implicit evolution of the integration layer is important. Now this is an example, but from a service-level agreement, there are other aspects, such as availability, performance, and throughput, that can impact the network.

Through the on-boarding process, an organization will need to deploy its own infrastructure, integrate their transactions into their own enterprise system, and complete a round of testing before they can actually start transacting. During their life on the network, the governing body may dictate that some audits should be performed on the participant's infrastructure to demonstrate adherence to the terms and conditions.

A situation that is often overlooked is the event of an organization off-boarding the network. There could be two events that cause this to occur:

- The participant's interest in the network changes and they no longer want to transact
- A breach of contract or a dispute causes the participant to be removed

No matter what the reason is, if there are no provisions for this event, there can be issues related to the ownership of the organization's data. While the transaction data is shared in the context of a legal agreement, the parties may agree to have the distributed ledger stored in everyone's peers, but once that agreement comes to an end, what happens?

Funding and fees

The network will not operate itself. There are smart contracts to develop, common infrastructure to deploy (ordered nodes, for example), legal agreements to be written, and so on.

The model that will be adopted here will vary widely depending on the chosen business model. A founder-led network may incur all the funding costs, but might in turn charge a fee that will not only cover the cost, but also generate a profit. On the other hand, a community-driven network may choose to have participants cover the cost of those common elements.

In any case, the governance should not only define the funding and fee structure, but should also consider how usage should be monitored and how billing is performed.

Regulation

This area will depend largely on the industry and geography in which the network is operating, but at that level, there should be an identification of the compliance requirements and the regulations that participants are meant to adhere to.

A good example is the **General Data Protection Regulation** (**GDPR**), which has recently come into effect. GDPR is a regulation proposed by the European Commission to strengthen and reinforce data privacy rules. Under the new law, users can request to have their personal data permanently erased from any organization. Ignoring such regulations could result in a smart contract that persists personal information, creating a major problem for all participants of the network when a request for erasure is received.

In this area, the focus should be on the following:

- Identifying the relevant regulations
- Auditing smart contracts and participants (where applicable) to ensure compliance is met

Education

This may not be applicable to all types of business model. For example, a community-driven model may choose not to provide education services, letting their participants manage it on their own, whereas a founder-led network may decide to invest in education to expedite the on-boarding process and recoup the investment faster.

Service life cycle

The service life cycle deals specifically with the technology side of the network. A lot of consideration needs to be put in up front, from the initial design and implementation to the operation of the network.

In the initial stages of the network, key decisions will include such areas as the following:

- Design authority and standards
- Data governance
- Configuration management
- Key management
- Testing processes

Once the network is ready for prime time, the operational aspect will then quickly surface:

- Infrastructure operation (network, server, storage)
- Changes, upgrades, release management, maintenance
- Business continuity plan, archiving, backups
- Security, controls, policy enforcement
- Capacity, scalability, and performance
- Incident and problem management

Disputes

Nobody likes to think about disputes any more than they would the off-boarding process; however, it is important to define a process to address these disputes. In that context, the governance should cover areas such as the following:

- **Raising grievances**: Where should those issues be raised? We will cover the governance structure in the next section, but what if you are working in a truly decentralized model? Do you have a forum to raise this?
- **Investigation**: How will facts be gathered? How will the issue be documented? If a smart contract transaction's output is questioned, will it (and its corresponding customer) be extracted from the ledger?
- **Resolution**: Disputes will not always have happy conclusions, but what is the process to resolve these? Is there a subset of participants that should decide on the issue? Should this become a legal prosecution?

Governance structure

So far, we have covered the various business models, looked at the impact of centralization versus decentralization, and explored the various kinds of decisions, along with the roles and responsibilities required to support those decisions.

We will now see how organizations have been structuring themselves to provide a coherent approach that deals with the different levels of focus that decision makers will have, depending on their role.

While the presentation of centralized and decentralized governance will appear very distinct from each other, in real applications there are shades of grey, where some functions may be centralized and others decentralized. Again, much of this will have to do with the business model and imperatives driving the network.

Centralized governance

While a network may adopt centralized or decentralized governance, each organization will also have their own mechanism to control who makes decisions. Typically, organizations will rely internally on centralized governance. The implication of this is that we need to consider not only network governance, but also each organization's structure, as shown in the following diagram:

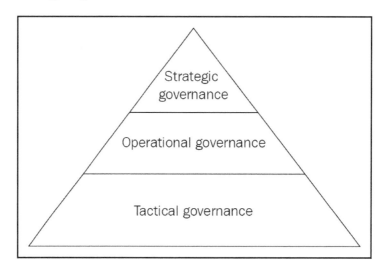

In a centralized model, decisions tend to flow from top to bottom, and only unresolved issues at the lower tiers of the organization percolate to the top. This creates a framework where there is a clear-cut process to deal with problems and vision, but which leaves little room for changes in structure.

In this model, we typically see three major layers of governance:

- **Strategic governance**
- **Operational governance**
- **Tactical governance**

The next subsections will define each one and explore the types of decision makers for each layer.

Strategic governance

Strategic governance represents the top of the decision pyramid. This governance tier requires executive sponsorship from the various organizations and business units, and is responsible for ensuring that the vision and strategy align with network objectives. It should also be focused on ensuring that the business benefits are realized.

Strategic governance will be focused on the following:

- Creating a common business vision
- Defining a clear mandate and governance structure (stakeholder-driven)
- Setting the agenda as to the priorities of the network
- Ensuring that the business objectives are met
- Developing and evolving network competencies

Operational governance

Operational governance focuses on converting the vision into a program with milestones that meet the requirements of the network. This will normally involve business stakeholders, directors, IT architects, legal counselor, and so on.

As a result of these concerns, the focus will be on the following:

- Defining ownership
- Developing and maintaining standards, privacy requirements, and regulation
- Creating a common approach for services and smart contracts

- Managing a common approach for defining business and technical requirements
- Common technology infrastructure

Tactical governance

Tactical governance is focused on the day-to-day activities that are centered around the running and operation of the network. At this level, the focus will be on aspects around the design, build, and operation of the network. It will include various stakeholders from business, legal, and technical teams. Tasks will include elements such as the following:

- Enforcing standards
- Smart contract code reviews
- Deployment planning
- Organization on-boarding
- Security audits
- Reporting

Decentralized governance

The decentralization of governance is a way to bring transparency and fairness to the decision process. Now keep in mind that every organizations have their own governance structure (The three tiers) and that those governance body need to come to an agreement on the decision. This is no trivial task considering that the strategic governance of each organization may have different imperative. This means that decisions need to be reached through a form of consensus—a voting process— which is fair, transparent and brings together the governance body of every organization of the network.

It also retains the same levels of governance (strategic, operational, and tactical) as a centralized network, but everything will be done in an open model where all topics are discussed in community calls/events. In such a model, the documentation of the decisions is even more important to ensure the proper level of transparency. Without a public audit trail, how can one know that the decision process is equitable?

It should be noted that while the model is decentralized and may be more lightweight/agile, it is no less important to properly document the model and see the participant's buy-in. Note that decentralized does not mean easier. In fact, while decentralized network governance might be more closely aligned to the nature of blockchain technologies, it introduces some interesting challenges.

For instance, since there is no central body that controls the strategic decision, how can a network move towards a common goal? How can you avoid a hard takeover or network fragmentation?

Such a model will work well while the business objectives are aligned. However, when a corporation's agenda is delayed because the majority of the community is voting for different priorities, this is bound to generate tension, disputes, and delays. As we have seen with the bitcoin block size debate, getting a consensus takes time and creates the opportunity for fragmentation. This is not to say that the solution lies in a centralized model—in fact, similar risks exist in that model too—but the decentralized nature of the decentralized model may mean that participants' business objectives are more loosely coupled.

Governance and the IT solution

So far in this chapter, we have been focusing primarily on the human side of governance. We have looked at the impact of the business model on governance, the business processes to consider, and the various potential structures, but what about the technology? What is the impact of the governance model on technology, and how does technology impact governance?

While blockchain projects might be primarily focused around solving business and enterprise issues, the foundation still relies on technology. In this section, we will look at the major phases of the life cycle of the network, from inception all the way to operation, and see how some of those activities can be automated and supported by technology.

We'll focus on the topic of on-boarding. As you now know, the system ledger is used to store the organizations, the policies, and the channels that make up the network. Storing configurations on the ledger means that any modifications need to be signed and approved. This is great from an audit perspective as it provides the configuration with the characteristics of the blockchain approach itself:

- **Consensus**: Configuration changes are endorsed and validated by members of the network according to the defined policies.
- **Provenance**: Configuration changes are signed by the initiator of the change and all other endorsers, thus preserving the provenance of the change.
- **Immutable**: Once the configuration block is added to the blockchain network, it cannot be modified. A subsequent transaction is required to further alter the configuration.

- **Finality**: As the transaction is recorded on the system ledger and distributed to all peers of the network, it provides a unique and final place to assert the configuration of the network. No need to look at configuration files to understand to which peer your anchor should communicate with.

Now while this is a highly valuable feature, it comes with a level of complexity. The high-level process to modify the configuration is as follows:

1. Retrieve the latest configuration block
2. Decode the configuration block and alter the configuration accordingly
3. Encode the block and calculate the delta/difference compared to the previous block to establish the RW set
4. Sign the transaction and share it with other participants so that they can sign it according to the network policy
5. Submit the signed transaction back to the network

These steps require a good understanding of the foundation of Hyperledger Fabric and a way to track and manage the signing by other parties. Given its decentralized nature, there might be a lot of different parties that need to be involved. This is one of the reasons the on-boarding process is so important to plan properly.

Networks should ensure that they define this process and the required automation early on. While organizations may build their own, they can also rely on prebuilt solutions. In the case of IBM, the IBM blockchain platform provides the ability to streamline the governance of the network. In the next section, we will look at how the on-boarding is done with the IBM blockchain platform.

Managed on-boarding

In order to follow through the exercise, you can:

1. **Sign up to the IBM Cloud here**: `https://console.bluemix.net/`
2. **Add the IBM blockchain platform service to your account using this link**:
   `https://console.bluemix.net/catalog/services/blockchain`

The starter plan should be selected and the reader should review the terms and conditions to understand the potential costs.

As the network is decentralized, an invitation can be issued by any organization of the network, unless the policies dictate otherwise.

The process starts with the issuance of an invitation through the following form, which can be accessed from the Membership menu of the dashboard:

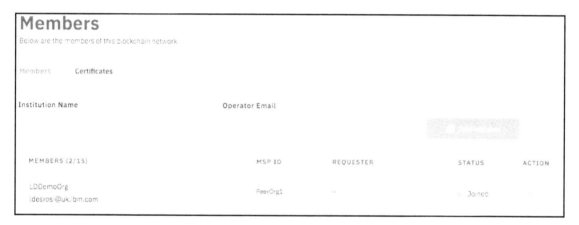

Upon submitting this form, the system will send a unique URL to the operator of the new organization. Behind the scenes, it also creates an enrollment request against the root fabric-ca of the network.

To accept the invitation, the operator signs up on the platform, provides the organization's name, and upon accepting the invitation, the system will automatically alter the network's configuration according to the defined policies and include the definition of the new organization. From this standpoint, the operator of the new organization gets access to the operational dashboard and can start joining channels and deploying smart contracts. The dashboard will look like the following screenshot:

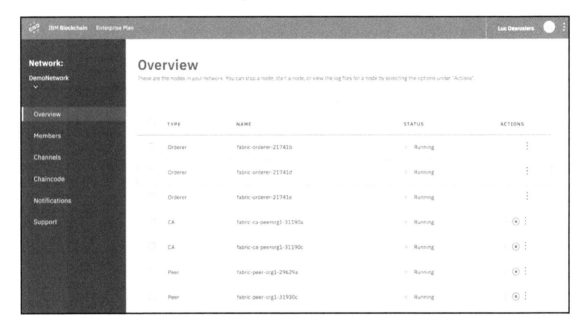

The operational dashboard

Now, since all interactions on the network are permissioned, the platform provides a voting mechanism that allows participants to accept or reject changes, as shown in the following screenshot:

Voting mechanism that allows participants to accept or reject changes

In this case, when the new organization is invited to join a channel, other organizations will get to vote on acceptance of the modification. They will be able to review the request in their notification portal and approve or reject it, as shown in the following screenshot:

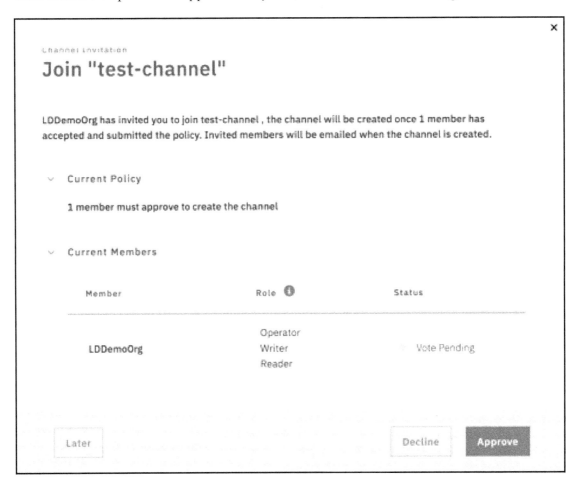

Reviewing the requests

While there are many more advantages and benefits to the IBM blockchain platform, the intent here was to show a way in which the IT solution can support and facilitate some of the key governance processes associated with an organization's on-boarding.

Summary

In a sense, governance is the human side of a business network. It is about how people come together and structure the decision-making process to ensure that all relevant parties are either consulted or responsible for the decision. Governance needs to cover a wide spectrum of topics.

Technologists might be less enthused about the topic than others, but having a basic view of what it entails is useful to understand our working environment.

To sum things up, in this chapter, we have explored how business models can have a profound impact on governance. Using these models, we then looked at how we can derive structures that meet business needs by addressing the key business processes. We have seen how organizations need to consider the approach of a centralized versus decentralized governance model. Finally, we learned that governance is required to support IT solutions, but in turn, IT solutions need to support the governance process.

A final point to keep in mind is that business models can be fluid things. While an initiative might start as a founder-led network, it can evolve into a consortium or a community-based project. This is important to note, because while we looked at each model in isolation, the reality is that they are bound to evolve over time, but need to remain aligned to the business value the network provides.

11
Hyperledger Fabric Security

Hyperledger Fabric is a modular blockchain system. It has been designed to allow a known set of actors to participate and perform actions in a blockchain network (the so-called **permissioned blockchain**). Due to its modular nature, it can be deployed in many different configurations. Different deployment configurations of Hyperledger Fabric have different security implications for the operator of the network, as well its users.

At its core, Hyperledger Fabric is a **public key infrastructure** (**PKI**) system and thus it inherits the security (and complexity) associated with such systems. At the time of writing this book, Hyperledger Fabric v1.1 has been released.

The security aspects of designing and implementing a blockchain network has been discussed in earlier application chapters, we intend to give a broader as well as a more in-depth view of the security features of Hyperledger Fabric here.

We will be covering the following topics in this chapter:

- Design goals impacting security
- Hyperledger Fabric architecture recap
- Network bootstrap and governance – the first step towards security
- Strong identities – the key to the security of the Hyperledger Fabric network
- Chain code security
- Common security threats and how Hyperledger Fabric mitigates them
- Hyperledger Fabric and quantum computing
- General data protection regulation (GDPR) considerations

Hyperledger Fabric design goals impacting security

To understand the security of Hyperledger Fabric, it is important to state the key design goals that impact security:

- **Existing members should determine how to add new members in the network**: The admission of new entities in the network must be agreed upon by existing entities in the network. This principle is at the foundation of creating a permissioned blockchain. Instead of allowing any entity to download software and connect to the network, network members must agree upon a policy to admit new members (e.g., by majority vote), which is then enforced by Hyperledger Fabric. Upon a successful vote, the digital credentials of a new member can be added to an existing network.

- **Existing members should determine how to update configuration/smart contract**: Similar to the first item, any change in the configuration of the network or deploying or instantiating a smart contract has to be agreed upon by the network members. Taken together, the first and second points give Hyperledger Fabric the capability to perform a permissioned blockchain.

- **The ledger and its associated smart contracts (chaincode) may be scoped to relevant peers to meet broader privacy and confidentiality requirements**: In public blockchain networks, all nodes have a copy of the blockchain ledger and execute smart contracts. To maintain confidentiality and scoping, it is necessary to create groups of peers that store the ledger associated with their transactions (channels and channel private data in Hyperledger Fabric). The smart contracts (chaincode in Hyperledger Fabric) that update such a ledger will be scoped to the members of such a group.

Only members participating in a channel have to determine how to update the configuration of that channel.

- **Smart contracts can be written in a general purpose language**: One of the main design goals of Hyperledger Fabric is to allow smart contracts to be written in general purpose languages such as Go and JavaScript. Obviously, allowing general purpose languages for smart contract execution exposes the system to a variety of security issues if there is no governance and process in place to verify and deploy smart contracts before execution. Even then, smart contracts written in a general purpose language should be reasonably isolated to limit the harm they may inadvertently cause.

- **Transaction integrity must be ensured**: A transaction is an execution of smart contract. The transactions must be created and stored in a way which will prevent them from being tampered with by other peers or will make it easy to detect any tampering. Typically, ensuring transaction integrity requires the use of cryptographic primitives.

- **Industry standards should be leveraged**: The system should leverage industry standards for asserting digital identities (for example, X.509 certificates), as well as for communication among peers (for example, TLS and gRPC).

- **Consensus separation from transaction execution and validation**: Existing blockchain networks combine transaction execution and validation with achieving consensus among nodes of a blockchain network. This tight coupling makes it difficult to achieve pluggability of the consensus algorithm.

- **Pluggability everywhere**: The system should have a modular design, and each module should be pluggable through standard interfaces. The ability to plug in modules specific to a network gives Hyperledger Fabric the flexibility to be used in a variety of settings. However, this pluggability also implies that two different instantiations of blockchain networks based on Hyperledger Fabric may possess different security properties.

To understand how these principles impact the security of Hyperledger Fabric, we will briefly explain the architecture of Hyperledger Fabric. Refer to earlier chapters for an in-depth architecture.

Hyperledger Fabric architecture

The Hyperledger Fabric architecture can be illustrated as follows:

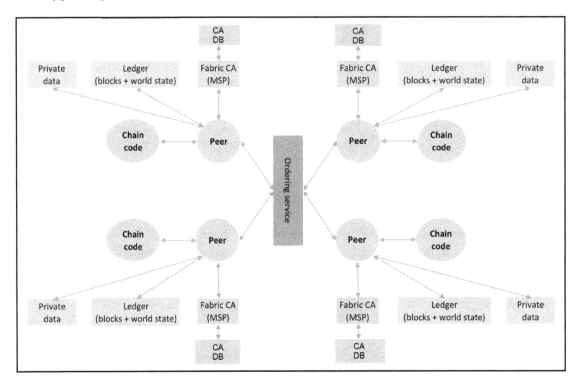

Hyperledger Fabric architecture

Fabric CA or membership service provider

The **membership service provider** (**MSP**) is responsible for creating digital identities for peers and users of the organization. The identities of peers must be configured in an existing network in order for a new entity to participate in the channel.

Fabric CA is an implementation of the MSP and provides a mechanism for registering users from a network member and issuing them digital identities (X.509 certificates). Fabric CA typically runs inside a Docker container. Each Fabric CA is configured with a backend database (the default being SQLite, with other options, such as PostgreSQL or MySQL) which stores the registered identities, as well as their X.509 certificates. Fabric CA does not store the private keys of the users.

Peer

A peer is an entity that participates in a Hyperledger Fabric network. Its identity is determined from its corresponding membership service provider. A peer is responsible for deploying and instantiating chaincode, updating the ledger, interacting with other peers to share private data associated with transactions, and interacting with the ordering service as well as smart contracts (chain code, in the preceding screenshot) that it runs. Similar to Fabric CA, a peer also typically runs inside a Docker container.

Smart contract or chaincode

Smart contract (**SC**) is application logic, written in a high-level language, such as Go or JavaScript; when successfully executed, it reads or writes data that eventually gets committed to the ledger. A smart contract does not have direct access to the ledger. A peer can deploy zero or more smart contracts that run as Docker containers. A peer can also deploy multiple versions of a smart contract.

Ledger

Each peer maintains a digital ledger, which contains a record of all committed transactions that a peer has received. The entries in the ledger are stored as key/value pairs. Updates to the same key will replace the current value of a key with a new value. The old value, of course, will stay in the ledger. To provide efficient querying of the latest value of a key, a node can store the latest value of each key in a database such as CouchDB. This database is referred to as a world state in Hyperledger Fabric.

Note that a peer will only receive blocks to commit to its ledger from the channels that it participates in.

A peer can be part of zero or more channels— the channels are not shown in the preceding diagram showing Hyperledge Fabric architecture.

Private data

With Hyperledger Fabric v1.1, peers can choose to selectively share private data with a subset of peers in the channel through the chain private data experimental feature (`https://jira.hyperledger.org/browse/FAB-1151`). The blocks on the ledger only contain hashes of such data, while the private data is stored off the ledger in a private state database.

Ordering service

The ordering service is responsible for receiving the executed transactions from peers, combining them into blocks, and broadcasting them to other peers on the same channel. The peers receiving the transaction blocks then validate it before committing it to their ledger. It is the responsibility of the ordering service to not mix the blocks intended for one channel on another channel.

In version 1.0 of Hyperledger Fabric, the peers would send a transaction (keys and associated values, along with the read/write set) to the ordering service. Thus, the ordering service had visibility into all data associated with transactions, which had implications from a confidentiality standpoint. In version 1.1 of Hyperledger Fabric, the client can send hashes of the transaction data (input and read/write set) to the ordering service while transferring the data associated with a transaction directly to the relevant peers.

Presently, the ordering service is implemented using Kafka and is **crash fault tolerant** (**CFT**), but not **Byzantine Fault Tolerant** (**BFT**). But this is a point in time statement as HyperLedger is purported to be pluggable that includes the consensus service. Pluggability implies that in future other consensus models may be available.

Although now shown in the diagram depicting Hyperledger Fabric architecture, peers, orderers, and fabric use a pluggable cryptography service provider, which allows them to plug in new crypto algorithms as well as hardware security modules (HSMs) (`https://en.wikipedia.org/wiki/Hardware_security_module`) for managing crypto keys.

Network bootstrap and governance – the first step towards security

When organizations decide to form a permissioned private blockchain network using Hyperledger Fabric, they need to consider several governance aspects, which will ultimately determine the overall security posture of the network. These governance aspects include, but are not limited to the following:

- **How shall the network be bootstrapped and the members verified to create the network?** Network bootstrap is the first step in creating a blockchain network. Different entities may come together to create a network. The entities may have an out-of-band communication to agree upon with the first set of members and establish governance policies, which will be discussed next.
- **What is the process for a new entity to join the network (or a channel)?** Defining a policy for admitting new members in the network is paramount and is governed by the business needs of the network.
- **Who can deploy and upgrade chaincodes on peers in the network?** Defining a process is important to prevent a malicious or buggy chaincode from being installed on one or more peers (see `Chapter 7`, *A Business Network Example*).
- **What is the data model that will be stored on the blockchain?** Members must agree upon a common data model that will be stored in the blockchain; the blockchain cannot be useful to its members otherwise. The data model should be devised so that it does not run afoul of any compliance regulations, such as **general data protection regulations** (**GDPR**) (`https://gdpr-info.eu/`).

Creating the network

When entities decide to create a network, they must decide on the following:

- Who will run the ordering service
- How many different instances of ordering service will be in the network

The role of the ordering service is critical because, depending on the configuration, it has visibility into transaction hashes or the transaction data across all channels that flow through it. Thus, the entities deciding to form a network may choose to trust one of the entities to act as the ordering service; they may also decide to trust a neutral third party to run the ordering service.

The ordering service can view all transactions (hashes or key/value pairs) across all channels that it serves. Thus, if it is necessary to hide the transaction data from the ordering service, only hashes of the read/write set in a transaction should be sent to the ordering service while exchanging the data directly between peers.

Once an ordering service has been established for a network, it must be configured with the digital identities of peers of founding members. This is typically done by configuring the digital certificates of peers in the ordering service genesis blocks. The peers must also be configured with the digital identity of the ordering service.

Adding new members

The founding members at the time of creation of a network or a channel must also define the policy on how new members will be admitted into the network or a channel. By default, this policy is simply the one chosen by the majority (namely two out of two, two out of three, three out of four, and so on). The members may decide on any other policy for admitting new members in the network. Any change in the policy to admit new members will typically be decided through a business agreement. Once an agreement is reached, the channel configuration can be updated per the current policy to reflect the new policy for admitting new members.

The creation of the genesis block, as well as subsequent transactions to update configurations, are privileged operations, and must be approved by the peer administrator before being confirmed.

Deploying and updating chaincode

Once members have decided to participate in a channel, they may choose to deploy and instantiate chaincode (a.k.a smart contract). A chaincode defines how key/value pairs which are scoped to a channel will be updated or read from. A chaincode can define its endorsement policy—that is, it may require a digital signature from some or all peers in the network. Due to the permissioned nature of Hyperledger Fabric, a chaincode requiring a digital signature from a peer (endorsement) must be installed and instantiated on a peer. See `Chapter 5`, *Exposing Network Assets and Transactions* and `Chapter 7`, *A Business Network Example*, for more details on deploying chaincode.

Before deploying chaincode on a channel, it is expected that network members will want to review the chaincode to ensure that it conforms to their policy. This process can be formalized into chaincode governance to require mandatory reviews from all relevant members who will instantiate the chaincode on their nodes.

 Establish a process for deploying chaincode on your peer, including manual reviews and the verification of a digital signature of the chaincode author.

Data model

The entities must agree upon a data model that will be stored in a blockchain, which in turn is determined by the chaincode. The founding members of a network or a channel deploying a chaincode will determine the key/value pairs that get stored in a channel. Furthermore, the member will decide which data they will share with other members, and which data they will keep private to themselves or a subset of members. The data model should be devised so that it is useful for the business functions that members desire to accomplish, is reasonably future-proof, and does not inadvertently leak information. Recall that all participating peers in a channel store the committed transactions (and their key/value pairs).

 Establish a process for defining the data model that will be stored in a channel.

The preceding steps can be summarized as follows:

1. Determine who will run the ordering service
2. Configure digital identities of founding members in the ordering service
3. Create channels and determine the channel policy for admitting new members
4. Define the governance for writing, distributing, deploying, and instantiating chaincode
5. Establish the data model

Strong identities – the key to the security of the Hyperledger Fabric network

Strong identities are at the heart of Hyperledger Fabric security. Creating, managing, and revoking these identities is critical to the operational security of Hyperledger Fabric-based deployment. The identities are issued by a MSP. As shown in the previous Hyperledger Fabric architecture diagram, one logical MSP is typically associated with one peer. An MSP can issue any appropriate cryptographically signed identities. Hyperledger Fabric ships with a default MSP, (Fabric CA), which issues X.509 certificates to the authenticated entities.

Bootstrapping Fabric CA

Fabric CA can be configured with a LDAP server or run in a standalone mode. When running in a standalone mode, it must be configured with a bootstrap identity that gets stored in the backend database of Fabric CA. By default, a SQLite database is used but, for production usages, a PostgreSQL or a MySQL database can be configured. Typically, the connection between the Fabric CA server and its database is over TLS if a standalone server is used.

For the rest of the chapter, we will refer to the bootstrap entity when running without the LDAP server as the `ca-admin`. The `ca-admin` and its password must be supplied on a bootstrap of the Fabric CA, when running without LDAP server.

In order for the `ca-admin` to interact with the server, it must submit a **certificate signing request** (**CSR**) to the Fabric CA server to obtain a X.509 certificate. This process is called **enrolling an identity**, or simply **enroll**. With a X.509 certificate in possession, the `ca-admin` can then add other users, which we will explain next.

 Keep the password of the admin user in a safe and secure place since this is the `root` user of your organization. Treat it as securely as you would treat the password of a `root` Linux user. Use it to create a new user with appropriate permissions, but never use this user for any other operation, except in the case of a security breach, where this user can be used to revoke the certs of all enrolled entities.

Fabric CA provides two key operations in the system, namely register and enroll. We will explain these operations next.

Register

The register operation adds a new entity specified by an identifier to Fabric CA. The register operation does not create a X.509 certificate for the user; that happens in the enroll operation. It is up to the administrator of the Fabric CA to define the policies and procedures for adding new users to the network.

There are some important points to consider while registering the users:

- If a policy is to register an email address then, upon subsequent enrollment, the user's email address will be encoded in the certificate. In Hyperledger Fabric, the certificate of the user issuing the transaction is stored in the ledger along with the committed transaction. Anyone can decode the certificate and determine the email address.

> Carefully determine how new entities will be registered within a Fabric CA, as their digital certificates will end up in the ledger when these entities issue transactions.

- Another important point to consider is how many enrollments are allowed for that user. Each enrollment results in a new certificate being issued to the user. In Hyperledger Fabric, a new user being registered can be enrolled a finite number of times, or can have unlimited enrollments. Typically, a new entity being enrolled should not be configured with unlimited number of enrollments.

> It is best to set the maximum number of enrollments to 1 for a new user. This setting ensures that there is 1-1 correspondence between an entity and its digital certificate, thus making management of entity revocation easier.

- With Hyperledger Fabric 1.1, it is now possible to define attributes for entities at the time of their registration. These attributes are then encoded in the X.509 certificate of an entity.

When used in standalone mode, upon successful registration, Fabric CA will create a unique password (if not supplied during registration). The `ca-admin` can then pass this password to the entity being registered, which will then use it to create a CSR and obtain a certificate through the enroll operation.

Default Fabric roles

To register an entity in the Fabric CA, an entity should have a set of roles. Fabric CA is configured with the following default roles:

```
hf.Registrar.Roles = client, user, peer, validator, auditor
```

A Fabric CA can register any entity that has one of these roles:

```
hf.Registrar.DelegateRoles = client, user, validator, auditor
```

A Fabric CA can revoke a role:

```
hf.Revoker = true
```

A Fabric CA can also register an intermediate CA:

```
hf.IntermediateCA
```

To register an identity in Fabric CA, an entity must have the `hf.Registrar`. Roles are attributed with a comma-separated list of values, where one of the values equals the type of identity being registered.

Secondly, the affiliation of the invoker's identity must be equal to or a prefix of the affiliation of the identity being registered. For example, an invoker with an affiliation of `a.b` may register an identity with an affiliation of `a.b.c`, but may not register an identity with an affiliation of `a.c`.

Enroll

The entity in possession of an ID and secret can then enroll itself with Fabric CA. To do so, it generates a public/private key pair, creates a CSR, and sends that to Fabric CA along with the registered ID and secret in the `Authorization` header. Upon successful authentication, the server returns an X.509 certificate to the entity being enrolled. The entity sending the enroll request is responsible for managing the private key. These private keys should be stored in a secure fashion (such as a hardware security module).

Which crypto protocols are allowed in certificate signing requests?

The CSR can be customized to generate X.509 certificates and keys that support the **Elliptic Curve Digital Signature Algorithm (ECDSA)**. The following key sizes and algorithms are supported:

Size	ASN1 OID	Signature Algorithm
256	prime256v1	ecdsa-with-SHA256
384	secp384r1	ecdsa-with-SHA384
521	secp521r1	ecdsa-with-SHA512

Revoking identities

Since Hyperledger Fabric is a PKI system, identities that must be removed from the system have to be explicitly revoked. This is done through standard **certificate revocation lists (CRLs)**. The CRLs need to be synchronized across all organizations to ensure that everyone detects the revoked certificate. The distribution of CRLs to other peers requires out of band mechanisms.

Practical considerations in managing users in Fabric CA

Typically, an organization has its own identity (LDAP) server for managing its employees. An organization may choose to participate in one or more Hyperledger Fabric networks, but only a subset of its employees may be onboarded to each network. The administrator of Fabric CA for each network may choose to register a subset of employees in each network.

Since an employee must generate and manage a private key to successfully participate in a Hyperledger Fabric network, the responsibility of managing the private key and its corresponding digital certificate lies with the employee of an organization. Managing private keys and digital certificates is non-trivial, and this can place an undue burden on an employee and may lead to inadvertent key exposures by the employee. Since an employee needs to remember their organization issued credentials (e.g., username and password) to log on to the organization systems, an organization can choose to manage the private keys and certificates on behalf of its employees that participate in one or more Hyperledger Fabric networks. Depending on the industry, the private keys may be stored in hardware security modules, which will make it infeasible to tamper with the keys. The precise configuration of hardware security modules is beyond the scope of this chapter.

Chaincode security

In Fabric, smart contracts, also known as **chaincode**, can be written in Go or JavaScript. The chaincodes must be installed on a peer and then explicitly initiated. When initiated, each code runs in a separate Docker container. The previous versions of chaincode also run in separate Docker containers.

The Docker container running the chaincode has access to the virtual network as well as the entire networking stack. If care is not taken in carefully reviewing the chaincode before it gets installed on the peer, and isolating the network access for that chaincode, it could result in a malicious or misconfigured node probing or attaching the peer attached to the same virtual network.

 An operator can configure a policy to disable all outgoing or incoming network traffic on the chaincode Docker containers, except white-listed nodes.

How is chaincode shared with other endorsing peers?

Organizations must establish a process for sharing chaincode with other other organizations participating in a Hyperledger Fabric network. Since the chaincode must be installed on all endorsing peers, it is necessary to ensure the integrity of the chaincode through cryptographic mechanisms while sharing it with other peers. Please refer to *Chapter 8, Agility in a Blockchain Network*, for more details on the approach to share the chaincode This issue was also highlighted in the security assessment of Hyperledger Fabric conducted by Nettitude `https://wiki.hyperledger.org/_media/security/technical_report_linux_foundation_fabric_august_2017_v1.1.pdf`

Who can install chaincode?

To install chaincode on a peer, an entity's certificate must be installed on the node (stored in the local MSP) of the peer. Since installing chaincode is a highly privileged operation, care should be taken that only entities with administrative capabilities have the ability to perform this operation.

Chaincode encryption

An entity can choose to encrypt the key/value pairs by using an AES encryption key at the time of chaincode invocation (`https://github.com/hyperledger/fabric/tree/master/examples/chaincode/go/enccc_example`). The encryption key is passed to the chaincode, which then encrypts the values before sending them in a proposal. The entities that need to decrypt the value (for example, to endorse a transaction) must be in possession of a key. It is expected that such encryption keys are then shared with other peers in an out-of-band manner.

Attribute-based access control

As you may remember from `Chapter 4`, *Designing a Data and Transaction Model with Golang*, one of the new features added with Hyperledger 1.1 is attribute-based access control. At the time of registering an entity, attributes can be specified for an entity, which then are added to the X.509 certificate upon enrollment. Examples of attributes include a role name such as an "auditor" that is agreed upon by the organizations participating in the network. When chaincode is executed, it can check if an identity has certain attributes before the invoke or query operation. At a simple level, this allows application-level attributes to be passed down into chaincode through a X.509 certificate.

Pros and cons of attribute-based access control

Encoding attributes in certificates has its own set of pros and cons. On one hand, all the information associated with an identity is encoded in the certificate, thus decisions can be made based on attributes. On the other hand, if an attribute has to be updated, for example, a user moves to a different department, the existing certificate must be revoked, and a new certificate has to be issued with a new set of attributes.

Common threats and how Hyperledger Fabric mitigates them

Hyperledger Fabric provides protection against some of the most common security threats, and assumes a shared responsibility model for addressing others. In the following table, we will summarize the most common security threats, whether Hyperledger Fabric addresses them and how or whether it is the responsibility of a node/network operator to address them:

Threat	Description	Hyperledger Fabric	Network/Node Operator
Spoofing	Use of a token or other credential to pretend to be an authorized user, or compromise a user's private key.	Fabric certificate authority generates X.509 certificates for its members.	Manage certificate revocation list distribution among network participants to ensure that revoked members can no longer access the system.
Tampering	Modify information (for example, an entry in the database).	Use of cryptographic measures (SHA256, ECDSA) make tampering infeasible.	Derived from Fabric.
Repudiation	An entity cannot deny who did what.	Tracks who did what using digital signatures.	Derived from Fabric.
Replay attacks	Replay the transactions to corrupt the ledger.	Hyperledger Fabric uses read/write sets to validate the transaction. A replay of transactions will fail due to an invalid read set.	Derived from Fabric.

Information disclosure	Data exposed through intentional breach or accidental exposure.	Hyperledger Fabric provides support for using TLSv1.2 for in-transit encryption. It does not encrypt ledger data at rest (the operator's responsibility). Information about all peers in the system and their transactions is exposed to the ordering service.	It is the operator's responsibility to prevent information disclosure by following information security best practices as well as at-rest encryption.
Denial of service	Makes it difficult for legitimate users to access the system.	It is the operator's responsibility.	It is the operator's responsibility to prevent denial of service to the system.
Elevation of Privileges	Gain high level access to the application.	Issued identities cannot upgrade their access (for example, create an identity) without manual review of access.	Hyperledger Fabric runs chaincode in Docker containers. It is the responsibility of the network/node operator to limit access and run chaincode containers with appropriate restrictions.
Ransomware	Using cryptographic or other means to prevent access to data on the file system.	It is the operator's responsibility.	It is the operator's responsibility to ensure that ransomware cannot prevent access to a node's ledger.

Transaction privacy in Hyperledger Fabric

One of the main design considerations for Hyperledger Fabric is to provide privacy and confidentiality of transactions. Hyperledger Fabric provides a number of knobs to achieve these goals.

Channels

A Hyperledger Fabric node that only intends to share data with a subset of nodes in the network can do so through channels. In these cases, only peers that participate in the channel can store transaction data; the peers that are not part of the channel do not have visibility into the transaction data, and thus cannot store it. However, this data is exposed to the ordering service. A robust Channel design will address the isolation, data privacy and confidentiality between participants and controlled/permissioned access with robust audit capability.

Private data

Peers in a channel can choose to determine which other peers they will share their data with. The private transaction data is passed peer-to-peer between the peers, while only the hashes of the transaction data are broadcasted to the ordering services and to peers with whom this data is not shared with.

Encrypting transaction data

Peers can also choose to encrypt the transaction data before sending it for endorsements. However, it may be necessary for peers endorsing the transaction to view the data. An out-of-band mechanism must be used to exchange encryption keys between such peers.

Hyperledger Fabric and Quantum Computing

Hyperledger Fabric uses elliptic curve cryptography for digitally signing that transactions. The elliptic curve cryptography relies on mathematical techniques which can be sped up using quantum computing (https://en.wikipedia.org/wiki/Post-quantum_cryptography). However, Hyperledger Fabric provides a pluggable cryptographic provider, which allows replacing these algorithms for digital signatures with others. Moreover, per the director of Information Technology Lab at NIST, the impact of quantum computing on the security of blockchain systems is at least 15 to 30 years from becoming a reality (https://www.coindesk.com/dc-blockchain-hearing-sees-call-for-congressional-commission/).

General data protection regulation (GDPR) considerations

General Data Protection Regulation (**GDPR**) (`https://gdpr-info.eu/`) is an EU law that defines how personal data is acquired, processed, and ultimately erased from a computing system. The definition of personal data in GDPR is quite broad—examples include name, email address, and IP address.

Blockchain, by design, creates an immutable, permanent, and replicated record of the data. A blockchain network based on Hyperledger Fabric will obviously encompass these three properties. Thus storing personal data on a blockchain network which cannot be deleted or modified can be challenging from the perspective of GDPR. Similarly, it is important to know who that personal data is shared with.

The channel and the channel private data feature of Hyperledger Fabric provides a mechanism for determining the entities with which data is shared. In the case of channel private data, the data is never stored on a blockchain, but its cryptographic hashes are stored on the chain. Though a governance process, peers can determine the other peers to share this data with. The channel private data feature in Hyperledger Fabric can potentially provide a mechanism to store personal data off the chain, determining who this data is shared with, while maintaining the integrity of this data through cryptographic hashes stored in the blockchain.

Hyperledger Fabric also stores the X.509 certificate of the entity creating the transaction in the digital ledger. These X.509 certificates can contain personal data. With version 1.1, Hyperledger Fabric provides a mechanism to prove the identity based on zero knowledge proofs, while hiding the actual value of the attribute. These zero-knowledge proof-based credentials are then stored in the ledger in lieu of a traditional X.509 certificate and can potentially help towards GDPR compliance.

Summary

In this chapter, we first covered design goals of Hyperledger Fabric that are tied to security. All the sets of points which were described are considered to keep Fabric security in mind. We briefly studied the Hyperledger Fabric Security and understood how strong identities are at the heart of Fabric security. We also took a look at chaincode security.

Hyperledger, by itself, is adept at handling threats. We dove into the common Hyperledger security threats and how Fabric mitigates them.

We also briefly looked at the impact of quantum computing on Hyperledger Fabric.

12
Introduction to Blockchain Technology

In this chapter, we give an overview of blockchain, along with its key concepts such as cryptography and hash algorithms, the distributed ledger, transactions, blocks, proof of work, mining, and consensus. We cover Bitcoin, the mother of blockchain technology, in detail. We briefly introduce Ethereum by pointing out some limitations of Bitcoin and how they are addressed by Ethereum. While Bitcoin and Ethereum are examples of public blockchains, IBM's Hyperledger is used as an example of enterprise blockchains. At the end of this chapter, we mention the evolution of the blockchain: blockchain 1.0, 2.0, 3.0, and beyond, based on their use cases. Specifically, we will cover the following topics on blockchain:

- A genealogical analogy for blockchain
- The Bitcoin consensus mechanism
- A brief discussion of Hyperledger
- Blockchain evolution

The genealogy analogy

One of the authors recently attended a Chinese university alma mater reunion event in Beijing, where blockchain became a hot discussion topic. A very well-regarded schoolmate and scholar, Professor Yang, who has authored books on cryptography and public data safeguards, used genealogy to describe a blockchain. This is a well-thought-out analogy since it explains blockchain intuitively and easily. The analogy is borrowed here to illustrate the basic ideas behind the technology.

Back in the old days in China, it was a custom for each family of a clan (sharing the same last name) to keep a copy of the genealogical tree of the clan. When members of a family changed due to either marriage or the birth of an offspring, as well as adoption, the new member's name would appear in each copy. However, the new member had to be accepted by the clan before the name could be added in. There were cases when a marriage was not endorsed by a majority of the clan due to various reasons. In this case, the new member's name would not be entered into the genealogy. In other words, when a new member joined in a family, the news was broadcast to other families of the clan. If the clan reached a consensus on accepting the new member, each family would update their copy of the genealogical tree to reflect the change. On the other hand, if the clan decided not to accept the new member, the name would not be added in. The genealogy could be used for verification purposes. For example, if a stranger made a claim to be a member of the clan, or two people with the same last name were eager to find out whether they shared the same ancestor, with the genealogy, it was easy to verify this. The outcome would be accepted since the genealogy was considered reliable thanks to the aforementioned consensus and decentralized records, which were difficult to manipulate unless the majority of families agreed.

A blockchain shares many of the characteristics of a genealogy. They are summarized as follows:

- Like a clan consisting of many related families, a blockchain network consists of nodes. Each node is like a family.
- Like every family keeping a copy of the clan's genealogy, each node of a blockchain maintains a copy of all transactions that have occurred on the chain, starting from the very beginning. The collection of all transactions is a **ledger**. This makes a blockchain a decentralized data repository.

- A genealogy starts with a common ancestor of the clan and names with direct relationships, such as parents and children, that are connected by a line for linkage. Similarly, a ledger consists of blocks. Each block contains one or multiple transactions depending on the type of blockchain. (As you will see later, blocks on Bitcoin or Ethereum host multiple transactions, while R3's Corda uses a block with only one transaction). Transactions are like names, and a block is similar to the invisible box containing a couple's names. An equivalent of the root ancestor is called the **genesis block**, which is the first block of a blockchain. Similar to a line linking parents and children, a hash, which will later be explained in more detail, points from the current block to its ancestor block.

- Like the consensus mechanism for adding new names to a genealogy, the Bitcoin blockchain uses a mechanism called Proof-of-Work to decide whether a block can be added to the chain. Like a genealogy, after a block is added to a chain, it is difficult to change (hack) unless one possesses the majority (which is called a 51% attack) of the computing power of the network.

- Genealogy provides transparency in a clan's history. Similarly, a blockchain allows a user to query the whole ledger or just a part of the ledger and find out about coin movements.

- Since every family kept a copy of the genealogy, it was unlikely to lose the genealogy even if many copies were lost due to a natural disaster, a war, or other reasons. As long as at least one family survived, the genealogy survived. Similarly, a decentralized ledger will survive as long as at least one node survives.

While genealogy is a good analogy to explain some key concepts of a blockchain, they are not the same. Inevitably, there are features that are not shared by them. For example, the blockchain uses cryptography and hashes extensively for data protection and deterring hackers. A genealogy does not have such a need. Therefore, next we move away from the genealogy analogy and explain key blockchain concepts chronically.

Bitcoin

Blockchain technology initially caught people's attention due to the **Bitcoin** blockchain, an idea outlined by a white paper authored by Satoshi Nakamoto and published in October 2008 on the cryptography mailing list at metzdowd.com. It describes the **Bitcoin digital currency** (**BTC**) and was titled *Bitcoin: A Peer-to-Peer Electronic Cash System*. In January 2009, Satoshi Nakamoto released the first Bitcoin software, which launched the network and the first units of the Bitcoin cryptocurrency: BTC coins.

Why Bitcoin

The creation of Bitcoin was right after the 2008 financial crisis, the most severe economic crisis since the Great Depression. This is not coincidental. The inventor of the Bitcoin cryptocurrency aimed at addressing people's disillusionment with financial institutions, whose epic failures in risk controls resulted in the 2008 financial crisis.

A fundamental role played by financial institutions is to be an intermediary entity and bring untrusting parties together to facilitate transactions. For example, a retail bank attracts residual money from individuals and lends to individuals or companies that need the money. The difference in interest paid to the money suppliers and borrowers is the fee a bank charges for providing the intermediary service. Financial institutions are very successful in providing these services and play a pivotal role in powering economies worldwide. However, there are many deficiencies associated with this business model. Here are some examples:

- **Slow**: It often takes days to complete a financial transaction. For instance, it takes three days (after an order is initially entered) to complete and settle a cross-border money transfer. To make it happen, multiple departments and application systems within an institution and across institutions have to work together to facilitate the transaction. Another example is stock trading. An investor hires a broker to enter an order to be routed to a stock exchange. Here, the broker is either a member of the exchange or routes the order to another intermediary institution with membership. After a match is found between a buyer and a seller at the exchange, the transaction details are recorded by two parties who send it to their back offices respectively. The back-office teams work with a clearing house for clearance and settlement. It takes T + 3 for both parties to complete the action of exchanging ownership of the security (stock) and the cash.
- **Expensive**: Financial intermediaries often charge hefty fees when providing these services. For example, a US bank could charge $10 to $30 USD to serve an individual by sending money from the US to a receiver in another country. In the case of stock trading, a full-service broker often charges tens of USD or more for a transaction. Even with a discount broker, an investor needs to pay $7 to $10 USD per transaction.
- **Prone to be hacked**: Since details on a customer and the transactions are saved in a centralized area within an institution, it is prone to being hacked and causing severe financial loss or leakage of confidential personal information about customers. Recently, there have been high-profile personal data leakage incidents at reputable companies such as JP Morgan (83 million accounts hacked in 2014), Target (up to 70 million customers' information hacked in 2013), and Equifax (148 million US consumers' information hacked in 2017).

- **Not transparent**: Financial institutions keep both detailed and aggregated information on transactions. However, most of the information is not open to the individual customer and this results in information imparity. In the example of cross-border money transfers, both the sender and receiver have to wait for three days to know whether the transaction has been completed successfully or not. If a transaction fails, a lengthy investigation has to be triggered. Imagine if the receiver was in an emergency and needed the funding immediately. Such a service is unsatisfactory despite the client having to pay a high fee.

With blockchain technology, the preceding problems are resolved elegantly. In the case of the Bitcoin blockchain, the underlying asset to be transferred is the digital coin, BTC. A cross-border BTC transaction can complete in no more than 1 hour. No settlement is needed since transaction and settlement are in one action. The cost of this transaction is a tiny fraction of a transfer via a bank. For example, a recent report published by the **Bank of America (BoA)** claims a transfer via blockchain costs 1/6000 of what BoA charges. However, for some clients, waiting an hour is still too long. **Ripple**, a payment provider for sending money globally, completes in under 1 minute.

The word Bitcoin often causes confusion as people use the word interchangeably for three things: the cryptocurrency, the blockchain, and the protocol. To avoid this confusion, we use BTC to refer to the cryptocurrency, and Bitcoin to refer to the blockchain and the corresponding network that uses the distributed ledger. For the protocol, we will fully spell out **Bitcoin protocol** or simply protocol.

A peer-to-peer network

To explain how Bitcoin works, let's look at what steps are involved with the existing business model for completing a cross-border transaction:

- A customer enters an order either by visiting a bank branch or via the web. The sender provides detailed information of an order such as the amount, sending currency, receiver name, receiving currency, receiver's bank name, account and branch numbers, and a SWIFT number. Here, **SWIFT** stands for the **Society for Worldwide Interbank Financial Telecommunications**, a messaging network used by financial institutions to transmit information and instructions securely through a standardized system of codes. SWIFT assigns each financial organization a unique code called, interchangeably, the **bank identifier code (BIC)**, SWIFT code, SWIFT ID, or ISO 9362 code.
- The sending bank takes the order and verifies that the sender has sufficient funds available.

- The bank charges a fee and converts the remaining amount from the sending currency to an amount in the receiving currency by executing an FX transaction.
- The sending bank enters a transferring message to SWIFT with all the needed information.
- Upon receiving the message, the receiving bank verifies the receiver's account information.
- Upon a successful verification and settling the funds between sending and receiving banks following the protocol, the receiving bank credits the amount to the receiver's account.

Since there are multiple steps, entities, and systems involved, the preceding activities take days to complete.

A Bitcoin network connects computers around the world. Each computer is a **node** with equal status, except for a subset of nodes called **miners**, which choose to play the role of verifying transactions, building blocks and linking to the chain. With Bitcoin, the business model for completing a money transfer involves the following steps:

1. A sender enters the number of BTCs, the addresses of Bitcoins to be taken from, and addresses of Bitcoins to be transferred to, using an **e-wallet.**
2. The transaction request is sent to the Bitcoin network by the e-wallet.
3. After miners have successfully verified the transaction and committed it to the network, the BTCs are now available for use by the receiver.

The Bitcoin transfer is a lot faster (in 1 hour, or minutes if using Ripple) for the following reasons:

- The transaction and settlement are one step. This avoids the need to go through a time-consuming and expensive reconciliation process.
- No FX trade is needed since BTC is borderless. It can move worldwide freely and rapidly.
- No fund settlement is needed between banks since the transaction requires no intermediary banks.

In a case where a sender or receiver prefers to use a **fiat currency** such as USD, GBP, CNY, or JPY, a cryptocurrency market can be used for a conversion between BTC and a fiat currency. A website, CoinMarketCap, lists these markets: `https://coinmarketcap.com/rankings/exchanges/`. As of September 21, 2018, there are 14,044 markets. In terms of market capitalization, the top three are Binance (`https://www.binance.com/`), OKEx (`https://www.binance.com/`), and Huopi (`https://www.huobi.pro`).

A peer-to-peer network can connect nodes worldwide. However, a merely physical connection is not enough to make two untrusting parties trade with each other. To allow them to trade, Bitcoin takes the following measures:

- Every node saves a complete copy of all transactions in a decentralized ledger. This makes any alteration to a transaction on the chain infeasible.
- The ledger transactions are grouped in blocks. A non-genesis block is linked to its previous block by saving the hash of all preceding blocks' transactions. Consequently, changing a transaction requires changing the current block of transactions and all subsequent blocks. This makes hacking the decentralized ledger extremely difficult.
- Bitcoin addresses the double-spending issue, that is the same BTC being spent twice, by using the Proof-of-Work consensus algorithm.
- Hashes are used extensively to protect the identities of parties and detect any changes occurring in a block.
- Public/private keys and addresses are used to mask the identities of trading parties and to sign a transaction digitally .

With these measures, untrusting parties feel comfortable to trade due to these reasons:

- The transaction is immutable and permanent. Neither party can nullify a transaction unilaterally.
- No double spending is possible.
- Transaction and settlement occur simultaneously; therefore, there is no settlement risk.
- Identities are protected.
- Transactions are signed by both parties, which will avoid any future legal disputes.

Cryptography and hash functions

Cryptography or cryptology is research on techniques for securing communication in the presence of adversaries. In the old days, cryptography was synonymous with encryption. Modern cryptography relies heavily on mathematical theory and computer science. It also utilizes works from other disciplines such as electrical engineering, communications science, and physics.

Cryptographic algorithms are designed around the assumption that with foreseeable computational hardware advances, it will not be feasible for any adversary to decipher encrypted messages based on these algorithms. In other words, in theory, it is possible to decode the encrypted message, but it is infeasible to do so practically. These algorithms are therefore defined to be computationally secure. Theoretical research (for instance, parallel or integer factorization algorithms) and computational technology advancements (for instance, quantum computers) can make these algorithms practically insecure and, therefore, encryption algorithms need to be adapted continuously.

Encryption is the process of converting plaintext into unintelligible text, called ciphertext. Decryption is the reverse, in other words moving from the unintelligible ciphertext back to plaintext.

The encryption algorithms used by Bitcoin mining are hash functions. A hash function is a function that maps data of any size to data of a fixed size. The values returned by a hash function are called hash values or simply hashes. A cryptographic hash function allows one to verify easily that some input data maps to a given hash value. However, the reverse – when the input data is unknown—it is practically infeasible to reconstruct the input plaintext from a hash value. In other words, hashing is a one-way operation. Another notable attribute of a hashing function is that a minor change in the input plaintext will result in a completely different hash value. This feature is desirable for safeguarding information as any tiny change to the original data by a hacker results in a visibly different hash.

Two common hash algorithms are MD5 (message-digest algorithm 5) and SHA-1 (secure hash algorithm):

- Developed by Ronald Rivest in 1991, MD5 maps input plaintext into a 128-bit resulting hash value. MD5 Message-Digest checksums are commonly used to validate data integrity when digital files are transferred or stored. MD5 has been found to suffer from extensive vulnerabilities.

- SHA-1 is a cryptographic hash function mapping input plaintext into a 160-bit (20-byte) hash known as a message digest – often displayed as a hexadecimal number, 40 digits long. SHA-1 was designed by the United States national security agency and is a US federal information processing standard.

SHA-256 is a successor hash function to SHA-1. It is one of the strongest hash functions available and has not yet been compromised in any way. SHA-256 generates an almost unique 256-bit (32-byte) signature for a text. For example, *My test string* maps to `5358c37942b0126084bb16f7d602788d00416e01bc3fd0132f4458d d355d8e76`. With a small change, the hash of *My test strings* is `98ff9f0555435 f792339d6b7bf5fbcca82f1a83fde2bb76f6aa95d66050887cc`, a completely different value. SHA-256 produces 2^256 possible hashes. There is yet to be a case where two different inputs have produced the same SHA-256 hash, an issue called collision in cryptography. Even with the fastest supercomputer, it will take longer than the age of our universe to hit a collision. As a result, SHA-256 is used by Bitcoin for encryption.

The distributed ledger, blocks, transactions, addresses, and UTXO

At a financial institution, a ledger is a book for recording financial transactions. Similarly, Bitcoin maintains a ledger for bookkeeping BTC transactions and balances by address. One key difference is that a bank's ledger is centralized and Bitcoin's ledger is decentralized. Consequently, a bank's ledger is much easier to be cooked. On the other side, Bitcoin's ledger is very difficult to cook as one has to change the ledger at all nodes worldwide.

A user submits a transaction containing the following information:

- Sources of the BTCs to be transferred from
- The amount of BTCs to be transferred
- Destinations the BTCs should be transferred to

As per the Wiki site, a transaction has a general structure shown as follows:

General format of a Bitcoin transaction (inside a block)		
Field	**Description**	**Size**
Version no	currently 1	4 bytes
Flag	If present, always 0001, and indicates the presence of witness data	optional 2 byte array
In-counter	positive integer VI = VarInt	1 - 9 bytes
list of inputs	the first input of the first transaction is also called "coinbase" (its content was ignored in earlier versions)	<in-counter>-many inputs
Out-counter	positive integer VI = VarInt	1 - 9 bytes
list of outputs	the outputs of the first transaction spend the mined bitcoins for the block	<out-counter>-many outputs
Witnesses	A list of witnesses, 1 for each input, omitted if flag above is missing	variable, see Segregated_Witness
lock_time	if non-zero and sequence numbers are < 0xFFFFFFFF: block height or timestamp when transaction is final	4 bytes

Both source and destination addresses are 64-character hashes. Here is an example of an address:
`979e6b063b436438105895939f4ff13d068428d2f71312cf5594c132905bfxy1`.

The term *address* is a bit confusing. A programmer may think it to be an address related to a disk or memory location. However, it has nothing to do with a physical location. Instead, it is a logical label for grouping BTCs that have been transferred from/to it. In a way, one can think of it as a bank account number, yet there are fundamental differences between them. For example, a bank has a centralized place where metadata on an account, for instance, owner name, account open date, and account type, is saved. In addition, the account balance is precalculated and saved. In Bitcoin, there is no metadata on an address and one has to query the entire ledger to find the balance of an address by counting the net BTCs being transferred in and out of the address. Addresses are referred to only in Bitcoin transactions. When the balance of an address falls to 0, any future request for taking BTCs from the address will fail the transaction validation due to insufficient funds.

Bitcoin utilizes the **UTXO** model to manage its BTC transfer. The term was introduced by cryptocurrency, where it refers to an *unspent transaction output*. This is an output of a blockchain transaction that has not been spent and can be used as an input for a future transaction. In a Bitcoin transaction, only unspent outputs can be used as an input, which helps to prevent double spending and fraud. As a result, a committed transaction results in deleting inputs on a blockchain and creating outputs in the form of UTXOs. The newly created unspent transaction outputs can be spent by the owner holding the corresponding private keys. In other words, UTXOs are processed continuously and a committed transaction leads to removing spent coins and creating new unspent coins in the UTXO database.

Like an address, a BTC is not associated with any physical object such as a digital token file or a physically minted coin. Instead, it only exists in transactions in the distributed ledger. For example, if one wants to know the total number of BTCs minted so far, one has to go through all nonzero balance addresses on the blockchain and add up all the BTCs. Since every node of Bitcoin keeps a copy of the ledger, it is only a matter of taking computing time to find an answer.

When a user enters a BTC transaction request at a node, Bitcoin software installed at the node broadcasts the transaction to all nodes. Nodes on the network will verify the validity of the transaction by retrieving all historical transactions containing the input addresses and ensuring that BTCs from these addresses are legitimate and sufficient. After that, the mining nodes start to construct a block by collecting the verified transactions. Normally, a Bitcoin block contains between 1,500 to 2,000 transactions. A miner who wins the race to resolve a difficult mathematical puzzle gets the role to build and link a new block to the chain. On the Bitcoin blockchain, a new block is created around every 10 minutes. As of September 21, 2018, approximately 542,290 blocks have been created on Bitcoin. The structure of a Bitcoin block is shown as follows:

Block structure

Field	Description	Size
Magic no	value always 0xD9B4BEF9	4 bytes
Blocksize	number of bytes following up to end of block	4 bytes
Blockheader	consists of 6 items	80 bytes
Transaction counter	positive integer VI = VarInt	1 - 9 bytes
transactions	the (non empty) list of transactions	<Transaction counter>-many transactions

Here, the block header contains the following fields:

Field	Purpose	Updated when...	Size (Bytes)
Version	Block version number	You upgrade the software and it specifies a new version	4
hashPrevBlock	256-bit hash of the previous block header	A new block comes in	32
hashMerkleRoot	256-bit hash based on all of the transactions in the block	A transaction is accepted	32
Time	Current timestamp as seconds since 1970-01-01T00:00 UTC	Every few seconds	4
Bits	Current target in compact format	The difficulty is adjusted	4
Nonce	32-bit number (starts at 0)	A hash is tried (increments)	4

The concept of a **nonce** will be explained in the subsection on mining. **hashPrevBlock** is the same value as **hashMerkleRoot**. The Merkle tree hash root is essentially the hash of all transaction hashes in the block via a binary tree aggregation structure. The following diagram explains the idea:

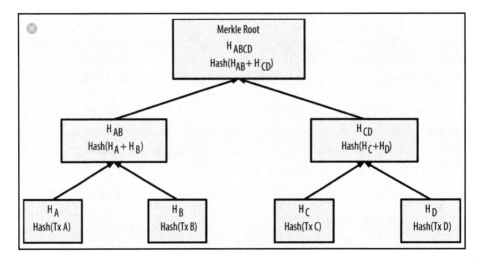

The consensus mechanism

If someone buys a bottle of water for $1, that person cannot spend the same $1 to buy a can of coke. If a person is free to double-spend a dollar, money would be worthless since everyone would have unlimited amounts and the scarcity, which gives the currency its value, would disappear. This is called the **double-spending problem**. With BTC, double spending is the act of using the same Bitcoin more than once. If this problem is not resolved, BTC loses its scarcity and cannot be used to facilitate a trade between two untrusting parties. The Bitcoin Core network protects against double spends via a consensus mechanism. To explain how the Bitcoin consensus mechanism works, we first describe the concepts of **PoW** (**Proof-of-Work**) and mining.

As explained earlier, a miner needs to solve a difficult mathematical puzzle ahead of other miners in order to receive the role of being a builder of the current new block and receive a reward for doing the work. The work of resolving the math problem is called **PoW**.

Why is PoW needed? Think of this: in a network consisting of mutually untrusting parties, more honest parties are needed than dishonest attackers in order to make the network function. Imagine if upon collecting sufficient transactions for a new block, a miner is allowed to build the new block immediately. This simply becomes a race for whoever can put enough transactions together quickly. This leaves a door wide open for malicious attackers to hack the network by including invalid or fake transactions and always win the race. This would allow hackers to double-spend BTCs freely.

Therefore, to prevent attackers from introducing bad transactions, a sufficient window of time is needed for participating nodes to verify every transaction's validity by making sure a BTC has not been spent yet. Since every node maintains a copy of the ledger, an honest miner can trace the history and ensure the following to confirm the validity of a transaction:

- The requestor of a transaction does own the BTCs.
- The same BTCs have not been spent by any other transactions in the ledger.
- The same BTCs have not been spent by other transactions within the candidate block.

This window of time is currently set to be around 10 minutes. To enforce the 10-minute waiting time, Bitcoin asks a miner to solve a sufficiently difficult mathematical puzzle. The puzzle requires only a simple computation. Miners have to repeat the same computation many times in order to burn enough CPU time to reach the network's goal of building a new block every 10 minutes on average. The process of repeated guessing is called **mining** and the device (specially made) is called a **mining rig**.

Since, in order to win the mining race, a miner needs to invest heavily in hardware, these miners are dedicated to the work of mining and aim to receive sufficient BTCs to cover the cost of running the mining operation and make a profit. As of the first half of 2018, the reward given to a winning miner is 12.5 BTCs. One can find the price of BTC by visiting the CoinMarketCap website (`https://coinmarketcap.com/`). As of September 21, 2018, one BTC is traded at around $6,710. Therefore, 12.5 BTC is worth about $83,875 USD.

Per Bitcoin protocol, mining is the only way for a new BTC to be issued (minted). Having a miner be rewarded handsomely serves three purposes:

- Compensates a miner's investment on hardware.
- Covers mining operational costs such as utility bills, which can be significant due to the large mining rigs being deployed at a mining site, human salaries, and site rentals.
- Gives miners incentives to safeguard the network from being attacked by malicious hackers. Miners are motivated to maintain the Bitcoin network in order not to lose value in their BTCs and their mining infrastructure. If Bitcoin is breached by hackers, Bitcoin's reputation will suffer badly and BTC prices would freefall. This is exactly what the Bitcoin inventor hoped for: having more good miners than bad miners to address the double-spending issue.

The total number of BTC that can be issued is fixed to be 21 million. As of today (September 19, 2018), around 17 million BTCs have been issued. The Bitcoin protocol defines a rule for dynamically adjusting the payout rate and the remaining 4 million coins aren't expected to be mined completely for another 122 years. The following point explains how the block creation payout rate is dynamically adjusted:

- The rate changes at every 210,000 blocks. It is a function of block height on the chain with genesis=0, and is calculated using 64-bit integer operations such as: (50 * 100000000) >> (height / 210000). The rate initially started with 50 BTCs, and fell to 25 BTCs at block 210,000. It fell to 12.5 BTCs at block 420,000, and will eventually go down to 0 when the network reaches 6,930,000 blocks.

Forking

A Bitcoin blockchain can diverge into two potential paths since miners do not necessarily collect transactions and contract block candidates in the same way, nor at the same time. Other reasons such as hacking or software upgrades can also lead to path divergence. The splitting patches are called **forks**. There are temporary forks and permanent forks.

If a permanent fork occurs due to, for example, malicious attacks, a hard fork occurs. Similarly, there is the concept of soft fork. Both hard fork and soft fork refer to a radical change to the protocol. Hard fork makes previously invalid blocks/transactions valid and a soft fork makes previously valid blocks/transactions invalid.

To remove a temporary fork, Bitcoin protocol dictates that the longest chain should be used. In other words, when facing two paths, a winning miner will choose the longer chain to link a new block. As a result, the longer path continues to grow and the blocks on the losing (shorter) path becomes orphaned. Bitcoin nodes will soon discard or not take the orphaned blocks. They only keep the blocks on the longest chain as being the valid blocks.

In the case of a permanent fork, nodes on the network have to choose which chain to follow. For example, Bitcoin Cash diverged from Bitcoin due to a disagreement within the Bitcoin community on how to handle the scalability problem. As a result, Bitcoin Cash became its own chain and shares the transaction history from the genesis block up to the forking point. As of September 21, Bitcoin Cash's market cap is around $8 billion, ranking fourth, versus Bitcoin's $215 billion.

Mining and difficulty level

There is one more issue that needs to be resolved: how to maintain the new block building rate of 10 minutes. If nothing is done, the mining rate will change due to the following factors:

- The number of miners on the network can vary in response to the BTC price
- Technology advancements make mining rigs progressively faster
- The total number of mining rigs varies

Bitcoin adjusts the **difficulty level** of the mathematical puzzle in order to keep the building rate at 10 minutes. The difficulty level is calculated from the rate at which the most recent blocks were added in. If the average rate of new blocks being added is less than 10 minutes, the difficulty level will be increased. If the average rate takes more than 10 minutes, it's decreased. The difficulty level is updated every 2,016 blocks. The following graph displays the historical trend in Bitcoin difficulty level.

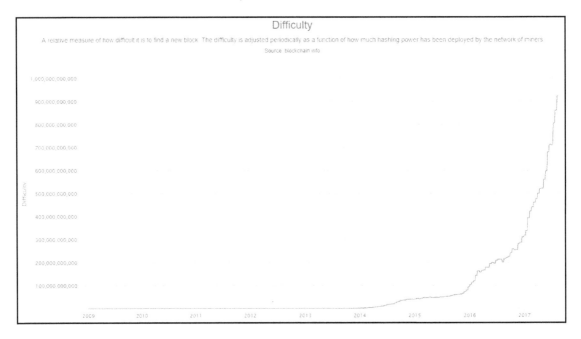

We have yet to talk about the actual mining algorithm. Assume the current difficulty level is to find the first hash value with the leading character to be 0. In Bitcoin, the process of solving a puzzle, that is, mining, requires a miner to follow these steps:

- First, find the SHA-256 hash of the block in construction.
- If the resulting hash has a leading 0, the miner solves the puzzle. The miner links the block to the ledger on the node and claims the trophy, 12.5 BTCs. The miner's node broadcasts the news to all nodes. All other nodes and miners on the network validate the answer (by mapping the block information plus nonce to get the same hash) and validate the entire history of the ledger, making sure that the block contains valid transactions.
- If it passes the checks, all nodes on the network add the block to their copies of the ledger. Miners start to work on the next new block.

- If the winning miner is a malicious attacker and includes bad transactions in the block, the validation of these transactions will fail and other miners will not include the block in their ledger copies. They will continue to mine on the current block. As time passes, the path containing the bad block will no longer be the longest path and, therefore, the bad block will become an orphaned block. This is essentially how all nodes on the network reach consensus to add only good blocks to the network and prevent bad blocks from sneaking in, therefore resolving the double-spending issue.

- If the resulting hash does not start with 0, then the miner is allowed to append a sequence number, known to be a nonce, starting from 0 to the input text, and retry the hash.

- If the resulting hash still does not contain a leading 0, the miner will add another sequence number, 1, to the input text and obtain a new hash. The miner will keep trying in this way until it finds the first hash with a leading zero.

The following is an example of how the plaintext and nonce work together. The original plaintext is *input string* and the nonce varies from 0 to 1:

- **input string**:
  f23f4781d6814ebe349c6b230c1f700714f4f70f735022bd4b1fb6942185999
  3

- **input string0**:
  5db70bb3ae36e5b87415c1c9399100bc60f2068a2b0ec04536e92ad2598b6bb
  b

- **input string1**:
  5d0a0f2c69b88343ba44d64168b350ef62ce4e0da73044557bff451fd5df6e9
  6

In Bitcoin, *adjusting difficult level* largely refers to changing the required number of leading zeros. (The actual adjustment involves some other miner tuning to the requirement.) Each addition of a leading zero will increase the average number of tries significantly and therefore will increase the computing time. This is how Bitcoin manages to maintain the average rate of 10 minutes for new blocks being added in. The current Bitcoin difficulty level is 18 leading zeros.

Hacking – the 51% problem

Thanks to the rising price of BTC, the mining operation has become more attractive. Investments are rushing in and large mining pools involving thousands of rigs or more have joined the network in order to gain an advantage in the race to solve the puzzle first and get the reward. For players without large capital from investments, they have a choice to participate in a mining pool. When the pool wins a race, the award will be allocated to each participant based on the computational power contributed.

This ever-growing computational power of a pool poses a real threat due to the so-called **51% problem**. This problem occurs when a miner manages to build up computational power to total at least 51% of the total computing power of the network. When this occurs, the miner will have a chance to outrun other miners. The miner can continue to grow the ledger with blocks containing bad transactions since this miner has more than a 50% chance of solving the puzzle first. Soon, the malicious miner's ledger will grow to be the longest path and all other nodes have to save this path based on Bitcoin's consensus protocol.

For a large and well-established network such as Bitcoin, the 51% problem is not as critical an issue, mainly due to the following reasons:

- A well-established network will attract a much larger number of participating parties and connect a very significant number of nodes. It will take an exorbitantly high initial investment for a hacker to purchase the necessary mining rigs. When such a network is attacked, the price of cryptography will drop quickly when the news becomes public and the hacker will have a low chance of recovering the investment.
- In the history of Bitcoin, there have been cases when a mining pool that accumulated dangerously high computing power approached this line. When the participating miners in the pool realized the problem, many of them chose to leave the pool. Soon, the computational power of the pool fell to a safe level.
- In the case of a small and immature network, it is not difficult for a miner to muster computing power of more than 51%. However, the cryptocurrency value of these networks is minimal and it gives hackers very little financial incentive to take advantage of the 51% problem.

Private keys and Bitcoin wallets

As discussed earlier, BTCs do not physically exist. The only evidence of their existence is when they are associated with addresses, which are referred to in transactions. When an address is initially created, a pair of public and private keys are generated with it. The public key is made known to the public and the private key is kept only by the owner of the address. When the owner wants to spend all or a portion of their BTCs, the owner provides a digital signature signed with the private key and sends the BTC request to the Bitcoin network. In other words, one has to know both the address and its private key to spend the BTC.

If an owner loses a private key, its associated BTCs will be lost permanently. Therefore, it is advised to keep this information in a safe place. It is generally good practice to keep the address and private keys in separate places. To prevent a digital copy getting lost, an owner should maintain physical copies of printouts. To make conversion easier, an owner can print a QR code and later scan the QR code whenever it is needed.

Bitcoin wallet applications are available to help a user manage keys and addresses. One can use a wallet to do the following:

- Generate addresses and corresponding public/private keys
- Save and organize a BTC's information
- Send a transaction request to the Bitcoin network

In Bitcoin, a private key is a 256-bit-long hash and a public key is 512 bits long. They can be converted into shorter lengths in hexadecimal representation. The following screenshot gives an example of a pair of public/private keys along with an address:

```
Private key:
a7f9c7ad318014b11cbad0a18587b374c339d91f55ca64c4c5e067776d0b65cb

Public key:
04d8fc7523fcd7caa825b6ed97d8564c78f59e8ba903bff5fe1e3c096a45d435937
942616f4dbccb353d3e19e822d707996143a603a6273cf237acfaf5bd029874

Wif:   5K6GJ5y9qSDSmrGZ1idLbWoXk4iaJpxFuDpiCC78cgngCXTSeDv

Address:   1GnUipq7cTjiPxEsCDzW6nYgbUyRa7eFYm
```

Bitcoin private keys can also be expressed in a string of 51 characters starting with a 5 and a public key in a string of 72 characters. A sample private key is `5Jd54v5mVLvy RsjDGTFbTZFGvwLosYKayRosbLYMxZFBLfEpXnp` and a sample public key is `BFCDB2DCE28D959F2815B16F81798483ADA7726A3C4655DA4FBFC0E1108A8FD17B448 A68`.

Bitcoin scripting

One can install the following development tools for programming Bitcoin operations:

- **NodeJS**: This is an open source, cross-platform JavaScript runtime environment that executes JavaScript code outside of a browser. It allows a programmer to write and execute scripts quickly and easily. These scripts can be written to be run in a web browser or on a server.
- **BitcoinJS**: This is a JavaScript library for working with Bitcoin and its cryptographic functions. BitcoinJS can be used to generate public/private keys and addresses.
- **Blockchain.info**: This is a public API that can be used to query the blockchain to find out balances and broadcast transactions to the network. It can be used to implement a Bitcoin node and install and run a Bitcoin node.

After installing the preceding tools, one can execute the following operations:

- Generate a new private key and compute a public key
- Check the balance for a certain address
- Generate addresses
- Construct a new transaction
- Send a transaction, which involves three steps:
    - Build a transaction with a list of inputs and outputs
    - Sign the transaction with the required private keys
    - Broadcast the transaction to the network
- Build an escrow account
- Broadcasts the transaction

Altcoins

Thanks to Bitcoin, blockchain technology has attracted worldwide attention. Like any new technology, it has its limitations. Many variations of Bitcoin were created to address a particular limitation of Bitcoin. Here, we mention a few of them:

- **Bitcoin Cash**: This is a hard fork of the Bitcoin chain that was created because a group of Bitcoin core developers wanted to use a different way of addressing the scalability issue.

- **Litecoin**: This is almost identical to Bitcoin except that the time for adding a new block was reduced from 10 minutes to 2 minutes.

- **Zcash**: This is based on Bitcoin but offers total payment confidentiality.

- **Monero and Zcash**: Both altcoins address the privacy issue by making transaction history untraceable, but they implement two different solutions.

- **Dash**: This mainly improves user-friendliness. For example, transactions are made untraceable and a user does not have to wait for several additional new blocks to be added before considering a transaction to be committed to the chain.

- **Namecoin**: This extends the use case of Bitcoin, which is for trading BTCs only, to providing domain name services.

- **Peercoin**: This altcoin addresses the deficiencies of PoW, which is environmentally unfriendly and is low in throughput. Instead, it adopts proof of stake for achieving consensus. Based on this rule, a miner validates block transactions according to how many coins a miner holds. In other words, the mining power of a miner is in proportion to the number of peercoins owned.

- **Primecoin**: A primecoin miner competes to be the first to find the next biggest prime number.

Ethereum

Regardless of the efforts made from the steps-mentioned altcoins in addressing some part of the Bitcoin's limitations, there are several fundamental issues that are not being addressed yet:

- Bitcoin and these altcoins are specific to one purpose: trading either BTC or an altcoin.

- Although a programmer can use tools such as BitcoinJS to interact with the network, the resulting code sits outside of the blockchain and is not guaranteed to run. The chain itself does not have a Turing complete programming language for coding directly on a blockchain.

- These blockchains are stateless and one has to search through the entire ledger to find an answer such as the total number of BTC minted.

In response to these problems, Vitalik Buterin, a Canadian cryptocurrency researcher and programmer, proposed the idea of Ethereum in late 2013. Funded by an online crowdsale, the system went live on 30 July 2015, with 11.9 million coins *premined* for the crowdsale.

The core idea for Ethereum was to build a general-purpose blockchain so users could solve a wide range of business problems not just limited to cryptocurrency transfer. Ethereum introduced a few new and critical concepts:

- The concept of saving a smart contract on a blockchain
- The concept of implementing a smart contract with a Turing complete programming language such as Solidity and running the piece of code on the blockchain

Solidity was initially proposed in August 2014 by Gavin Wood. The Ethereum project's Solidity team led by Christian Reitwiessner later developed the language. It is one of the five languages, (Solidity, Serpent, LLL, Vyper, and Mutan) designed to target the **Ethereum virtual machine** (**EVM**).

Nick Szabo, a programmer and lawyer, initially proposed the term *smart contract* in 1996. In his blog, Nick Szabo described it as the granddaddy of all smart contracts, the vending machine.
A vending machine shares the exact same properties as a smart contract on a blockchain today. A vending machine is built with hardcoded rules that define what actions to execute when certain conditions are fulfilled, for example:

- If Susan inputs a dollar bill in the vending machine, then she will receive a bag of pretzels.
- If Tom puts in a five-dollar bill, Tom will receive a bag of pretzels and also change of four dollars.

In other words, rules are defined and enforced by a vending machine physically. Similarly, a smart contract contains rules in program code that are run on the blockchain and triggered when certain conditions are met.

The introduction of the smart contract concept is significant:

- A smart contract is a scripted legal document.
- The code built into the contract is stored on the Ethereum blockchain and cannot be tampered with or removed. This greatly increases the credibility of the legal document.

- This code cannot be stopped, meaning any party—regardless of how powerful the party is—cannot order or interfere with the running of the smart contract code. As long as certain conditions are met, the code will run and the legally defined actions will be fulfilled.
- Ethereum to blockchain is like an OS to a computer. In other words, the platform is generic, no longer serving only one specific purpose.
- It now has a Turing complete language: Solidity.

Enterprise blockchain – Hyperledger

The arrival of Ethereum revolutionized blockchain technology. Applying technology to resolve business problems well beyond the financial industry has become feasible. However, there are many scenarios where Ethereum is not enough. Ethereum's issues include the following:

- Real enterprise applications, particularly in the financial industry, require a high throughput, which can mean billions of transactions a day. The current form of Ethereum has a maximum capacity of 1.4 million a day. Bitcoin is even worse: 300,000 transactions a day. During a stress test, Bitcoin Cash reached 2.2 million. Ethereum 2.0 under development aims at getting to a billion transactions a day while maintaining a decentralized and secure public blockchain.
- Many financial markets, for instance OTC Derivatives or FX, are permission-based. A public blockchain supported by Ethereum or Bitcoin does not meet such a need.

To satisfy their needs, well-established companies across industries form consortiums to work on enterprise blockchain projects, which are permission-based only. In other words, a node has to receive approval before it can join in the blockchain network. Examples of enterprise blockchains are Hyperledger and R3's Corda.

In December 2015, the **Linux Foundation** (**LF**) announced the creation of the Hyperledger Project. Its objective is to advance cross-industry collaboration by developing blockchains and distributed ledgers. On 12 July 2017, the project announced its production-ready **Hyperledger Fabric** (**HF**) 1.0.

Currently, Hyperledger includes five blockchain frameworks:

- **Hyperledger Fabric** (**HF**): A permissioned blockchain, initially contributed by IBM and Digital Asset, it is designed to be a foundation for developing applications or solutions with a modular architecture. It takes plugin components for providing functionalities such as consensus and membership services. Like Ethereum, HF can host and execute smart contracts, which are named chaincode. An HF network consists of peer nodes, which execute smart contracts (chaincode), query ledger data, validate transactions, and interact with applications. User-entered transactions are channeled to an ordering service component, which initially serves to be HF's consensus mechanism. Special nodes called Orderer nodes validate the transactions, ensure the consistency of the blockchain, and send the validated transactions to the peers of the network as well as to **membership service provider** (**MSP**) services that are implemented to be a certificate authority.
- **Hyperledger Iroha**: Based on HF, it is designed for mobile applications. Iroha was contributed by Soramitsu, Hitachi, NTT Data, and Colu. It features a modern and domain-driven C++ design. It implements a consensus algorithm called Sumeragi.
- **Hyperledger Burrow**: Contributed initially by Monax and Intel, Burrow is a modular blockchain that was client-built to follow EVM specifications.
- **Hyperledger Sawtooth**: Contributed by Intel, it implemented a consensus algorithm called **Proof of Elapsed Time** (**PoET**). PoET is designed to achieve distributed consensus as efficiently as possible. Sawtooth supports both permissioned and permissionless networks. Sawtooth is designed for versatility.
- **Hyperledger Indy**: Contributed initially by the Sovrin foundation, it is intended to support independent identity on distributed ledgers. Indy provides tools, libraries, and reusable components, which are implemented to provide digital identities.

Early members of the initiative include the following:

- Blockchain ISVs, (Blockchain, ConsenSys, Digital Asset, R3, Onchain)
- Technology platform companies such as Cisco, Fujitsu, Hitachi, IBM, Intel, NEC, NTT DATA, Red Hat, and VMware
- Financial institutions such as ABN AMRO, ANZ Bank, BNY Mellon, CLS Group, CME Group, the **Depository Trust and Clearing Corporation** (**DTCC**), Deutsche Börse Group, J.P. Morgan, State Street, SWIFT, and Wells Fargo
- Software companies such as SAP

- Academic institutions such as Cambridge Centre for Alternative Finance, blockchain at Columbia, and UCLA blockchain lab
- Systems integrators and other firms such as Accenture, Calastone, Wipro, Credits, Guardtime, IntellectEU, Nxt Foundation, and Symbiont

The evolution of blockchain

Blockchain technology is still at an early stage. It will take many years before it becomes mature and its potential is fully explored and harnessed. Currently, there is no universally agreed way to classify or define blockchain generation.

In her book on blockchain, Melanie Swan defined blockchain 1.0 to 3.0 based on the use scenarios that blockchain platforms are created to serve:

> *"Blockchain 1.0 is currency, the deployment of cryptocurrencies in applications related to cash, such as currency transfer, remittance, and digital payment systems.*
>
> *Blockchain 2.0 is contracts, the entire slate of economic, market, and financial applications using the blockchain that are more expensive than simple cash transactions: stocks, bonds, futures, loans, mortgages, titles, smart property, and smart contracts.*
>
> *Blockchain 3.0 is blockchain applications beyond currency, finance, and markets - particularly in the areas of government, health, science, literacy, culture, and art."*

Some others divided blockchain evolution into four generations from blockchain 1.0 to 4.0:

- **Blockchain 1.0**: With Bitcoin being the most prominent example in this segment, use cases were based on the **distributed ledger technology** (**DLT**) where financial transactions could be executed. Cryptocurrency was used as cash for the Internet.
- **Blockchain 2.0**: With Ethereum being the most prominent example in this segment, the new key concept was Smart Contracts, which are stored and executed on a blockchain.

- **Blockchain 3.0**: The keyword is DApps, an abbreviation for decentralized applications, which avoided centralized infrastructure. They use decentralized storage and decentralized communication. Unlike a smart contract which only involves a backend or server-side code, a DApp can have frontend code and user interfaces, i.e. client-side code to interact with its backend code on a blockchain. Like the smart contract code, a DApp's frontend can be stored and executed on decentralized storage such as Ethereums Swarm. In summary, a DApp is frontend plus contracts running on Ethereum.

- **Blockchain 4.0**: Blockchain platforms in this segment are built to serve for Industry 4.0. Industry 4.0 refers, in a simple way, to automation, enterprise resource planning, and integration of different execution systems.

Regardless of how the blockchain technology is divided into versions, it is certain that the technology growth is far from being over. New ideas and implementations will be incorporated into the existing platforms to deal with challenges for real-life problems. In other words, blockchain technology will be nimble and is self-adjusted to be an enabler in resolving business problems.

Summary

Blockchain is an emerging technology. Thanks to its immutability, transparency, the consensus mechanism for avoiding double spending, along with other clever designs such as blocks chained with the hashes of the previous blocks, the technology allows untrusting parties to trade with each other. In this chapter, we explained the basic concepts of its important features. Most of the discussions were about Bitcoin, which is the mother of the technology. We briefly talked about Ethereum, which extended Bitcoin and introduced the concept of smart contracts. The introduction of smart contracts makes the Ethereum blockchain generic and allows us to develop applications beyond the borderless cash payment use case for which Bitcoin was invented. The concept of an enterprise chain, along with one of the examples, Hyperledger, was mentioned as well. Finally, we briefly touched on the evolution of blockchain to give readers an idea of the trend in the technology. In the next chapter, we will discuss the concepts of Ethereum in detail.

13
Ethereum Fundamentals

Ethereum is an open source public blockchain and is considered to be an alternative coin to Bitcoin. A Canadian cryptocurrency researcher and programmer, Vitalik Buterin, proposed the idea in late 2013. Founded by an online crowdsale that took place in the middle of 2014, the platform went live at the end of July 2015. *The DAO* event in 2016 led to a hard fork, resulting in a split into **Ethereum** (**ETH**) and **Ethereum Classic** (**ETC**).

In this chapter, we cover the following topics about Ethereum:

- Overview of Ethereum
- Basic concepts such as ether, ERC20 tokens, smart contracts, EVM, gas, accounts, and oracles
- The Ethereum performance issue and ongoing efforts to address the issue, such as PoS, Casper, Plasma, and Sharding

An overview of Ethereum

In late 2013, Vitalik Buterin sent an email to the blockchain community announcing a white paper outlining the idea for Ethereum. He described it as a universal platform with internal languages, so anyone could write an application. According to Vitalik, the original idea for Ethereum was to create a general-purpose blockchain for fintech. Ethereum is a variation on Bitcoin. Unlike Bitcoin, which is a blockchain focusing on payments, Ethereum is a programmable, general-purpose blockchain. The introduction of smart contracts is the key to differentiating Ethereum from Bitcoin.

A well-known analogy to describe Ethereum and smart contracts, which bring together untrusting parties trading digital or digitized physical assets, is a vending machine, as described at the end of `Chapter 12`, *Introduction to Blockchain Technology*.

After a vending machine is made, nobody, including the machine owner, can change the rules. A buyer does not need to worry about the owner altering the rules prior to or during the transaction. As a result, a buyer can trust the machine to behave in the expected way and feels comfortable enough to go ahead with a transaction. Of course, the vending machine does not necessarily provide a perfect solution. A customer could occasionally face a malfunctioning machine and insert $1, yet nothing happens. If the vending machine does not provide a refund solution, such as posting a contact phone, the customer would permanently lose the $1. On the other hand, Ethereum's solution is much more robust. The rules in the form of smart contracts are distributed to all nodes. The same smart contracts will run on thousands of nodes (or even more) worldwide at approximately the same time. As long as at least one node runs, the transaction is successfully executed. In other words, Ethereum is truly a world computer.

Some blockchain enthusiasts responded to Vitalik's email and formed a core group in advancing and executing the idea. (This groundbreaking paper, titled *A Next-Generation Smart Contract and Decentralized Application Platform*, is available at `https://github.com/ethereum/wiki%20Wiki/`, archived from the original on 28 March 2015 with 169 revisions as of August 22, 2018.) In January 2014, the Ethereum Foundation was created. Soon (in early 2014), a British computer science PhD, Gavin Wood, published a yellow paper titled *Ethereum: A Secure Decentralized Generalized Transaction Ledger* (`https://ethereum.github.io/yellowpaper/paper.pdf`). Gavin's paper unified multiple initiatives for implementing the Ethereum idea and served as a blueprint for future development work.

Before talking about the Ethereum crowdsale event, we need to first explain the concept of **crowdfunding**. Crowdfunding refers to the practice of funding a project or an initiative by raising money from a large number of people, commonly on the internet. Crowdfunding is an alternative way of financing an initiative. In the case of blockchain projects, crowdfunding often takes place in the form of a project owner selling a portion of a hardcoded (preminted) total number of digital coins in circulation, exchanging them for an amount in a fiat currency or another established digital currency such as Bitcoin.

From July to August 2014, an online crowdfunding sale took place. The event led to selling 11.9 million coins of *premined* Ether—Ethereum's native cryptocurrency. This is about 12% of the total Ether coin supply: 102,431,467. Funded by the proceeds from this crowdfunding sale, development started. The core Ethereum team consisted of Vitalik Buterin, Mihai Alisie, Anthony Di Iorio, and Charles Hoskinson. The real development of the Ethereum project was started by a Swiss company, Ethereum Switzerland GmbH (EthSuisse). The platform went live on 30 July 2015.

Stephan Tual, an ex-Ethereum CMO, formed a company called the *The DAO* on April 30, 2016. The purpose of this entity was to manage the process of selecting which smart contract to deploy. *The DAO* came up with the clever idea of selecting contracts based on investments. Completed smart contracts were posted on the internet. A potential investor would declare an amount to be invested in a smart contract. Smart contracts with the top amounts would be chosen for deployment. *The DAO* raised a record US $150 million via crowdfunding sales to fund the project. *The DAO* was hacked in June and lost US $50 million worth of Ether due to bugs in its software. The hacking ignited a heated debate within the Ethereum community on how to deal with it. Two contesting opinions emerged:

- Enhance the Ethereum code to make a similar attack in future not feasible and deploy the code to all nodes
- Make no changes to the core Ethereum code and take the risk of future attacks

Vitalik made a call for a hard fork solution and publicly asked all Ethereum nodes to stop trading for the deployment of patch code. Within hours, all of the thousands of nodes worldwide were completely shut down. The majority of the nodes voted for adopting the hard fork approach and upgraded their core Ethereum code with the patch, yet a small portion of nodes chose not to take the patch and still run the same code.

This hard fork event split the Ethereum blockchain into two. The nodes running the old code maintaining the original blockchain became Ethereum Classic, with the coin symbol ETC, and the nodes with the patched code, maintaining a forked Ethereum blockchain, became Ethereum, with the coin symbol ETH. The fork occurred exactly at block number 1,920,000. The hard fork created a rivalry between the two networks. Now, the ETH price has gone up more than 130 times and ETC is worth only one-tenth of ETH's price, due to its unpopularity and the concerns of suffering a future *The DAO* type of attack.

After the *The DAO* hard fork, Ethereum forked twice in Q4 of 2016 to deal with new attacks. While the hard forks resolved past hackers' attacks, this is obviously not a scalable solution as one cannot always rely on creating a hard fork to resolve every future hack. Consequently, Ethereum has increased its protection by preventing new spam attacks by hackers.

While hard forks are used to address hacking, soft forks are used by Ethereum for protocol upgrades, which are important changes affecting the underlying functionality and/or incentive structures of Ethereum. Some notable soft forks are as follows:

- **Homestead** was for improvements to transaction processing, gas pricing, and security. The soft fork took place on 31 July 2015.
- **Metropolis part 1**: **Byzantium** was for changes to reduce the complexity of the EVM and add more flexibility for smart contract developers. The soft fork took place on 16 October 2017.
- Two more protocol upgrades are planned in the future: **Metropolis part 2**: *Constantinople* helps to lay the foundations for the transition to proof-of-stake.

In March 2017, blockchain startups, research groups, and major companies created the **Enterprise Ethereum Alliance** (**EEA**) consisting of 30 founding members. In May, the nonprofit organization expanded to include 16 enterprise members with household names such as Cornell University's research group, Samsung SDS, Microsoft, Intel, J. P. Morgan, DTCC, Deloitte, Accenture, Banco Santander, BNY Mellon, ING, and National Bank of Canada. By July 2017, the list had increased to 159 members.

Despite the many improvements made since its initial launch, Ethereum continues to evolve. Ethereum 2.0 sets out to address one of the weakest links, scalability, and is expected to launch in 2019, in phases, as per Vitalik's recent comments.

Ethereum basic concepts

Ethereum builds on top of the Bitcoin blockchain, including key features such as a distributed ledger containing chained blocks, the proof-of-work algorithm, and so on. However, its biggest addition is the introduction of smart contracts, which are coded in a Turing-complete scripting language. Because of this new addition, unlike Bitcoin or its non-smart contract close relatives, Ethereum allows developers to address generic business problems.

Before getting to the basic concepts, we summarize some useful facts on Ethereum as follows:

- Ethereum has three main ingredients:
    - **Decentralization**: For guaranteed execution
    - **Hashes**: For safeguarding the world state
    - **Signatures**: For authorizing programs and transactions

- Since Ethereum is a blockchain, it uses mathematical algorithms to replace intermediary entities and bring untrusting parties together to do businesses.
- Ethereum blockchain brings trust in data due to its ability to verify the validity of data on a node via its consensus mechanism.
- It uses total validation to replace central control.
- Like a transaction, a digital signature is required for deploying a smart contract. A deployed smart contract is permanent and is immutable.
- A smart contract is assigned with an address.
- Suppose a smart contract has a bug and requires a fix. The patched smart contract will be deployed with a newly assigned address and therefore is treated as a completely new smart contract with no relationship to the old one.
- In May 2017, Ethereum had 25,000 reachable nodes worldwide, consisting of full nodes and light nodes.
- A full node has the full blockchain downloaded and available. The Ethereum ledger can be pruned. Full nodes verify transactions in a block in construction. A miner node has to be a full node.
- A light node does not store the entire blockchain, but it stores the parts it cares about from someone it trusts.
- Scripts of a contract code are executed via the **Ethereum virtual machine** (**EVM**) on full nodes. A smart contract's address stores bytecode, called opcode, that runs on the EVM.
- Since a smart contract runs on full nodes on tens of thousands of machines, it truly is worldwide. In other words, writing a smart contract to a blockchain is global and permanent.
- Since smart contract scripts are stored in a decentralized way, it provides an additional layer of security. This is true as all full nodes know that other nodes store the same code. It is not feasible for a hacker to push malicious scripts to all good nodes worldwide and crash them.
- A smart contract is a scripted legal document and is guaranteed for execution. Since a smart contract is signed at its deployment and a transaction that invokes it is also signed, there should not be a dispute between the two trading parties in the transaction. In other words, with a decentralized blockchain such as Ethereum, the need for a judge disappears! node and can grow to a full network.
- Thanks to the nature of permanence and immutability, data and programs on Ethereum blockchain are auditable. This could be of special interest to the government for enforcing regulation and compliance requirements.
- Ethereum is open source. Anyone can download the code and create his or her own version of an Ethereum network. Of course, the issue is about how to convince others of its value so they join the network.

- Ethereum is decentralized. As a result, there is no master node that controls or dictates the whole network. The network operates via consensus, as per its protocols.

- Ethereum provides fault tolerance as well. As long as at least one full node survives during a catastrophic attack, the network can be rebuilt from the surviving node and grow to a full network.

- While Ethereum provides extreme robustness, the flip side is the problem of how to stop it when it is out of control. Like in the example of the *The DAO* hack, the network had to rely on Vitalik and his authority to shut it down completely. Compared to today, the network then was many times smaller. As the network continues to grow in size, this approach will become harder. In future, the network may grow to tens of millions of nodes or more. As long as one node does not respond to an authoritative call, the Ethereum network is still alive. In other words, it becomes extremely difficult to shut down a network completely. Of course, this is what a decentralized blockchain is all about: no centralized authority dictating to everyone else!

- Ethereum allows for recursive calls to other smart contracts. Poorly written smart contracts can lead to infinite loops. To address this issue, Ethereum builds in a circuit breaker mechanism, Gas, which is explained later in detail.

- On a big data platform, a task is divided into chunks that are distributed to nodes on the network and the work is shared by nodes. However, Ethereum's full nodes execute the same pieces of scripts. That means every full node of the Ethereum blockchain stores and computes the same data; this is reliable but not scalable. The scalability issue is one of the major criticisms of Ethereum. As we will discuss later, multiple efforts are underway to address this issue.

- Ether is the native cryptocurrency of Ethereum. Ethereum allows a user to issue their own digital coins called tokens. ERC-20/ERC-721/ERC 1400 are common technical standards to be followed for issuing Ethereum tokens.

- Ethereum can be seen as the third generation of the internet. This could be one reason that Ethereum's JS API was called Web3. There are discussions on rewriting the internet with blockchain technology.

- The practice of providing centralized services on top of a decentralized internet (such as Google providing a centralized searching functionality on a decentralized internet) will apply to blockchain as well.

Ether

Since Ethereum is built on top of Bitcoin, it is considered to be a Bitcoin altcoin. Ether to Ethereum is similar to BTC to Bitcoin. Ethereum is the name used when referring to the protocols, the blockchain, the client software, and the mainnet.

The Ethereum mainnet is the blockchain network that is used by clients for transferring a digital asset from a sender to a recipient. In other words, it is the network where actual transactions take place on a distributed ledger. Mainnet is equivalent to a production environment. The Ethereum testnet is for development. As mentioned at `https://www.ethernodes.org/network/2`, as of October 8, 2018, the mainnet had 13,662 nodes and the testnet had 29 nodes. Since the actual transactions take place on the mainnet, Ether has a real value only on the Ethereum mainnet. In other words, on the testnet, it is worth nothing. Ether coins (ETH and ETC) are listed and exchanged in tens of thousands of digital currency markets. Their prices vary greatly. For example, on October 8, 2018, ETH was traded at around $223 and ETC at $11.

Ether can be transferred between addresses (accounts). It is used to pay miners for their computational work; they are paid in transaction fees and also for gas consumption resulting from executing a transaction. Here, the concept of gas is essential for Ethereum and it is discussed later in more detail.

Ether is the largest denomination. There are other units. The smallest is called WEI, named after the digital money pioneer, Wei Dai, who is the inventor of B-money. B-money was his proposal for an anonymous, distributed electronic cash system. Other units include Gwei, microether, and milliether. They all have a second name. For example, milliether is also called finney, named after another digital money pioneer, Harold Thomas Finney II, who in 2004 wrote the world's first implemented cryptocurrency, RPOW (reusable proofs of work) before Bitcoin. The following table gives the conversion rate between ether and other units:

Unit	Wei value	Wei
Gwei (shannon)	10^9 Wei	1,000,000,000
microether (szabo)	10^{12} Wei	1,000,000,000,000
miliether (finney)	10^{15} Wei	1,000,000,000,000,000
ether	10^{18} Wei	1,000,000,000,000,000,000

ERC20 tokens

Ethereum is a generic blockchain. It allows developers to build a DApp and trade digital assets. Correspondingly, it allows a developer to define a user-specific coin called a token. The majority of these tokens are ERC20 tokens. ERC refers to Ethereum Request for Comment, and 20 is the number that was assigned to this request. In other words, ERC-20 is a technical standard used for smart contracts on the Ethereum blockchain for implementing tokens. According to Etherscan.io, as of October 8, 2018, a total of 125,330 ERC-20 compatible tokens were found on the Ethereum main network.

ERC-20 defines a list of rules for Ethereum tokens to follow. By doing so, it allows for interaction and conversion between Ethereum tokens within the larger Ethereum ecosystem. Currently, Ether does not conform to the ERC-20 standard. However, since Ether is the native coin of Ethereum, it can be converted into other tokens. The ERC-20 specification defines an interface containing methods and events.

The following is list of required methods (github.com):

- `name`: It returns the name of the token, for instance, `HelloToken: function name() view returns (string name)`.
- `symbol`: It returns the symbol of the token, for instance, `HTC: function symbol() view returns (string symbol)`.
- `decimals`: It returns the number of decimals the token uses; for instance, 8 means to divide the token amount by 100,000,000 to get its user representation: `function decimals() view returns (uint8 decimals)`.
- `totalSupply`: It returns the total token supply: `function totalSupply() view returns (uint256 totalSupply)`.
- `balanceOf`: It returns the account balance of another account with `address _owner: function balanceOf (address _owner) view returns (uint256 balance)`.
- `transfer`: It transfers a specified number (`_value`) of tokens to the `_to` address, and MUST fire the transfer event. The function should throw an error if the `_from` account balance does not have enough tokens to spend: `function transfer(address _to, uint256 _value) returns (bool success)`.
- `transferFrom`: It transfers a specified amount (`_value`) of tokens from the `_from` address to the `_to` address, and MUST fire the Transfer event. The function should throw an error unless the `_from` account has deliberately authorized the sender of the message via some mechanism: `function transferFrom (address _from, address _to, uint256 _value) returns (bool success)`.

- `approve`: It allows `_spender` to withdraw from your account multiple times, up to the `_value` amount. If this function is called again, it overwrites the current allowance with `_value`: `function approve (address _spender, uint256 _value) returns (bool success)`.
- `allowance`: It returns the amount that `_spender` is still allowed to withdraw from `_owner`: `function allowance (address _owner, address _spender) view returns (uint256 remaining)`.

The list of required events is as follows:

- `transfer`: Must trigger when tokens are transferred, including zero value transfers. A token contract that creates new tokens SHOULD trigger a `Transfer` event with the `_from` address set to 0x0 when tokens are created: `event Transfer (address indexed _from, address indexed _to, uint256 _value)`.
- `approval`: Must trigger on any successful call to approve `(address _spender, uint256 _value)`: `event Approval (address indexed _owner, address indexed _spender, uint256 _value)`.

Although Ethereum allows for a person to create his or her own money, Ethereum's true value is its guaranteed execution of a smart contract. Ether and ERC20 token creation are mainly for initial crowdfunding purposes to support a project and are used for payment during the transaction to circumvent a bank. Without a real business use case, a token is worth nothing.

Smart contracts

The term *smart contract* was initially coined by Nick Szabo, who is a computer scientist, a legal scholar, and the inventor of Bit Gold, in 1994. He is a living legend in the world of cryptocurrency for his research into digital contracts and digital currency. He is even considered to be Satoshi Nakomoto by some people, although he rejected that claim.

Nick Szabo originally defined smart contracts as follows:

> *"A smart contract is a computerized transaction protocol that executes the terms of a contract. The general objectives of smart contract design are to satisfy common contractual conditions (such as payment terms, liens, confidentiality, and even enforcement), minimize exceptions both malicious and accidental, and minimize the need for trusted intermediaries. Related economic goals include lowering fraud loss, arbitration and enforcement costs, and other transaction costs."*

With a vending machine, transaction rules are built into the machine hardware. Transaction rules on a digital asset are built into scripts. That is, the smart contract consists of code. Here are some useful facts on smart contracts:

- A smart contract is immutable.
- A smart contract is permanent.
- A smart contract is timestamped.
- A smart contract is globally available.
- A smart contract is a digitized legal document.
- A smart contract is a computer protocol intended to facilitate, verify, or enforce an agreed contract between trading parties digitally.
- Smart contracts allow for execution of transactions without the third party as an intermediary. The transactions are auditable and irreversible.
- A smart contract moves digital coins, executes a conventional payment, or transfers a digital asset, or even delivers real-world goods and services.
- For a third-party-involved business transaction, for instance, buying/selling a house, escrow accounts are often used to temporarily store the trading parties' money. With a smart contract, no escrow account is needed. Smart contracts eliminate the need for escrow accounts since they are guaranteed to be executed for transferring the money and assets.
- Smart contracts provide more security than traditional contract law and their transaction costs are only a fraction of other transaction costs associated with contracting.
- In the interpretation used by the Ethereum Foundation, a smart contract does not necessarily refer to the classical concept of a contract. It can be any kind of computer program.
- To deploy and run a smart contract, one has to digitally sign the deployment, similar to sending other data or transactions on the Ethereum blockchain.
- Smart contracts can be public and are open to developers. This leads to a security issue. If a smart contract has a bug or security loophole, it is visible to all developers. To make the issue worse, such a bug or loophole is not easily fixable, due to its immutability. This gives hackers plenty of time to explore weaknesses and initiate attacks on the Ethereum blockchain. *The DAO* event was a high-profile example of this issue.

An Ethereum smart contract can be developed in one of four languages: solidity (inspired by JavaScript), Serpent (inspired by Python, no longer used), LLL (inspired by Lisp), and Mutan (inspired by Go, no longer used). Regardless of the language used, smart contracts are coded in a high-level programming language which needs to be compiled into a low level, machine-runnable language. In the Ethereum smart contract implementation, a VM approach similar to the concept of Java VM (JVM) is used. The Ethereum VM is called **EVM**. Smart contract scripts are converted to EVM-runnable code called **bytecode**. The opcode is then deployed to the Ethereum blockchain for execution. Currently, a research-oriented language is under development, which is called Vyper and is a strongly typed Python-based language.

Ethereum virtual machines

In the sixties, when computers had just been invented, coding was in a lower level language, for instance an assembly language (assembler). For example, an assembler code line, *ADD R1 R2 R3*, is an instruction to add the contents of register 1 and register 2 with the result being placed in the third register, R3. A register is a temporary storage area built into a CPU. With a 32-bit CPU, a register is 32 bits long.

The code in an assembly language is then converted to a machine language in 0 and 1 sequences, which is machine-executable. Coding in a low-level language is tedious and time-consuming. When high-level languages such as ALGOL or BASIC were invented, coding time was greatly reduced. However, the underlying process remained the same: compiling the code into a machine executable language in 0 and 1 sequences. Java, Python, JavaScript and C++ are currently popular high-level languages.

While the compiling approach works well, it does have one inconvenience: lack of portability. A piece of code that is compiled on a computer is machine-dependent. In other words, it is not portable. To address this issue, the concept of the virtual machine was introduced. A **virtual machine** (**VM**) is an emulation of a computer system. There are two types of virtual machine: **system virtual machine** (also called full virtualization), which provide a substitute for a real machine, and **process virtual machines,** which are for executing computer programs in a platform-independent environment. It is the process of VM that we refer to in our preceding discussion.

A program written in a high-level language is compiled into VM-executable code. As long as a computer supports such a VM, the compiled code can run on it without the need to be recompiled. For example, JVM is a well-known Java VM that enables a computer to run Java programs compiled into Java bytecode.

In the case of Ethereum, smart contracts are written in a high-level language, mostly solidity. A smart contract is compiled to opcodes, which are executable on a VM built specifically for Ethereum, the **EVM**. The EVM brings portability along with robustness, since EVM performs runtime checks to prevent crashes. These types of checks do have a performance penalty though.

Since Ethereum contracts can be written in any one of the four languages: solidity, serpent, LLL, and Mutan, there are four compilers to convert each of the four languages' coded smart contracts into opcodes for running on the EVM. Another relevant concept is the **Ethereum client**, which refers to a collection of software being installed on a node for parsing and verifying blockchain transactions, smart contracts, and everything related. The Ethereum client is implemented in one of eight languages: Python, C++, Go, JavaScript, Java, Haskell, Ruby, and Rust. Implemented EVMs are an essential part of the Ethereum client. As a result, opcodes can run on any one of the eight client implementations. EVM was originally designed for currency transactions and later extended to other digital assets. As a result, there are restrictions on supporting certain features. Developers face some severe restrictions (for instance, the use of string or local registers).

Ethereum gas

An Ethereum transaction can call a smart contract, which can in turn call another smart contract, and then another, and so on. When smart contracts are buggy, it can lead to infinite loops. Outside a blockchain, it is easy to resolve an infinite loop issue. One can stop the out-of-control program by simply shutting down a server, rebooting it, debugging the program, fixing the faulty logic in the code, recompiling it, and redeploying.

With the Ethereum blockchain, this approach simply does not work! Imagine if tens of thousands of nodes went into infinite loops at approximately the same time worldwide. In order to stop infinitely looping smart contracts, all the nodes need to be shut down within a short time window. As long as one node fails to comply, the infinitely looping smart contract would still be alive and running. It is a logistical nightmare to coordinate and shutdown all these nodes.

To resolve this issue, the concept of **gas** was introduced. A vehicle relies on an engine burning gas to move. When an engine runs out of gas, the vehicle stops. Ethereum introduced the gas concept to achieve the same effect. When submitting a transaction to the Ethereum blockchain, the requester is required to provide a max gas amount. For example, in the following example, a transaction request is submitted to call a **HelloWorld** smart contract with the maximum consumption not exceeding a specified gas value:

When this request is validated by mining nodes, the **HelloWorld** smart contract is invoked. Every operation running on the EVM consumes a predefined quantity of gas. For example, ADD (sum operation) consumes three gas and MUL (multiplication operation) uses five gas. For illustration purposes, suppose a smart contract was badly written and contains an infinite loop. Furthermore, we assume each loop consists of an ADD operation and a MUL operation. Therefore, a loop will consumes eight gas (three gas for ADD and five gas for MUL). After EVM executes enough loops, the specified maximum gas value will be consumed. Consequently, EVM stops executing the contract. Therefore, all nodes would stop running at approximately the same time. Another advantage of gas is to make spamming monetarily expensive and, therefore, reduce the risk of hacking.

Gas is a metering unit for measuring consumption, just as the kilowatt is the unit for measuring electricity usage. Suppose that, in a month, a family uses 210 KW. Before sending a bill to the family, the utility company first converts 210 KW into USD, based on a predefined conversion rate. Suppose a unit of KW costs $0.2 USD, the total charge for the month is 0.2 * 210 = $42 USD. Similarly, gas usage is converted to Ether and charged to a requester. Ethereum allows a requester to specify the conversion rate when the transaction is submitted. A miner has the right to selectively process transactions by giving higher priority to transactions with higher rates. If a requester does not specify a rate, EVM uses a default rate, which varies. For example, in 2016 the rate was 1 gas = 0.00001 ETH. In 2018, one gas = 0.00000002 ETH.

Account

In *Chapter 12*, *Introduction to Blockchain Technology*, we discussed addresses, an account-like concept, which is used to *host* balances of BTC. Bitcoin uses the UTOX model to manage the transfer of BTCs between addresses. However, one has to retrieve the entire ledger to find the balance of an address, which is very inconvenient. This inconvenience is due to the fact that Bitcoin does not support an on-chain Turing-complete programming language and it does not have the concept of states. On the other hand, Ethereum blockchain supports scripting languages and smart contracts; it can maintain state. Ethereum transactions manage state transitions by calling smart contract methods. Ethereum no longer needs to rely on UTOX to manage payments. Instead, it operates using accounts and balances via state transitions. State denotes the current balance of all accounts, along with other data. State is not stored on the blockchain. It is saved off-chain in a Merkle Patricia tree. This is because state is mutable data, while a block is not mutable. As with Bitcoin, a cryptocurrency wallet can be used to manage public and private *keys* or accounts, which are for receiving or sending ETH. In other words, Ethereum introduced the concept of **accounts**.

Ethereum supports two types of account: externally owned accounts (controlled by human users via ownership of private keys) and contract accounts.

- **An externally controlled account**:
    - Has an Ether balance
    - Can initiate transactions for either transferring Ether or triggering smart contract code
    - Is controlled by users via private keys
    - Has no associated smart contract code

- **A contract account**:
    - Has an Ether balance
    - Has associated smart contract code
    - Smart contract code execution is triggered by transactions or calls received from other contracts

- **For both types of account, there are four components**:
    - `nonce`: For an externally owned account, it refers to the number of transactions sent from the account's address; for a contract account, nonce is increased every time this contracts calls another contract
    - `balance`: It is the number of Wei owned by this address

- `storageRoot`: A 256-bit hash of the storage contents of the account
- `codeHash`: The hash of the code of this account is EVM; this is the code that gets executed when the address receives a call

When Ether is transferred from contract accounts to an externally owned account, there is a fee, for instance 21,000 gas. When Ether is sent from an externally owned account to a contract account, the fee is higher, and depends on the smart contract code and data being sent in the transaction.

Ethereum addresses have the following format:

1. Start with the prefix 0x, a common identifier for hexadecimal
2. Rightmost 20 bytes of the Keccak-256 hash (big-endian) of the ECDSA public key

Since, in hexadecimal, two digits are stored in one byte, a 20-byte address is represented with 40 hexadecimal digits. A sample address is `0xe99356bde974bbe08721d77712168fa074279267`.

Oracle

As we already learned, identical Ethereum smart contracts are executed on nodes worldwide. What we have not emphasized yet is that all these nodes take the same set of inputs and should yield the same outputs. This is called **determinism**. Ethereum relies on this determinism since, in order to verify the validity of smart contracts and transactions, mining nodes have to yield the same results while running the same code with the same inputs.

This determinism raises a challenge. On one side, Ethereum is a generic platform that can be used to transfer any digital or digitized assets. Its smart contracts require data or inputs from external sources such as the internet, for example, stock prices, macroeconomic or microeconomic indices, and so on. Without access to these sources of information, use cases for smart contracts will be restricted to only a tiny fraction of their potential. On the other side, even with a tiny time difference, nodes may retrieve different information from an external source. With different inputs, nodes will end up with different outputs. Consequently, the determinism property does not hold. As a result, smart contracts are not permitted to call an internet URL or directly pull data from an external source. To address the paradox, the concept of the **oracle** is implemented.

According to Merriam-Webster, one of the definitions of oracle is *a shrine in which a deity reveals hidden knowledge or the divine purpose through such a person*. In the blockchain world, an oracle refers to the third-party or decentralized data feed services that provide external data. Oracles provide interfaces from the real world to the digital world. Oracle data is not part of the blockchain. It is saved off-chain.

There are different types of oracle. Two of them are software oracles and hardware oracles:

- **Software oracles**: Normally refer to easily accessible online information such as stock index close prices, FX rates, economic news or weather forecasts, and so on. Software oracles are useful since they provide smart contracts with wide varieties and up-to-date information.
- **Hardware oracles**: Normally refers to scanned information such as UPS delivery scanning, registered mail scanning, or supplier goods delivery scanning. This feed can be useful to activate a smart contract that is triggered upon an event's occurrence.

Other concepts

Since Ethereum is built on top of Bitcoin, many of the basic concepts were already discussed in `Chapter 12`, *Introduction to Blockchain Technology*. For the rest of this subsection, we briefly cover a few of them with a focus on the key differences.

- **Consensus algorithms**:
    - Like Bitcoin, PoW is its consensus algorithm. Unlike Bitcoin, Ethereum is working on switching to another consensus algorithm called **Proof-of-Stake (PoS)** to significantly improve performance with its next release tag of serenity.
- **Private blockchain**:
    - In general, both Bitcoin and Ethereum are public blockchains since the network is open to anyone and a node can join freely.
    - Ethereum has variants on private chains. With private Ethereum, a node needs approval prior to joining a network. These blockchains are called private blockchains. Private blockchains are suitable for enterprise applications. Hyperledger and JPM Morgan's Quorum are examples of well-known private blockchain variants of Ethereum. Another example is Brainbot's hydrachain.

- **Off-chain data**:
    - With the Bitcoin blockchain, we do not talk much about the concept of off-chain data. With the Ethereum blockchain, this topic needs to be discussed. There are multiple scenarios where data cannot be stored on-chain:
        - The first case is state variables. All data stored in a blockchain is immutable since the contents of a block are hashed and blocks are linked via these hashes. A tiny change in the contents of a block will lead to the reconstruction of all the blocks afterwards, which is obviously not feasible. However, state variables are, for instance, used to hold balances. They do change content to reflect the balance move. A solution is to save them off-chain.
        - Oracles are another example, where information pulled from external sources is saved off-chain to be fed to smart contracts.
        - Ethereum was invented to allow for trading generic digital or digitized assets. Metadata describing the underlying assets is saved off-chain.
        - With Bitcoin, the distributed ledger has to be saved on all nodes in order to provide the information required for transaction validation. In the case of Ethereum, the balance of a cryptocurrency or digital asset can be directly retrieved from state variables. There is no need to browse the ledger to obtain balances in order to determine whether a _from address has sufficient funds. As a result, a full node can choose to keep only a portion of the ledger, that is, trim a ledger. The blocks being trimmed can be saved off-chain at a centralized location for future inquiries.

- **Testing**:
  - It is vital to thoroughly test, double-test, and triple-test a smart contract. Safety testing is critical. As explained earlier, in Ethereum's short history, there have been several high-profile hacking events, which occurred mainly due to buggy smart contract code.
  - Ethereum is less safe than Bitcoin because of bugs introduced in smart contracts. Ethereum smart contracts are saved in chained blocks and are not encrypted. Hackers can easily spot and explore the vulnerability of buggy contract code and engage in attacks. On the other hand, like Bitcoin, data and transactions on Ethereum are relatively secure and not vulnerable to hacking. It is only the contract that a hacker can construct malicious transactions to call and abuse.
  - After a smart contract is deployed, it is permanent and immutable. Deployment of revised code will become a new contract with a different address. It has different state variables with new balances.
  - Deployment of a smart contract is not free. It burns gas.
- **Digital signature, encryption, and public/private keys**:
  - Bitcoin is a multi-signature process. In order for a transaction to be executed, both sides have to sign it. Ethereum is similar. In addition, deployment of a smart contract also requires digital signatures.
  - Like Bitcoin, with an Ethereum blockchain one can take a wallet application and generate a pair of public and private keys at the same time. An address is derived from a public key; that is, an address is just the hash of a public key. A sender uses a private key to sign a transaction and a receiver uses a public key to verify the authenticity of a signature. In general, a pair of public and private keys can be used to support the following two types of activity:
  - **Sending a secret message**: The public key is used to encrypt a message and the private key is used to decrypt the message.
  - **Signature**: A private key is used to encrypt and generate a signature. The public key is used to decrypt for signature verification.
  - Block transaction contents in both Bitcoin and Ethereum are currently not encrypted. On the other hand, block contents in Zcash are encrypted.

- Since every Ethereum transaction, including smart contracts, has to be digitally signed, a node only needs to accept digitally signed requests, potentially without the need to verify the entire transaction history. This approach can help to improve performance.

- **DAO**:

  - DAO refers to a decentralized autonomous organization. One should not confuse it with the organization called *The DAO*, which is famously linked to a hacking event that resulted in the split of **Ethereum** into **Ethereum (ETH)** and **Ethereum Classic (ETC)**.
  - DAO can be considered to consist of smart contracts, which is in term-built form decentralized codes, that is, a hierarchical structure of decentralized core → smart contract → DAO.
    - Decentralized code is saved in multiple nodes. It will definitely run and cannot be stopped.
    - Smart contracts move money and digital assets.
    - DAO consists of smart contracts and creates an independent entity or community.

- **DApp**:

  - DApp is a big topic. We briefly mention it due to restrictions on the size of the book:
    - DApp refers to decentralized application and uses decentralized code.
    - Ethereum is a general-purpose DApp platform.
    - An Ethereum DApp, like any other blockchain DApp, has a decentralized backend (for instance, smart contracts) and a centralized frontend (a client-side application for interacting with the blockchain). This architecture is due to the performance and limitations of today's blockchain.
    - As discussed before, a large portion of the backend, the database and business logic, is hosted off-ch.

- **Ethereum issues**:
    - Ethereum suffers from issues inherited from Bitcoin:
        - Data can get lost due to forking or splitting. When there are two competing chains, the chain that cannot manage to grow fast has to be discarded in order to maintain data consistency on all nodes. Transactions on the short chain will get lost if they are not included in blocks of the winning chain without even being known by their original requesters!
        - Since data on-chain is not encrypted, a blockchain is not anonymous and not confidential.
        - Addresses are not verified. This is bad. When a receiver's address is wrongly entered, the coins being transferred to it will be permanent as transactions are permanent and coins are locked forever!
        - The PoW algorithm consumes a huge amount of power. It is reported that some large mining operations in China require dedicated power stations to supply electricity.

Performance

Another problem inherited from Bitcoin is that Ethereum is slow. It is many magnitudes slower than other platforms that host transaction data, for instance a traditional database. For example, it takes an average of 10 minutes to build a new record for Bitcoin. As a rule of thumb, after waiting for six new blocks to be built, a transaction is considered to be finalized (the same as a commitment in a database). This means that, on average, a requester will wait for one hour to see a request completed. In Ethereum, the average time for miners to build a block is 17 seconds and it is recommended you wait for 12 blocks before a transaction is confirmed. This is 12 * 17 = 204 seconds, or 3.4 minutes' waiting time for a user. Here, waiting for a few subsequent blocks to be built before confirming a transaction is useful. At any point, Ethereum can have competing chains. The waiting gives Ethereum sufficient time to work out the issue of having competing chains and reach a consensus.

Throughput

Throughput is a measure of how many units of information a system can process in a given time window. To measure performance on a transaction platform, throughput is expressed in terms of **TPS**, transactions per second:

- For Bitcoin, TPS can be computed as follows. A Bitcoin block normally contains 1,500-2,000 transactions. Let's use the high-end number, 2,000. Since it takes 60 minutes to confirm these 2000 transactions, its TPS = 2,000 / (60*60) = 0.56; that is, only half a transaction per second. A similar calculation for Ethereum yields a TPS = 2,000 / 204 = 9.8, almost 10 transactions per second—much better than Bitcoin. Led by Vitalik, the Ethereum Foundation is working on the sharding approach, targeting at increasing TPS by 80 times.

- For comparison, VISA has an average TPS of 2000 with a peak at 40,000. A high-performance database such as VoltDB can handle over a million insertions per second. A stock exchange can match thousands of trades per second.

- However, this comparison is not complete. From a business point of view, a credit card or exchange transaction is finalized only when it is cleared and settled. For credit cards, a billing cycle is normally 2-3 months. A stock exchange takes three days to settle a transaction. In this sense, Ethereum is much faster, since on the blockchain transaction and settlement occur simultaneously.

- When compared with a database, Ethereum is at a disadvantage. A database commitment can take place right after the insertion, updating, or deletion of a transaction.

- These are the reasons causing Ethereum's slowness:
    - Every full node must execute the same smart contract code.
    - As the Ethereum network becomes larger, the time for reaching a consensus will take longer, as it takes time to transfer data between a growing number of nodes to verify transactions, access info, and communicate.

- There are ways to increase the throughput. The following are a few:
    - When the block size is increased, more transactions can be hosted in a block and a higher TPS can be obtained.
    - Running multiple chains in parallel. Enterprise chains such as Hyperledger Fabric and R3's Corda use this approach.

- State channel design helps to increase throughput. An example of a state channel implementation for Ethereum is Raiden. Micro Raiden was launched in November 2017. The idea behind state channels is to use off-chain for a transaction between two parties and use on-chain for the settlement of the transaction. Off-chain transactions are another topic worth an in-depth discussion, but not in this book.

Proof-of-Stake (PoS)

The PoS consensus algorithm is based on the principle that when a miner owns more coins, the miner has more power to mine or validate transactions, a higher chance of building new blocks, and therefore a higher chance of receiving more reward coins. PoS is energy-efficient and can reach a consensus much faster.

Several randomization methods are available for selecting a miner to build the next block, not just based on Ether balances of externally owned accounts, in order to avoid a scenario where the richest miner is always selected:

- **Randomized block selection**: Uses a formula to look for the lowest hash value in combination with the size of the stake for selecting a miner.
- **Coin age-based selection**: Coins owned for long enough, say 30 days, are eligible to compete for the next block. A miner with older and larger sets of coins has a better chance of being granted the role.
- **Delegated Proof-of-Stake**: This implementation chooses a limited number of nodes to propose and validate blocks to the blockchain.
- **Randomized Proof-of-Stake**: Each node is selected randomly, using a verifiable random beacon to build the new block.

Ethereum is working on replacing PoW with PoS in a new tagged release.

Casper

PoS is being worked on as a replacement to the computationally inefficient PoW algorithm. PoS is not being fully implemented and upgraded on mainnet due to concerns about an issue such as emerging of a set of centralized supernodes (which receive an outsized role in building the new blocks). Casper is the Ethereum community's effort to transition from PoW to PoS.

In the Per Casper protocol, validators (the Ethereum equivalent of miners in Bitcoin) set aside a portion of their Ether as a stake. When a validator identifies a candidate block to build, Ether is bet on that block by the validator. If the block is indeed added to the chain, the validator is rewarded based on the size of his or her bet. Validators acting maliciously will be penalized by having their stakes removed. Casper has two main projects: Casper FFG and Casper CCB.

Casper FFG (Friendly Finality Gadget; Vitalik's version of Casper) is a hybrid algorithm running on PoW but treating every 50th block on the network as a PoS checkpoint. Validators vote on the finality of these blocks and write them into the blockchain. FFG is meant to be an intermediate step in a transition to a complete adoption of PoS. FFG is already running on a test network. It will soon be implemented completely on mainnet. The Casper **CBC** (**Correct by Construction**, Vlad's Casper) is more dramatic. CBC focuses on designing protocols where one can extend local views of a node's estimate of safety to achieve consensus safety. So far, the approach has been merely researched and no release plan is available for making it to Ethereum.

Plasma

In 2017, Buterin and Joseph Poon presented their idea, which called for scaling up Ethereum's performance, that is, increasing TPS. Like the state channel design, plasma is a technique for conducting off-chain transactions while relying on the underlying Ethereum blockchain to provide its security. Therefore, plasma belongs to the group of *off-chain* technologies. Truebit is another example in this group.

Plasma works as follows:

- Smart contracts are created on the main-chain and served to be the roots for Plasma child-chains. They define rules for child chains and are called to move assets between the main-chain and child-chains.
- A child-chain is created with its own consensus algorithm, for instance, PoS.
- Deploy smart contracts, which define the actual business rules, to the child-chain.
- Digital assets being created on the main-chain are transferred onto the child-chain by calling the plasma rooting contracts.
- The block builders on the child-chain periodically commit a validation to the main-chain, proving that the current state of the child-chain is valid, in accordance with the consensus rules. A user sends and gets requests executed without ever interacting with the main-chain directly.

Plasma has these advantages:

- Allows an Ethereum blockchain to handle larger datasets
- Enables more complicated applications to run on the blockchain
- Increases throughput greatly

The Ethereum community is actively working on the implementation of Ethereum plasma. Plasma-MVP (minimum viable product) is being worked on first, to gain experience and test its viability. There is the possibility of releasing plasma-mvp by the end of 2018. Plasma's release will follow in one or more quarters.

Sharding

Vitalik initially proposed the sharding idea for scaling Ethereum blockchain. His proposal was to chop the blockchain into hundreds or thousands of independent pieces: shards. All shards share the same consensus algorithm and security model. These shards will not handle different types of task and do not need to be validated by all full nodes. Instead, each shard serves a single purpose and therefore is very efficient at it. In summary, sharding splits up the state of the network into multiple shards, where each shard has its own transaction history and a portion of the network's state. To implement the sharding idea on the blockchain, a Validator Management Contract is needed, which is a smart contract. It verifies each shard's block headers, maintains validators' stakes, and selects validators between shards pseudo-randomly. Sharding provides an alternative way to increase Ethereum's performance dramatically and could be implemented as early as 2020.

Summary

Ethereum was developed on top of Bitcoin by introducing smart contracts along with Turing-complete scripting languages such as solidity. Ethereum is a general-purpose platform for DApp development. The platform is very popular. However, Ethereum is not mature yet. Compared to Bitcoin, it is more vulnerable to hacking, since any human errors in writing a smart contract are visible to everybody. It inherited the performance issue from Bitcoin. Many initiatives are ongoing to address this scalability problem. In the next chapter, we will dive into the details of solidity, the most popular language for writing Ethereum smart contracts.

14
Overview of Solidity Programming

Solidity is a smart contract programming language. It was developed by Gavin Wood, Christian Reitwiessner, Alex Beregszaszi, and several Ethereum core contributors. It is a JavaScript-like, general-purpose language designed to target the **Ethereum virtual machine** (**EVM**). Solidity is one of four languages in the Ethereum protocol at the same level of abstraction, the others being Serpent (similar to Python), **LLL** (**Lisp-like language**), Vyper (experimental), and Mutan (deprecated). The community has slowly converged on solidity. Usually, if anyone today talks about smart contracts in Ethereum, they implicitly mean solidity.

In this chapter, we will discuss the following topics:

- What is solidity?
- Tools for the solidity development environment
- Introduction to smart contracts
- Common smart contract patterns
- Smart contract security
- Case study – crowdfunding campaign

What is solidity?

Solidity is a statically typed contract language that contains state variables, functions, and common data types. Developers are able to write decentralized applications (DApps) that implement business logic functions in a smart contract. The contract verifies and enforces the constraints at compile time, as opposed to runtime. Solidity is compiled to EVM executable byte code. Once compiled, the contracts are uploaded to the Ethereum network. The blockchain will assign an address to the smart contract. Any permissioned user on the blockchain network can call a contract function to execute the smart contract.

Here is a typical flow diagram showing the process from writing contract code to deploying and running it on the Ethereum network:

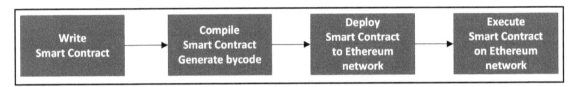

Tools for solidity development environment

Smart contract development is still in its infancy. Creating such contracts and interacting with them in a convenient manner can be done in a multitude of ways. The following powerful tools can be used to build, monitor, and deploy your smart contracts for development on the Ethereum platform.

Browser-based IDE

In this section, we will be looking at onlien browser based tools such as Remix and EthFiddle.

Remix

Remix is a powerful, open source, smart contract tool that helps you write solidity code just from the browser. It supports compile, run, analysis, testing, and debugger options. The following three types of environments are available with Remix when developing and testing:

- **JavaScript VM**: Remix comes with five Ethereum accounts, and each account is deposited with 100 ethers as default. This is convenient for testing smart contracts in the development phase. Mining is not required as it is done automatically. This option is a good choice when you are a beginner.

- **Injected Web3**: This option will directly invoke injected browser web3 instances such as MetaMask, an Ethereum network browser extension. MetaMask provides you with many functions and features, and, like regular Ethereum wallets, it allows you to interact with DApps.

- **Web3 provider**: Remix also supports Web3 provider. The web3.js library is the official Ethereum JavaScript API. It is used to interact with Ethereum smart contracts. You can connect to the blockchain network through web3j API. Web3j supports three different providers: HTTPProvider, WebsocketProvider, and IpcProvider. In Remix Web3, you can give the HTTP URL to connect the remote blockchain instance. The URL can point to your local private blockchain, test-net, and other instance endpoints.

Start by using the Remix solidity IDE: `https://remix.ethereum.org`. The following is the screenshot for the UI of Remix:

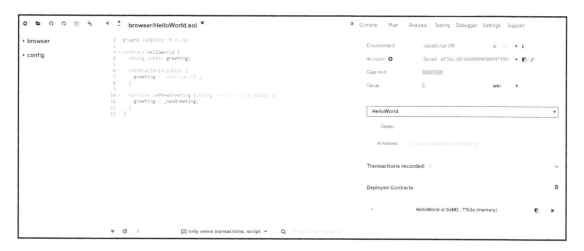

EthFiddle

EthFiddle is a very simple solidity browser-based development tool. You can quickly test and debug smart contract code, and share a permalink to your code. One feature that makes EthFiddle stand out is its potential to perform security audits. The following screenshot shows the software interface:

Interface of EthFiddle software

Here is the EthFiddle solidity IDE link: `https://ethfiddle.com`.

Command-line development management tools

The command-line tools are server-side Ethereum tools used to create a basic structure of a DApp project.

Truffle

Truffle is a popular development environment and testing framework, and is an asset pipeline for Ethereum. Truffle's major features include the following:

- Built-in smart contract compilation, linking, deployment, and binary management
- Automated contract testing with Mocha and Chai s Truffle site link: http

- Scriptable deployment and migrations framework
- Network management for deploying to many public and private networks
- Interactive console for direct contract communication
- We will discuss in more detail in the next chapter, and we will use Truffle to development DApp for ERC20 token
- Here is Truffle's site link: `https://truffleframework.com/`

Introduction to smart contracts

Let's begin with the most basic smart contract example, `HelloWorld.sol`, shown as follows:

```
pragma solidity ^0.4.24;

contract HelloWorld {
  string public greeting;

  constructor() public {
    greeting = 'Hello World';
  }

  function setNewGreeting (string _newGreeting) public {
    greeting = _newGreeting;
  }
}
```

Solidity's file extension is `.sol`. It is similar to `.js` for JavaScript files, and `.html` for HTML templates.

Layout of a solidity source file

A solidity source file is typically composed of the following constructs: pragma, comments, and import.

Pragma

The first line containing the keyword pragma simply says that the source code file will not compile with a compiler earlier than version 0.4.24. Anything newer does not break functionality. The ^ symbol implies another condition—the source file will not work either on compilers beyond version 0.5.0.

Comments

Comments are used to make the source code easier for humans to understand the function of the program. Multi-line comments are used for large text descriptions of code. Comments are ignored by the compiler. Multi-line comments start with /* and end with */.

In the HelloWorld example, there are comments for the set and get methods:

- Method: The setNewGreeting (string _newGreeting) {} function
- @param: This is used to indicate what parameters are being passed to a method, and what value they're expected to have

Import

The import keyword in solidity is very similar to JavaScript's past version, ES6. It is used to import libraries and other related features into your solidity source file. Solidity does not support export statements.

Here are a few import examples:

```
import * as symbolName from "solidityFile"
```

The preceding line shown will create a global symbol called symbolName, containing the global symbol's member from the import file: solidityFile.

Another solidity-specific syntax equivalent to the preceding import is the following:

```
import solidityFile as symbolName;
```

You can also import multiple symbols, and name some of the symbols as alias, demonstrated as follows:

```
import {symbol1 as alias, symbol2} from " solidityFile";
```

Here is an example where an ERC20 token is created using the zeppelin solidity libraries:

```
pragma solidity ^0.4.15;
import 'zeppelin/contracts/math/SafeMath.sol';
....
contract ExampleCoin is ERC20 {
```

```
    //SafeMath symbol is from imported file SafeMath.sol'
    using SafeMath for uint256;
        ...
}
```

For the example shown in the preceding code snippet, we imported the `SafeMath` library from Zeppelin and applied it to `uint256`.

Paths

When importing a solidity file, the file path follows a few simple syntax rules:

- Absolute paths: `/folder1/ folder2/xxx.sol` starting from `/`, the path location is from same solidity file location to the imported files. In our ERC 20 example, this is shown as follows:

  ```
  import 'zeppelin/contracts/math/SafeMath.sol';
  ```

The actual project structure appears as follows:

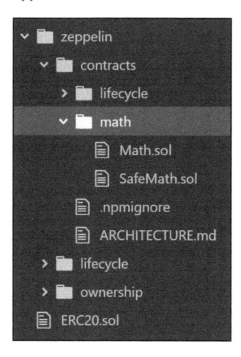

Relative paths

`../folder1/folder2/xxx.sol`: these paths are interpreted relative to the location of the current file, `.` as the current directory, and `..` as the parent directory.

In the solidity path, it is possible to specify path prefix remappings. As an example, if you want to import `github.com/ethereum/dapp-bin/library`, you can first clone the GitHub library to `/usr/local/dapp-bin/library`, and then run the compiler command, shown as follows:

```
solc github.com/ethereum/dapp-bin/library=/usr/local/dapp-bin/library
```

Then, in our solidity file, you can use the following `import` statement. It will remap to `/usr/local/dapp-bin/library/stringUtils.sol`:

```
import "github.com/ethereum/dapp-bin/library/stringUtils.sol " as
stringUtils;
```

The compiler will read the files from there.

Structure of a contract

A contract includes the following constructs: state variables, data type, functions, events, modifiers, enum, struct, and mapping.

State variables

State variables are values that are permanently stored in contract storage, and are used to maintain the contract's state.

The following is an example of the code:

```
contract SimpleStorage {
    uint storedData; // State variable
    //...
}
```

Data type

Solidity is a statically typed language. Developers familiar with language such as JavaScript and Python will find Solidity syntax easy to pick up. Each variable needs to specify the data type. The variable, which will always be passed by value, is called value types, it is built-in or predefined data types.

The value types in solidity are as follows:

Types	Operators	Example	Note
Bool	!, &&, ||, ==, !=	bool a = true;	The Booleans are true or false expressions.
Int (int8 to int256)	Comparison operators: <=, <, ==, !=, >=, >, Bit operators: &, |, ^, +, -, unary -, unary +, *, /, %, **, <<, >>	int a = 1;	Signed integer, signed of 8 up to 256 bits, in the step of 8.
Uint (uint8 to uint256)	Comparison operators: <=, <, ==, !=, >=, > Bit operators: &, |, ^, +, -, unary -, unary +, *, /, %, **, <<, >>	uint maxAge = 100;	Unsigned integer, unsigned of 8 up to 256 bits, in the step of 8.
Address	<=, <, ==, !=, >=, >	address owner = msg.sender; address myAddress = 0xE0f5206B...437b9;	Holds a 20 byte value (size of an Ethereum address).
<address>.balance		address.balance()	Addresses members and <indexentry content="value types, solidity:.balance">returns the balance of the address in Wei.
<address>.transfer		beneficiary.transfer(highestBid)	Addresses members and sends ether (in units of Wei) to an address. If the transfer operation fails, it <indexentry content="value types, solidity:.transfer">throws an exception, and all of the changes in a transaction are reverted.
<address>.send		msg.sender.send(amount)	Addresses members and send ether (in units of Wei) to an address. If the send operation fails, it returns false.

`<address>.call`		`someAddress.call.`
		`value(1ether)`
		`.gas(100000) ("register", "MyName")`
			Executed code of another contract, returns false in the event of failure, forwards all available gas, adjustable, should be used when you need to control how much gas to forward.

`<address>.delegatecall`		`'` `_library.delegatecall(msg.data);`	Executed code of another contract, but with the state (storage) of the calling contract.
Fixed size byte array (bytes1, bytes2, ..., bytes32)	Comparison operators: <=, <, ==, !=, >=, >, Bit operators: &, |, ^, ~,<<, >>, get array data : array[index]	`uint8[5] memory traits =` `[1,2,3,4,5];`	Fixed size byte arrays are defined using the keyword byteN, the N being any number from 1 to 32, it limits the size, it will be a lot cheaper and will save you gas.

Dynamically-sized array bytes string		`/**bytes array **/`
		`bytes32[] dynamicArray`
		`function f() {`
		`        bytes32[] storage`
		`storageArr = dynamicArray`
		`        storageArr.length++;`
		`}`
		`/**string array **/`
		`bytes32[] public names`
			Solidity supports a dynamically-sized byte array and a dynamically-sized UTF-8-encoded string.

Hexadecimal literals		`hex"1AF34A"`	Hexadecimal literals are prefixed with the keyword hex and are enclosed in single or double quotes.
Address literals		`0x5eD8Cee6b63b1c6AFce` `3AD7c92f4fD7E1B8fAd9F`	It is hexadecimal literals that pass the address checksum test.
String literals		`"Hello"`	String literals are normally written with either single or double quotes.

Enum type

Enum is a type with a restricted set of constants values. Here is an example, as follows:

```solidity
pragma solidity ^0.4.24;
  contract ColorEnum {
    enum Color {RED,ORANGE,YELLOW, GREEN}
    Color color;
    function construct() public {
     color = Color.RED;
    }
    function setColor(uint _value) public {
      color = Color(_value);
    }
  function getColor() public view returns (uint){
      return uint(color);
    }
}
```

Struct type

A struct is a type that contains named fields. New types can be declared using struct. Here is an example in the following code:

```solidity
struct person {
        uint age;
        string fName;
        string lName;
        string email;
    }
```

Mapping

Mappings act as hash tables that consist of key types and corresponding value type pairs. Here is an example, as follows:

```solidity
pragma solidity ^0.4.24;
contract StudentScore {
    struct Student {
        uint score;
        string name;
    }
    mapping (address => Student) studtents;
    address[] public studentAccts;
    function setStudent(address _address, uint _score, string _name) public
```

```
    {
        Student storage studtent = studtents[_address];
        studtent.score = _score;
        studtent.name = _name;
        studentAccts.push(_address) -1;
    }
    function getStudents() view public returns(address[]) {
        return studentAccts;
    }
    function getStudent(address _address) view public returns (uint,
string) {
        return (studtents[_address].score, studtents[_address].name);
    }
    function countStudents() view public returns (uint) {
        return studentAccts.length;
    }
}
```

Functions

Functions are the executable units of code within a contract. Here is a function structure in solidity, as follows:

```
function (<Input parameters>) {access modifiers}
[pure|constant|view|payable] [returns (<return types>)]
```

Input parameters

Function can pass input parameters. The input parameters are declared the same way as variables are.

In the previous `HelloWorld` example, we define `setNewGreeting` using the input parameter, `string _newGreeting`. Here is an example of this step:

```
function setNewGreeting (string _newGreeting) {
  greeting = _newGreeting;
}
```

Access modifiers

Solidity access modifiers are used to provide access control in Solidity.

There are four types of access modifiers available in Solidity, listed as follows:

- **Public**: Accessible from this contract, inherited contracts, and externally
- **Private**: Accessible only from this contract
- **Internal**: Accessible only from this contract and contracts inheriting from it
- **External**: Cannot be accessed internally, only externally

Output parameters

The output parameters can be declared after the `return` keyword, as shown in the following code snippet:

```
function getColor() public view returns (uint){
    return uint(color);
}
```

In solidity, `pure` functions are functions that are promised not to modify, or read the state.

```
pure|constant|view|payable
```

If the function modifier is defined as view, it indicates that the function will not change the storage state.

If the function modifier is defined as pure, it indicates that the function will not read the storage state.

If the function modifier is defined as constant, it indicates that the function won't modify the contract storage.

If the function modifier is defined as payable, modifier can receive funds.

```
uint amount =0;
function buy() public payable{
    amount += msg.value;
}
```

In the preceding example, the buy function has a payable modifier, which makes sure you can send ethers to the buy function. A function without any name, and annotated with a payable keyword, is called a payable fallback function.

```
pragma solidity ^0.4.24;
// this is a contract, which keeps all Ether to it with not way of
// retrieving it.
contract MyContract {
    function() public payable { }
}
```

Modifiers

In solidity, the modifier is used to change the behavior of a function. They can automatically check a condition prior to executing the function. Here is an example, as follows:

```
pragma solidity ^0.4.24;
contract Modifiers {
        address public admin;
    function construct () public {
       admin = msg.sender;
    }
    //define the modifiers
    modifier onlyAdmin() {
        // if a condition is not met then throw an exception
        if (msg.sender != admin) revert();
        // or else just continue executing the function
        _;
    }
    // apply modifiers

    function kill() onlyAdmin public {
        selfdestruct(admin);
    }
}
```

Events

Events are used to track the execution of a transaction sent to a contract. There are convenient interfaces with the EVM logging facilities. Here is an example, as follows:

```
pragma solidity ^0.4.24;
contract Purchase {
    event buyEvent(address bidder, uint amount); // Event
    function buy() public payable {
        emit buyEvent(msg.sender, msg.value); // Triggering event
    }
}
```

Constructor

The constructor method is a special method for creating and initializing a contract. In solidity v0.4.23, Solidity introduced this new constructor notation and the old one was deprecated.

```
//new
pragma solidity ^0.4.24;
contract HelloWorld {
  function constructor() public {
    // ...
  }
}
//deprecated
pragma solidity ^0.4.22;
contract HelloWorld {
  function HelloWorld () public {
    // ...
  }
}
```

Constant state variables, unit, and functions

The value of a constant cannot change through reassignment, and it can't be redeclared after compile time. In solidity, a state variable can be declared as constant. It does not allow reassignment to blockchain data (for example, this `.balance`, `block.blockhash`), or execution data (`tx.gasprice`), or make calls to external contracts.

The following table out the solidity global variables and their built-in functions:

Global variables / functions	Description
`msg.sender(address)`	`msg.sender` is the address currently interacting with the contract call message.
`msg.data(bytes)`	`msg.data` is the address currently interacting with the contract complete call. The data is in bytes.
`msg.value(unit)`	`msg.value` is the address currently interacting with the number of Wei sent with message as per the contract.
`msg.sig`	`msg.sig` is the address currently interacting with the contract that returns the first four bytes of the call data.
`gasleft() returns (uint256)`	API to check the gas remaining.
`tx.origin`	API to check the sender of the transaction.
`tx.gasprice`	API to check the gas price of the transaction.
`now`	Get current unix timestamp.
`block.number`	API to retrieve the current block number.
`block.difficulty`	API to retrieve the current block difficulty.
`block.blockhash(uint blockNumber) returns (bytes32)`	API to get the hash of the given block; the result only returned the 256 most recent blocks.
`block.gasLimit(unit)`	API to get the current block gas limit.
`block.coinbase ()`	Returns the current block miner's address.
`keccak256(...);`	Returns (bytes32) compute the Ethereum-SHA-3 (Keccak-256) hash of the (tightly packed) arguments.
`sha3(...)`	Returns (bytes32): an alias to keccak256.
`assert(bool condition)`	`assert` can be used to check for conditions. It indicates something that should never be false under any circumstances. Furthermore, `assert` uses the `0xfe` opcode to cause an error condition.
`require(bool condition)`	The `require` function should be used to ensure valid conditions. It can return false when the user enters something inappropriate. Furthermore, `require()` uses the `0xfd` opcode to cause an error condition.
`revert()`	`revert` will still undo all state changes.
`<address>.balance`	It checks the balance of the address in Wei (uint256).
`<address>.send(uint256 amount) returns (bool)`	API sends the amount of Wei to address and returns false in the event failure.
`<address>.transfer(uint256 amount)`	API transfer the amount of Wei to the address, and throws error when transfer fails.
`this`	The current contract, explicitly convertible to address.
`super`	The contract one level higher in the inheritance hierarchy.
`selfdestruct(address recipient)`	`self-destruct` will destroy the current contract, and storage associated with it is removed from the Ethereum's world state.
`suicide(address recipient)`	An alias to self-destruct.

Ether units

Solidity ether is dividable into Wei, Kwei, Mwei, Gwei, Szabo, Finney, Kether, Mether, Gether, and Tether. The following are the conversion units:

- 1 ether = 1,000 Finney
- 1 Finney = 1,000 Szabo
- 1 Szabo = 1,000 Mwei

- 1 Mwei = 1,000 Kwei
- 1 Kwei = 1,000 Wei

Time units

A solidity time unit is dividable into seconds, minutes, hours, days, weeks, and years. The following are the conversion units:

- 1 = 1 second
- 1 minute = 60 seconds
- 1 hour = 60 minutes
- 1 day = 24 hours
- 1 week = 7 days
- 1 year = 365 days

Inheritance, abstract, and interface

Many of the most widely used programming languages (such as C++, Java, Go, and Python, and so on) support **object-oriented programming** (**OOP**) and support inheritance, encapsulation, abstraction, and polymorphism. Inheritance enables code reuse and extensibility. Solidity supports multiple inheritance in the form of copying code, which includes polymorphism. Even if a contract inherits from multiple other contracts, only a single contract is created on the blockchain.

In solidity, inheritance is pretty similar to classic oriented-object programming languages. Here are a number of examples, as follows:

```
pragma solidity ^0.4.24;
contract Animal {
    constructor() public {
    }
    function name() public returns (string) {
        return  "Animal";
    }
    function color() public returns (string);
}
contract Mammal is Animal {
    int size;
    constructor() public {
    }
    function name() public returns (string) {
        return  "Mammal";
```

```
    }
    function run() public pure returns (int) {
        return 10;
    }
    function color() public returns (string);
}
contract Dog is Mammal {
    function name() public returns (string) {
        return  "Dog";
    }
    function color() public returns (string) {
        return "black";
    }
}
```

Dog inherits from `Mammal`, whose parent contract is `Animal`. When calling `Dog.run()`, it will call its parent method `run()` and return ten. When calling name, `Dog.name()` will override its patent method and return the output from `Dog`.

In solidity, a method without a body (no implementation) is known as an abstract method. A contract that contains an abstract method cannot be instantiated, but can be used as a base.

If a contract inherits from an abstract contract, then the contract must implement all the abstract methods of abstract parent class, or it has to be declared abstract as well.

Dog has a concrete `color()` method, which is a concrete contract and can be compiled, but the parent contract—mammal, and the grandparent contract—animal, are still abstract contracts.

Interfaces in solidity are similar to abstract contracts; they are implicitly abstract and cannot have implementations. An abstract contract can have instance methods that implement a default behavior. There are more restrictions in interfaces, as follows:

- Cannot inherit other contracts or interfaces
- Cannot define constructor
- Cannot define variables
- Cannot define structs
- Cannot define enums

```
pragma solidity ^0.4.24;
//interface
contract A {
    function doSomething() public returns (string);
}
```

```
//contract implements interface A
contract B is A {
    function doSomething() public returns (string) {
        return "Hello";
    }
}
```

In the preceding example, the contract is an interface, `contract B` implements `interface A`, and has a concrete `doSomething()` method.

Common smart contract patterns

In this section, we will discuss some common design and programming patterns for the smart contract programming language.

Access restriction

Access restriction is a solidity security pattern. It only allows authorized parties to access certain functions. Due to the public nature of the blockchain, all data on the blockchain is visible to anyone. It is critical to declare your contract function, state with restricted access control, and provide security against unauthorized access to smart contract functionality.

```
pragma solidity ^0.4.24;
contract Ownable {
 address owner;
 uint public initTime = now;
 constructor() public {
 owner = msg.sender;
 }
 //check if the caller is the owner of the contract
 modifier onlyOwner {
 require(msg.sender == owner,"Only Owner Allowed." );
 _;
 }
 //change the owner of the contract
 //@param _newOwner the address of the new owner of the contract.
 function changeOwner(address _newOwner) public onlyOwner {
 owner = _newOwner;
 }
 function getOwner() internal constant returns (address) {
 return owner;
 }
 modifier onlyAfter(uint _time) {
```

```
require(now >= _time,"Function called too early.");
_;
}
modifier costs(uint _amount) {
require(msg.value >= _amount,"Not enough Ether provided." );
_;
if (msg.value > _amount)
msg.sender.transfer(msg.value - _amount);
}
}
contract SampleContarct is Ownable {


mapping(bytes32 => uint) myStorage;
constructor() public {
}
function getValue(bytes32 record) constant public returns (uint) {
return myStorage[record];
}
function setValue(bytes32 record, uint value) public onlyOwner {
myStorage[record] = value;
}
function forceOwnerChange(address _newOwner) public payable
onlyOwner onlyAfter(initTime + 2 weeks) costs(50 ether) {
owner =_newOwner;
initTime = now;
}
}
```

The preceding example shows the access restrict pattern applied to a contract. We first define a parent class called Ownable with onlyOwner, changeOwner, and onlyAfter function modifiers. Other contracts can inherit from this contract to use defined access restriction. SampleContract inherits from Ownable contract and therefore, only the owner can access setValue function. Furthermore, forceOwnerChange may only be called two weeks after the contract creation time with 50 ether cost, and only the owner has permission to execute the function.

State machine

State machine is a behavior design pattern. It allows a contract to alter its behavior when it's internal state changes. A smart contract function call typically moves a contract state from one stage to the next stage. The basic operation of a state machine has two parts:

- It traverses through a sequence of states, where the next state is determined by the present state, and input conditions.
- It provides sequences of outputs based upon state transitions.

To illustrate this, let's develop a simple state machine. We will use washing dishes as an example. The process typically is *scrub, rinse, dry, scrub, rinse, dry*. We defined state machine stages as an enumerated type. As this is an extensive use case, only the state machine related code is presented. Any logic for detailed action implementation, such as `rinse()`, `dry()` and so on are omitted. See the following example:

```solidity
pragma solidity ^0.4.24;
contract StateMachine {
 enum Stages {
 INIT,
 SCRUB,
 RINSE,
 DRY,
 CLEANUP
 }


 Stages public stage = Stages.INIT;
 modifier atStage(Stages _stage) {
 require(stage == _stage);
 _;
 }
 function nextStage() internal {
 stage = Stages(uint(stage) + 1);
 }
 modifier transitionNext() {
 _;
 nextStage();
 }

 function scrub() public atStage(Stages.INIT) transitionNext {
 // Implement scrub logic here
 }


 function rinse() public atStage(Stages.SCRUB) transitionNext {
```

```
  // Implement rinse logic here
  }


  function dry() public atStage(Stages.SCRUB) transitionNext {
  // Implement dry logic here
  }


  function cleanup() public view atStage(Stages.CLEANUP) {
  // Implement dishes cleanup
  }
}
```

We define function modifier `atStage` to check if the current state allows the stage to run the function. Furthermore, `transitionNext` modifier will call the internal method `nextStage()` to move state to next stage.

Smart contract security

Once a smart contract has been deployed on the Ethereum network, it is immutable and public to everyone. Many of the smart contract functions are account payment related; therefore, security and testing become absolutely essential for a contract before being deployed on the main network. Following are security practices that will help you better design and write flawless Ethereum smart contracts.

Keep contract simple and modular

Try to keep your smart contract small, simple, and modularized. Complicated code is difficult to read, understand, and debug, it is also error-prone.

Use well-written library tools where possible.

Limit the amount of local variables.

Move unrelated functionality to other contracts or libraries.

Use the checks-effects-interactions pattern

Be very careful when interacting with other external contracts, it should be the last step in your function. It can introduce several unexpected risks or errors. External calls may execute malicious code. These kinds of calls should be considered as potential security risks and avoided if possible.

```
pragma solidity ^0.4.24;
// THIS CONTRACT is INSECURE - DO NOT USE
contract Fund {
    mapping(address => uint) userBalances;
function withdrawBalance() public {
    //external call
        if (msg.sender.call.value(userBalances[msg.sender])())
            userBalances[msg.sender] = 0;
}
}
contract Hacker {
    Fund f;
    uint public count;
    event LogWithdrawFallback(uint c, uint balance);
    function Attacker(address vulnerable) public {
        f = Fund(vulnerable);
    }
    function attack() public {
        f.withdrawBalance();
    }


    function () public payable {
        count++;
        emit LogWithdrawFallback(count, address(f).balance);
        if (count < 10) {
          f.withdrawBalance();
        }
    }
  }
}
```

The line `msg.sender.call.value(userBalances[msg.sender])` is an external call, when `withdrawBalance` is called, it will send ether with the `address.call.value()`. The hacker can attack fund contracts by triggering the hack fallback function, which can call the `withdrawBalance` method again. This will allow the attacker to refund multiple times, draining all ether in accounts.

The preceding contract vulnerabilities is called reentrancy. To avoid this, you can use the checks-effects-interactions pattern, shown in the following example:

```
pragma solidity ^0.4.24;
contract Fund {
    mapping(address => uint) userBalances;
    funct
ion withdrawBalance() public {
        uint amt = userBalances[msg.sender];
        userBalances[msg.sender] =0;
        msg.sender.transfer(amt);
    }
}
```

We first need to identify which part of the function involves external calls, `uint amt = userBalances[msg.sender]; userBalances[msg.sender] =0;`.

The function reads `userBalances` value, and assigns it to a local variable, then it resets `userBalances`. These steps are to make sure message sender can only transfer to their own account, but can't make any changes to state variables. The balance of a user will be reduced before the ether is actually transferred to user. If any error occurs during the transfer, the whole transaction will be reverted, including the reduction transfer amount of balance in the state variable. This approach can be described as *optimistic accounting*, because effects are written down as completed, before they actually take place.

DoS with block gas limit

The Ethereum blockchain transaction can only process a certain amount of gas due to the block gas limit, so be careful to look without fixed limited integration. When a number of iteration costs go beyond the gas limit, the transaction will fail and the contract can be stalled at a certain point. In this case, attackers may potentially attack the contract, and manipulate the gas.

Handle errors in external calls

As we discussed earlier, solidity has some low-level call methods: `address.call()`, `address.callcode()`, `address.delegatecall()`, and `address.send()`. These methods only return false when the call encounters an exception. So handling errors in external calls is very important in contracts, as shown in the following code snippet:

```
// good
if(!contractAddress.send(100)) {
```

```
                // handle error
        }
        contractAddress.send(20);//don't do this
        contractAddress.call.value(55)(); // this is doubly dangerous, as it will
        forward all remaining gas and doesn't check for result
        contractAddress.call.value(50)(bytes4(sha3("withdraw()"))); // if withdraw
        throws an exception, the raw call() will only return false and transaction
        will NOT be reverted
```

Case study – crowdfunding campaign

In this section, we will implement and deploy the smart contract for the crowdfunding campaign use case.

The idea of crowd funding is a process of raising funds for a project or venture from the masses. Investors receive tokens that represent a share of the startup they invested. The project sets up a predefined goal and a deadline for reaching it. Once a project misses the goal, the investments are returned, which reduces the risk for investors. This decentralized fundraising model can supplant the fund need for startup, and there is no need for a centralized trusted platform. Investors will only pay the gas fees if the fund returns. Any project contributor gets a token, and they can trade, sell, or keep these tokens. In a certain stage, the token can be used in exchange for real products as the physical reward.

Define struct and events, shown as follows:

```
pragma solidity ^0.4.24;

contract CrowdFunding {

    Project public project;
    Contribution[] public contributions;
    //Campaign Status
    enum Status {
        Fundraising,
        Fail,
        Successful
    }
    event LogProjectInitialized (
        address owner,
        string name,
        string website,
        uint minimumToRaise,
        uint duration
    );
    event ProjectSubmitted(address addr, string name, string url, bool
```

```
initialized);
    event LogFundingReceived(address addr, uint amount, uint currentTotal);
    event LogProjectPaid(address projectAddr, uint amount, Status status);
    event Refund(address _to, uint amount);
    event LogErr (address addr, uint amount);
    //campaign contributors
    struct Contribution {
        address addr;
        uint amount;
    }
    //define project
    struct Project {
        address addr;
        string name;
        string website;
        uint totalRaised;
        uint minimumToRaise;
        uint currentBalance;
        uint deadline;
        uint completeAt;
        Status status;
    }
    //initialized project
    constructor (address _owner, uint _minimumToRaise, uint
_durationProjects,
        string _name, string _website) public payable {
        uint minimumToRaise = _minimumToRaise * 1 ether; //convert to wei
        uint deadlineProjects = now + _durationProjects* 1 seconds;
        project = Project(_owner, _name, _website, 0, minimumToRaise, 0,
deadlineProjects, 0, Status.Fundraising);
        emit LogProjectInitialized(
            _owner,
            _name,
            _website,
            _minimumToRaise,
            _durationProjects);
    }
```

Define modifiers, shown in the following code:

```
    //check if project is at the required stage
    modifier atStage(Status _status) {
        require(project.status == _status,"Only matched status allowed." );
        _;
    }
    //check if msg.sender is project owner
    modifier onlyOwner() {
        require(project.addr == msg.sender,"Only Owner Allowed." );
        _;
    }
    //check if project pass the deadline
    modifier afterDeadline() {
        require(now >= project.deadline);
        _;
    }
    //Wait for 6 hour after campaign completed before allowing contract
destruction
    modifier atEndOfCampain() {
        require(!((project.status == Status.Fail || project.status ==
Status.Successful) && project.completeAt + 6 hours < now));
        _;
    }
```

Define smart contract functions, shown as follows:

```
    function () public payable {
        revert();
    }

    /* The default fallback function is called whenever anyone sends funds
to a contract */
    function fund() public atStage(Status.Fundraising) payable {
        contributions.push(
            Contribution({
                addr: msg.sender,
                amount: msg.value
                })
            );
        project.totalRaised += msg.value;
        project.currentBalance = project.totalRaised;
        emit LogFundingReceived(msg.sender, msg.value,
project.totalRaised);
    }
    //checks if the goal or time limit has been reached and ends the
campaign
    function checkGoalReached() public onlyOwner afterDeadline {
```

```
        require(project.status != Status.Successful &&
project.status!=Status.Fail);
        if (project.totalRaised > project.minimumToRaise){
            project.addr.transfer(project.totalRaised);
            project.status = Status.Successful;
            emit LogProjectPaid(project.addr, project.totalRaised,
project.status);
        } else {
            project.status = Status.Fail;
            for (uint i = 0; i < contributions.length; ++i) {
              uint amountToRefund = contributions[i].amount;
              contributions[i].amount = 0;
              if(!contributions[i].addr.send(contributions[i].amount)) {
                contributions[i].amount = amountToRefund;
                emit LogErr(contributions[i].addr,
contributions[i].amount);
                  revert();
              } else{
                project.totalRaised -= amountToRefund;
                project.currentBalance = project.totalRaised;
                emit Refund(contributions[i].addr,
contributions[i].amount);
              }
            }
        }
        project.completeAt = now;
    }
    function destroy() public onlyOwner atEndOfCampain {
        selfdestruct(msg.sender);
    }
}
```

Let's use Remix to test our campaign. We select the JavaScript VM option.

1. Initialize the campaign by clicking the **Deploy** button with the following input. This will start our campaign by means of the call constructor. We assign the first account as the project owner. The minimum funds raised is 30 ether, deadline set to five minutes for testing purposes. Put the following input code in the text box beside the **Deploy** button. Here are input parameters for constructor:

   ```
   0xca35b7d915458ef540ade6068dfe2f44e8fa733c, 30, 100, "smartchart",
   "smartchart.tech"
   ```

   The following is the screenshot for the Remix editor screen for this step:

Remix editor screen

2. Switch to the second account and, in the Remix value input field, enter 20 ether, and then click **(fallback)** button. This will add 20 ether to **totalRaised**. To check project information, click project button, and you should see that the **totalRaised** is 20 ethers now. Enter 0 uint in the **contributions** input field, and we can a see second account contribution address, and a fund amount of 20 ethers:

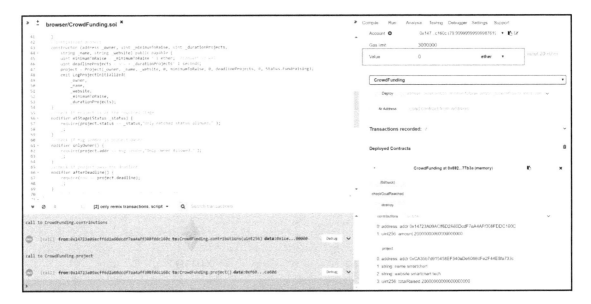

Remix value input field

3. Switch to the third account, enter `15` ethers in the **Value** field to add funds for the project. Click **(fallback)**, and we can see the project total fund raised to **35** ethers. At this moment, the project has achieved the campaign goal:

Adding funds to the project

4. Switch back to project owner, which is the first account, and click **checkGoalReached.** We can see that the transaction has been successfully executed. In the logs, the project status is updated to "successful". `LogProjectPaid` is triggered. If we check Remix account 1, 2, 3, the project owner account now contains a total in the region of 135 ethers. Our campaign smart contract was successfully tested in Remix:

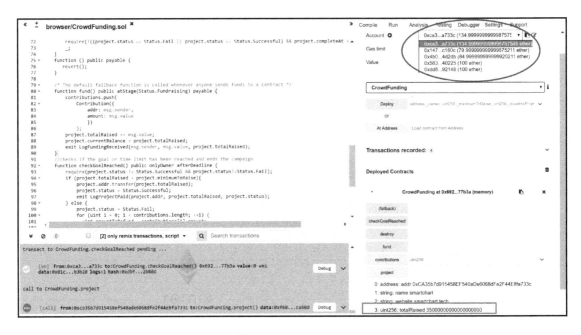

Successfully testing the campaign in smart contract

Summary

In this chapter, we learned the basic features of solidity programming. We also overviewed current popular smart contract development tools. By exploring common patterns and security best practices, we learned how to write better code to avoid contract vulnerabilities. Finally, we wrote a crowd funding campaign contract, and used Remix to deploy and test our example.

In the next chapter, we will build a Decentralize application (DApp) for crowdfunding.

15
Building an Ethereum Blockchain Application

In the previous chapter, we reviewed the basic features of smart contracts and how to write a crowdfunding smart contract example. After we deployed the smart contract to the blockchain, we needed to write the web application to interact with the smart contract. Ethereum blockchain provides the web3 API by calling smart contract functions and getters.

In this chapter, we will cover the following topics:

- What is a **decentralized application** (**DApp**)
- web3js quick overview
- Setting up an Ethereum development environment
- Developing and testing a DApp

Decentralized application overview

A **decentralized application** (or **DApp**) is an application that uses smart contracts to run. Smart contracts are deployed on the **Ethereum virtual machine** (**EVM**). It is similar to a client-server low-tier architecture. A DApp can have a frontend (web) that makes calls to its backend (smart contract) through the web3.js API.

The following structure is what we are going to build for our crowdfunding DApp:

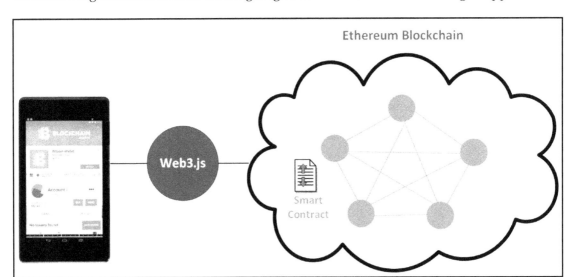

Strucuture of what we will be building for crowdfunding DApp

web3.js quick overview

web3.js is an Ethereum JavaScript API, that provides a collection of libraries to interact with a local or remote Ethereum network. The connection between web3js and Ethereum is made by using the HTTP or IPC protocol. In the following table, we quickly review a number of important web3.js API concepts:

API reference	Description	Example
web3-eth	This package provides an API to interact with the Ethereum blockchain and smart contracts	`getBalance, sendTransaction, coinbase, getBlockNumber, getAccounts`
web3-shh	This package provides an API to interact with the whisper protocol for broadcasting	`web3.shh.post({` `    symKeyID: identities[0],` `    topic: '0xffaadd11',` `    payload: '0xffffffddddddd1122'` `}).then(h => console.log(`Message` `with hash ${h} was successfuly sent`))`

web3-bzz	This package provides an API to interact with the Ethereum swarm, the decentralized file storage platform	`web3.bzz.currentProvider`
		`web3.bzz.download(bzzHash [,`
		`localpath])`

web3-utils	This package provides a collection of utility functions for Ethereum DApps and other web3.js packages	`web3.utils.toWei(number [, unit])` `web3.utils.isAddress(address)`

Provider

A provider abstracts a connection that talks to the Ethereum blockchain. It will issue queries and send transactions to the blockchain. web3 provides `JsonRpcProvider` and `IpcProvider`, which allow you to connect to a local or remote Ethereum node, including Mainnet, Ropsten testnet, Kovan testnet, Rinkeby testnet, and custom **remote procedure call** (**RPC**), like Ganache. Below is the code snippet to show how we can use web3 API to connect an Ethereum node.

```
var Web3 = require('web3');
var web3 = new Web3('http://localhost:8545');
// or
var web3 = new Web3(new
Web3.providers.HttpProvider('http://localhost:8545'));
// change provider
web3.setProvider('ws://localhost:8546');
// or
web3.setProvider(new
Web3.providers.WebsocketProvider('ws://localhost:8546'));
```

DApp development tools

There are some popular blockchain web development tools used being by developers for creating a basic structure of a DApp project. The following sections list a few of these.

Truffle

Truffle is an Ethereum DApp end-to-end development tool that provides a development environment for writing, compiling, and deploying test smart contracts and DApps. You can write HTML, CSS, and JavaScript for the frontend; Solidity is for smart contracts, and uses the web3.js API to interact with the UI and smart contract. Truffle Boxes provide helpful boilerplates, which contain helpful modules, solidity contracts and libraries, frontend code, and many other helpful files. The Truffle Boxes help developers to quickly get started with their DApp project.

The Truffle command line uses the following formats:

- `truffle [command] [options]`

Here are the frequently used options in command-line tools:

command	Description
`compile`	Compile solidity contract files.
`console`	Command-line interface to interact with deployed smart contracts.
`create`	This command helps to create a new contract, new migration file, and basic test.
`debug`	Experiment on a particular transaction in debugger sessions.
`deploy/migration`	Deploy a contract to the blockchain network.
`develop`	Interact with a contract via the command line in the local development environment.
`init`	Install a package from the Ethereum package registry.

Ganache

Ganache is a private Ethereum blockchain environment that allows to you emulate the Ethereum blockchain so that you can interact with smart contracts in your own private blockchain. Here are some features that Ganache provides:

- Displays blockchain log output
- Provides advanced mining control
- Built-in block explorer
- Ethereum blockchain environment
- Ganache has a desktop application as well as a command-line tool

This is what the desktop version of Ganache looks like:

The command line uses the following format:

```
ganache-cli <options>
```

These are the frequently used options of the command-line tools:

Options	Description
-a or --accounts	The number of accounts to generate at startup.
-e or --defaultBalanceEther	Configure the default test account ether amount. The default is 100.
-b or --blockTime	Specify the block time in seconds as a mining interval. If this option is not specified, Ganache will instantly mine a new block when a transaction is invoked.
-h or --host or --hostname	Specify hostname to listen on. The default is 127.0.0.1.
-p or --port	Specify the port number. The default is 8545.
-g or --gasPrice	Specify the gas price in Wei (defaults to 20000000000).
-l or --gasLimit	The block gas limit (defaults to 0x6691b7).
--debug	Display VM opcodes for debugging purpose.
-q or --quiet	Run ganache-cli without any logs.

Setting up an Ethereum development environment

Follow these instructions to obtain the Ethereum development tools and start up an Ethereum private local blockchain environment (primarily used to run/deploy your smart contract to a local blockchain).

Installing Truffle

Open up the command line and run the following command:

```
npm install -g truffle
```

Installing Ganache

Open up the command line and install Ganache's command-line interface as follows:

```
npm install -g ganache-cli
```

Creating a Truffle project

To initialize a new DApp project, we can run the truffle `init` command to initialize an empty Truffle project. This will create the DApp directory structure, including apps, contracts, and tests with Truffle configurations. Since Truffle Boxes provide many working templates, in our DApp example, we will use pet-shop box—a JQuery version of a JavaScript UI library—to develop our crowdfunding DApp example.

Create a folder called `Crowdfunding`, open a command-line prompt, navigate to the `Crowdfunding` folder, and run the following command:

```
truffle unbox pet-shop
```

The project structure is as follows:

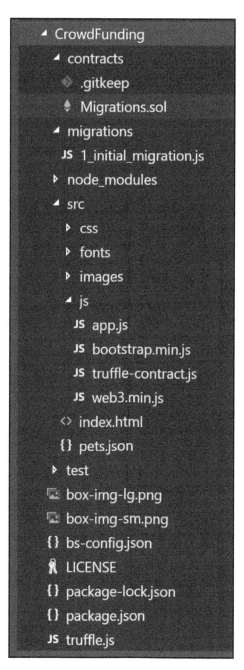

We wrote the crowdfunding smart contract in the previous chapter. Let's copy the `CrowdFunding.sol` file into the contracts folder under `Crowdfunding`.

Launching the Ganache environment

Open a new Terminal window and run the following command:

```
Ganache-cli
```

This will run `Ganache-cli` on port `8545`, and Ganache will create 10 default accounts for us. Each account will have 100 ether by default. You should see something like this in your console:

```
Ganache CLI v6.1.0 (ganache-core: 2.1.0)

Available Accounts
==================
(0) 0x1bd9143fd20a5abac181bce06c4589b8dad2eb74
(1) 0xc52674afe27e13d1db178d80d09cc7b67560b9b3
(2) 0xbecb8195da2b87287fda98cf0d625ed256e0c32e
(3) 0x7d070b0689ec30302661640c93e157aa33ec2267
(4) 0xc1937d9f1b5e384d2acb6a1216ba4444ed6d9278
(5) 0x142994a3ed8c6ab8ed73f41e7a0bd97df4088020
(6) 0xee5ba816088e35eb4e43bbcbfd08428f6df5873d
(7) 0x97dea4cda2fb9af1bd8b09ee9dabb1bd111cab57
(8) 0x1e007b99e62533ab61096e6a49b71d3900b382d4
(9) 0x45c4631122edd53736bb67dc9ff59c709bb8aba4

Private Keys
> eth_blockNumber
eth_blockNumber08c17bc237c500a0063c96f75ec72bcd6eb50a3494e2918cf5d9c
eth_blockNumberfae90a7098113b051ac13727c138b12471413367ab7aa0c6f44fb
eth_blockNumberbd803de3f5b717a4f1077d050fc623e77abef7e0bad21575862a8
eth_blockNumberec98db349e1baa694ccf43a0bff570d8fa3a7d7223907e53f7c94
eth_blockNumber7e186319e4557584ae77eca3f86117d8411f6e5cf51eca8ebf838
eth_blockNumbere5bdfb5425dc27151f11824116d135f7832ada926006e178852a8
eth_blockNumber65cd1a16a82d6cc20ed4997e924a384a1fac33d60cc90c34fa86b
eth_blockNumberb4ae7624798ea4e4231cc8de1172057fea309b3e1787c5c1f39f8
eth_blockNumberadf66dc8371615150b37ebb019d8aef33da6bfd643318cb530a1b
eth_blockNumberee810ceb16cdf6e40060837901243317e31308027ed50eef283ec
eth_blockNumber
```

In our Truffle project, `truffle.js` defined `7545` as the default port number. We need to update the port number to `8545` to match with the Ganache port number, as follows:

```
module.exports = {
  networks: {
    development: {
      host: "127.0.0.1",
      port: 8545,
      network_id: "*" // Match any network id
    }
  }
};
```

Deploying a smart contract

As you might have noticed, two migration-related files were created by the previous command, `Migrations.sol` and `1_initial_migration.js`. `Migrations.sol` stores a number that corresponds to the last applied "migration" script. When you add a new contract and deploy the contract, the number of the last deployment in stores will increase. After the contract has run once, it will not run again. The numbering convention is `x_script_name.js`, with x starting at 1, that is `1_initial_migration.js`. Your new contracts would typically come in scripts starting at `2_....`.

In our case, we will add a new migration contract to deploy `CrowdFunding`. Let's create a file called `2_deploy_contracts.js`.

`CrowdFunding.sol` defines the constructor as follows:

```
constructor (address _owner, uint _minimumToRaise, uint _durationProjects,
        string _name, string _website)
```

To deploy a contract, with optional constructor arguments, you can call the truffle deploy function, `deployer.deploy(contract, args..., options)`.

We will use the first account given to us by Ganache as the owner account, as follows:

```
var CrowdFunding = artifacts.require("./CrowdFunding.sol");
module.exports = (deployer, network, accounts) => {
  const ownerAddress = accounts[0];
  deployer.deploy(CrowdFunding, ownerAddress, 30, 60, "smartchart",
"smartchart.tech");
}
```

Let's deploy the smart contract to our network. Run the `truffle` command, as follows:

```
truffle migrate
```

The following screenshot displays the result for running the command for `truffle migrate`:

```
Using network 'development'.

Running migration: 1_initial_migration.js
  Deploying Migrations...
  ... 0xd2e9f62dbbcfca6da38b09e5bbb82a4019fa09e87d00ebfd45416b757f676c48
  Migrations: 0x77ab1ca444797a862e1555e418c73b7aeaf03b90
Saving successful migration to network...
  ... 0xc221d7e60f0f46d0fc7c5f00281918b7837f5a412d9149600c11a8d5f57c525c
Saving artifacts...
Running migration: 2_deploy_contracts.js
  Deploying CrowdFunding...
  ... 0x1b163aac8f62076039081896afb0b897bdae27470536485546f474a2ef4f2084
  CrowdFunding: 0x9e24eea74f385e95cf61df1d5f441108a6715356
Saving successful migration to network...
  ... 0xeef193b79458260af8abdc2ab8d8f96d88e672a8a963e24efa7f965aa4389e9a
Saving artifacts...
```

This deploys our crowdfunding smart contract in a local Ganache blockchain environment.

To bring your local node server up, run the following command, which will bring up the pet store page in our browser:

```
npm run dev
```

Writing a campaign decentralized application

We just deployed our smart contract on our local Ganache blockchain environment. Now, we will start to write UI code to trigger smart contract functions through an RPC call. The source code for this chapter is available at `https://bit.ly/2X8xPBL`.

Selecting a web3 provider

When we load a web page, we need to connect to a web3 provider. If you have already installed a provider such as MetaMask, you can use your correct provider option, as follows:

```
App.web3Provider = web3.currentProvider;
```

In our crowdfunding example, for the sake of simplicity, we will directly connect to our local Ganache server, as follows:

```
App.web3Provider = new
Web3.providers.HttpProvider('http://localhost:8545');
```

Loading account information

To load accounts, we define a drop-down menu with empty content, as follows:

```
<div class="form-group">
        <label for="exampleFormControlSelect1">Accounts</label>
        <select class="form-control" id="accts">
        </select>
    </div>
```

When we load the page, we will use `web3.eth.accounts` to get all 10 default accounts. Notice that the first account has an ether balance of 99.84; this is because we used the first account as the owner account to deploy the contract and burned some gas as the transaction fee, as shown in the following code:

```
web3.eth.accounts.forEach( function(e){
    $('#accts').append($('<option>', {
        value:e,
        text : e + " (" +web3.fromWei(web3.eth.getBalance(e), "ether")
+ " ether)"
    }));
})
```

Once the accounts are loaded, it will be displayed as follows:

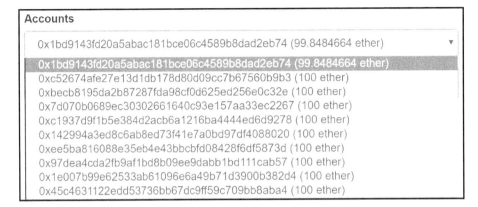

Loading project information

In crowdfunding, we defined a project struct that contains fundraising information, as follows:

```
struct Project {
        address addr;
        string name;
        string website;
        uint totalRaised;
        uint minimumToRaise;
        uint currentBalance;
        uint deadline;
        uint completeAt;
        Status status;
    }
```

Let's define some related information in HTML, for example:

```
<table class="table table-hover table-striped">
                <tbody>
                  <tr>
                    <th scope="row">address</th>
                    <td><span class="text-info" id="address"></span
</td>
                  </tr>
                  <tr>
                    <th scope="row">name</th>
                    <td><span class="text-info" id="name"></span></td>
```

```
                    </tr>
                    <tr>
                        <th scope="row">website</th>
                        <td><span class="text-info"
    id="website"></span></td>
                    </tr>
                    <tr>
                        <th scope="row">totalRaised</th>
                        <td><span class="text-info"
    id="totalRaised"></span></td>
    ...
                    </tbody>
                </table>
```

The `CrowdFunding.deployed()` function will create an instance of `CrowdFunding` that represents the default address managed by `CrowdFunding`. The code here shows us how to display project information:

```
    App.contracts.CrowdFunding.deployed().then(function(instance) {
        crowdFundingInstance = instance;
        return crowdFundingInstance.project();
    }).then(function(projectInfo) {
        $("#address").text(projectInfo[0].toString());
        $("#name").text(projectInfo[1]);
        $("#website").text(projectInfo[2]);
        $("#totalRaised").text(projectInfo[3].toString());
        ..
        if(projectInfo[6].toString().length>0) {
            var deadline = new
    Date(Number(projectInfo[6].toString())*1000);
            deadlineDate = moment(deadline).format("YYYY-MM-DD h:mm:ss");
            $("#deadline").text(deadlineDate);
        }
        if(projectInfo[7].toString().length>0 &&
    projectInfo[7].toString()!='0') {
            console.log(projectInfo[7].toString());
            var completeAt = new
    Date(Number(projectInfo[7].toString())*1000);
            completeAtDate = moment(completeAt).format("YYYY-MM-DD h:mm:ss");
            $("#completeAt").text(completeAtDate);
        }
    }).catch(function(error) {
    ..
    });
```

The result will be displayed as follows:

Project	
address	0x1bd9143fd20a5abac181bce06c4589b8dad2eb74
name	smartchart
website	smartchart.tech
totalRaised	0
minimumToRaise	30000000000000000000
currentBalance	0
deadline	2018-11-15 7:29:49
completeAt	
status	Fundraising

Handling the fund function

To raise funds, we need to call the fund function, which is defined in our crowdfunding smart contract. In our web page, we use the HTML range input slider component to contribute fund amounts, as follows:

```
<form id="fund-form" method="post" role="form" style="display: block;">
                            <div class="form-group row">
                                <div class="row">
                                    <div class="col-lg-12">
                                        <input type="range"
name="ageInputName" id="ageInputId" value="0" min="1" max="100"
oninput="ageOutputId.value = ageInputId.value">
                                        <div style="display:
inline;"><output name="ageOutputName" id="ageOutputId">0</output>
<span>ether</span></div>
                                    </div>
                                </div>
                            </div>
                            <div class="form-group">
                                <div class="row">
```

```
                                        <div class="col-lg-12">
                                            <button type="button"
    id="fundBtn" class="btn btn-primary pull-left">Submit</button>
                                        </div>
                                    </div>
                                </div>
                            </form>
```

The `Crowdfunding fund` function is a payable fallback function; therefore, we need to pass `msg.sender` and `msg.value` from the UI to call it, as follows.

```
    function fund() public atStage(Status.Fundraising) payable {
        contributions.push(
            Contribution({
                addr: msg.sender,
                amount: msg.value
                })
            );
......
    }
```

You can define the sending address and value parameters as follows:

```
    handleFund: function(event) {
      event.preventDefault();
      var fundVal = $('#ageOutputId').val();
      var selectAcct = $('#accts').find(":selected").val();
      $("#displayMsg").html("");
      App.contracts.CrowdFunding.deployed().then(function(instance) {
        return instance.fund({ from: selectAcct, value:web3.toWei(fundVal,
    "ether"), gas:3500000});
      }).then(function(result) {
        App.loadProject();
      }).catch(function(err) {
        console.error(err);
        $("#displayMsg").html(err);
      });
    },
```

Once we get the result back, we will call the `loadProject` function to refresh the project information. We can see that the current balance fund increased, as shown in the following screenshot:

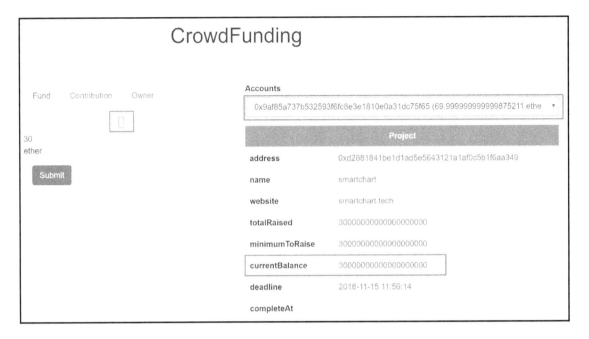

checkGoalReached

Once the funding goal is reached, the crowdfunding owner will collect of the all funds by running the `checkGoalReached` method.

The HTML is just a simple button, as shown in the following code:

```
<button type="button" id="checkGoal" class="btn btn-
success">CheckGoal</button>
```

Similar to the fund function, we call the smart contract in JavaScript using the following code:

```
instance.checkGoalReached({ from: selectAcct, gas:3500000});
```

Here is the detailed logic:

```
handleCheckGoal: function(event) {
  event.preventDefault();
  $("#displayMsg").html("");
  var selectAcct = $('#accts').find(":selected").val();
  App.contracts.CrowdFunding.deployed().then(function(instance) {
    return instance.checkGoalReached({ from: selectAcct, gas:3500000});
  }).then(function(result) {
    App.loadProject();
  }).catch(function(err) {
    console.error(err);
    $("#displayMsg").html(err);
  });
},
```

The result will display as follows:

If you followed the whole example and run this step, congratulations! You are now able to write and run a crowdfunding DApp.

Summary

In this chapter, we learned DApp basics and we now understand the web3.js API. By running Ganache as our local Ethereum environment, we could use the Truffle development tool to create a crowdfunding project and write a DApp component. Finally, we deployed and launched the crowdfunding DApp. In the next chapter, we will start to explore the most popular enterprise blockchain—Hyperledger Fabric.

16
Exploring an Enterprise Blockchain Application Using Hyperledger Fabric

The previous chapter, we discussed the Ethereum blockchain. Ethereum is a public blockchain; anyone can read the blockchain data and make legitimate changes. Anyone can write a new block into the chain. Ethereum is fully autonomous and is not controlled by anyone. The smart contract is written in Solidity, as a nearly Turing complete language, that can run on the **Ethereum virtual machine** (**EVM**) to execute various transactions. Developers can build and deploy **decentralized applications** (**DApps**) using these smart contracts. Ether is a cryptocurrency in Ethereum, and acts as fuel for every operation in Ethereum, including executing smart contracts, DApps, transactions, and so on. However, this is not the only way to build a blockchain.

Blockchains that require an access control layer built into the blockchain nodes to read restricted information on the blockchain can be created. This will limit the number of participants in the network who can transact in the consensus mechanism of the blockchain's network. This kind of blockchain is called a permissioned blockchain.

The differences between public and permissioned blockchains are shown in the following table:

	Permissionless	Permissioned
Public	Everyone can read the transaction data. Everyone can validate a transaction in the block. • **Speed**: Poor • **Consensus**: Proof-of-Work • **Blockchain**: Bitcoin, Ethereum • **Token**: Needed	Everyone can read the transaction data. Only predefined users can validate a transaction. • **Speed**: Good • **Consensus**: Proof-of-Work • **Blockchain**: Ethereum after Casper • **Token**: Needed
Private	Only predefined users can read transaction data. Only predefined users can validate a transaction. • **Speed**: Good • **Consensus**: **Federated byzantine agreement (FBA)** • **Token**: Not needed	Only predefined users can read transaction data. Only entitled users can validate a transaction. • **Speed**: Good • **Consensus**: **Practical Byzantine Fault Tolerance Algorithm (PBFT)** • **Blockchain**: Hyperledger Fabric • **Token**: Not needed

Hyperledger Fabric is one such private permissioned blockchains. In this chapter, we will discuss the Hyperledger Fabric blockchain.

Hyperledger Fabric is an open source enterprise blockchain technology. The project was initially contributed by IBM and digital asset. Hyperledger Fabric is one of the blockchain projects hosted by the Linux foundation. The smart contract in Hyperledger Fabric is called *chaincode*, which defines the business logic for Fabric applications. The modular architecture design enables Fabric to support high degrees of confidentiality, resiliency, flexibility, and scalability. The components in Fabric, such as consensus and membership services, can be plug and play.

In this chapter, we will cover the following topics:

- Issuance claim
- Setting up a Hyperledger Fabric environment
- Write a chaincode
- Configuring Hyperledger Fabric

Issuance claim

In this section, we will explore and implement an issuance claim use case.

No one wants to have an insurance claim, but when things do go wrong and accidents happen, this may result in financial losses. These losses will be covered by your insurance policy. The traditional insurance claims process has stayed the same for decades, as there are a number of key issues in the process, including false claims, fraud detection, slow and complex claims processing, human error, undesirable customer experience, and inefficient information flows in reinsurance.

With blockchain, the transaction record in the ledger is immutable and the state data can only be updated when all parties agree. The record in the blockchain can be shared in real time. This allows insurers to move quickly, as most of the required information for claims verification can be processed in no time. Insurers can track the use of asset data in the blockchain. The paperwork can be eliminated and customers can submit claims via a web application.

Let's take a look at the insurance claim process, as shown in the following screenshot. For demonstration purposes, we simplified the claim process, as it can be much more complex in a real-world use case:

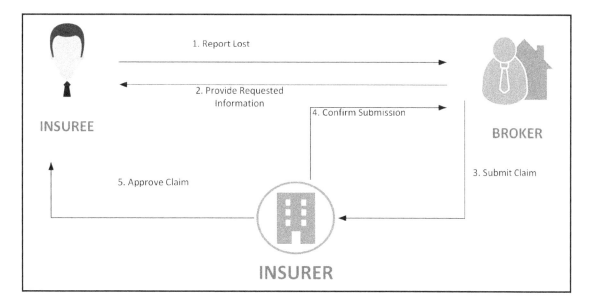

For the preceding process, the steps are as follows:

1. An insuree reports a claim to a broker
2. A broker provides requested information
3. A broker submits a claim to an issuer
4. An issuer confirms the claim
5. An issuer process and approves the claim

Setting up a Hyperledger Fabric environment

So far, we have learned about the key concepts of Hyperledger Fabric. In this section, we will set up a Hyperledger Fabric development environment. Before continuing with the installation steps, let's take a look at the prerequisites for fabric installation.

Installation prerequisites

The following are the prerequisites for installing the required development tools.

Ubuntu Linux 14.04 / 16.04 LTS (both 64-bit), or macOS 10.12	Docker Engine: Version 17.03 or higher
Docker-Compose: Version 1.8 or higher	Node: 8.9 or higher (note version 9 is not supported)
npm: v5.x	git: 2.9.x or higher
Python: 2.7.x	

We will use Ubuntu for our development environment. We can download the prerequisites using the following commands:

```
curl -O https://hyperledger.github.io/composer/latest/prereqs-ubuntu.sh
chmod u+x prereqs-ubuntu.sh
./prereqs-ubuntu.sh
```

It may prompt for your password, since it uses `sudo` during its execution.

Installing Hyperledger Fabric

Create and navigate to the project folder called `insurance-claim`, as follows:

```
mkdir ~/insurance-claim && cd ~/insurance-claim
```

Enter the following command to install the Hyperledger Fabric platform-specific binaries:

```
curl -sSL
https://raw.githubusercontent.com/hyperledger/fabric/release-1.3/scripts/bo
otstrap.sh | bash
```

After this executes, it downloads the following platform-specific binaries in the `bin` folder, which is located under the `fabric-samples` folder. You can set `fabric-samples/bin` as a `PATH` variable as follows:

```
export PATH=<path to download location>/bin:$PATH
```

We also provide `bootstrap-hyperledger.sh` from the code files in this book, and you can download it from the Packt site. Once you get the file, you can directly run the following script, and it will create a bin folder and download binaries to this folder:

```
===> List out hyperledger docker images
hyperledger/fabric-ca          1.3.0-rc1    784b38dab5ba    5 days ago     244MB
hyperledger/fabric-ca          latest       784b38dab5ba    5 days ago     244MB
hyperledger/fabric-tools       1.3.0-rc1    693f6ae1c95c    5 days ago     1.5GB
hyperledger/fabric-tools       latest       693f6ae1c95c    5 days ago     1.5GB
hyperledger/fabric-ccenv       1.3.0-rc1    04415e10d1f2    5 days ago     1.38GB
hyperledger/fabric-ccenv       latest       04415e10d1f2    5 days ago     1.38GB
hyperledger/fabric-orderer     1.3.0-rc1    4f5d3e993eb8    5 days ago     145MB
hyperledger/fabric-orderer     latest       4f5d3e993eb8    5 days ago     145MB
hyperledger/fabric-peer        1.3.0-rc1    3286d6b8fe00    5 days ago     151MB
hyperledger/fabric-peer        latest       3286d6b8fe00    5 days ago     151MB
hyperledger/fabric-zookeeper   0.4.12       bca71b814159    12 days ago    1.39GB
hyperledger/fabric-zookeeper   latest       bca71b814159    12 days ago    1.39GB
hyperledger/fabric-kafka       0.4.12       58b901c762ea    12 days ago    1.4GB
hyperledger/fabric-kafka       latest       58b901c762ea    12 days ago    1.4GB
hyperledger/fabric-couchdb     0.4.12       fe8d64d1233c    12 days ago    1.45GB
hyperledger/fabric-couchdb     latest       fe8d64d1233c    12 days ago    1.45GB
```

These components will be part of our Hyperledger Fabric network.

Writing chaincode

Chaincode is similar to a *smart contract*. It defines and executes the business logic invoked by authorized participants in a specific network. A chaincode is written in Go or Node.js. In our example, we will use Go.

There are many IDEs and tools to support Golang. Here are some popular IDEs that work great with Golang.

Development tools

There are various tools that support Go development. Some popular IDEs are listed in the following sections.

LiteIDE

LiteIDE is an open source Go IDE that was directly designed for Golang. There are a bunch of useful features available for Go developers, including a configurable code editor, customized build commands, many building options, and Golang support.

JetBrains Gogland

Gogland has a powerful built-in autocomplete engine, errors detection, code refactoring tools, and more.

Visual Studio Code

You can install Go extension in Visual Studio Code. It provides code hints and the ability to debug code.

In this chapter, we will use LiteIDE to develop our chaincode. Follow the official LiteIDE installation guide to set up your local IDE environment, which is available from the following link:

```
https://github.com/visualfc/liteide/blob/master/liteidex/deploy/welcome/en/
install.md.
```

Chaincode key concept and APIs

There are three important functions in Fabric chaincode: `Init`, and `Invoke`, `Query`. Every chaincode program must implement the chaincode interface, as follows:

```
type Chaincode interface {
    Init(stub ChaincodeStubInterface) pb.Response
    Invoke(stub ChaincodeStubInterface) pb.Response
}
```

`Init()` is called when the application initializes its internal data for other chaincode functions to use. It is triggered when a chaincode receives an instantiate or upgrade transaction.

When the application client proposes an update or query transaction, the `Invoke();` function is called.

`Query()` is called when a chaincode queries a chaincode state. Hyperledger Fabric uses LevelDB (key/value store) as the default database to store world;state data. You can use a key to get the current ledger state data. The query function reads the value of a chaincode state by passing in the key value.

The shim package provides APIs for the chaincode to access its state variables, transaction context, and call other chaincodes.

`ChaincodeStubInterface` is one of the important interfaces. It provides various functions that let you query, update, and delete assets in the ledger. These are as follows:

`GetState(key string) ([]byte, error)`	`GetState` returns the value of the specified key from the ledger
`PutState(key string, value []byte) error`	`PutState` puts the specified key and value into the transaction's writeset as a data-write proposal
`DelState(key string) error`	`DelState` records the specified key to be deleted in the writeset of the transaction proposal

Defining an issuance claim

Let's write a chaincode. Open LiteIDE and create a new file called `claimcontract.go`, as follows:

In the insurance claim use case analysis, we analysed the participants in the issuance claim process. There are three participants for whom we need to define a chaincode: insuree, broker, and insurer, as shown in the following example:

```go
type Insuree struct {
        Id              string `json:"id"`
        FirstName       string `json:"firstName"`
        LastName        string `json:"lastName"`
        SSN             string `json:"ssn"`
        PolicyNumber    string `json:"policyNumber"`
}
```

In `Insuree`, we define `Id`, `firstname`, `LastName`, `SSN`, and `policyNumber`.

In Go language, it allows the first letter of a field name as to be either uppercase or lowercase. When we need an exported field to be public for any piece of code to use it, it needs to be a capitalized letter. You can use encoding in the JSON package to unmarshal data into struct, which defines the field name in JSON as the `firstName` key, as shown in the following format:

```
type Member struct {
  Name string `json:"member_name"`
}
```

The broker and insurers data models are similar and only different in type. We define them as follows:

```
type Company struct {
        Id    string `json:"id"`
        Type string `json:"type"`
        Name string `json:"name"`
}
```

In the issuance claim process, `Insuree` initializes a claim request. The claim document will keep track of each step of the process in the blockchain. It records all necessary information, including status, user claim description, `insueeId`, `brokerId`, `insurerId`, process time at each step, and comments entered from an authorized party, as shown in the following example:

```
type Claim struct {
        Id         string `json:"id"`        //the fieldtags are needed to
keep case from bouncing around
        Desc       string `json:"desc"`      //claim description
        Status     string `json:"status"`    //status of claim
        InsureeId string `json:"insureeId"` //InsureeId
        BrokerId   string `json:"brokerId"`  //BrokerId
        InsurerId string `json:"insurerId"` //InsurerId
        Comment    string `json:"comment"`   //comment
        ProcessAt string `json:"processAt"` //processAt
}
```

Initializing the chaincode

Next, we'll implement the Init function. Init() allows the chaincode to initialize the insuree data to start the claim request. In our case, we will set up and register the insuree person information, as follows:

```
func (c *ClaimContract) Init(stub shim.ChaincodeStubInterface) pb.Response
{
        args := stub.GetStringArgs()
        if len(args) != 5 {
                return shim.Error("Incorrect arguments. Expecting a key
and a value")
        }
        insureeId := args[0]
        firstName := args[1]
        lastName := args[2]
        ssn := args[3]
        policyNumber := args[4]
        insureeData := Insuree{
                Id:           insureeId,
                FirstName:    firstName,
                LastName:     lastName,
                SSN:          ssn,
                PolicyNumber: policyNumber}
        insureeBytes, _ := json.Marshal(insureeData)
        err := stub.PutState(insureeId, insureeBytes)
        if err != nil {
                return shim.Error(fmt.Sprintf("Failed to create asset:
%s", args[0]))
        }
        return shim.Success(nil)
}
```

ChaincodeStubInterface.GetStringArg gets the input arguments. It expects that the length of the arguments should be 5. With all required insurer data, we build Insurer JSON data and encode it to JSON byte strings —json.Marshal(insureeData. Then, we store the key and the value on the ledger. If all went well, it returns a peer.Response object with success to Fabric's client.c.

Invoking the chaincode

To trigger the invoke function, you can call the name of the chaincode application function and pass `shim.ChaincodeStubInterface` as the signature. In the insurance claim case, we defined several functions to support our use case, for example:

`AddCompany`, `ReportLost`, `RequestedInfo`, `SubmitClaim`, `ConfirmClaimSubmission`, `ApproveClaim`.

We also defined a query to keep track of the current claim request and `getHistory` to get all of the historical claim transaction records, as follows:

```
func (c *ClaimContract) Invoke(stub shim.ChaincodeStubInterface)
pb.Response {
        function, args := stub.GetFunctionAndParameters()
        if function == "AddCompany" {
                return c.AddCompany(stub, args)
        } else if function == "ReportLost" {
                return c.ReportLost(stub, args)
        } else if function == "RequestedInfo" {
                return c.RequestedInfo(stub, args)
        } else if function == "SubmitClaim" {
                return c.SubmitClaim(stub, args)
        } else if function == "ConfirmClaimSubmission" {
                return c.ConfirmClaimSubmission(stub, args)
        } else if function == "ApproveClaim" {
                return c.ApproveClaim(stub, args)
        } else if function == "query" {
                return c.query(stub, args)
        } else if function == "getHistory" {
                return c.getHistory(stub, args)
        }


        return shim.Error("Invalid function name")
}
```

AddCompany

`AddCompany` is similar to how we added insuree at the Init step. Chaincode can register brokers and insurers through this function. The company type can be a *broker* or *insurer*, as follows:

```
func (c *ClaimContract) AddCompany(stub shim.ChaincodeStubInterface, args
[]string) pb.Response {
```

```
        id := args[0]
        name := args[1]
        companyType := args[2]
        companyData := Company{
                Id:    id,
                Type: companyType,
                Name: name}
        companyBytes, _ := json.Marshal(companyData)
        stub.PutState(id, companyBytes)
        return shim.Success(companyBytes)

}
```

ReportLost

In this step, the insuree reports the lost item to the broker with all the claim information. This function also records the current system process time at the `processAt` field. `currentts.Format(2006-01-02 15:04:05)` is a Go custom format; it will convert the current time into YYYY-MM-dd hh:mm:ss format, as shown in the following example:

```
func (c *ClaimContract) ReportLost(stub shim.ChaincodeStubInterface, args
[]string) pb.Response {
        claimId := args[0]
        desc := args[1]
        insureeId := args[2]
        brokerId := args[3]
        currentts := time.Now()
        processAt := currentts.Format("2006-01-02 15:04:05")
        //initialized claim
        claimData := Claim{
                Id:        claimId,
                Desc:      desc,
                Status:    "ReportLost",
                InsureeId: insureeId,
                BrokerId:  brokerId,
                InsurerId: "",
                Comment:   "",
                ProcessAt: processAt}
        claimBytes, _ := json.Marshal(claimData)
        stub.PutState(claimId, claimBytes)
        return shim.Success(claimBytes)

}
```

RequestedInfo

After the insuree reports a loss, the next step is for the broker to return `RequestedInfo`, as follows:

```
func (c *ClaimContract) RequestedInfo(stub shim.ChaincodeStubInterface,
args []string) pb.Response {
        return c.UpdateClaim(stub, args, "RequestedInfo")
}
func (c *ClaimContract) UpdateClaim(stub shim.ChaincodeStubInterface, args
[]string, currentStatus string) pb.Response {
        claimId := args[0]
        comment := args[1]
        claimBytes, err := stub.GetState(claimId)
        claim := Claim{}
        err = json.Unmarshal(claimBytes, &claim)
        if err != nil {
                return shim.Error(err.Error())
        }
        if currentStatus == "RequestedInfo" && claim.Status !=
"ReportLost" {
                claim.Status = "Error"
                fmt.Printf("Claim is not initialized yet")
                return shim.Error(err.Error())
        } else if currentStatus == "SubmitClaim" && claim.Status !=
"RequestedInfo" {
                claim.Status = "Error"
                fmt.Printf("Claim must be in RequestedInfo status")
                return shim.Error(err.Error())
        } else if currentStatus == "ConfirmClaimSubmission" &&
claim.Status != "SubmitClaim" {
                claim.Status = "Error"
                fmt.Printf("Claim must be in Submit Claim status")
                return shim.Error(err.Error())
        } else if currentStatus == "ApproveClaim" && claim.Status !=
"ConfirmClaimSubmission" {
                claim.Status = "Error"
                fmt.Printf("Claim must be in Confirm Claim Submission
status")
                return shim.Error(err.Error())
        }
        claim.Comment = comment
        if currentStatus == "RequestedInfo" {
                insurerId := args[2]
                claim.InsurerId = insurerId
        }
        currentts := time.Now()
        claim.ProcessAt = currentts.Format("2006-01-02 15:04:05")
```

```
        claim.Status = currentStatus
        claimBytes0, _ := json.Marshal(claim)
        err = stub.PutState(claimId, claimBytes0)
        if err != nil {
                return shim.Error(err.Error())
        }
        return shim.Success(claimBytes0)
    }
```

Since the remaining process functions are quite similar, we define `UpdateClaim` as a common function to share with the remaining steps.

The `UpdateClaim` function first gets `claimId` and the current participant comment from input arguments. It then queries and gets a claim from the blockchain to decode the claim data and turns it into a JSON string—`json.Unmarshal(claimBytes, &claim)`.

Before updating the claim content, it will validate the input claim status and make sure it is on the expected step. If all goes well, we will update the claim status, participant comment, and process time.

Finally, we update the claim data with `claimId` as a key on the ledger.

SubmitClaim, ConfirmClaimSubmission, ApproveClaim

Submitting, confirming, and approving the claim are very similar to `RequestedInfo`, and these steps are called by the `UpdateClaim` function. Only the comment, status, and process time values are different.

Query

Queries are how you read data from the ledger. The query function is used to query the chaincode's state. As we put claim data in the ledger with `claimId`, in order to read the current claim, we call `GetState`, passing `claimId` as key, as follows:

```
func (c *ClaimContract) query(stub shim.ChaincodeStubInterface, args
[]string) pb.Response {
        var ENIITY string
        var err error
        if len(args) != 1 {
                return shim.Error("Incorrect number of arguments. Expected
ENIITY Name")
```

```
        }
        ENIITY = args[0]
        Avalbytes, err := stub.GetState(ENIITY)         if err != nil {
                jsonResp := "{\"Error\":\"Failed to get state for " +
ENIITY + "\"}"
                return shim.Error(jsonResp)
        }
        if Avalbytes == nil {
                jsonResp := "{\"Error\":\"Nil order for " + ENIITY + "\"}"
                return shim.Error(jsonResp)
        }
        return shim.Success(Avalbytes)
}
```

getHistory

As its name indicates, the `gethistory` function reads a claim of all historical values records for a key, as well as the `TxId` and claim value.

We first define the `AuditHistory` struct, which has `TxId` and value. `GetHistoryForKey` returns the list of results with `resultsIterator`, which contains all historical transaction records. We iterate through these records and add them to an array of `AuditHistory`. Later, we convert it to JSON byte and send the data back as a response, as follows:

```
func (c *ClaimContract) getHistory(stub shim.ChaincodeStubInterface, args
[]string) pb.Response {
        type AuditHistory struct {
                TxId   string `json:"txId"`
                Value Claim  `json:"value"`
        }
        var history []AuditHistory
        var claim Claim
        if len(args) != 1 {
                return shim.Error("Incorrect number of arguments.
Expecting 1")
        }
        claimId := args[0]
        fmt.Printf("- start getHistoryForClaim: %s\n", claimId)


        // Get History
        resultsIterator, err := stub.GetHistoryForKey(claimId)
        if err != nil {
                return shim.Error(err.Error())
        }
        defer resultsIterator.Close()
```

```
            for resultsIterator.HasNext() {
                    historyData, err := resultsIterator.Next()
                    if err != nil {
                            return shim.Error(err.Error())
                    }
                    var tx AuditHistory
                    tx.TxId = historyData.TxId
                    json.Unmarshal(historyData.Value, &claim)
                    tx.Value = claim                //copy claim over
                    history = append(history, tx) //add this tx to the list
            }
            fmt.Printf("- getHistoryForClaim returning:\n%s", history)


            //change to array of bytes
            historyAsBytes, _ := json.Marshal(history) //convert to array of
    bytes
            return shim.Success(historyAsBytes)
    }
```

This covers our issuance claim chaincode. We will learn about Hyperledger Fabric configuration in the next section.

Configuring Hyperledger Fabric

There are three entities in the insurance claim network—insuree, broker, and insurer. All of these participants will register in Fabric as a peer node. The following table describes the three peer roles and MSP information:

User ID	Role	Organization MSP ID
user_001	INSUREE	Org1MSP
broker_001	BROKER	Org2MSP
insurer_001	INSURER	Org3MSP

We have one insuree who joins the organization with MSP ID org1, one broker who joins the organization with MSP ID org2, and one insurer who joins the organization with MSP ID org3. For bootstrapping the fabric network, we need to first generate crypto material for all three components that we need to run.

Generating the certificate

We need to define `crypto-config.yaml` and use the cryptogen tool to generate the certificates for each peer. Cryptogen is available in the tools image. `crypto-config.yaml` contains the following information:

- **OrdererOrgs**: Definition of organizations managing orderer nodes
- **PeerOrgs**: Definition of organizations managing peer nodes

OrdererOrgs contains the following information about the ordered node in the cluster:

- **Name**: Name of the orderer
- **Domain**: Domain URL for orderer; in our case, it is ic.com
- **Hostname**: Hostname for the orderer

Here is an example:

```
OrdererOrgs:
  - Name: Orderer
    Domain: ic.com
    Specs:

      - Hostname: orderer
```

PeerOrgs contains the following information about the peer node in the cluster:

- **Name**: Name of the organization; we have three different orgs : `Org1`, `Org2`, and `Org3`
- **Template count**: Number of peer nodes for an organization
- **Users count**: Number of users for an organization

Here is an example:

```
PeerOrgs:
  # --------------------------------------------------------------------
  ----
  # Org1
  # --------------------------------------------------------------------
  ----
  - Name: Org1
    Domain: org1.ic.com
    Template:
      Count: 2
    Users:
```

```
       Count: 1
  #  ---------------------------------------------------------------
----
  # Org2
  #  ---------------------------------------------------------------
----
  - Name: Org2
    Domain: org2.ic.com
    Template:
      Count: 2
    Users:
      Count: 1
  #  ---------------------------------------------------------------
----
  # Org3
  #  ---------------------------------------------------------------
----
  - Name: Org3
    Domain: org3.ic.com
    Template:
      Count: 2
    Users:
      Count: 1
```

The following is the command thats used to generate the crypto material:

```
cryptogen generate --config=./crypto-config.yaml
```

After running the cryptogen tool, you should see the following output in the console:

```
##############################################################
##### Generate certificates using cryptogen tool ##########
##############################################################

org1.ic.com
org2.ic.com
org3.ic.com
```

Generating an orderer genesis block

After generating the certificate, the next step in the process is to generate the orderer genesis block. The `configtxgen` command allows users to create and inspect channel config. The `configtxgen` tool's output is largely controlled by the content of `configtx.yaml`, as follows:

```
Profiles:
    ICOrgsOrdererGenesis:
        Orderer:
            <<: *OrdererDefaults
            Organizations:
                - *OrdererOrg
        Consortiums:
            InsuranceClaimConsortium:
                Organizations:
                    - *Org1
                    - *Org2
                    - *Org3
    ICOrgsChannel:
        Consortium: InsuranceClaimConsortium
        Application:
            <<: *ApplicationDefaults
            Organizations:
                - *Org1
                - *Org2
                - *Org3
Organizations:
    - &OrdererOrg
        Name: OrdererOrg
        ID: OrdererMSP
        MSPDir: crypto-config/ordererOrganizations/ic.com/msp
    - &Org1
        Name: Org1MSP
        ID: Org1MSP
        MSPDir: crypto-config/peerOrganizations/org1.ic.com/msp
        AnchorPeers:
            - Host: peer0.org1.ic.com
              Port: 7051
    - &Org2
        Name: Org2MSP
        ID: Org2MSP
        MSPDir: crypto-config/peerOrganizations/org2.ic.com/msp
        AnchorPeers:
            - Host: peer0.org2.ic.com
              Port: 7051
    - &Org3
```

```
        Name: Org3MSP
        ID: Org3MSP
        MSPDir: crypto-config/peerOrganizations/org3.ic.com/msp


        AnchorPeers:
            - Host: peer0.org3.ic.com
              Port: 7051
    Orderer: &OrdererDefaults
        OrdererType: solo
        Addresses:
            - orderer.ic.com:7050
        BatchTimeout: 2s
        BatchSize:
            MaxMessageCount: 10
            AbsoluteMaxBytes: 20 MB
            PreferredMaxBytes: 512 KB
        Kafka:
            Brokers:
                - 127.0.0.1:9092
        Organizations:
    Application: &ApplicationDefaults


        Organizations:
```

We defined three organizations in the `Organizations` section of the `configtx` file; we specified each organization name, `ID`, `MSPDir`, and `AnchorPeers`. `MSPDir` describes cryptogen generated output MSP directories. `AnchorPeers` points to the peer node's host and port. It updates transactions in order to enable communication between peers of different organizations and finds all active participants of the channel, as follows:

```
configtxgen -profile ICOrgsOrdererGenesis -outputBlock ./channel-
artifacts/genesis.block
```

An output similar to the following will be displayed on the console:

```
###########################################################
######### Generating Orderer Genesis block #############
###########################################################
2018-10-03 18:32:04.833 UTC [common/configtx/tool] main -> INFO 001 Loading configuration
2018-10-03 18:32:04.860 UTC [common/configtx/tool] doOutputBlock -> INFO 002 Generating genesis block
2018-10-03 18:32:04.862 UTC [common/configtx/tool] doOutputBlock -> INFO 003 Writing genesis block
```

Generating a channel configuration transaction

configtxgen writes a channel creation transaction to channel.tx by executing a channel configuration transaction, as follows:

```
configtxgen -profile ICOrgsChannel -outputCreateChannelTx ./channel-
artifacts/channel.tx -channelID icchannel
```

An output similar to the following will be displayed on the console:

Output for executing channel configuration transaction

Overview of Hyperledger Fabric Docker composer configuration files

Hyperledger Fabric utilizes Docker compose to define fabric application services. The docker-compose-cli.yaml service section is the place for defining all peer services and related containers. Hyperledger Fabric's *first-network* provides a .yaml template to help you quickly start to create yaml files from scratch:

https://github.com/hyperledger/fabric-samples/tree/release-1.2/first-network.

In docker-compose-cli.yaml, we define the following information:

- networks: Definition of the blockchain network name. In our case, it is icn
- services: Definition of all peer services and related Docker containers
- cli: Definition of the Cli container that is used to replace the SDK client, and environment variables for Docker compose command-line behavior

Here is an example configuration for the network and service section:

```
networks:
  icn:
services:
  orderer.ic.com:
    extends:
      file:   base/docker-compose-base.yaml
      service: orderer.ic.com
```

```
        container_name: orderer.ic.com
        networks:
          - icn
    peer0.org1.ic.com:
        container_name: peer0.org1.ic.com
        extends:
          file:  base/docker-compose-base.yaml
          service: peer0.org1.ic.com
        networks:
          - icn
```

As you can see, there is a file extension directory: `base/docker-compose-base.yaml`. Docker compose supports sharing common configuration for individual services with the *extends* field. We will discuss more on `docker-compose-base.yaml` later.

Here is an example of configuration for `cli` section:

```
cli:
    container_name: cli
    image: hyperledger/fabric-tools
    tty: true
    environment:
      - GOPATH=/opt/gopath
      - CORE_VM_ENDPOINT=unix:///host/var/run/docker.sock
      - CORE_LOGGING_LEVEL=DEBUG
      - CORE_PEER_ID=cli
      - CORE_PEER_ADDRESS=peer0.org1.ic.com:7051
      - CORE_PEER_LOCALMSPID=Org1MSP
      - CORE_PEER_TLS_ENABLED=true
      -
CORE_PEER_TLS_CERT_FILE=/opt/gopath/src/github.com/hyperledger/fabric/peer/
crypto/peerOrganizations/org1.ic.com/peers/peer0.org1.ic.com/tls/server.crt
      -
CORE_PEER_TLS_KEY_FILE=/opt/gopath/src/github.com/hyperledger/fabric/peer/c
rypto/peerOrganizations/org1.ic.com/peers/peer0.org1.ic.com/tls/server.key
      -
CORE_PEER_TLS_ROOTCERT_FILE=/opt/gopath/src/github.com/hyperledger/fabric/p
eer/crypto/peerOrganizations/org1.ic.com/peers/peer0.org1.ic.com/tls/ca.crt
      -
CORE_PEER_MSPCONFIGPATH=/opt/gopath/src/github.com/hyperledger/fabric/peer/
crypto/peerOrganizations/org1.ic.com/users/Admin@org1.ic.com/msp
    working_dir: /opt/gopath/src/github.com/hyperledger/fabric/peer
    command: /bin/bash -c './scripts/script.sh ${CHANNEL_NAME} ${DELAY};
sleep $TIMEOUT'
    #for mapping the directories that are being used in the environment
configurations
    volumes:
        - /var/run/:/host/var/run/
```

```
        - ./chaincode/:/opt/gopath/src/github.com/chaincode
        - ./crypto-
config:/opt/gopath/src/github.com/hyperledger/fabric/peer/crypto/
        -
./scripts:/opt/gopath/src/github.com/hyperledger/fabric/peer/scripts/
        - ./channel-
artifacts:/opt/gopath/src/github.com/hyperledger/fabric/peer/channel-
artifacts
    depends_on:
      - orderer.ic.com
      - peer0.org1.ic.com
      - peer0.org2.ic.com
      - peer0.org3.ic.com
    networks:
      - icn
```

The `docker-compose` tool uses the `docker-compose-cli.yaml` file to initialize the fabric runtime environment. Blow are some of the most common commands you will use when using `docker-compose-cli.yaml` file:

`TTY`	TTY basically means *a console*, and we set it as true.
`Image`	Points to the fabric-tools image directory.
`Environment`	Specifies environment variables, for example, GOPATH, a TLS-related file location generated by the cryptogen tool.
`working_dir`	Sets the working directory for the peer.
`command`	Specifies the command that is issued when the container starts.
`volumes`	Maps the directories that are being used in the environment configurations.
`depends_on`	Starts services in dependency order.

It then generates four fabric-peer transaction node containers, one fabric-order orderer node container, and one fabric-tools cli container.

Fabric project directory structure

In our Fabric sample first-network, the project structure is similar to the following:

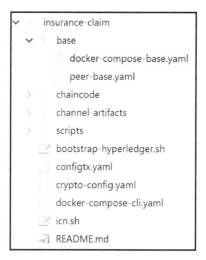

As we discussed previously, the `docker-compose-cli.yaml` service extends from `base/docker-compose-base.yaml`. There are two file base directories: `peer-base.yaml` and `docker-compose-base.yaml`.

Docker-compose-base.yaml

This file contains the base configurations, including each peer and orderer container environment and port number. This defines the overall topology of the insurance claim network, as follows:

```
services:
  orderer.ic.com:
    container_name: orderer.ic.com
    image: hyperledger/fabric-orderer
    environment:
      - ORDERER_GENERAL_LOGLEVEL=debug
      - ORDERER_GENERAL_LISTENADDRESS=0.0.0.0
      - ORDERER_GENERAL_GENESISMETHOD=file
      -
ORDERER_GENERAL_GENESISFILE=/var/hyperledger/orderer/orderer.genesis.block
      - ORDERER_GENERAL_LOCALMSPID=OrdererMSP
      - ORDERER_GENERAL_LOCALMSPDIR=/var/hyperledger/orderer/msp
      # enabled TLS
```

```
        - ORDERER_GENERAL_TLS_ENABLED=true
        -
ORDERER_GENERAL_TLS_PRIVATEKEY=/var/hyperledger/orderer/tls/server.key
        -
ORDERER_GENERAL_TLS_CERTIFICATE=/var/hyperledger/orderer/tls/server.crt
        - ORDERER_GENERAL_TLS_ROOTCAS=[/var/hyperledger/orderer/tls/ca.crt]
      working_dir: /opt/gopath/src/github.com/hyperledger/fabric
      command: orderer
      volumes:
      - ../channel-
artifacts/genesis.block:/var/hyperledger/orderer/orderer.genesis.block
      - ../crypto-
config/ordererOrganizations/ic.com/orderers/orderer.ic.com/msp:/var/hyperle
dger/orderer/msp
      - ../crypto-
config/ordererOrganizations/ic.com/orderers/orderer.ic.com/tls/:/var/hyperl
edger/orderer/tls
      ports:
        - 7050:7050


  peer0.org1.ic.com:
    container_name: peer0.org1.ic.com
    extends:
      file: peer-base.yaml
      service: peer-base
    environment:
      - CORE_PEER_ID=peer0.org1.ic.com
      - CORE_PEER_ADDRESS=peer0.org1.ic.com:7051
      - CORE_PEER_GOSSIP_EXTERNALENDPOINT=peer0.org1.ic.com:7051
      - CORE_PEER_LOCALMSPID=Org1MSP
    volumes:
        - /var/run/:/host/var/run/
        - ../crypto-
config/peerOrganizations/org1.ic.com/peers/peer0.org1.ic.com/msp:/etc/hyper
ledger/fabric/msp
        - ../crypto-
config/peerOrganizations/org1.ic.com/peers/peer0.org1.ic.com/tls:/etc/hyper
ledger/fabric/tls
      ports:
        - 7051:7051
        - 7053:7053
.....
```

Peer-base.yaml

This file defines peer network configuration for the insurance claim `docker-compose-base.yaml`, as follows:

```
services:
  peer-base:
    image: hyperledger/fabric-peer
    environment:
      - CORE_VM_ENDPOINT=unix:///host/var/run/docker.sock
      - CORE_VM_DOCKER_HOSTCONFIG_NETWORKMODE=${COMPOSE_PROJECT_NAME}_icn
      - CORE_LOGGING_LEVEL=DEBUG
      - CORE_PEER_TLS_ENABLED=true
      - CORE_PEER_GOSSIP_USELEADERELECTION=true
      - CORE_PEER_GOSSIP_ORGLEADER=false
      - CORE_PEER_PROFILE_ENABLED=true
      - CORE_PEER_TLS_CERT_FILE=/etc/hyperledger/fabric/tls/server.crt
      - CORE_PEER_TLS_KEY_FILE=/etc/hyperledger/fabric/tls/server.key
      - CORE_PEER_TLS_ROOTCERT_FILE=/etc/hyperledger/fabric/tls/ca.crt
    working_dir: /opt/gopath/src/github.com/hyperledger/fabric/peer
    command: peer node start
```

The command in the peer gets the peer to install the system chaincode and other configurations.

We have an overview of the critical Hyperledger Fabric configuration files, so let's start our insurance claim network using the following code:

```
      - CORE_PEER_TLS_KEY_FILE=/etc/hyperledger/fabric/tls/server.key
      - CORE_PEER_TLS_ROOTCERT_FILE=/etc/hyperledger/fabric/tls/ca.crt
    working_dir: /opt/gopath/src/github.com/hyperledger/fabric/peer
    command: peer node start
```

Starting the Hyperledger Fabric network

Now, it is time to bring up our Hyperledger Fabric network. We will use Docker commands to kick off the new Docker compose initially:

```
docker-compose -f docker-compose-cli.yaml up
```

The Docker container will trigger the command defined in `docker-compose-cli.yaml`, as follows:

```
command: /bin/bash -c './scripts/script.sh
```

`script.sh` is a script that contains a series of instructions to fabric deployment and test commands. We also define some business-specific shell script functions in `utils.sh`.

Creating a channel

First, we need to create a channel to build a genesis block. Run the following command:

```
peer channel create -o orderer.ic.com:7050 -c icchannel -f ./channel-
artifacts/channel.tx
```

This command reads a genesis block from `channel.tx` that is then used to join the channel and creates the icchannel channel. Here is the result on the console:

Output for the console that joins and creates the channel

Joining channels

After the ordering service creates the channel, we can add the peers to the channel, as follows:

```
peer channel join -b icchannel.block
```

Here is the result on the console:

Adding peers to the channel

We can see that `peer0.org1`, `peer0.org2`, and `peer0.org3` are joined in the channel.

Updating the anchor

The last operation that we need to complete before we start to interact with our issuance claim network is to update the anchor peers. Anchor peers receive and broadcast transaction updates to the other peers in the organization. Anchor peers are searchable in the network. Therefore, any peer registered as an anchor peer can be discovered by an order peer or any other peer, for example:

```
peer channel update -f ./channel-artifacts/Org1MSPanchors.tx -c icchannel -o orderer.ic.com:7050 --tls true --cafile $ORDERER_CA
```

Here is the console output for this step:

Getting discovered by an order peer or any other peer

Installing chaincode

After the previous steps, we are almost ready to use our issuance claim blockchain application. However first, we need to install `claimcontract.go` chaincode on our network, as follows:

```
peer chaincode install -n iccc -v 1.0 -l golang -p
github.com/chaincode/claimcontract
```

We will see the output of the preceding command:

Installing chaincode to our network

Instantiating the chaincode

After installing the chaincode, we need to instantiate it. As we discussed previously, we will onboard insuree in the `init()` chaincode. Therefore, we need to pass the required arguments to create an insuree participant, as follows:

```
peer chaincode instantiate -o orderer.ic.com:7050 -C icchannel -n iccc -l
golang -v 1.0 -c '{"Args":[ "user_001","John","Smith",
"9999","4394497111/1"]}' -P "OR    ('Org1MSP.member'
```

Here is the output for this step:

Creating an insuree participant

We query the insuree to verify that the record has been created in the blockchain, as follows:

```
peer chaincode query -C $CHANNEL_NAME -n iccc -c
'{"Args":["query","user_001"]}'
```

We can see from this output that the insuree (`user_001`) was added in our blockchain:

Insuree added in our block chain

Invoking add broker

Let's onboard a broker to our insurance claim blockchain, as follows:

```
peer chaincode invoke -o orderer.ic.com:7050 -C icchannel -n iccc -c
'{"Args":["AddCompany","broker_001","BROKER","BNC Brokerage"]}'
```

Here is the result:

Onboarding a broker to our insurance claim blockchain

Invoking add insurer

Add the last party insurer to the insurance claim blockchain, as follows:

```
peer chaincode invoke -o orderer.ic.com:7050 -C icchannel -n iccc -c
'{"Args":["AddCompany","insurer_001","INSURER","Western Insurance"]}'
```

The output that's displayed is as follows:

Adding a last party insurer to insurance claim blockchain

Invoking ReportLost

All of the participants have joined the network, and it is time to start the insurance claim process. An insuree reports a claim to a broker, Here is the command to invoke 'ReportLost' chaincode.

```
peer chaincode invoke -o orderer.ic.com:7050 -C icchannel -n iccc -c
'{"Args":["ReportLost","claim_001", "I was in Destiny shopping center and
lost my IPhone 8", "user_001", "broker_001"]}
```

The following output will be displayed:

Isuree reporting a claim to a broker

Invoking RequestedInfo

A broker provides the requested information, as follows:

```
peer chaincode invoke -o orderer.ic.com:7050 -C icchannel -n iccc -c
'{"Args":["RequestedInfo","claim_001", "Broker processsed user John Smith
report and sent Requested Info to user.", "insurer_001"]}'
```

The following output will be displayed:

Providing the requested information

Invoking SubmitClaim

A broker submits a claim to an issuer, as follows:

```
peer chaincode invoke -o orderer.ic.com:7050 -C icchannel -n iccc -c
'{"Args":["SubmitClaim","claim_001", "Broker submitted a claim"]}'
```

The following output will be displayed:

Submitting a claim to the issuer

Invoking ConfirmClaimSubmission

An issuer confirms the claim, as follows:

```
peer chaincode invoke -o orderer.ic.com:7050 -C icchannel -n iccc -c
'{"Args":["ConfirmClaimSubmission","claim_001", "Insurer received and
confirmed a claim"]}'
```

The following output will be displayed:

Confirming the claim

Invoking ApproveClaim

An issuer processes and approves a claim, as follows:

```
peer chaincode invoke -o orderer.ic.com:7050 -C icchannel -n iccc -c
'{"Args":["ApproveClaim","claim_001", "Insurer processed and approved the
claim."]}'
```

The following output will be displayed:

Processing and approving the claim

Querying claim history

After an issuer approves the claim, the entire process flow is done and we can use the Fabric API to query the entire life cycle of the claim, as follows:

```
peer chaincode query -C icchannel -n iccc -c
'{"Args":["getHistory","claim_001"]}'
```

From the output obtained from this query, we can see the entire Fabric transaction history of the claim request.

This ends our test execution.

End-to-end test execution

We have gone over each step of insurance claim fabric execution. To simplify the entire end-to-end application flow, you can navigate to the `insurance-claim` folder and then run the following command:

```
cd ~/insurance-claim
#change path if insurance-claim directory is different
export PATH=/home/ubuntu/insurance-claim/bin:$PATH
./icn.sh -m up
```

The output result will be as follows:

Simplifying the entire end to end application flow

The final output is as follows:

Insurance claim End to End Test completes

Summary

In this chapter, we have learned about the basics of Hyperledger Fabric's. After setting up a development environment, we wrote a chaincode for an insurance claim use case. We then studied fabric composer configuration. Finally, we ran the end-to-end fabric test execution for our insurance claim application. We can see that it is quite complex to use Hyperledger Fabric to implement an insurance claim application. In the next chapter, we will learn how to use Hyperledger Composer to quickly write an insurance claim application.

17
Implementing Business Networks Using Hyperledger Composer

Hyperledger Composer is a high-level toolset and framework that was made to quickly build and run applications on top of a Hyperledger Fabric blockchain.

We learned about Hyperledger Fabric in the previous chapter, so you already know that developing a Fabric-based application is quite complex as it needs to handle many configurations at the network level.

In this chapter, we will discuss the following topics:

- Hyperledger Composer—a quick overview
- Setting up a Hyperledger Composer environment
- Analyzing business scenarios
- The business network archive
- Implementing business transaction functions

Hyperledger Composer – a quick overview

Hyperledger Composer is a set of JavaScript-based high-level toolsets and frameworks that simplify and quickly build and run an application on top of a Hyperledger Fabric blockchain. Business owners and developers can quickly create smart contracts and applications via the composer tool. The composer tool generates a RESTful endpoint to interact with fabric channels. Instead of writing chaincode using Golang, Composer uses model language to generate a business network archive (.BNA) file for the blockchain network.

Here is an example of a Hyperledger Composer solution architecture:

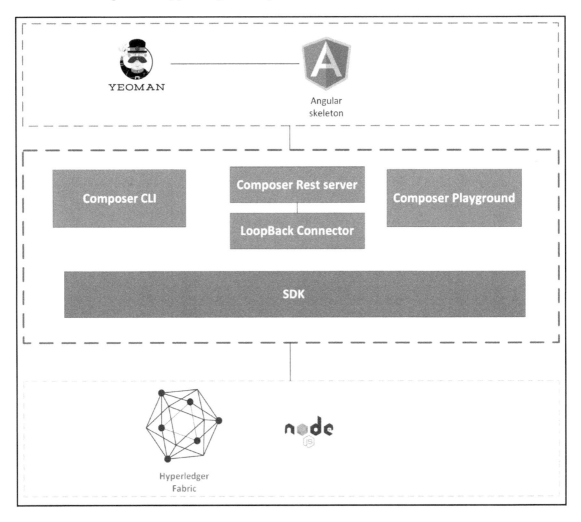

Hyperledger Composer contains the components that are listed in the following sections.

Yeoman generator

The npm module generator-hyperledger-composer in Yeoman is used to make templates for Hyperledger Composer. It supports and generates three different types of templates:

- CLI application
- Angular 2 application
- Skeleton business network

You can use Yeoman's generated angular skeleton to connect to the Hyperledger Composer REST server.

Composer REST server

Composer's REST server utilizes a standalone Node.js process and exposes a set of RESTful API endpoints from a deployed composer business network. These generated APIs can interact with fabric chaincode. The side code can then trigger **create**, **read**, **update**, **delete** (**CRUD**) for assets, participants, and transactions.

LoopBack connector

The LoopBack connector utilises the Node.js LoopBack framework to expose GET/POST/PUT/DELETE operations for the assets, participants, and transactions defined in the business network.

JavaScript SDK

The JavaScript SDK API is used to interact with the deployed business network. It is comprised of the client and admin APIs.

The client APIs provide query, create, update, and delete resources (asset and participant), and submit transactions from client applications.

The admin API is used to deploy the business network.

Composer playground

The Hyperledger Composer playground is a browser-based interface to create and test business networks. You can use the playground to build and test your business network.

Composer-cli

Composer-cli is a command-line tool that lets you deploy and manage business networks.

Here is a list of some commands:

Command	Description
composer archive create	Command to create a business network archive file (nba).
composer archive list	Verifies the contents of a business network archive.
composer card create	Creates a business network card from individual components.
composer card delete	Deletes a business network card from individual components.
composer card list	Lists all business network cards stored in the local wallet.
composer network deploy	Deploys a business network archive from local disk to a Hyperledger Fabric network.
composer network list	Lists the details of the business network card.
composer network ping	Tests the connection to a deployed business network.

Setting up a Hyperledger Composer environment

We just reviewed the Hyperledger Composer solution architecture. In this section, we will set up the Hyperledger development environment.

Installation prerequisites

Before we install the composer tools, make sure you have the required prerequisites by following the *Setup of Hyperledger Fabric environment—installing prerequisites* section.

Installing the development environment

The following are the installation commands for developing the environment:

- Installing the CLI tools:

  ```
  npm install -g composer-cli@0.20
  ```

- Installing `composer-rest-server`:

  ```
  npm install -g composer-rest-server@0.20
  ```

- Installing Hyperledger Composer generator:

  ```
  npm install -g generator-hyperledger-composer@0.20
  ```

- Installing Yeoman:

  ```
  npm install -g yo
  ```

- Installing playground:

  ```
  npm install -g composer-playground
  ```

- Installing fabric runtime:

  Download and install fabric runtime for the composer as follows:

  ```
  mkdir ~/fabric-devserver && cd ~/fabric-devserver
  curl -O https://raw.githubusercontent.com/hyperledger/composer-
  tools/master/packages/fabric-dev-servers/fabric-dev-servers.zip
  unzip fabric-dev-servers.zip
  export FABRIC_VERSION=hlfv12
  ./downloadFabric.sh
  ```

At this step, you have installed everything required for the typical composer development environment.

Analyzing business scenarios

In Chapter 16, *Exploring an Enterprise Blockchain Application Using Hyperledger Fabric*, we discussed the blockchain use case for the insurance claim. It includes the following steps:

1. An insuree reports a claim to a broker
2. A broker provides requested information

3. A broker submits a claim to an issuer
4. An issuer confirms the claim
5. An issuer processes and approves the claim

In this chapter, we will use the same insurance claim use case, but also build the end-to-end application via Hyperledger Composer.

Business network archive

Composer business is comprised of four different types of files: model file (.cto), script file (.js), access control list (ACL) file (.acl), and query file (.qry).

Network model file (.cto)

A CTO file is composed of the following elements:

Element	Description
A single namespace	Defines the composer model namespace; every .cto model file requires a namespace.
Resources - asset	Anything of value that can be exchanged between parties.
Resources - participant	Business network member.
Resources - enum	A data type consisting of a set of named values.
Resources - concept	Any object you want to model that is not one of the other types.
Resources - transactions	Defines the blockchain business logic.
Resources - events	Blockchain transaction notification.
Import	Imports resources from other namespaces.

The composer model language, like other programming languages, has data types including String, Double, Integer, and so on.

Let's see some samples of assets, participants, transactions, and events.

IBM Bluemix provides a browser version playground without installation; we can use this tool to do a quick prototype. Here is the link: https://composer-playground.mybluemix.net/.

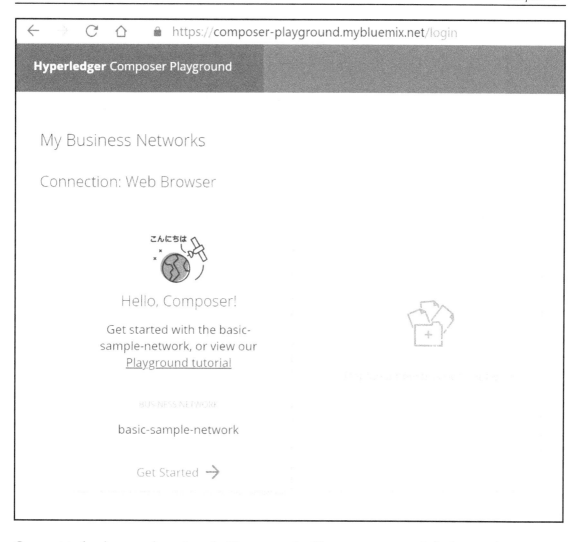

Connect to **basic-sample-network**. Playground will generate some default sample assets, participants, transactions, and events for you, for example:

```
sample.cto
/**
* Sample business network definition.
*/
namespace org.example.basic
asset SampleAsset identified by assetId {
  o String assetId
  --> SampleParticipant owner
  o String value
```

```
}
participant SampleParticipant identified by participantId {
  o String participantId
  o String firstName
  o String lastName
}
transaction SampleTransaction {
  --> SampleAsset asset
  o String newValue
}
event SampleEvent {
  --> SampleAsset asset
  o String oldValue
  o String newValue
}
```

A `namespace org.example.basic` was defined in `sample.cto.SampleAsset` and is an example of an `Asset` class. It defines an asset whose name is followed by an identifying field.`o String assetId`: a field of the `SampleAsset.--> SampleParticipant owner`: field point to `SampleParticipant instance.SampleParticipant` is an example of a `Participant` class, the syntax is similar to `SampleAsset.SampleTransaction` is an example of a transaction `class.SampleEvent` is an example of an event class.

Script file (.js)

We define transactions and events in the model file, a script file that implements these transaction functions. Decorators within *comments* are used to annotate the functions with metadata required for transaction processing, for example:

```
/**
 * Sample transaction processor function.
 * @param {org.example.basic.SampleTransaction} tx The sample transaction
instance.
 * @transaction
 */
async function sampleTransaction(tx) {  // eslint-disable-line no-unused-
vars
..
    emit(event);
}
```

In the `sampleTransaction` function, the `@param` tag is followed by the resource name of the transaction that triggers the transaction processor function. `@transaction` marks this function as a transaction processor function.

Access control list (ACL) file (.acl)

An ACL file defines the permission of the participants in the business network, for example:

```
rule OwnerHasFullAccessToTheirAssets {
    description: "Allow all participants full access to their assets"
    participant(p): "org.example.basic.SampleParticipant"
    operation: ALL
    resource(r): "org.example.basic.SampleAsset"
    condition: (r.owner.getIdentifier() === p.getIdentifier())
    action: ALLOW
}
```

In the preceding ACL example, it specifies that the participant is `SampleParticipant`. Any instance registered as `SampleParticipant` can perform `ALL` operations on all instances of `org.example.SampleAsset`. This transaction is triggered when the `SampleAsset` owner is the same as the participant who submitted a transaction.

Query file (.qry)

A query file defines the queries that are used to return data about the blockchain world state. The query syntax is quite similar to SQL language, for example:

```
query queryName {
    description: "Select SampleAsset by assetId "
    statement:
        SELECT org.example.basic.SampleAsset
            WHERE (_$assetId = assetId)
}
```

Designing business models

Now that we have reviewed the basic composer model language and structure, it is time to implement an insurance claim using Hyperledger Composer.

For simplicity's sake, we will allow participants to have permission to read and write for all resources in this example. Remove the sample resource related to ACL and update the rule as follows:

```
rule EverybodyCanReadEverything {
    description: "Allow all participants read access to all resources"
    participant: "**"
    operation: READ
    resource: "com.packt.quickstart.claim.*"
    action: ALLOW
}
rule EverybodyCanSubmitTransactions {
    description: "Allow all participants to submit transactions"
    participant: "**"
    operation: CREATE
    resource: "**"
    action: ALLOW
}
```

With simplified ACL, we start to work on our model file as follows:

1. Rename `sample.cto` as `insurance-claim.cto`
2. Change namespace to `com.packt.quickstart.claim` and remove the remaining code
3. Define the participants and assets

   We wrote a chaincode called `claimcontract.go` in *Chapter 16*, *Exploring an Enterprise Blockchain Application using Hyperledger Fabric*, that defines a struct for insuree, broker insurer, and claim. We can define participants and assets similar to this struct. It is quite straightforward, as follows:

   ```
   namespace com.packt.quickstart.claim
   participant Insuree identified by id {
     o String id
     o String firstName
     o String lastName
     o String ssn
     o String policyNumber
   }
   participant Company identified by id {
     o String id
     o String type
     o String name
   }
   asset Claim identified by id {
     o String id
   ```

```
        o String desc
        o Integer status
        o String insureeId
        o String brokerId
        o String insurerId
        o String comment
        o String processAt
    }
```

4. Define the transactions and events. By using the `Init` function, we onboard insuree, as follows:

```
transaction Init {
    o String insureeId
    o String firstName
    o String lastName
    o String ssn
    o String policyNumber
}
event InitEvent {
    --> Insuree insuree
}
```

5. Composer's JavaScript API provides CRUD to create resources, including the participant. For the insurer and broker, we will use this approach. We will explain this in more detail when we do testing.

6. Define `ReportLost`: An insuree reports a claim to a broker—this starts a claim, as follows:

```
transaction ReportLost {
    o String claimId
    o String desc
    o String insureeId
    o String brokerId
}
event ReportLostEvent {
    --> Claim claim
}
```

7. Define `RequestedInfo`: A broker provides the requested information, as follows:

```
transaction RequestedInfo {
  --> Claim claim
}
event RequestedInfoEvent {
  --> Claim claim
}
```

8. Define `SubmitClaim`: A broker submits a claim to an issuer.
9. Define `ConfirmClaimSubmission`: An issuer confirms the claim.
10. Define `ApproveClaim`: An issuer process and approves the claim.

Step 8, 9, and 10 are transaction functions, and are very similar to step 7.

We have defined all of our transactions, participants, and assets in the model file. As a next step, we will implement the transaction we defined in the model file.

Implementing the business transaction function

We learned how to implement a transaction function in the previous section by reviewing `SampleTransaction`. Following a similar approach, we will implement an insurance claim transaction function. Rename `sample.js` to `logic.js`.

Implement the `Init` function, as follows:

```
Init() function is used to register insuree person information.
/**
  * Create the insuree
  * @param {com.packt.quickstart.claim.Init} initalAppliation - the
InitialApplication transaction
  * @transaction
  */
 async function Init(application) { // eslint-disable-line no-unused-vars
    const factory = getFactory();
    const namespace = 'com.packt.quickstart.claim';
    const insuree = factory.newResource(namespace, 'Insuree',
application.insureeId);
    insuree.firstName = application.firstName;;       insuree.lastName =
application.lastName
```

```
    insuree.ssn = application.ssn;;
    insuree.policyNumber = application.policyNumber;;
    const participantRegistry = await
getParticipantRegistry(insuree.getFullyQualifiedType());
    await participantRegistry.add(insuree);
    // emit event
    const initEventEvent = factory.newEvent(namespace, 'InitEvent');
    initEventEvent.insuree = insuree;
    emit(initEventEvent);
}
```

Implement `ReportLost` and, set up and create a claim, as follows:

```
/**
  * insuree report lost item
  * @param {com.packt.quickstart.claim.ReportLost} ReportLost - the
ReportLost transaction
  * @transaction
  */
 async function ReportLost(request) {
    const factory = getFactory();
    const namespace = 'com.packt.quickstart.claim';
    let claimId = request.claimId;
    let desc = request.desc;
    let insureeId = request.insureeId;
    let brokerId = request.brokerId;
    const claim = factory.newResource(namespace, 'Claim', claimId);
    claim.desc = desc;
    claim.status = "ReportLost";
    claim.insureeId = insureeId;
    claim.brokerId = brokerId;
    claim.insurerId = "";
    claim.comment = "";
    claim.processAt = (new Date()).toString();
    const claimRegistry = await
getAssetRegistry(claim.getFullyQualifiedType());
    await claimRegistry.add(claim);
    // emit event
    const reportLostEvent = factory.newEvent(namespace,
'ReportLostEvent');
    reportLostEvent.claim = claim;
    emit(reportLostEvent); }
```

Implement `RequestedInfo` to verify and update the claim status, as follows:

```
/**
 * broker send Requested Info to insuree
 * @param {com.packt.quickstart.claim.RequestedInfo} RequestedInfo - the
RequestedInfo transaction
 * @transaction
 */
 async function RequestedInfo(request) { // eslint-disable-line no-unused-
vars
    const factory = getFactory();
    const namespace = 'com.packt.quickstart.claim';
    let claim = request.claim;
    if (claim.status !== 'ReportLost') {
        throw new Error ('This claim should be in ReportLost status');
    }
    claim.status = 'RequestedInfo';
    claim.processAt = (new Date()).toString();
    const assetRegistry = await
getAssetRegistry(request.claim.getFullyQualifiedType());
    await assetRegistry.update(claim);
    // emit event
    const requestedInfoEventEvent = factory.newEvent(namespace,
'RequestedInfoEvent');
    requestedInfoEventEvent.claim = claim;
    emit(requestedInfoEventEvent); }
```

Implement `SubmitClaim`, `ConfirmClaimSubmission`, and `ApproveClaim`. These functions are similar to `RequestedInfo`.

Testing in the playground

We just implemented all model and logic files in the previous section, so it is time to test our composer application:

1. Click on the **Deploy changes** button on the left bottom panel of the playground. This will deploy the composer code.
2. Click **Test** link on the top navigation bar. It will pop up the submit transaction page. Select the init method from the transaction type drop down. Enter the JSON value, as shown in the following screenshot; the input data is the same as what we tested in Chapter 16, *Exploring an Enterprise Blockchain Application using Hyperledger Fabric*. Instantiate the fabric chaincode step. Submit the transaction, as follows:

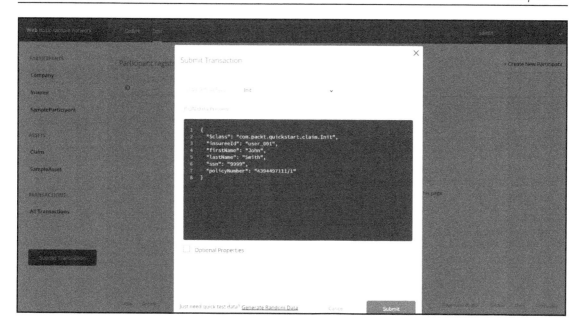

If transaction submission is successful, we will be able to see that the insuree participant has been created, for example:

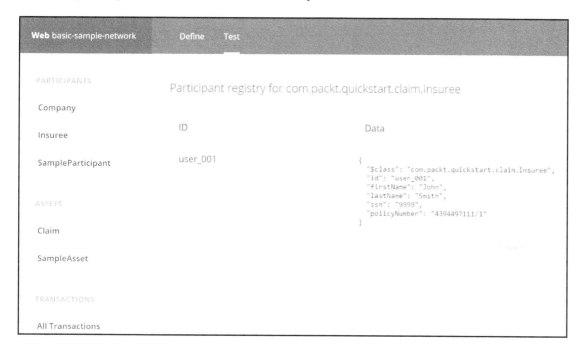

3. Now, let's onboard the broker and insurer. Click company in the participant section and click **Create New Participant**. Enter the broker data in, the same way that we did it for the `chaincodeInvokeAddBroker` step in *Chapter 16, Exploring an Enterprise Blockchain Application using Hyperledger Fabric.* Click **Create New,** as follows:

If the transaction submission succeeds, this will onboard the broker. Repeat this same step to onboard the insurer, as follows:

	Participant registry for com.packt.quickstart.claim.Company	
PARTICIPANTS		
Company		
	ID	Data
Insuree		
SampleParticipant	broker_001	`{ "$class": "com.packt.quickstart.claim.Company", "id": "broker_001", "type": "BROKER", "name": "BNC Brokerage" }`
ASSETS		
Claim		
	insurer_001	`{ "$class": "com.packt.quickstart.claim.Company", "id": "insurer_001", "type": "INSURER", "name": "Western Insurance" }`
SampleAsset		
TRANSACTIONS		

4. Submit `ReportLost`, as follows:

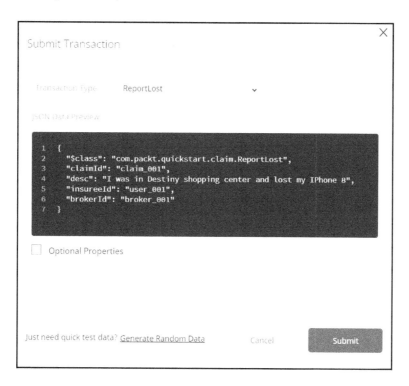

Here is the result:

5. Test `RequestedInfo` with the following result:

```
1  {
2    "$class": "com.packt.quickstart.claim.RequestedInfo",
3    "claim": "resource:com.packt.quickstart.claim.Claim#claim_001"
4  }
```

Asset registry for com.packt.quickstart.claim.Claim

ID	Data
claim_001	`{ "$class": "com.packt.quickstart.claim.Claim", "id": "claim_001", "desc": "I was in Destiny shopping center and lost my IPhone 8", "status": "RequestedInfo", "insureeId": "user_001", "brokerId": "broker_001", "insurerId": "", "comment": "", "processAt": "Sat Oct 06 2018 03:22:15 GMT-0400 (Eastern Daylight Time)" }`

The remaining steps (`SubmitClaim`, `ConfirmClaimSubmission`, and `ApproveClaim`) are very similar to `RequestedInfo`.

Deploying a business network

We have tested the composer application in the playground, so next we will deploy it to the blockchain:

1. Create a folder called `insurance-claim-network`, and navigate to the folder.
2. Generate a business network project template, as follows:

```
yo hyperledger-composer:businessnetwork
```

It will prompt a few questions. Enter `insurance-claim-network` as the network name and choose the empty template network, as shown in the following screenshot:

```
Welcome to the business network generator
? Business network name: insurance-claim-network
? Description: create insurance claim
? Author name:  brian wu
? Author email: brian.wu@smartchart.tech
? License: Apache-2.0
? Namespace: com.packt.quickstart.claim
? Do you want to generate an empty template network? Yes: generate an empty template network
   create package.json
   create README.md
   create models/com.packt.quickstart.claim.cto
   create permissions.acl
   create .eslintrc.yml
```

This will generate a few files with a default template. Replace the contents of `com.packt.quickstart`
`.claim.cto` with our earlier tested model file.

Create a new folder called `lib`, under the `lib` folder, and copy the tested `logic.js` in here.

Replace `permissions.acl` with the tested `acl` file, as follows:

```
├── lib
│   └── logic.js
├── models
│   └── com.packt.quickstart.claim.cto
├── package.json
├── permissions.acl
└── README.md
```

3. Start Hyperledger Fabric, as follows:

```
cd ~/fabric-devservers
    export FABRIC_VERSION=hlfv12
    ./startFabric.sh
    ./createPeerAdminCard.sh
```

This will create `PeerAdminCard`, as shown in the following screenshot:

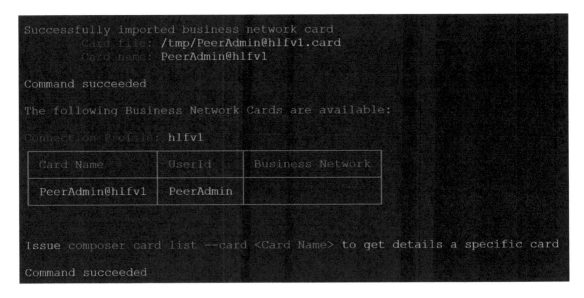

4. Generate a business network archive. From the `insurance-claim-network` directory, run the following command:

```
composer archive create -t dir -n
```

This will generate `insurance-claim-network@0.0.1.bna`.

5. Install the business network. From the `insurance-claim-network` directory, run the following command:

```
composer network install --card PeerAdmin@hlfv1 --archiveFile
insurance-claim-network@0.0.1.bna
```

6. Start the business network. From the `insurance-claim-network` directory, run the following command:

```
composer network start --networkName insurance-claim-network --
networkVersion 0.0.1 --networkAdmin admin --networkAdminEnrollSecret
adminpw --card PeerAdmin@hlfv1 --file networkadmin.card
```

7. Import the network admin card. From the `insurance-claim-network` in directory, run the following command. This will import `insurance-claim-network` to the network:

```
composer card import --file networkadmin.card
```

8. Check if the business network has been deployed successfully. From the `insurance-claim-network` directory, run the following command:

```
composer network ping --card admin@insurance-claim-network
```

The result should look as follows:

Checking if the business network been deployed successfully

Integrating with REST server

We just deployed `insurance-claim-network` in the fabric network. The next step is to build an insurance-claim client API to interact with the smart contract function in the network. The Hyperledger Composer REST server can be used to generate a REST API. A REST client can call these end point functions and interact with the business network chaincode from the Fabric blockchain.

Generating the Hyperledger Composer REST API

Run the following command to generate a composer server API:

```
composer-rest-server
```

Enter `admin@insurance-claim-network` from the business network card, as shown in the following screenshot:

```
ubuntu@ip-172-31-5-222:~/fabric-dev-servers/insurance-claim-network$ composer-rest-server
? Enter the name of the business network card to use: admin@insurance-claim-network
? Specify if you want namespaces in the generated REST API: never use namespaces
? Specify if you want to use an API key to secure the REST API: No
? Specify if you want to enable authentication for the REST API using Passport: No
? Specify if you want to enable the explorer test interface: Yes
? Specify a key if you want to enable dynamic logging:
? Specify if you want to enable event publication over WebSockets: Yes
? Specify if you want to enable TLS security for the REST API: No

To restart the REST server using the same options, issue the following command:
    composer-rest-server -c admin@insurance-claim-network -n never -u true -w true

Discovering types from business network definition ...
Discovering the Returning Transactions..
Discovered types from business network definition
Generating schemas for all types in business network definition ...
Generated schemas for all types in business network definition
Adding schemas for all types to Loopback ...
Added schemas for all types to Loopback
Web server listening at: http://localhost:3000
Browse your REST API at http://localhost:3000/explorer
```

Entering business network card

This will a generate the REST API and expose it as `http://serverIP:3000` and `http://serverIP:3000/explorer`.

Open the explore URL. You will see the generated REST endpoints, as follows:

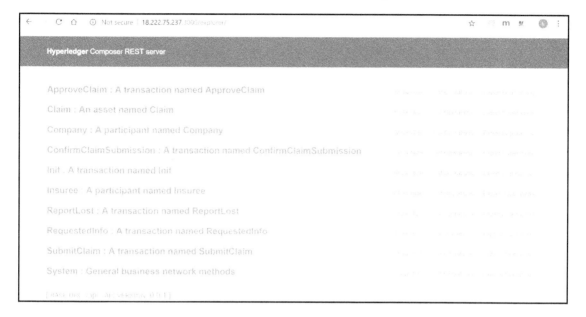

Let's try a number of methods to demonstrate how these endpoints interact with the fabric network.

Select the `init Post` method from endpoints, provide the post JSON data, and click the Try it out! button. The example of JSON data is shown as follows:

```
{
  "$class": "com.packt.quickstart.claim.Init",
  "insureeId": "user-001",
  "firstName": "John",
  "lastName": "Smith",
  "ssn": "9999",
  "policyNumber": "string"
}
```

Here is a screenshot that shows the result after clicking the **Try it out!** button:

```
Try it out!    Hide Response

Curl

curl -X POST --header 'Content-Type: application/json' --header 'Accept: application/json' -d '{ \
   "$class": "com.packt.quickstart.claim.Company", \
   "id": "insurer_001", \
   "type": "INSURER", \
   "name": "Western Insurance" \
 }' 'http://18.222.75.237:3000/api/Company'

Request URL

 http://18.222.75.237:3000/api/Company

Response Body


   {

     "$class": "com.packt.quickstart.claim.Company",

     "id": "insurer_001",

     "type": "INSURER",

     "name": "Western Insurance"

   }


Response Code

 200

Response Headers

 {
   "date": "Tue, 09 Oct 2018 01:00:00 GMT",
   "x-content-type-options": "nosniff",
   "etag": "W/\"6e-5ndzT6iGpj2E7RLnJjIh1jHCzW0\"",
   "x-download-options": "noopen",
   "x-frame-options": "DENY",
   "content-type": "application/json; charset=utf-8",
   "access-control-allow-origin": "http://18.222.75.237:3000",
   "access-control-allow-credentials": "true",
   "connection": "keep-alive",
   "vary": "Origin, Accept-Encoding",
   "content-length": "110",
   "x-xss-protection": "1; mode=block"
 }
```

Example of JSON data

The API will call the `Init` chaincode in the fabric network and return the response to the browser.

Select a company using a post method to create an insuree. Enter this JSON request as follows:

```
{
    "$class": "com.packt.quickstart.claim.Init",
    "insureeId": "user-001",
    "firstName": "John",
    "lastName": "Smith",
    "ssn": "9999",
    "policyNumber": "string"
}
```

You should see a successful response, similar to the one shown in the following screenshot:

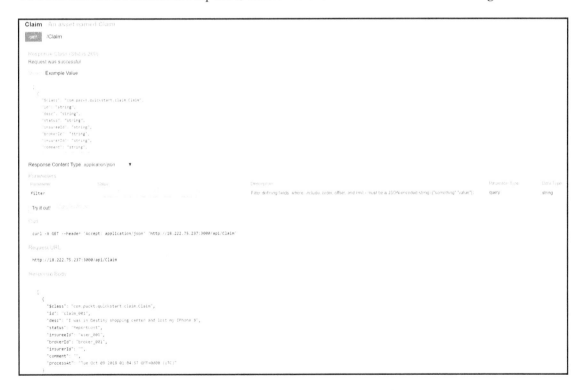

Selecting a company using a post method to create insuree, enter this JSON request

Select the `ReportLost Post` method from endpoints, provide the post JSON data, and click **Try it out!**:

```
{
  "$class": "com.packt.quickstart.claim.ReportLost",
  "claimId": "claim_001",
  "desc": "I was in Destiny shopping center and lost my IPhone 8",
  "insureeId": "user_001",
  "brokerId": "broker_001"
}
```

You should see a success response back from the blockchain.

To verify that the claim was successfully created in the network, you can select the claim get method and click **Try it out!** You should be able to get the claim result, as follows:

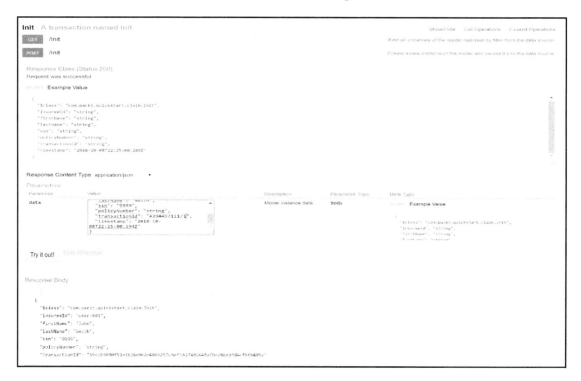

Verifying if the claim was sucessfully created in the network

Other insurance claims endpoint APIs will be quite similar to the ones we have explored.

Summary

We have reached the end of this chapter. In this chapter, we have overviewed Hyperledger Composer and installed the related tools. We used composer model language to develop the same insurance claim use case as in *Chapter 16*, *Exploring an Enterprise Blockchain Application Using Hyperledger Fabric*, and deployed it to the fabric network. Lastly, we integrated the application with a composer REST server to generate a client API and interacted with these APIs from the web.

At this point, you should be comfortable working with Hyperledger Composer. Now that we're at the end of this chapter, we have learned about the two most popular public and enterprise blockchains. As a blockchain developer, you should have the basic blockchain knowledge to be able to write your blockchain application. In the next chapter, we will discuss the various real world blockchain use cases.

18
Blockchain Use Cases

After completing the first six chapters, you should have sufficient knowledge to think about how to apply your newly acquired skills to resolving real-life problems. As discussed earlier, blockchain is considered to be a game-changing technology, which can potentially disrupt existing business models by making intermediary services obsolete and inspire the creation of new and cost-effective business models. However, this technology can not resolve all issues and its value can only be fully realized by combining it with other mature or emerging technologies, such as big data platforms, cloud computing, data science/AI, and IoT.

In this chapter, we first talk about popular blockchain use cases across industries, including financial, civil services, supply chain, IoT, and healthcare, at a high level. We will then proceed to a discussion of factors for consideration, before determining proper use cases and developing a successful DApp. Finally, we take the health data sharing use case and comment, at a high level, on building a DApp for it. Specifically, we cover the following topics:

- Examples of blockchain uses cases
- How to choose a proper use case
- In-depth discussion of the use case of healthcare data sharing

Blockchain use case examples

The evolution of technology has fundamentally changed people's lives. Throughout human history, machines have replaced humans for performing various tasks. For example, in agriculture, farming vehicles made farming work less labor-intensive and greatly increased productivity. In the US, as of 2008, less than 2 % of the population directly work in agriculture. They not only supply the food needed for the other 98% of the population, but also make the US the biggest agricultural products exporter. Examples in other areas include programmable telephone switchboards replacing telephone operators, and automatic elevators replacing elevator operators.

This trend of machines replacing humans sped up in the last several decades, largely due to the invention of computers. So far, there have been three computer-led revolutions in technology. Each of these revolutions fundamentally affected existing business models and inspired new ways of doing business. We are now at the dawn of the fourth phase: a blockchain technology-led revolution. The following are the phases:

- **Invention of mainframe and PC**: Computers replaced humans for performing repetitive computations faster and better. Applications of computers driving automation are numerous and everywhere.
- **Internet**: The internet refers to a globally interconnected network of computers. The arrival of the internet fundamentally changed the way services are delivered. For example, in the 90s, renting a video cassette or CD/DVD at a local rental store was a popular family entertainment activity on the weekends. Blockbuster was a household name offering rental services, and its business model worked well. In 2004, Blockbuster employed 84,300 people worldwide and had 9,094 stores in total. With the internet, new companies such as Netflix emerged and disrupted the reign of companies such as Blockbuster. Families no longer need to make a trip to a physical rental store to pick up a CD/DVD. Instead, they can downloaded a virtual copy of a movie from the internet. In 2010, Blockbuster filed for bankruptcy. Today, Netflix is a 145B company. The same story has repeated itself many times in other areas.
- **Social media sites**: Social media sites such as Facebook, Twitter, or YouTube not only changed existing business models, they changed the way people obtain news and how news is distributed. Papers and radio/TV-based news distribution are no longer the only channels for news dissemination. Many news publishers were forced to shut down due to the loss of subscribers. On the other hand, freelance news reporters started emerging via YouTube and so on. Social media sites have also fundamentally impacted governments as news censorship became more difficult.

Phase 4—blockchain technology: Even with social media sites, censorship—although more difficult—is still possible since information is hosted and processed at a centralized server, so censorship can be implemented at that centralized server. With a blockchain network, censorship is not practical thanks to the decentralized design of blockchain technology. The only way is to shut down all the nodes of the network within a country. The biggest impact of blockchain on existing business models comes from the fact that this technology will make intermediary services obsolete. It will particularly affect the financial industry, where most financial services are essentially intermediary. This technology is about to bring changes not just to the financial industry, but to virtually every other industry.

Next, we cite a few examples of potential blockchain technology applications. We use the word *potential,* since the technology is still evolving and its current form has many limitations. There is no guarantee that these use cases can be implemented. It will take a while before many of these use cases become a reality, and some may never come to fruition. Regardless of whether a use case can be implemented or not, we focus our discussions on business problems and on ideas of how business *pain points* can potentially be addressed via this technology. As the technology advances, for example with improvements in performance, some use cases will become a reality. We first talk about use cases in the financial industry.

Payment and settlement services

Reconciliation of transactions between banks is costly and time-consuming when performed traditionally. For example, in 2016, the US alone had 70B debit card transactions. In the same year, VisaNet (one of world's largest electronic payment networks) processed an average of 150 million transactions a day. With these high volumes, even a tiny saving in each transaction can lead to a huge reduction in the overall cost of doing business. In the case of stock trading, the complete cycle of a trade plus clearing and settlement take three days. A failure in reconciling a transaction could result in a significant monetary loss. (Therefore, a clearinghouse such as DTCC implements an insurance mechanism to mitigate settlement risks.) With blockchain technology, payment processing is increasingly moving towards instant payment worldwide. For example, Ripple can complete a cross-board payment in minutes. The technology combines transaction and settlement. It dramatically reduces the associated transaction costs. The steps of a transaction are visible to a requester. A recent research report claimed Ripple's payment cost is only 0.1% of the cost associated with a traditional transaction. Similarly, for stock trading, since a blockchain implementation merges trading and clearing/settlement into one action, there is no longer a settlement risk. An exchange member firm will not need to pay a premium for settlement insurance and will not require a large back office team dedicated to handling settlements. This will significantly reduce the cost of doing business for the firm.

Import and export finance

In goods trading, importers and exporters respectively use their banks for issuing **letter of credit** (**LC**) and settling payments. Blockchain will allow banks to simplify document management. It provides transparency to the parties involved and mitigates the potential risk of document fraud. It makes transaction reconciliation between and within financial institutions a lot simpler, leading to significant savings. The decentralized ledger provides auditable transaction logs, making legal disputes less likely and simpler to settle.

Immutable ledger

Book or record keeping methods, such as using a ledger, become increasingly complicated due to the increasing number of participants and the complexity of transactions. The traditional way of maintaining a ledger is for it to be centralized. This approach lacks transparency, leading to frequent disputes legally or not legally. It is also difficult to identify an error as parties involved in a transaction do not have an efficient real-time method to check and verify transaction facts against the ledger. Blockchain technology can resolve the issues seamlessly. The decentralized and immutable ledger maintained on the chain virtually eliminates any chance of a dispute and brings trust between parties in transactions. Blockchain allows for real-time queries and permits parties to ensure their correctness. Unlike the traditional way, where two trading parties kept entries in their respective ledgers, possibly leading to discrepancies, the blockchain ledger allows all parties to maintain a unified ledger, eliminating the possibility of inconsistencies.

Regulatory compliance and auditing

With its immutability, regulators can trust any information that they extract from transactions recorded on enterprise blockchains. Financial companies do not have to take steps to prepare data and invest heavily in implementing data governance to ensure the correctness of data. As a result, blockchain technology can potentially help lower the cost of regulatory compliance and auditing for financial companies in areas such as security trading, **anti-money laundering** (**AML**), and **know your customer** (**KYC**).

Identity theft detection

The decentralized blockchain system deters bank theft and hacking activities. The adoption of blockchain technology will make detection of identity theft easier. If a thief steals an identity and opens a bank account or makes a fraudulent tax claim, the affected individual can see all the accounts under his/her name and identify the suspicious activities. The person can then report them to a bank or the IRS immediately, preventing them from suffering further loss.

Funds back-office operation

Blockchain can be used to improve the efficiency of implementing measures to satisfy the regulation requirements of AML and KYC while onboarding a new client. It can help with funds' net present value calculation, as well as other back-office activities such as reconciliation and handling corporate actions (such as, stock splitting, company mergers and acquisitions, and so on).

Collateral management

In a traditional way, regardless of a bilateral or tri-party transaction, information on collateral is not available in real time to parties involved in a transaction. Blockchain can be used to provide a decentralized system for collateral management. It provides real-time transparency and maintains one copy of state on collateral usage, which removes the possibility of having inconsistent information on collateral due to parties keeping their individual records as well as a traditional collateral management approach.

In the previous section, we discussed examples of use cases for the financial industry. Next, we cover examples beyond the financial industry.

Healthcare systems

Blockchain can help to address the issue of lacking a way to manage health data efficiently. The adoption of blockchain technology can simplify medical data management. For example, a patient's medical history, diagnostic information, and test results are kept at their respective doctors' offices. Sharing medical information among doctors, for instance a patient's family physician and specialists, is time-consuming and difficult. This could lead to a delay in diagnosis or generatre redundant medical tests. The blockchain can make data sharing easier, while the confidential data is well protected. The detailed medical records can then be aggregated. The aggregated information can be made available to medical researchers, government agencies, and pharmaceutical or insurance companies. With simplification and worldwide access, health data sharing helps promote cooperation among researchers and pharmaceutical companies in the development of new treatments and drugs. Based on real health data, government agencies can make improved health policies. Medical insurance firms can utilize data to calculate the premiums for plans and reduce the cost of collecting the required data. The same goes for decentralizing the results of clinical trials. In summary, blockchain can revolutionize how health data is stored, managed, and shared. It will profoundly impact the development of the health industry as a whole.

Real estate trading and rental markets

In the US, realtors charge a broker fee, typically 5 to 6% of the selling price, for bringing a seller and a buyer together to make a real estate transaction. Lawyers charge hundreds of dollars for providing legal services to a buyer or seller. In New York city, a real estate broker typically charges a customer one month of rent, which is often thousands of USD, for facilitating a rental transaction. This is quite expensive compared to the limited services provided. Blockchain provides a much lower cost solution with the added value of providing transparency. A real estate blockchain network matches untrusted buyers/sellers or tenants/landlords for a deal. The scripted legal document, a smart contract, replaces mos legal services provided by a real estate lawyer, thus rendering them nonessential. No escrowsing accounts are required since blockchain combines transaction and settlement into one action. In other words, transferring ownership of a house and payment occur at the same time. A similar solution is applicable in the case of property rentals. This will lead to dramatic savings in transactions by both parties. Facing the threat posed by blockchain technology, realtors will either have to find an innovative way of providing value added services or change to a different occupation.

IP market

IP refers to intellectual property. This can be a digital or digitized asset such as a novel, a song, a movie, a painting, a patent, or a piece of software. Blockchain technology can potentially be used to set up a market for buying and selling IPs. This will allow an owner to sell an IP asset to a buyer. For example, upon completion of a novel, an author can generate a predetermined number of digital copies of the novel and sell directly to readers. Each digital copy has a pair of public/private keys and an address. Upon paying the price of the book, the title of this copy is transferred to a buyer. The buyer can in future resell the copy at a secondary IP market. This new business model does not involve a publisher. An author can pocket most of the proceeds from book sales.

Elections

The current way of conducting an election has multiple downsides. First, it often requires the physical presence of the person casting the vote. Many elections still rely on paper voting. This makes counting the result very time-consuming, labor-intensive, and expensive. It also may lead to a lengthy recount, which happened during the previous US presidential elections in several close-call states. The recounting took weeks or longer to complete. Manipulating the outcome, double voting, or faking a vote are other frequently cited problems, even during several highly watched elections in other countries.

Blockchain technology can be used to address these issues. With a blockchain-based election DApp, casting a vote can take place worldwide. Every voter is uniquely assigned an account, an address, making double voting infeasible. The result of an election is immutable. Therefore, manipulation of an election outcome is not possible. The technology brings another advantage by making worldwide, cross-border referendums feasible on issues such as environmental topics.

HR and recruiting

A common issue faced by the HR department at a large company is how to identify a candidate with the right skills, work experience, and educational background. Often, the solution is to hire a professional recruiter or headhunter, who either identifies candidates via personal networking or through scanning social media sites such as LinkedIn. The fee paid to a recruiter is equal to a month's salary for the hired candidate or more. Blockchain can be utilized to build a decentralized database of professionals. This can serve two purposes. First, it provides transparency to match employers and candidates. Second, every company can learn the history of a potential employee and the person's current employment status. This can help to filter out potential fraudsters getting employed by a company.

Public records

The government's civic administration office maintains different types of record, for example on citizens, tax returns, holders of deed and property titles, building permits, zoning information, patents, water pipeline and sewage layouts, and so on. They require continuous updates. In addition, these offices receive frequent inquiries. Keeping these records on paper is expensive since the government has to hire a team of office clerks to manage the records manually.Even in the case where records are electronically filed, hands are still needed to respond to inquiries. With a digital ledger hosted on a blockchain, inquiries can be met via software query tools instead of via an office clerk. This solution will safeguard the data from being altered for malicious purposes. This can help to reduce identity theft as well.

Reduce contract disputes

Blockchain is used internally by IBM for resolving contract disputes between partners on the network. According to IBM's estimates, an average of 0.9% of its 2.9 million transactions result in disputes. These disputes lead to around US $100 million in capital being tied, up and unable to be put to work to make a profit. The capital financing cost for $100 million is not trivial. There are also significant costs associated with resolving the disputes. With the blockchain solution, IBM can combine data provided by participants in the network and create a comprehensive view of all transactions. The blockchain provides strong privacy and confidentiality controls via an access-entitling governance mechanism. This solution has greatly reduced the number of disputes.

Sharing economy

Blockchain technology can be used to create a market to promote the sharing or rental of the residual value of an item or services to others. For example, one may have an underused computer that can be rented out to another user who needs a temporary boost in computational capacity. In this case, the blockchain sharing market can be used to complete such a rental arrangement. The platform essentially allows individuals to run a private rental business on virtually anything that is shareable. The blockchain technology-based market is suitable for any device whose usage can be conveniently shared digitally, such as a computer. The market can be used to facilitate the sharing of general services as well. For example, in a European country young people provide nursery services to elders in exchange for credits. The accumulated credits can be used to recieve similar services when a person becomes old. With the blockchain solution, the person will receive digital coins that may be called *ServiceCoin* for the services being provided to others and can spend the coins later to recieve a service. This can potentially be a solution to addressing the problem of the high cost of nursery care in the US.

Integration with IoT

IoT refers to Internet of Things. IoT is a network of many different types of things, such as physical devices, vehicles, home appliances, and sensors. These things are connected and can collect and share data. When combining blockchain technology and IoT, we can potentially implement many meaningful applications. They can have a lot of benefits such as providing convenience in people's lives, saving lives, and reducing the cost of conducting business. The following are a few possible use cases:

- A smart contract can be automatically called to place an order for additional laundry detergent when an embedded sensor detects the level of detergent is down the preset level.
- A health wristband or embedded sensor in clothing may detect vital statistics on a person pointing to the likelihood of a potential heart attack. It then automatically triggers a smart contract to send an order to a pharmacy store and an SMS or email alert to the person. When implemented well, this kind of application can save many lives.

- A built-in sensor in a refrigerator can detect the quantity of vegetables or meat and trigger a smart contract to order additional vegetables/meat from a local farmer and a meat supplier without the involvement of a grocery store. This will avoid costs added to grocery products by stores and lead to savings for consumers.
- When a hotel guest is ready to check out, the guest can simply drop a room key (or smart key) at a designated place. A sensor triggers a checkout smart contract. When triggered, the smart contract will access the data being collected via other sensors in the room, such as information on consumption of snacks/drinks at a mini-bar or possible damage to room facilities. Based on the collected data, the smart contract will calculate a final amount and complete the guest's checkout by invoking and completing a payment transaction. With such a solution, a guest does not need to visit the hotel reception desk and this saves the guest time. It also helps the hotel reduce operating costs since the hotel does not need to hire an employee to man the reception desk.

Facilitate commercial and social relationships

The Australian government entity, the **CSIRO** (**Commonwealth Scientific and Industrial Research**) Organisation , carried out scientific research for the benefit of Australia. The agency pointed out that the blockchain can be used as a database system that facilitates commercial and social relationships. An effective use of blockchain technology lies in complex markets with multiple organizations interacting with each other.

How to choose a proper use case

With so much speculation about blockchain technology and its potential impacts on existing business models, it is a time to be realistic. In Gartner's most recent *Hype Cycle for Emerging Technologies* report, blockchain is said to have entered the *trough of disillusionment* phase, the third phase of the company's *hype cycle* metric, as shown in the following screenshot:

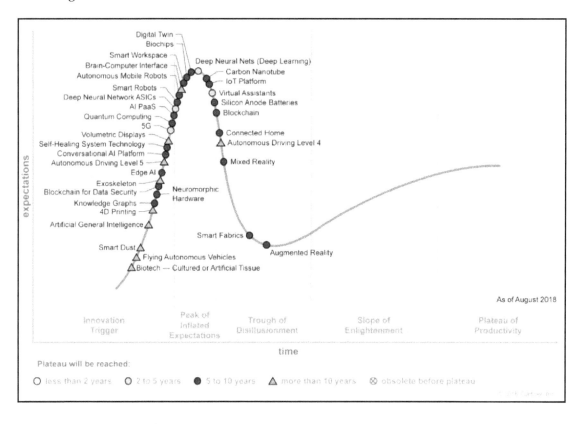

Between Q4 2017 and Q1 2018, the price of 1 BTC reached above 19K and then quickly dropped down 10k in a matter of days. It is 3.4K on December 11, 2018. This eye-popping roller-coaster in BTC price has led to the cooling down of frantic speculations on cryptocurrencies and consequently a reduction in investment in cryptocurrency projects. In addition, the limitations of the technology are also a factor, making the technology unsuitable for certain use cases. A well known issue is the low rate of **transactions per second (TPS)** inherited by most blockchain platforms from Bitcoin, as discussed in `Chapter 13`, *Ethereum Fundamentals*. Successful blockchain applications are still scarce and they are mainly concentrated in the financial industry. Ripple is a success story, which focuses on cash payments.

Since blockchain technology is not suitable for all use cases, it is important to choose a proper use case before jumping into action. The following comments can be useful to help you in determining which use case to work on and how to choose a blockchain platform for its implementation along with other architectural considerations:

- Not every use case is suitable for blockchain. For instance, many use cases can be implemented with traditional technology. It is true that blockchain is a data repository. If the sole purpose is to host data, choosing a regular database may be sufficient. Currently writing to a blockchain is still much slower than writing to a database. Insertion into a blockchain takes seconds or minutes. Insertion into a database takes only milliseconds. This makes databases a better choice in many use cases requiring high throughput, such as capturing credit/debit card transactions or equity trading market data. In the future, as performance and scalability improve, blockchain technology can be used for these use cases.

- In IoT use cases, an issue to consider is how to integrate an IoT device with a blockchain network. An IoT device is not a computer. As a result, an IoT device cannot be a node of the blockchain network. One possible solution is to link the device with a node on the network via APIs. The node interacts with the blockchain ledger and triggers the corresponding smart contracts upon receiving a signal from the IoT device. Performance is also an issue. Some IoT devices, such as airplane sensors, generate high-frequency measurements. A low TPS blockchain network cannot respond quickly to requests from these devices.

- The block size of a blockchain platform is limited. For example, Bitcoin has a block size restricted to around 1 MB. The following graph (from `blockchain.com`) shows its average block size history up to October 2018. For use cases such as an IP market for selling a novel or a movie, detailed information on a digital asset requires a lot of storage space. One can consider an architectural design of combining on-and off-chain storage to resolve the limited block size issue. Details about a digital asset can be saved off-chain at a centralized location. Ethereum has already adopted the on-and off-chain data storage approach:

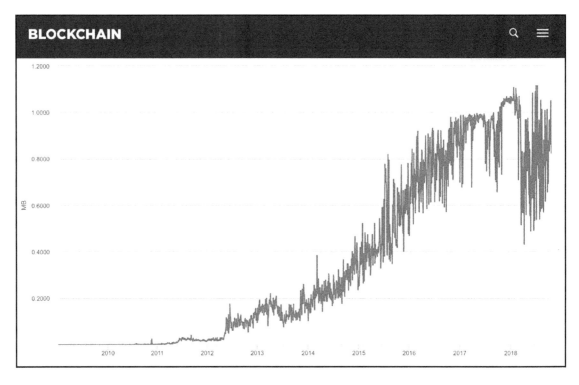

- If a use case involves a digitized asset, a few issues need to be addressed for managing the underlying physical assets:
    - The physical asset needs to be notarized in order to prove its authenticity.
    - A solution is needed to ensure that the underlying asset remains the same and is not changed between the time it is notarized andwhen it is transferred in its title.
    - Similar to the digital coin double spending issue, a solution is needed to ensure that a physical asset is mapped to one and only one digital asset.

- Valuable physical assets require secured places for storage. When ownership is transferred digitally, the corresponding ownership on the underlying asset needs to be recorded and transferred. A possible solution could be borrowed from bullion (gold) trading. The physical gold can be stored at a safe place, like the NY Fed gold vault. When a pile of gold bars changes ownership, the physical gold bars do not leave the vault.

- Although Ethereum is a generic platform supporting DApp development, its implementation involves a digital coin. Whenever a cryptocurrency is part of a solution, one may need to deal with legal complications associated with it. For example, in the US, BTC is defined as an asset, not a currency. In other words, there is a tax implication (for instance, sales tax) when a BTC is sold to a buyer. Certain countries such as China prohibit cryptocurrency trading. As a result, an enterprise blockchain solution such as **Hyperledger Fabric** (HF) may be preferred since its implementation does not involve a cryptocurrency.

- Many use cases such as healthcare data sharing or credit data digitization are not suitable for public use. A permission-based enterprise (or private) blockchain is needed instead of a public blockchain such as Ethereum.

- Another advantage of a private chain such as HF or R3's Corda over Ethereum is that both HF and Corda support development in Java, while Ethereum requires a programmer to learn a new language such as Solidity. Given the scarcity of talent in Solidity, it is difficult and expensive to find qualified developers. On the other hand, turning a Java programmer into a HF or Corda developer could be an easier solution.

- Blockchain technology implies the guaranteed execution of a scripted legal document, a smart contract, which makes untrusting parties feel comfortable doing transactions. If a use case does not require a guaranteed transaction, then it is not a suitable use case. For instance, blockchain is not needed to replace the traditional internet dating site. Dating is very personal and it does not lead to a guaranteed transaction—a marriage.

- If blockchain is only used for the purpose of being a distributed ledger, it is not justifiable due to the cost associated with a blockchain solution. If fault tolerance and providing transparency are the primary goals, a distributed ledger can be implemented in a traditional way by making identical copies of the ledger at multiple nodes without the need to involve additional components, such as Bitcoin's mining and consensus mechanism. The consensus component was introduced to resolve the double spending issue. A distributed ledger does not involve double spending. In other words, blockchain is overkill if one only needs a distributed ledger.

- Blockchain currently is still not a suitable solution for many use cases requiring high throughput, such as stock trading or credit card transactions. Existing blockchain platforms are many magnitudes slower than other platforms (for instance, traditional databases) for hosting transaction data. For example, a specialized database, KDB, is needed to save market data in terms of billions of records a day.

- Since smart contracts are scripted legal documents, there are legal challenges to be dealt with:
  - Are local laws applicable when a smart contract runs? If the answer is yes, how do you deal with conflicts with local laws, a scenario when the contract is legal at some locations of nodes and not at other locations of nodes?
  - Regulations and laws are not fully developed on blockchain and cryptocurrency. A US lawmaker recently pushed the IRS to clarify regulations on blockchain.
  - Since the execution of a smart contract is automatic and unstoppable, a blockchain application could be ruled to be unlawful when it cannot sufficiently address illegal activities such as money laundering.
  - Cryptocurrency receives different statuses in different countries. For example, in the US it is defined as an asset and in Singapore, it is considered to be a currency.

DApp use case – healthcare data sharing

In this subsection, we look at one use case in more detail and talk about steps leading to the implementation of a DApp. The use case of healthcare data sharing will be examined further. Here, only ideas are discussed, which are not necessarily implementable. Most of the discussions focus on business and architectural considerations.

The business problem

Before getting to implementing a DApp, one should start with the business problem by asking questions such as *What are the challenges or the pain points*? In the case of healthcare data, examples of challenges are as follows:

- **Digitization**: Many patients' medical records are available only on paper. This is particularly true for family physician offices, which are usually small. When a patient visits a physician's office, it is still a common scene for a doctor's office receptionist to search the file cabinets and pull out a folder with the patient's medical history. The records are then handed over to the physician. The physician reads the records while talking to the patient. This approach is not scalable and risky. A natural disaster such as flooding or fire can easily destroy these records. When a patient changes physician, the old records are not transferred. The new physician's office will set up a new folder and start to accumulate the medical history for the patient. Due to the loss of old records, some medical tests may need to be redone, resulting in additional costs and inconvenience to the patient. More importantly, the loss of history could lead to losing precious time that could be used for curing a disease.

- **Timeliness**: Since a patient's medical records are physically maintained at multiple offices, sharing the records, for example between the patient's family physician and a specialist, is difficult and time-consuming. To facilitate sharing the records, the patient first gives his/her physician's contact information to the specialist's office. Then, a specialist's office receptionist contacts the physician's office. The physician's office makes an arrangement to send the information via fax or regular mail. This approach is slow, expensive, and insecure. A patient's medical information can potentially be seen by unauthorized parties during the information transfer and the stolen insurance information can be used for malicious purposes.

- **Ownership**: Medical records are the health history of a patient. The patient should be the owner of the medical data. A doctor's office is merely the custodian. In reality, this is rarely the case. Whoever maintains the medical records becomes the de facto owner and makes decisions on how the data is used or accessed.

- **Transparency**: Since medical records are on paper and scattered at doctors' offices, individual and institutional users such as medical researchers, government agencies, and insurance companies do not have a convenient way to access aggregated medical information for legislative and other purposes. Access to the aggregated medical information, which does not involve confidential information about individuals, can be beneficial for the advancement of medical research, prioritizing medicine development, or making government health policies.

A blockchain solution

After identifying a business problem and its *pain points*, the next step is to search for a proper solution. For the previous business problem, a general solution is needed to build a computer-based healthcare data sharing platform. The platform will allow authorized parties such as doctors, researchers, government agencies, insurance companies, and pharmaceutical firms to access the medical data. Developing such a platform requires a tremendous amount of work. Digitization of existing paper records alone is well beyond our capability and requires the involvement of many groups and organizations. Since this book focuses on blockchain technology, we will concentrate on the blockchain part of a solution without worrying too much about the feasibility of its actual implementation.

Blockchain technology combined with other technologies, such as big data platforms and data science, is proposed. The blockchain will be used for hosting transactions. The big data platform provides sufficient space for hosting the bulk of the healthcare data at the detailed and aggregation levels. The data science-based analytics component computes the aggregated medical data and derives the analytical summaries.

- **Data repository**: The size of patient healthcare data can easily be in terabytes. It is not feasible to host healthcare data on-chain only. It is logical to choose the approach of combining on- and off-chain records for saving detailed medical data. In fact, the Ethereum blockchain has already used the idea of maintaining state variables off-chain, while having transactions and smart contracts saved on the chain. The body of a patient's medical information can be saved off-chain and its hash is saved on the chain. The hash is used here to prevent medical records from being modified without authorization. Each patient's medical record will be assigned with an address. When a patient's medical record is updated, a transaction with the type *update* is generated on chain. A new hash corresponding to the updated medical records of a patient is generated and saved on the chain. The updated records will have a new address. Similarly, when a user accesses a patient's medical records, a transaction with the type *access* is saved on chain. The digital assets of these transactions are the medical records.

- **Choice of blockchain platform**: Choosing a proper blockchain platform is an important architectural decision. There are technical and non-technical factors to be considered. One key non-technical consideration is the legal implication if a DApp solution involves a cryptocurrency, as different countries have different laws on cryptocurrency trading. Trying to work out a coin-based DApp following these laws is a daunting task and is not worth the effort. The purpose of our DApp is to resolve a business problem, not to issue a digital coin. A generic public blockchain platform such as Ethereum involves a digital coin or token. An enterprise blockchain platform such as Hyperledger Fabric does not involves a cryptocurrency. Therefore, HF should be considered. Since HF is permission-based, its consensus algorithm does not require heavy and lengthy computations. Therefore, HF provides a higher TPS. It also contains an access entitlement and control component, which is required for managing medical information access.

- **Analytics component**: An analytical component is needed to perform tasks such as aggregating detailed medical information and providing useful statistics. The aggregation is mandatory in order to mask confidential individual information and make the medical information usable by users such as medical researchers, government agencies, or insurance/pharmaceutical companies. A patient's detailed medical information should only be used by the patient's doctor with the patient's permission. The aggregated data should, as a minimum, make it impossible to reverse-engineer the information for any patient.

- **Data protection**: With any DApp implementation, protecting digital assets hosted on the platform is a key requirement. There are many examples of hackers attacking blockchain platforms, cryptocurrency exchanges, or wallets and stealing millions of USD in digital coins. Some well known incidents are Mt Gox and Bitfinex being hacked a few years ago. Attaching on Zaif is a more recent example. In addition, protection of a patient's privacy is legally required. Failure to comply with privacy laws will lead to the shutdown of a DApp application and result in costly legal suits. To protect a patient's medical information, we can encrypt off-chain data. When a patient grants permission to a doctor to access medical records, a temporary key will be provided. The doctor's office uses the temporary key to obtain a masked private key for decrypting the records. The private key should not be visible to the doctor's office afterward. Only the temporary key is visible and is valid for a short period of time. A new temporary key will be generated for the next access request. The aggregated information may not need to be encrypted. However, access to the information is strictly controlled based on a well defined authentication and entitlement model.

- **Backend component**: The backend component refers to smart contract development. Multiple contracts are needed to provide rules governing transactions, including uploading medical records, accessing detailed medical records, or querying the aggregated data. Since these transactions are on the chain, they provide an auditing trail of data being uploaded and how data is accessed. With these audit trails, a patient can easily monitor his/her medical information use and effectively protect his/her privacy and personal health information.

- **Frontend component**: To complete a DApp, a frontend component is needed. This component includes interfaces with users and interactions with the HF ledger or the analytics component. Interfaces with users allow a user such as a doctor's office receptionist to upload or update medical records. It also contains GUI tools for users to access both detailed and aggregated medical information. Any request to access medical information is first passed to an authorization verification module. After the request passes the permission check, it is then sent to the modules, which interact with a HF node to trigger the corresponding smart contracts and execute the request. These modules also interact with the blockchain network for data uploads.

The following chart displays how users interact with health data sharing platform components:

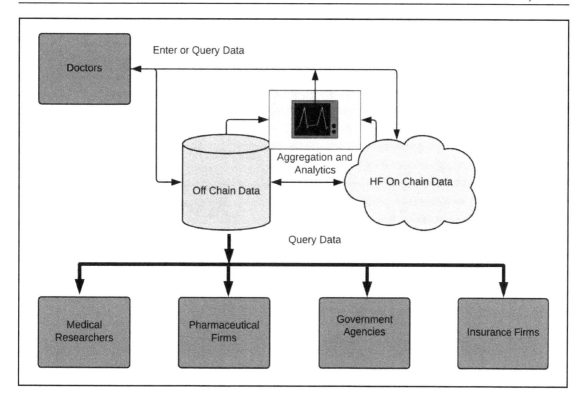

Users interaction with the health data sharing platform's components

The implementation of both frontend and backend components requires in-depth knowledge of blockchain and GUI development. IDE preparation and setup alone are not an easy task. Several startups step in to fill in the gaps and make these tasks easier. With these tools, a user no longer needs to write code to perform repetitive tasks such as environment setup, testing, and deployment. Instead, the user simply clicks on a few buttons. As a result, developers can focus on resolving a real business problem.

- **Parties involved**: The platform involves several parties. Doctor's offices are the primary data uploaders, as well as the users of the patient's detailed medical records. Medical researchers, government agencies, pharmaceutical companies, and insurance companies are users of the aggregated medical information.

- **Architectural diagram**: The following architectural diagram shows a layered design for implementing the healthcare data sharing platform. The top layer contains the frontend components. The middle layer is for off-chain data processing and analytics. The bottom layer is for backend components containing smart contracts, along with other HF components:

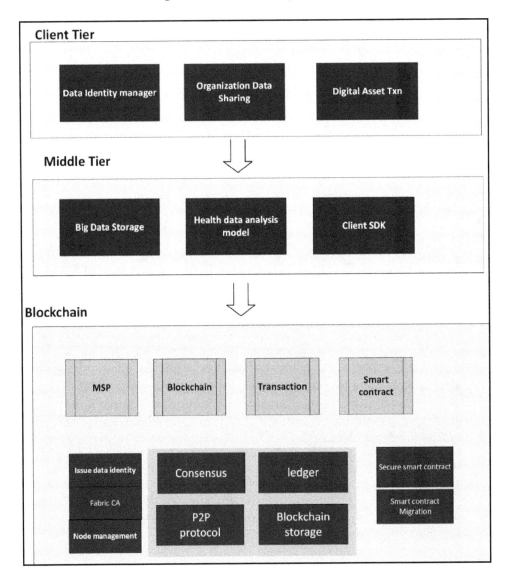

- **Project funding**: Sufficient funds need to be raised to support the healthcare data sharing project. One idea is to set up a blockchain startup and lobby potential investors to fund efforts. Nowadays, setting up and running a startup are much easier thanks to emerging technologies and online services. For example, cloud computing vendors such as Linode provide the affordable hardware supplies needed by a startup. Similarly, by utilizing WeChat members of a startup can have visual meetings worldwide without incurring any cost. Google Drive, Slides, Docs, and Sheets can serve as a virtual team's document collaboration and sharing software. GitHub is for software sharing and version control. For financial auditing, firms such as BitAudit (`http://www.bitaudit.vip/`) specialize in providing auditing services for blockchain technology firms. This is helpful given the fact that laws on cryptocurrency and blockchain technology have not matured yet and are still evolving.

Summary

As was the case for the internet in the nineties, blockchain is at the dawn of the Blockchain age. This technology will disrupt existing business models and give birth to new models. It will inspire the emergence of community economies built on a blockchain network, where every participant makes contributions to, and receives benefits from, the community. There is no longer a single entity that controls and receives dividends from the economy.

In this chapter, we have discussed use cases across industries to give you a flavor of potential blockchain applications. Given the limitations of the existing technology, not all these cases can be immediately implemented. As the technology progresses, more use cases can be tackled. Finally, we talked about important factors to be considered in selecting a proper use case and the steps to be followed in developing a complete DApp through an in-depth discussion on the healthcare data sharing use case.

Other Books You May Enjoy

If you enjoyed this book, you may be interested in these other books by Packt:

Blockchain for Business 2019

Peter Lipovyanov

ISBN: 978-1-78995-602-3

- Understand the fundamentals of blockchain and how it was developed
- Gain a good understanding of economic concepts and developments
- Develop a base for concepts such as cryptography, computer networking, and programming
- Understand the applications of blockchain and its potential impact on the world
- Become well versed with the latest developments in the blockchain space
- Explore blockchain frameworks, including decentralized organizational structures, networks, and applications

Blockchain Developer's Guide

Brenn Hill, Samanyu Chopra, Paul Valencourt and Narayan Prusty

ISBN: 978-1-78995-472-2

- Understand how various components of the blockchain architecture work
- Get familiar with cryptography and the mechanics behind blockchain
- Apply consensus protocol to determine the business sustainability
- Understand what ICOs and crypto-mining are, and how they work
- Create cryptocurrency wallets and coins for transaction mechanisms
- Build DApps using Solidity and Web3.js
- Create your own Ethereum wallets
- Explore the consortium blockchain

Leave a Review - Let Other Readers Know What You Think

Please share your thoughts on this book with others by leaving a review on the site that you bought it from. If you purchased the book from Amazon, please leave us an honest review on this book's Amazon page. This is vital so that other potential readers can see and use your unbiased opinion to make purchasing decisions, we can understand what our customers think about our products, and our authors can see your feedback on the title that they have worked with Packt to create. It will only take a few minutes of your time, but is valuable to other potential customers, our authors, and Packt. Thank you!

Index

www.ingramcontent.com/pod-product-compliance
Lightning Source LLC
LaVergne TN
LVHW081506050326
832903LV00025B/1397